William Scott Ament
and the
Boxer Rebellion

William Scott Ament and the Boxer Rebellion

Heroism, Hubris and the "Ideal Missionary"

LARRY CLINTON THOMPSON

McFarland & Company, Inc., Publishers
Jefferson, North Carolina, and London

Frontispiece: Ament (1851–1909), missionary to
China of the American Board of Commissioners for
Foreign Missions (Porter, *William Scott Ament*, 1911).

LIBRARY OF CONGRESS ONLINE CATALOG

Thompson, Larry Clinton, 1941–
William Scott Ament and the Boxer Rebellion : heroism, hubris and
the "ideal missionary" / Larry Clinton Thompson.
p.   cm.
Includes bibliographical references and index.

ISBN 978-0-7864-4008-5
softcover: 50# alkaline paper ∞

1. Ament, William Scott, 1851–1909.   I. Title.

2008053862

British Library cataloguing data are available

©2009 Larry Clinton Thompson. All rights reserved

*No part of this book may be reproduced or transmitted in any form
or by any means, electronic or mechanical, including photocopying
or recording, or by any information storage and retrieval system,
without permission in writing from the publisher.*

On the cover: portrait of Ament, 1877; background ©2008 Shutterstock.

Manufactured in the United States of America

*McFarland & Company, Inc., Publishers
Box 611, Jefferson, North Carolina 28640
www.mcfarlandpub.com*

For my wife, Kay,
sunny and warm

Table of Contents

List of Maps ix
Prologue 1

1. The Fists of Righteous Harmony — 3
2. Will Ament in China — 17
3. Red-Headed Devils in Peking — 29
4. The Semi-Siege — 40
5. Admiral See-No-More — 51
6. The Empress Dowager — 63
7. The Assassination of the Baron — 75
8. In the British Legation — 83
9. Herbert Hoover and Smedley Butler — 96
10. A Tour of the Defenses — 106
11. The Tartar Wall — 118
12. The Conquest of Tientsin — 129
13. The Darkest Days — 139
14. Life Under Siege — 147
15. Not Massacred Yet — 155
16. Marching to Peking — 163
17. Rescue — 174
18. Ament's Palace — 185
19. The Looting of Peking — 194
20. Mark Twain and Will Ament — 205

Epilogue 215
American and Canadian Missionaries in the Siege at Peking 221
Chapter Notes 223
Bibliography 231
Index 237

List of Maps

Ament's Mission Territory	4
Peking—1900	34
Military Operations in Northern China—1900	60
The Battle for the Taku Forts	72
The British Legation	84
The Defenses of the Legation Quarter	108
The Night Attack on the Tartar Wall—July 3	126
Tientsin and Vicinity	136
The Race to Peking	176

Prologue

China awoke in 1900 and the world has never been the same. That summer, a peasant movement known as the Boxers tried to destroy its oppressors from the West.

The paramount event of the Boxer Rebellion was the siege of the legations in Peking, called by the New York *Sun*—with only modest hyperbole—"the most exciting episode ever known to civilization."[1] Peking was isolated, leaving the world to speculate on the fate of the foreigners within its walls. It was known that the diplomatic legations were surrounded by a horde of brightly dressed, acrobatic, anti–Western, and anti–Christian Boxers. China's rulers, led by the mysterious Empress Dowager, took the side of the Boxers, declared war on the world, and dedicated their armies to the destruction of the "red-headed devils." The rescue of the foreigners in Peking proved difficult. The Western powers quickly assembled a multinational expeditionary force to march to Peking. The Boxers and the Chinese Imperial Army defeated it—shocking the complacent and superior Western countries.

Now, a month after the siege began, newspapers reported that the Chinese had massacred Americans and Europeans in Peking to the last man, woman, and child. The London *Daily Mail* pronounced the purported massacre as "the greatest tragedy of the century."[2] Warships bearing tens of thousands of fresh soldiers from eight countries steamed toward China to rescue their citizens in Peking, if any were still alive, or avenge their deaths—if the tales of the massacre proved to be true.

The story of the siege at Peking is dramatic: stalwart soldiers, pious missionaries, haughty diplomats, poltroons and fools, heroes and martyrs, a courageous American woman at the barricades with the men, a diet of horsemeat and musty rice in a drawn out agony of heat, dust, and death. It was a pageant and tragedy of comprehensible scale. Fewer than five hundred soldiers and a like number of civilians, one-half of them women and children, defended the legations and the Peitang, the North Cathedral of the Roman Catholic Church, from the Boxers and the Imperial armies. They battled within sight of the Forbidden City, the center of the Chinese empire. Another siege, which also had its hazards and heroes, including a future president of the United States, took place in Tientsin, 80 miles from Peking.

Drama begets tragedy. In 1900, tens of thousands of Chinese died at the hands of other Chinese only because they were Christians and more tens of thousands of Chinese died at the hand of Western soldiers only because they were Chinese. The defeat of China and the Boxers by the West was perhaps the last war of imperialism embarked on with enthusiasm and moral surety. A few people now began to ask a question: Did the Christian nations have the right to impose their culture and religion on China?

* * *

It was the age of Rudyard Kipling when European and American men and women confidently shouldered the white man's burden and journeyed to the further corners of the earth to bestow the benefits of civilization and Christianity on the heathen. The merchant came to China to peddle his products to four hundred million customers, the mass of them wretchedly poor, but a rich market for textiles, kerosene, and opium. The scholar, the aesthete, and the artist found in China a treasure house of art and a gracious tradition of living for the privileged few. The diplomat came to protect the citizens and expand the commerce of his country and to ensure that the Chinese government lived up to laws and treaties imposed on it by the force of Western arms.

The most resolute and numerous of the foreigners in China were the missionaries: Protestants from Great Britain, the United States, and Scandinavia, and Catholics from France and Italy. China was the ultimate challenge for the soldiers of Christ: one-fourth of the world's population, living in a heathen condition and urgently requiring that the gospel of salvation be preached to them by the best and the brightest of God's legions, the China missionaries.

One of the most distinguished of the China missionaries was the American William Scott Ament, a brave and resourceful man whose heroism was tarnished by hubris and looting. Mark Twain, the most famous American of the day, attacked Ament. Did Ament become a character of infamy while lesser men of greater sin escaped censure? The reader must judge whether Ament was maligned unfairly.

* * *

Scholars agree that animosity toward Christian missionaries was a major cause of the Boxer Rebellion against the West. Oddly enough, however, most accounts of the Boxers neglect the missionaries, focusing instead on the diplomats and soldiers who weathered the siege and defeated the Chinese in battle. This book aims to give equal due to the missionaries, their work, the impact they had on China, and the controversies arising in the aftermath of the Boxer Rebellion. William Ament was the outstanding exemplar of his profession, the "ideal missionary" in the words of one author.[3]

A difficulty in writing about China in 1900 is converting Chinese characters and pronunciation of names and place names to English. The system most used in 1900 to romanize Chinese characters was Wade-Giles. The system now used is called Pinyin. The differences in romanization can be minor or major. In 1900, the capital city of China was Peking; today, we spell and pronounce it Beijing. Tientsin in 1900 is now Tianjin; Paoting is now Baoding; the Dowager Empress, Tzu Hsi, is now Cixi. Moreover, different authors rendered Chinese words as they saw fit: the capital city of China was usually Peking, but sometimes Pekin or Peching. Some readers may be confused. After much internal debate I decided to use Wade-Giles romanizations, the system in use in 1900, although I simplified it to eliminate apostrophes. Thus, in this book, the name of the Manchu dynasty ruling China in 1900 is rendered Ching rather than Ch'ing — or Qing as it is now known. Present-day Beijing is called Peking as it was in 1900. To clear up any confusion, I have listed both Wade-Giles and Pinyin versions of names and places in the index. For example, the entry for Peking in the index is: Peking (Beijing).

My aim is to tell the story of the foreigners living in northern China in 1900, especially Americans — missionaries, soldiers, diplomats, and others — who were caught up in the Boxer Rebellion. The sources were mostly old, hard-to-find books, magazine articles, and dusty archives. I wish to extend my thanks to the following libraries and their always helpful librarians: the Universities of North Carolina at Greensboro and Chapel Hill, Duke, Virginia Tech, Howard University Divinity School, Herbert Hoover Presidential Library, the University of Illinois at Urbana-Champaign, the Presbyterian Historical Society, and the Library of Congress. A special word of thanks is due to my friend, Bill Lenderking, who read and commented on an early draft of this book.

1

The Fists of Righteous Harmony

On a cold morning on the last day of 1899, a young Anglican missionary, Sidney M. Brooks, left his home to visit several churches and the small groups of Chinese Christians scattered around the countryside of Shantung province. Snow was falling. Brooks hired a donkey and a passenger wheelbarrow, wrapped himself in blankets, and nestled down for a jolting ride along the narrow, rutted tracks that ran through brown, bare fields between villages.

Twelve miles from home, a gang of six Chinese men set upon Brooks. They hit him on the head and arms with swords. They stripped him of his outer clothing and tied him up, looped a rope around his neck and led him around on a leash, displaying him as a trophy to villagers. Brooks begged for freedom. He promised a ransom of silver, but the men paid no heed. Tiring of this sport, his captors stopped at a roadside inn for their afternoon meal. The kindly Chinese innkeeper gave Brooks water and pleaded for his life. The captors seemed to agree to ransom Brooks and the party headed for a nearby village with a Christian Church to arrange the ransom. Brooks, however, broke free and ran toward the village. Three men on horseback pursued, circled him, and knocked him to the ground with blows from their swords. The horsemen dismounted at the side of the beaten and bloodied missionary. Brooks knelt and cried out for mercy, but one of the men chopped off his head, and threw it into a ditch.

Brooks was the first foreigner killed by the members of a secret society spreading like wildfire over the north China plain. They called themselves I Ho Chuan, the Fists of Righteous Harmony. An American missionary dubbed them Boxers and the name stuck.[1]

* * *

Several months before Brooks' murder the American missionary William Scott Ament in Peking wrote that "the air is full of rumors and the [Chinese] people seem to have a dull apprehension that in some way or other the foreigners are going to injure them or their country."[2] Brooks' murder confirmed Ament's premonition. A collective chill passed down the spine of thousands of missionaries in China.

In March 1900 — three months after Brooks was killed — Ament had his first encounter with the Boxers. Messengers from his churches in the small towns and cities of north China told stories of being threatened by fanatical, anti-foreign, anti–Christian neighbors formed into village societies of Boxers. The countryside south of Peking was coming under their control. Ament, 48 years old, was the spiritual father of twenty-two fledgling churches counting a thousand members and inquirers. He rushed to assist his flock. His urgent errand to the country churches would be dangerous but his life's work was the Chinese he had so laboriously converted to Christianity. He was a hardy, talkative, dedicated man who, in the words of a colleague, was "the best evangelistic worker and the most successful organizer" of the Protestant missionaries in northern China.[3] "I suppose there can be little doubt that Dr. Ament is the best Chinese [language] preacher in the city," said his colleague Charles Ewing. "He is exceedingly

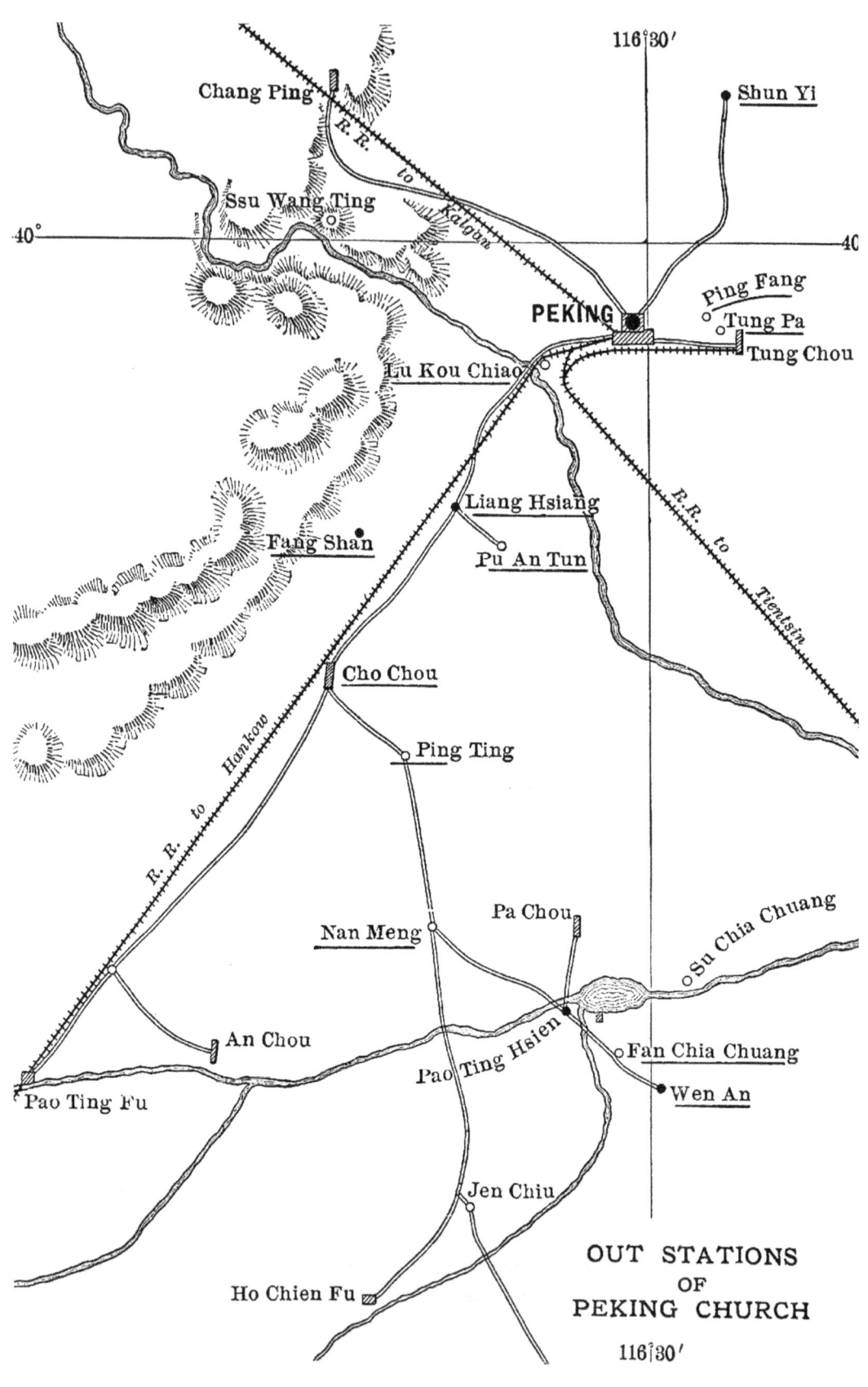

good in personal work, taking an interest in men individually and winning them.... How he gets through so much work, I don't know. I always said that he could do two men's work."[4]

Ament asked other missionaries to accompany him but they found reasons to excuse themselves from going outside the safety of Peking. Finally, William B. Stelle, a Baptist and a "brave, chivalric young man," volunteered to go along. The two missionaries left Peking in the clear, cold and biting wind of a March day. They stuck revolvers in their belts beneath their coats. It was common in 1900 for male missionaries to arm themselves, especially when they were traveling to unfriendly regions where the Chinese government was unable or unwilling to ensure their safety.

The missionaries traveled by train through the market city of Cho Chou and disembarked near Ping Ting fifty-five miles south of Peking. They quickly found evidence of Boxer influence. The people of Ping Ting were in "the throes of a well-cleaning craze. It was reported," Ament wrote, "that the wells had been poisoned by the Christians and they all had to be cleaned out. Having been a very dry season, this wasting of a large quantity of good water will be a serious matter. Our enemies [the Boxers] had thrown little packages of purported medicine in the wells. They also claimed that they alone had antidotes to the poison and sold their medicine in great quantities to the deluded people and reaped large gains thereby. The people were greatly excited and we were repeatedly warned not to proceed." Ament and Stelle ignored the warning and traveled on, running into a hostile crowd at a country fair five miles away. However, once they told the crowd they were Protestants and not Catholics the people became friendly. More numerous than Protestants, Catholics were, the Americans believed, the targets of the Boxer's animosity.

Ament and Stelle continued on to Nan Meng to visit a native pastor. Here they met face-to-face a company of brightly dressed Boxers who had recently arrived in the town to spread their anti-foreign doctrine and gain recruits. "We looked well to our firearms (very modest revolvers) as we had no desire to be put out of the way ... by cowards who would run from a pop-gun. Here we passed a camp of Boxers who came out and stared at us, starting the report that we were the advance guard of a large army, and that accounted for our boldness. We found most of our Christians, including the pastor, in a pitiable state of fright, and they assured us that we should certainly be killed if we did not leave immediately. The pastor had already sent away his family."

Undaunted by their first encounter with the Boxers, Ament and Stelle continued southward and found Chinese Christians there in an equal state of panic. No one had been hurt so far, but the Christians had been threatened by men armed with knives and spears who came to the doors of their houses and reviled them in the high-pitched wail of Chinese oratory. The two missionaries spent the Sabbath with their flock. Here, they saw the aftermath of a battle between Catholics and Boxers.

> Many Boxers were returning from the battle-field in Jen Chiu where they had been defeated by the Romanists [Roman Catholics] and imperial soldiers. Dead men were carried past us and some wounded. At least one thousand Boxers had gathered at a place called Liang Cho to exterminate the Catholics. A hundred soldiers had been sent to calm them down but they were afraid of the Boxers and refused to fight. About seventy Catholics were behind their walls. They had good guns and when the Boxers with no guns, only swords and spears, came on, the Catholics shot them down. The Boxers seemed devil-possessed and did not know what they were doing, going up to the walls and hacking at them with their swords. The brave soldiers, seeing that the Boxers were not really impervious to bullets, took a hand in shooting after the Catholics had gained the victory. The 1,000 Boxers scattered taking their dead and wounded with them.

Opposite: Ament's Mission Territory. Ament established many small Chinese Christian churches in the cities and towns in the Cho Chou region about fifty miles south of Peking (Porter, ***William Scott Ament,*** 1911).

Ament and Stelle, ignoring the pleas of Chinese Christians, traveled on to Wen An, near the battlefield. To their pleasant astonishment four Chinese were brave enough to come forward and request baptism. Boxers, wearing red or yellow sashes and turbans and carrying long swords and wooden pikes, abounded in the village. They had thrown bricks at the little church but the town magistrate had taken the side of the Christians and jailed three of the attackers. From Wen An, the missionaries visited a small village occupied by eighty Boxers to investigate a report that a prominent Christian of the village planned to renounce his faith and pay blackmail to the Boxers. Here began a contest of East and West. At one end of the village, Ament bolstered the courage of the Chinese Christians with a sermon; at the other end the Boxers demonstrated their sword-waving, gymnastic routines. The Boxers sent messengers to demand that the villagers seize and bind the missionaries. Ament and Stelle pulled their revolvers and allowed as how they were not going to be detained. They remained the afternoon and left unmolested, but their mission was a failure; the Christian would not withdraw his renunciation. However, two of his sons affirmed the strength of their faith by saying they would rather die than recant.

Breathing easier, the missionaries journeyed back to Peking. Ament, on his return, called on the United States minister* Edwin H. Conger to tell the diplomat about his experiences.[5] Conger was disturbed. The Boxers were closer to Peking and more aggressive than he had imagined. Relying on Ament's report, he sent a protest note to the Chinese government demanding that Chinese authorities halt the persecution of Chinese Christians by the Boxers. Conger also shared Ament's story with the diplomats of the other ten countries represented in Peking. The diplomats were perplexed with this new movement, the so-called Boxers, although they discounted them as just another of the inexplicable peasant uprisings which broke out suddenly and disappeared just as rapidly in China.

The diplomats gave only routine attention to the missionary's warnings and pleas for protection. Disputes among missionaries, their Chinese converts, and non–Christian Chinese were daily events and reluctant diplomats were drawn frequently into the disputes. American diplomats in China spent one-half their working day dealing with problems caused by the presence of the missionaries. Somewhat in awe at his prominence, one young missionary, Charles Ewing, said in 1894: "I find here a U.S. consul and vice consul, ready to protect my interests.... If I am insulted all I have to do is report it to the consul and he will see to it that a proclamation is issued, or something is done, that will prevent a recurrence of the insult.... The government [of China], so far from failing to respond, has issued proclamation after proclamation, until as one of our missionaries says the Chinese are almost afraid to look at a foreigner."[6]

The Chinese were afraid to look at a foreigner because the Western countries, and more recently Japan, had been chipping away at Chinese sovereignty for sixty years. Due to several wars between West and East, which the Chinese lost, unequal treaties were imposed under which foreigners and foreign organizations in China received special privileges and immunity from Chinese law. The missionaries were forthright in demanding their rights and the rights of their converts. The legations, the consulates, and the Chinese government drowned in a sea

---

*An explanation of diplomatic titles used in 1900 may be helpful. A minister was the chief diplomatic representative of one country to another. Ambassador is the more common title in use nowadays. When I refer to ministers in this book I speak of diplomats rather than Christian clergy. A minister was stationed in the capital city of the country to which he was accredited and his offices were called a legation, which would be called an embassy today. The minister's subordinates were secretaries, e.g. first secretary, second secretary, Chinese secretary, etc. Chancellor and attache were also diplomatic titles used by some countries. Scattered around China in other major cities were consulates and consulates-general in charge of consul generals, consuls, and vice consuls in descending order of rank. Consulates and their staffs were under the general supervision of the minister. At the American Legation in Peking, Conger was the minister, Herbert G. Squiers was the first secretary, William E. Bainbridge was the second secretary, and Fleming D. Cheshire was the Chinese language interpreter. The only other American diplomat in China who figures in this story is James W. Ragsdale, American consul in Tientsin. All American diplomats in Peking lived and worked within the walls of the legation compound.

of missionary demands for adjudication of disputes, punishment of malefactors, and rectification of offenses, including, one supposes, insults offered to the young Reverend Ewing. Small wonder that tales of anti–Christian Boxers aroused no urgency among the diplomats. They heard complaints every day from missionaries. Their usual response was to draft a diplomatic note explaining the problem and suggesting a solution, carry it over to the appropriate representative of the Chinese government, and then wait for the creaking wheels of Chinese bureaucracy to find a course of action to satisfy the complainant while preserving the dignity of both governments. If it were an especially serious incident, the diplomat might allude to the fact that gunboats were standing by at Tientsin, eighty miles away, and off the Taku Banks in the Gulf of Chihli and a failure by China to meet its treaty obligation to protect the right of foreigners and Chinese Christians to practice and preach their religion could "not fail to be most extremely serious to the Chinese government."[7] Charles Ewing commented, "In case of necessity the United States, Great Britain, France, Germany, and Russia are thus represented." He continued with an unprophetic remark. "Armed resistance on the part of civilians, however interesting and exciting it might be, will hardly be called for, while we have the gunboats at hand. Why, the very presence of these armed creatures is enough to terrify the natives."[8]

* * *

The Boxers were a whirlwind, an indigenous movement in the troubled Chinese countryside among peasants and laborers. Although some authorities believe they originated earlier, for practical purposes the Fists of Righteous Harmony were born in 1898 in Shantung province, more than 200 miles south of Peking. The Boxers were related to long-existing secret societies such as the Big Swords. They were ephemeral, their organization rudimentary, their leadership shadowy, their growth spontaneous, and their beliefs expressed in lurid posters and shouted slogans. Their war cries were, "Support the Ching [Manchu dynasty]! Destroy the Foreigner!" and "Sha! Sha!" (Kill! Kill!) The *North China Herald* spoke contemptuously of the "droll drill of the Boxers" and the "flummery and rigmarole" of their rituals.[9]

The Boxers, mostly poor and young, wore red and yellow headbands and armbands and wide sashes around their middle. They brandished swords and spears. Their rituals included whirling and twirling of swords, violent prostrations, and incantations to Taoist and Buddhist saints. When a supplicant chanted the correct incantation, the god descended and possessed his body, and with much frothing at the mouth, he acquired invulnerability and superhuman skills with sword and lance. The Boxers imitated the martial arts performers they saw in the traveling shows that visited every village — and find an echo in the Chinese martial arts movies of our own day. The supernatural gave the Boxers much of their appeal. Thousands testified they had seen Boxers withstand blows of cannon, rifle ball, and knife. On one occasion a man stood in front of a loaded cannon to demonstrate his invulnerability. When the cannon was fired, he was cut in two. This failure might have thrown a pall over the proceedings, but, no, it was explained, the man had not entirely possessed the spirit. The experiment failed but the principle was the same. A collection from the onlookers was taken up for the father of the unfortunate celebrant and the ceremony continued.[10]

The Boxers practiced monk-like austerity. They were forbidden to eat meat or drink tea. Their diet was wheat cakes and water. They avoided sexual contact with women, as women were unclean and a yin impurity would destroy the efficacy of their spells and trances. Women were technically equal, however, and a woman's auxiliary, the Red Lanterns, was founded. The Boxers had a distinctive jargon. They renamed modern devices such as the railroad to excise foreign words from the Chinese language. They celebrated special days and set apart times for fasting and prayer.

The Boxers feared the threat that the growing number of foreigners in China represented to a culture more than three thousand years old. They were akin to religious fundamentalists of all faiths. Powerful foreign religious and secular culture assaulted their beliefs on every side and they retreated into a hysterical world of reaction in which they aimed to restore the glories of an idealized tradition. The American missionary Arthur Smith made the point in a little story. On one of his peregrinations in Shantung about 1887 Smith saw an old man squatting by the roadside staring at him in a surly manner and muttering to himself: "One unceasing stream!" Smith read his thoughts. "He could remember when there were no foreigners throughout the whole region; then there was one a year, or three in two years. After that they began to appear in pairs, later still in droves, with women and children, and now it is 'one unceasing stream.' He did not like it — why, he might or might not have been able to tell, but it was evident that he thought he had fallen upon evil days, and that the old were better."[11]

The Boxers' posters and broadsheets appeared everywhere in northern China. A sample gives the flavor of their appeal to a beleaguered people:

> Foreign devils come with their teaching, and converts to Christianity, Roman Catholic and Protestant, have become numerous. These [churches] are without human relations, but being most cunning have attracted all the greedy and covetous as converts, and to an unlimited degree they have practiced oppression, until every good official has been corrupted, and, covetous of foreign wealth, has become their servant. So telegraphs have been established, and machine-shops have been a delight to their evil nature. Locomotives, balloons, electric lamps, the foreign devils think excellent. Though these foreigners ride in sedans unbefitting their rank, China yet regards them as barbarians of whom God disapproved, and He is sending down spirits and genii for their destruction.
>
> The first of these powers which has already descended is the Light of the Red Lamp, and the Volunteer Associated Fists [Boxers] who will have a fight with the devils. They will burn down the foreign buildings and restore the temples. Foreign goods of every variety they will destroy. They will extirpate the evil demons, and establish right teaching — the honor of the spirits of the sages; they will cause their sacred teaching to flourish.
>
> The purpose of Heaven is fixed; a clean sweep is to be made. Within three years all will be accomplished.[12]

A Boxer in Tientsin. This is one of the few photographs of a Boxer decked out in his ceremonial garb (National Archives, 1900).

* * *

The last refuge of a hopeless people is magic and the Boxers were a magical fantasy. They rose in the venerable Chinese tradition of secret societies, the populist and clandestine organizations which had formed a shadowy counterpart to authoritarian rule for hundreds of years. At their best, secret societies were the voices of the common man in an absolutist society, an indirect but powerful influence on rulers. At their worst, they were crime syndicates whose power dominated government. Whatever their stated purpose secret societies had a history of becoming rebellious sects to challenge declining dynasties. Thus, secrecy was necessary to avoid persecution by the authorities.

The Ching or Manchu dynasty which had governed China for more than two hundred and fifty years repressed secret societies and, also, as possible sources of sedition, the Buddhist and Taoist priesthoods. The Manchus were well aware that a revolt led by a nationalistic secret society, the White Lotus, had overthrown the Mongol dynasty in the fourteenth century. The Manchus were an ethnic minority conquering and ruling China and they wanted no nationalistic banners raised by ethnic Han Chinese to threaten their rule. The pigtail worn by Chinese men was a symbol of their subjugation by the Manchus. (For simplicity's sake, I will call all the people of China and the government itself Chinese unless it is necessary to make a distinction between ethnic Chinese, Manchus, and the many other minorities who also live in China. Moreover, by 1900, most differences between Han Chinese and Manchus had been erased by time and contact.)

Secret societies flourish in times of trouble and in the late nineteenth century in northern China there was plenty of that. First was the weather, always the first concern in a country where a large majority of the people lived on the land. A drought in 1897 caused a poor harvest and in 1898 famine ravaged Shantung. The drought and famine continued into 1899 and spread north to near Peking. One natural disaster followed another. The Yellow River, appropriately called "China's sorrow," overflowed in 1898 and inundated the Shantung plain, already in distress from the drought. Crowds of starving farmers flocked to the provincial cities. The government's relief effort was corrupt and inefficient. By the spring of 1900, Sir Claude MacDonald, the tall, angular British minister in Peking, could still opine that favorable weather would dissolve the Boxer movement. "I am now convinced that a few days heavy rainfall, to terminate the long-continued drought which has helped largely to excite unrest in the country districts, would do more to restore tranquility than any measures which either the Chinese government or foreign governments can take."[13]

MacDonald was probably correct. Drought and flood are frequent in north China and only 20 years before a drought had caused one of the worst famines of history. The rural population still had horrific recollections of starvation and death and every reason to be anxious and to look to supernatural factors as both a cause and a solution to the drought. The Boxers saw the foreigners in China as the disharmony that caused drought. One of their slogans was: "Heaven is now sending down eight millions of spirit soldiers to extirpate these foreign religions, and when this has been done there will be a timely rain."[14]

The Christian missionaries, of course, ridiculed the Boxers' faith in heathen charms, slogans, and prayers for rain. Luella Miner said that the Boxers were "plainly the work of the devil, saturated with superstition and witchcraft, reeking with cruelty, diabolical to the last degree, an open revolt against Jehovah and his Annointed."[15] In the correct Christian manner, the missionaries also prayed for rain and saw in its absence the evidence of an ineffable plan by God to convert the Chinese to Christianity.

Prayers for rain are not unknown in our own enlightened era. "Even in modern secular America, with its general trust in scientific explanation of the physical world and its extraordinary technological capability, when a serious drought hit the Midwest in the summer of 1988, Jesse Jackson, then campaigning for the Democratic nomination for president, prayed for rain in the middle of an Iowa cornfield, and an Ohio florist flew in a Sioux medicine man from one of the Dakotas to perform a rainmaking ceremony which thousands came to watch." According to press reports, most of the people attending these ceremonies seemed to have some faith they would be efficacious.[16]

Nor were the Boxer's claims to invulnerability to Western bullets unique. Ten years before in the United States another beleaguered people, the American Indians, had been swept up in the Ghost Dance movement which included incantations to the gods and predictions that white oppressors would be swept away, the buffalo herds would return, and true believers would be immune to bullets. The massacre at Wounded Knee in 1890 destroyed the American Indian spirit soldiers just as Western arms would destroy the Chinese spirit soldiers in 1900. People on opposite sides of the world, unaware of each other, reacted in similar ways to a situation in which white invaders threatened their culture and economy. Scholar Paul Cohen calls the phenomena death anxiety and says of the Boxers, and other similar movements, "Their religious and magical practices had as a paramount goal the affording of protection and emotional security in the face of a future that was indeterminate and fraught with danger and risk."[17]

Other causes of Chinese discontent also contributed to the Boxer outbreak. The railroads were a new irritation. The railroad from Tientsin to Machia Pu, one and one-half miles outside the walls of Peking, was completed in 1897 by a Franco–Belgian syndicate. The building of the railroad had two consequences. First, it offended the Chinese folk superstition of *feng shui*. Running straight as a string across the landscape and cutting through sacred ground, the railroad let enter evil spirits, brought down calamity, and disturbed the calculations of the soothsayers. Adding to the offense, the railroad violated innumerable cemeteries in the course of its run. Nothing was more sacred to the Chinese than the graves of their ancestors. Dark rumors of human sacrifice also circulated. The blood and body of a Chinese child was said to reinforce every wooden sleeper underlying the track and every pier of every bridge of the railroad. The Catholics were known to collect street children for their orphanages. Why did they want these children if not for some devilish rite of their barbarous religion? One is reminded of present day rumors in many countries around the world that foreigners kidnap children and steal their organs for transplants.

An equally serious grievance against the railroad was economic. From time immemorial, commerce from Tientsin to Peking had been by boat up the muddy, winding Pei Ho or North River to Tungchou. At Tientsin the commerce from the well-watered south and the austere plains and deserts of the north met. Tea, pressed into bricks, was the most valuable product moving north. Five thousand cargo and passenger boats plied the Pei Ho. They departed Tientsin in an endless procession, each boat with its square, bamboo-slatted sail and crew to pole and pull, inching up the river at tortoise speed to arrive — with favorable winds and waters — at Tungchou in three or four days. At Tungchou, a walled city with an ancient pagoda, a new American flour mill, and Christian-owned North China College, caravans of two-humped Bactrian camels met the boats, loaded the brick tea on the ungainly beasts, and set off for the vast interior of Asia.

The traveler also left the boats behind at Tungchou and made the passage to Peking, most commonly in a cramped and uncomfortable hired cart pulled by mules over an execrable track that wandered over the plain through the mud and dust, paralleling, crossing, and sometimes following a centuries-old but never repaired stone highway. The stone highway showed the glory that had been China. It was raised about five feet above the level of the ground, more than 25 feet wide, and its surface was of fitted flat stones 16 inches thick and as much as eight feet long and two and one half feet wide. Near Peking were seventy miles of stone highways. Monumental stone gateways leading to shady and well-tended cemeteries lined the ancient highways.[18] The traveler, shaken to the marrow by the jolting on the muddy tracks and stone highways, finally arrived at the massive walls of Peking. This was how visitors made their way to the capital of China until 1897.

The railroad destroyed this pattern. In 1900 a traveler and a bale of tea traveled by rail from Tientsin to Peking in four hours. The tea caravans, rather than meeting the riverboats at Tungchou, met the railroad just outside Peking. The boatmen, the carters, the Pei River, and the city of Tungchou were bypassed and antiquated by the railroad. Thousands lost their livelihoods and from their ranks came many Boxer recruits.

Land and power grabs by Western countries added to the woes of China. Japan — a Western power, geography to the contrary — began the process of dismembering China into spheres of influence. In 1894 and 1895, the Japanese, little regarded until then, defeated China in a brief war. Japan demanded a monetary indemnity of $300 million and, but for the pressure of the other powers, would have occupied Manchuria while China raised cash to pay the indemnity. However, the Europeans persuaded Japan to pull out of Manchuria in exchange for lesser concessions elsewhere in China.

Inspired by Japan, the rapacious and ambitious Europeans sliced off pieces of a weak and failing Chinese empire. Russia had its eye on Manchuria and, in a charade of benevolence, extended to China a long-term loan to pay one-half of the indemnity to Japan, but extracted permission to build a railroad in Manchuria and to station Russian troops there to guard the railroad. In 1898, the Russians forced the Chinese into another agreement allowing them to lease Port Arthur, now called Lushun, the terminus of the Manchurian railroad. Russian influence in China now rivaled that of the British. It appeared that the partition of China was underway, British and American objections notwithstanding. The Anglo Saxons were the status quo foreign powers in China. The British possessed Hong Kong and 60 percent of Chinese foreign trade; the Americans, following the British lead, had commercial rather than colonial, interests in China. Both countries sought to keep China intact to preserve their domination of China's trade — and, in the American case, a traditional antipathy to colonialism.

The French, envious of the British and second to none in colonial ambitions, could hardly allow the Russians and Japanese to gain prizes without extracting their pound of flesh. They demanded ports and trade concessions in the south. Even the Italians got into the act. Italy desired to lease a port to establish a sphere of influence in Chekiang province. However, the decrepit Chinese government retained enough perspective not to be intimidated by Italy and turned down its request in March 1899.

Germany was not to be denied. A latecomer to the game of imperialism and running fast to catch up, the Germans were keen to try their hand at bringing German civilization to the heathen world. In 1897, the propitious murder of two German Catholic missionaries in Shantung furnished a pretext. To avenge the insult a German fleet steamed to Chiao Chou Bay on the southern coast of the parrot's beak of Shantung, occupied the area and forced China to lease the bay and the city of Tsingtao to them. Germany also secured generous development rights, including mining and railroads. The Germans followed up their naval operations with punitive expeditions to burn the villages and punish the villagers where Christians had been persecuted. By 1898, a substantial piece of Shantung province, birthplace of the sages Confucius and Mencius, became, in effect, a German colony.

In sending the fleet, Kaiser Wilhelm exploded with bombastic fervor. "Thousands of German Christians will breathe more easily when they know that the German Emperor's ships are near; hundreds of German traders will revel in the knowledge that the German Empire has at last secured a firm footing in Asia; hundreds of thousands of Chinese will quiver when they feel the iron fist of Germany heavy on their necks; and the whole German nation will be delighted that its Government has done a manly act." The Kaiser sent his brother Henry to the East with additional ships for the expedition and instructed him that "if anyone should undertake to insult us in our rights or wish to harm us, then drive in with the mailed fist and, as God wills it, bind about your brows the laurels which no one in this entire German Empire will begrudge us."[19]

The world's most influential newspaper, *The Times* of London, enthused. The Germans were decisive "instead of wasting time making remonstrances at Peking, which would assuredly have been met as usual by the innumerable dilatory devices of Chinese diplomacy."[20] The common view of the West was that "force and fear are the only things that count ... with regard to almost all Asiatics."[21] Some American missionaries also applauded German vigor and would have welcomed a similar, forthright action on the part of the United States to intimidate the Chinese. "The German government deserves the admiration of all right minded people the world over. The immediate effect throughout Shantung province is to strengthen every form of mission work."[22] Even the American and British missionaries who did not go so far as to approve the German military expeditions were scornful of the cautious policies of their own countries. Will Ament expressed a common view: "Our government does not allow any threats or strong measures to be taken and the Chinese foreign office fears nothing but force."[23]

However, the more astute missionaries later saw German frightfulness as a major cause of the Boxer Rebellion. Arthur Smith said that the German military expeditions were "a fatal dart which never for an instant failed to rankle in the Chinese body politic."[24] A few months after the Chinese felt the Germans' mailed fist in Shantung, the Boxers rose in the same province.

* * *

The missionaries are the most arguable element in an examination of why the Boxers erupted and killed Chinese Christians and foreigners in 1900. Prince Kung of the Imperial Ching Court expressed the Chinese brief against the West succinctly: "Take away your missionaries and your opium and you will be welcome."[25] Opium was the great trade item of the British with China and Great Britain had cultivated the trade with its gunboats and diplomats. China had lost two wars with Great Britain attempting to staunch the import of opium, and now had no choice but to tolerate the noxious opium trade. In Chinese eyes, Christianity was the other great infliction visited upon China by the West. Missionaries were the visible symbols of that infliction. The businessmen stayed in their concessions and treaty ports; the diplomats worked and lived in their legations; marines and sailors were on their ships patrolling the coasts of China. The foreigner the Chinese saw in his village and his neighborhood was the missionary. By and large, he did not like what he saw.

To paraphrase writer Pat Barr, why the Aments of Owosso, Michigan, were so feverishly determined to convert the Wangs of Peking to their brand of Christianity is a mystery to the lay mind of today, as it was to many of Ament's contemporaries.[26] One factor was that becoming a missionary satisfied a young man's or woman's desire for adventure while permitting them to pursue what they saw as idealistic and humanitarian aims. In addition, the species *Homo sapiens* seems to have an unquenchable compulsion to persuade others to share his opinions and beliefs and can usually find a justification for action to further that objective. All religions have been spread by missionaries. Buddhism came to China with Indian missionaries in the second century and the Arabs spread Islam with sword and book in the seventh century. The nineteenth century was the great century for Christian, especially Protestant, endeavor to deliver the doctrine of Christ throughout the world. The "evangelization of the world in this generation" was the missionary motto: "Let us arise and resolve, at whatever cost of self-denial, to grapple in right earnest, as we have never yet done, with the stupendous work of supplanting the three thousand years' consolidated empire of Satan in these vast realms by the establishment of Messiah's reign."[27]

It is easy to condemn the missionaries as agents of imperialism and Western commerce and to laugh at their follies. But the missionary of the nineteenth century believed — as did most of his countrymen — that Christianity was the cornerstone and pre-requisite of civilization. "No social revolution and no intellectual education," said a British diplomat, "could so thoroughly advance the moral and material evolution of China as the willing adoption of the Christian faith."[28] A missionary journal said it even more succinctly: "We contend that a true Civilization cannot exist apart from Christianity."[29] Therefore, China was backward because it was not Christian. By converting the Chinese, the missionary was not only saving souls but bringing the benefits of modern civilization to a benighted empire.

Arthur Henderson Smith, the widely-read missionary author, cited the benefits of Christianity: "It will sanctify childhood, ennoble motherhood, dignify manhood, and purify every social condition," says Smith.[30] A writer to *The New York Times* was more emphatic. "The greatest force in the world today to bring about that great ideal, the brotherhood of the whole human race, is the work of Christian missionaries, whose one great aim is to put into the hearts of men and women in all the lands of the earth the common love for Jesus Christ."[31] One of the greatest of China missionaries, Timothy Richard, wrote that, "Christianity, wherever it goes, brings material blessings with it. Whatever country is lacking in Clothing, in Agriculture, in Art, in Industries and in Commerce is sure to be benefited in all these departments by Christianity."[32]

Will Ament differed from his colleagues in equating the material with the spiritual. "The oldest Chinese Christian in Peking, the first man baptized, to this day has no faith in foreign medicine, nor any interest whatever in foreign devices or machinery.... Is there not too much of practically making the acceptance of Western ideas synonymous with acceptance of Christianity?"[33] Although inconsistent on the subject of foreign intervention in Chinese affairs, Ament came down on the enlightened side more often than not: "China must be left to work out her own salvation by her own methods, foreign nations giving only such help and encouragement as they are invited to do."[34]

We moderns have abandoned the idea that Christianity and civilization are inseparably linked, but the related view that Western culture and civilization are synonymous is still prevalent. Democracy, private enterprise, human rights, and free trade have replaced Christianity as the sacred sacraments of the West. Today most missionaries are secular, concerning themselves with social justice, economic development, humanitarian aid, and political freedom. But they are missionaries just as William Ament and Arthur Smith were. They aim to bring a true civilization to a people they judge to lack that blessing. If Ament were alive today, he would probably not be a Christian missionary. He might instead head a no-nonsense program of economic assistance in a poor country. Arthur Smith might be a prolific writer and tireless campaigner for human rights. Neither would be adverse to calling on the U.S. Marines to invade and protect their freedom to spread their views. Missionary fervor is not dead in the West. We look back on the missionaries of a hundred years ago with condescension, but the inhabitants of this planet one hundred years from now will look back the same way at the secular missionaries of today, amused at their quaint beliefs of what constitutes truth and justice, irritated at their strident surety, and appalled at their pushiness. However, despite their errors, conceits, and overweening sense of their worthiness, missionaries of all ages are worthy of qualified respect, for at least they have the intention, however misguided, of improving the state of mankind.

* * *

The missionary issue in China is two: the Roman Catholics and the Protestants. By 1900 the Catholics had been in China three hundred years and had gained a membership of half a million Chinese, impressive at first appearance, except that half a million represents little more than one-tenth of 1 percent of the total population of China. Catholics lived apart from Chinese society under the authority of a foreign bishop who maintained discipline and obedience.

Until the late nineteenth century the Catholic Church was only a minor sect in the Chinese pantheon, but the expansion of Western power led to its expansion in membership, influence, and arrogance.

Seven hundred and fifty foreign priests from Italy and France lived in China in 1900. The French government appointed itself the protector of all Catholics in China and confirmed that status in treaties. The French had little trade with China and latched onto the Catholics to enhance their influence and keep a strong hand in Chinese affairs. That the French government was, on occasion, anti-clerical in France at the same time it defended the faith in China did not trouble the expedient Gauls. France also derived a benefit by sponsoring the Catholic Church: the finest intelligence network of any Western country. After three centuries of difficult survival, Catholics were attuned to every nuance of Chinese behavior and hint of threat. They communicated their insights to the French Legation in Peking.

By contrast, Protestant missionaries had been in China less than a century and in significant numbers only since 1860 when a military expedition by Great Britain and France forced the government to open the whole country to the purveyors of Western goods and religion. The next forty years was an era of missionary expansion. By 1900, 2,500 Protestant missionaries — men, women, and children — lived in China.[35] About 1,000 were American, 1,400 British, and 100 European. The Protestants had only 80,000 converts — far fewer than the Catholics — but their membership rolls were growing more rapidly.[36]

The *modus operandi* of the two faiths differed. The foreign Catholic priests lived apart "in a state of mysterious seclusion which the native vainly attempts to penetrate, and about which he invents the most wonderful stories."[37] The Protestants were on the streets, preaching to anyone who would listen, and many who would not. Their churches and chapels were open to all. The Protestant was a glad-hander, the Catholic a recluse. The Catholics were ingrown, protective of their hard-won privileges and members. The Protestants were outgoing, with nothing to lose, save their lives and their dignity.

The Catholics had the premium on arrogance. The Protestants were obnoxious and offensive; the Roman Catholics were an *imperium in imperio*. The Catholic missionary came armed with the authority of Rome, nearly two thousand years of tradition, a hierarchic and authoritarian bureaucracy, and a history of attempting to dominate secular authorities. They built massive Gothic cathedral-fortresses that offended *feng shui* no less than did the railroads. Their bishops adopted "the rank of a Chinese Governor, and wear a button on their caps indicative of that fact, traveling in a sedan chair with the number of bearers appropriate to that rank, with outriders and attendants on foot, an umbrella of honor borne in front, and a cannon discharged upon their arrival and departure."[38]

Will Ament — boldness dominated his character — broke the mold of Protestant missionaries by calling on Catholic churches to meet Catholic priests. His opinions, however, were hardly favorable or atypical of Protestants. Although complimentary of some aspects of Catholicism, and admiring the discipline and unity of doctrine of the Catholics, he saw its missionary effort as one to "convert the Chinese to a Church rather than to Christ." He criticized the ostentation and pomposity of Roman Catholic priests with wry humor: "We have never yet seen a priest whose appearance indicated nightly flagellations or whose penances impeded a good digestion."[39]

Catholics and Protestants shared characteristics which made Christianity hateful to the Chinese. The first was intolerance. The Chinese, it may be said, were not intolerant of other religions, but rather too tolerant. Religion in China was a blend of folk superstition, Taoism, Buddhism, and Confucianism, with Confucian philosophy important among the upper, educated classes while Taoism and Buddhist attracted the lower classes. The Chinese were untroubled by the coexistence of different, often conflicting strains of religion in their society. However,

Christianity demanded to be the one and only faith of the people, unwilling or unable to accommodate itself to other religions, and requiring of its converts a renunciation of much of Chinese culture, most importantly, ancestor worship, folk celebrations and ceremonies, and much-loved theatricals.

The Chinese associated Christianity with the opium trade, the disastrous Taiping Rebellion — led by a Chinese visionary who claimed to be the younger brother of Jesus — the unequal treaties, and the doctrine of extra-territoriality under which citizens of Western countries were not subject to the jurisdiction of Chinese courts. The missionary, in Chinese eyes, was a pathfinder for the consuls and generals, the vanguard of foreign armies that would subject China to rule by the West. Not surprisingly, the outcasts of Chinese society made up many of those embracing Christianity. Chinese Christians, especially the Roman Catholics, formed a community apart from the mainstream and — as Western influence expanded — they extracted privileges and advantages, chief among them protection by the missionaries and the diplomats from the laws of the land.

The mass of Chinese regarded the Christian religion with a mixture of contempt, fear, and ignorance. Foreigners were "hairy ones"; Chinese Christians were "second-class hairy ones"; and Chinese who sold or used foreign goods were "third-class hairy ones."[40] Witness the following excerpt from an anti–Christian pamphlet widely distributed in China in the 1860s. "During the first three months of life the anuses of all [Christian] infants are plugged up with a small hollow tube, which is taken out at night. They call this 'retention of the vital essence.' It causes the anus to dilate so that upon growing up sodomy will be facilitated. At the junction of each spring and summer boys procure the menstrual discharge of women and, smearing it on their faces, go into Christian churches to worship."[41]

Another pamphlet titled "Death to the Devil's Religion" was printed in more than 800,000 copies in the 1890s. The scurrilous pamphlet addresses Chinese suspicions that an economic motive lay behind the missionaries. "In the case of death, the priest drives out of the house all the relatives and friends, and amid all kinds of formulas and behind locked doors he puts the body in the coffin. Before he does so, he secretly cuts both of the eyes out of the head. The reason is the following: out of every one hundred pounds of Chinese lead eight pounds of silver can be secured.... However, the only way in which this silver can be extracted is to mix it with the eyes of dead Chinese. The eyes of foreigners are perfectly useless for this purpose."[42]

Jesus was depicted as a crucified hog in anti–Christian pamphlets. The Chinese language is rich in double entendre and the words "Tien Chu Chiao" meaning "the religion of the Lord of Heaven" can be written in characters having the same pronunciation but meaning "the squeak of the celestial hog." Missionaries were called "pig-goat devils" and their converts "the sons and grandsons of pig-goat devils."[43]

A British military attache in 1897 described the Chinese brief against the missionary. "It is, perhaps, not strange in this country that though the foreigner is despised, the native who follows the creed of the foreigner frequently obtains power and influence to which he could not otherwise attain. The reason for this is that the mass of the upper classes regard the missionaries as political agents and fear them. The poor know this, and look, in many cases, to the missionary — the honest for protection, the dishonest to further their own ends. These ends may be the evasion of recovery of a debt, or some similar dispute in which they know that their connection with the Church will influence the Magistrate.[44]

A German observer commented in a similar vein.

> No doubt most of the missionaries are entirely unselfish; but their great fault is that, in order to make a convert, they close their eyes to many faults. It is a great disgrace for a Chinaman to abandon the religion of his fore fathers, to turn his back upon Confucian morals. To cease honoring his ancestors in the accustomed manner is equivalent to a complete severance of the bonds between him, his

family, and his country. The natural consequence is that, in villages where "converts" are to be found, two parties are formed — the Chinese who acknowledge the authority of the officials, and a minority of "converts," who are under the protection of the missionary. This protection is only too often abused, and the "Christians" in this way obtain victories over the "heathens." When the influence of the missionaries was increased enormously under treaty rights, this meant a new triumph for the Chinese "Christians," who soon showed such arrogance that riots were inevitable. They found many adherents who regarded the new faith solely as a protection for their crimes; for if among the missionaries there are many who act in good faith, among the "converts" there are but few who deserve respect. In all Shanghai papers the words "no converts" are invariably added to the "help wanted" advertisements. The great mistake of the missionaries is that they think themselves bound to protect against the authorities every rascal who calls himself a Christian. Equal justice would do much to preserve quiet. It may be necessary for the missionaries and their adherents to show greater tolerance to those who do not share their beliefs.[45]

In 1889, Lieutenant Wood of the US Navy was even more critical: "It is not extravagant to say that the work of the missionaries in China and Korea is absolutely without any result, except to hold them up to the ridicule of the natives. It has before been stated, and I concur in the belief, that there is not a Chinese convert to Christianity of sound mind to-day within the entire extent of China."[46] That was too harsh. Slowly but surely, the missionary endeavor had built up churches and developed Chinese Christians of conviction and courage.

The growth in missionary influence generated its counter-reaction. In 1891, a writer predicted the future for the missionaries in China as "pillage and massacre at intervals followed by pecuniary indemnification, an indefinite struggle with the hatred of a whole nation; compensated by a certain number of genuine converts to their faith."[47] He was accurate.

For all their faults the missionaries were, in general, persons of good heart and good intention, but the hardships they suffered, the indignities heaped upon them, and their failure to bring more than a tiny fraction of Chinese to Christianity caused in many a barely-concealed hostility to their host country and its people. The missionaries praised the virtues of the common man and asserted that the Chinese peasant was receptive to the doctrines of Christianity. The machinations of the upper classes stymied the spread of the gospel. Therefore, it would be a good thing if the upper classes of China — the gentry, mandarins, and Manchu overlords — were defeated and humiliated. Again, the voice of Charles Ewing: "For the best of China herself, most of the missionaries here seem to think that a thorough-going defeat [in the Sino-Japanese war of 1894] will be advantageous."[48] The British missionary Griffin John said, "War is going to be a source of great blessing to China. It is an awful chastisement, but China needed it, and will be the better for it."[49] A humiliated China would come to Christ. The missionaries were not entirely mistaken. The Boxer debacle led to successes by the missionaries. After 1900 they attracted to Christianity prominent Chinese men and women who saw in the culture and religion of the foreign devils the means by which China could survive and hope to regain its customary position at the center of the world.

2

Will Ament in China

In 1877, when William Ament came to China, the mission field of Peking, capital and heartland of the Ching dynasty, was still new. North China was the citadel of Chinese conservatism, less receptive to alien ideas than the coastal cities of the south which had been forced to deal with foreign intruders for decades. The Chinese were contemptuous of foreign devils; the atmosphere for evangelical work was hostile, the harvest of souls meager, the possibility of martyrdom ever-present. Seven years before, twenty foreigners, including priests, nuns, and the French consul, had been killed in Tientsin. The Tientsin Massacre was set off by rumors that the Catholics were killing Chinese children in their rites. A Chinese mob rampaged through the city and destroyed the hated foreigners. Ament and other Protestants assured themselves that the arrogance of the Roman Catholic Church incited the Tientsin Massacre. The Protestants—and the Anglo-Saxons—were different from the Romanists, they told themselves, but they also worried that the Chinese could not distinguish one foreign devil from another.

Ament was typical of American Protestant missionaries in their golden period of enthusiasm. The evangelical juices of missionary pioneers from New England had run thin and Ament and many of his contemporaries came from the Midwest. Ament was a sensible rather than an emotional Christian, a self-confident leader, and certain of the moral and intellectual superiority of his faith. Caught up in the industrial age, Ament saw much to admire and emulate in the success of American business. The vivid images of military conquest stirred him. No otherworldly halo hung over the pious heads of Ament and his colleagues; they were practical men and women of action.

Ament was born September 14, 1851, in Owosso, Michigan, a village near where the thriving corn belt met the cold, north woods.[1] His father was a hard-working blacksmith with a pioneer's determination to grow rich on his labors. Soon, he was the proprietor of a hotel—the only brick building in the village—and a stage line. Will Ament's mother, Emily, was plain-faced and church-going in contrast to her ambitious, rough-hewn husband.

Young Will Ament learned hard work from his father—at eleven he was driving a team of horses—and piety from his mother. He grew into a solid, dependable, and conscientious lad, traits that might have led him to build on his father's achievements to become a captain of industry or, under the influence of his mother, to devote his life to religion. When he was fourteen years old, his father died and the scales tipped in favor of his gentle mother and religion. The most adventurous of the promising, well-educated sons and daughters of Midwestern families often chose the life of a missionary in foreign lands. For Ament, the virility of the missionary enterprise was appealing. He was "hearty, aggressive, and fearless," a fine horseman, and a good athlete. He played second base on Owosso's championship baseball team, the Blue Sox, and was called "Home Run Ament."

Ament was the first son of Owosso to graduate from college. He chose to attend the liberal arts college of Oberlin in the town of the same name in Ohio. Oberlin College was a unique institution, the Puritan and Congregational tradition of New England moved west. The leadership of the college was evangelical with the objective of graduating young men and women of conspicuous Christian piety and determined ambition to spread the gospel of salvation. Oberlin was reformist, confident in its virtue, advanced in its social agenda—the school was co-educational and admitted "negroes"—strict in its regulation of students, and, most of all, possessed of unlimited Christian energy. The curriculum was laden with biblical studies. Morning prayers and a daily chapel were mandatory, and students had to attend both Sunday morning and evening religious services and abstain from recreation on the Sabbath. Faculty members prayed or led a hymn at the start of each class and a Thursday lecture for all students was usually a sermon. Oberlin excelled as a seedbed of missionaries and William Ament became one of them. He had "the brisk air of a young business man, an athletic build, an alertness of mind and robustness of soul."[2]

After Ament graduated from Oberlin and Andover Theological Seminary in Massachusetts, he applied to America's oldest and most venerable missionary organization, the Congregationalist American Board of Commissioners for Foreign Missions, the ABCFM or American Board, to become a missionary. His letter of application was a model of reasoned piety. His desire to be a missionary had been the "result of gradual growth." He had not received any "visions or special revelations on this subject, but a deepening and ever increasing conviction" of his duty. He declared himself in perfect health and engaged to a young lady fully supportive of his aspirations and "consecrated to the work from infancy." He was confident: "Difficulties do not appall me, for I rest assured that as my day is so my strength shall be."[3] "Strong" was a word that Ament often used; he often described fellow missionaries as "not strong," meaning they were not quite up the arduous task of being a China missionary.

Ament affirmed that he accepted the doctrines of the Congregational Church. His beliefs would "place as central and most important the doctrine of the Deity of Christ.... I would preach much concerning the Love of God as revealed in His glorious redemptive plan."[4] No fire-breathing, Bible-thumping mystic was Will Ament. He was the strong, sensible, reliable, and intelligent Christian the American Board sought.

Ament was accepted for assignment to the North China Mission, the pinnacle of missionary aspirations. Letters of recommendations for him were highly favorable, although one reference made the criticism that "on occasions in which cautious deliberation would be needed he might possibly decide too quickly."[5] The comment was apt. Ament, to the ruin of his reputation, would never conquer his tendency to rush ahead when "cautious deliberation" might be more advisable. This caveat notwithstanding, Ament was an outstanding candidate. Even his choice of wife was exemplary. She was Mary Alice Penfield, born July 4, 1856, the daughter of a retired Oberlin professor of Greek and Latin.[6] The young couple, in whirlwind fashion, prepared for their life together among the heathen. They were married in Cleveland on August 23, 1877. William Ament was 25 years old; Mary Penfield was just 21. After a few frantic weeks of preparation, they took a train to California on the first leg of their journey to a newly-created missionary station in Paoting, ninety miles south of Peking. Ament wrote from Oakland, California, before his departure. "We sail October 17. Our steamer is the *China*. I am favorably impressed with the Chinese whom we daily see. I await with impatience the study of the language that I may make known the riches of the Gospel."

Twenty-seven days later the Aments arrived in Japan and after a brief visit with missionaries in Kobe were off to China. Bad weather off the China coast at the Taku banks delayed them six days. After finally crossing the treacherous banks their ship navigated thirty miles up the Pei river to Tientsin where they were greeted by the humorous and good-natured Arthur and Emma Smith, seven years in China. Arthur Henderson Smith was on his way to becoming a missionary author and the fount of all Christian wisdom on China. Emma seems a pleasant if

Will and Mary Ament. Will was twenty-five and Mary twenty-one when they married in 1877 and left shortly thereafter for China (Porter, *William Scott Ament*, 1911).

simple-minded purveyor of biblical verses at every opportunity. They helped the Aments arrange to travel the one hundred miles to Paoting overland. The usual route was by riverboat but, December upon them, the river was frozen. They procured three Peking carts, three wheelbarrows, and a mule litter for Mary Ament and jounced over the frozen north China plain for five days to reach Paoting. Ament commented dryly that they had "the usual experience with Chinese inns" along the way, the usual experience being uncomfortable and unpleasant, but stimulating fascinated amazement at the number and variety of insects inhabiting a Chinese inn. Mary Ament was the first white woman to traverse this region by land. She suffered from idle and persistent curiosity from the Chinese, most of whom had apparently never contemplated the possibility that foreign devils could be of the female sex. The attention was not necessarily sexual. Western women were repulsive to Chinese men. "First, there is your hair," said missionary doctor Emma Martin. "It looks as if rats had nested in it. Then there are your shameless breasts, sticking out on your chest, instead of being bandaged close to the body. And most of all, your feet. They look like gunboats."[7]

The American Board had opened Paoting as a mission station in 1873. The city had a population of 100,000 and was the capital of a prefecture or *fu* with twenty walled cities, several hundred towns and villages and a population of more than three million people. When the Aments arrived in Paoting as missionary recruits, the complement of the mission consisted of Isaac Pierson, his wife, and his sister. They were the only Protestant missionaries in Paoting-fu with a population "half that of the State of New York." The Catholics had churches in the north and south suburbs but the Protestants did not anticipate — nor receive — any welcome from their brothers in Christ of the Romanist persuasion. Protestants and Catholics ignored each other.

The history of the Paoting Mission illustrates the difficulties of working in China. The first task of Isaac Pierson on arriving in 1873 had been to find premises for the mission and living quarters. Pierson took up residence at an inn and immediately began searching for a property to rent or buy for the mission. "The people," he said, "were afraid to sell to us" and only after several months was he able to negotiate an agreement to rent the inn where he was staying. The inn was long and narrow in shape, with rooms built around two courtyards. One of the front rooms served as a chapel and the remainder was living quarters for the missionaries.

After another year of effort Pierson was able to rent a street chapel. Street chapels were the fundamental tool of the Protestants to attract new members. They rented shops on crowded streets and at principal intersections and installed an altar, religious pictures, and a few benches. There, a missionary went each afternoon for two or three hours to preach to anyone who entered the chapel — or sometimes to stand on the street and invite passers-by in — to give away or sell pamphlets and Bibles, and to meet with Chinese Christians and inquirers.

However, the Chinese, who tolerated the missionaries while they stayed behind the high walls of their mission compounds, took a dim view of the establishment of street chapels serving as retail outlets for public marketing of Christianity. Pierson opened his street chapel on a Sunday with a sermon to a full house of Chinese inquirers. By sundown, the magistrate of Paoting had been informed of this new activity of the Christians and had sent runners to inquire what was going on. Threats were made against the Chinese who had rented the street chapel to the foreign devils and Pierson feared that "we have a siege before us." The Catholic Church had been driven out of a rented building in Paoting two years before and the fate of the Protestants might be the same. However, Pierson was persistent and stubborn and, slowly, the furor against the street chapel died down. For a poor Chinese, a street chapel was a good place to sit and rest — although the price to be paid was to have to listen to a hairy foreigner braying in atrocious Chinese an incomprehensible notion of man's relationship to the spirit world.

By the time the Aments arrived, the Piersons had overcome the early hardships. Two cozy rooms, heated by a wood stove, were ready for them. Their new, sanctified lives as missionaries to the heathen of China had begun. Will Ament took to the new life with enthusiasm. In the midst of the long, cold winter, he wrote, "My life here is one of unalloyed happiness." Each morning from nine until one the Aments wrestled with the complexities, tones, and characters of Mandarin Chinese with a teacher. Afterwards they put in long hours of study. "To acquire the Chinese language," Ament said, quoting another missionary, "is a work for men with bodies of brass, lungs of steel, heads of oak, hands of spring-steel, eyes of eagles, hearts of apostles, memories of angels, and lives of Methuselahs!"[8] The intricacies of a language do not always surrender to the bull rushes of a determined male. Ament, however, conquered Chinese more rapidly than average. Scarcely one year after his arrival he went into the countryside alone — "alone" meaning without another foreigner although Chinese assistants and servants usually accompanied him. A brave man was Will Ament to try his wings as a preacher so soon. Most missionaries devoted two years to language study to master enough Chinese to teach and preach — and many never learned the language well. "My idioms," Ament said, "are very imperfect and words and ideas considerably mixed, but I manage in some way to get through a sermon."[9] Mary Ament, an intelligent, efficient young woman, learned Chinese even faster than her husband.[10]

Despite the frustrations of learning Chinese, life in Paoting fascinated Ament with the "heathen processions," colorful lanterns, the men and women carrying bundles of incense and colored paper to be ceremoniously burned "before their idols" in the New Year's celebrations. Kite flying was the most popular recreation and he described the grotesque forms of the "whirring monsters" that filled the sky. The winter night skies over the dry north China plain, so much clearer than the humid atmosphere of his native Michigan, entranced him. He denied "the shock to the nervous system which one is apt to feel on coming for the first time into the midst of heathenism." He professed to admire the Chinese and expressed confidence that he would become a "successful harvester of souls."[11]

Ament's arrival in Paoting coincided with the beginning of one of the greatest calamities of human history, the drought and great famine in northern China from 1877 to 1879. Timothy Richard, the British missionary, was one of the first to report on the famine. "That people pull down their houses, sell their wives and daughters, eat roots and carrion, clay and leaves, is news which nobody wonders at. It is the regular thing. If this were not enough to move one's pity, the sight of men and women lying helpless on the roadside, or if dead, torn by hungry dogs and magpies should do and the news which has reached up, even the last few days, of children being boiled and eaten up, is so fearful as to make one shudder at the thought."[12] The famine region began at Paoting and extended south and west. William Ament, novice missionary, lived in Paoting.

Ten million people died in north China of starvation and disease, mostly typhus, during the great famine. Missionaries estimated that one district saw 25 percent of its population die, another 19 percent, another 33 percent, and a fourth an astonishing 73 percent.[13] The famine gave missionaries "the greatest opportunity of the century" to demonstrate that the religion of Christianity had an earthly practicality in addition to its heavenly promise.[14]

Richard's graphic descriptions of starvation, cannibalism, and slavery among the peasants of north China led to an outpouring of contributions from the business community in Shanghai and the collection of relief funds in London and other cities. Sixty-nine foreigners, including Protestant and Roman Catholic missionaries and volunteers from Imperial Maritime Customs, a Chinese government agency managed by foreigners, joined the effort to distribute relief supplies. Four died of typhus. Arthur Smith nearly died and many others were stricken. The famine would also result in a significant number of conversions to Christianity as desperate Chinese—"rice Christians" they were called derisively—embraced Christianity.

The famine was the testing ground for the mettle of William Ament. In May 1878, Ament and Isaac Pierson departed Paoting—now full of beggars and disease—with cart loads of food and heavy bags of silver. They visited villages and did a quick census of families and inhabitants. Based on their findings, they provided enough money to the villagers for ten days of food. Ament worked only on the edge of the famine area. Food was available if the poor had money to buy it and, thus, the usual assistance given to the needy was small sums of money. Toward the interior, in the center of the famine area, food was unattainable at any price and only a trickle of rice and wheat entered on the backs of mules and camels.

Shortly, Pierson departed to take up new duties in Peking and Ament was left in the countryside. "Imagine a young man alone, not an English speaking man within oceans of miles, possessing only a smattering of the language, living in a low room of a Chinese inn, with black walls and brick floor, sleeping on a Chinese brick bed, the abode of fleas and worse inhabitants, having to deal with men whose business it is to cheat and lie, surrounded each day by hundreds of people whose bones protrude for want of food, separated from his source of supplies, so that he had no food but the coarse grain the natives sold him."[15] Ament saw the heads of robbers suspended in cages on the streets as object lessons to the populace; he traveled by cart over hundreds of miles of rutted tracks, the carts drawn by mules as poor as the people he was trying to serve; he visited villages, registered the inhabitants as best he could and distributed money and food. Ament "felt the sensations of a soldier under fire" as he saw his colleagues succumb to disease. Ament himself left the field in August, more dead than alive from an attack of dysentery, the hardy, young missionary setting a new speed record of three days travel by horseback from Paoting to Peking.

That summer's work crystallized Ament's attitudes about Chinese character. "I am not dismayed by the depravity of nature thus revealed to me," he said, "but think that I can discern the germs that may be developed into a noble manhood under the genial influences of the Gospel. The Chinese are very susceptible to kindness and fully appreciate honesty, so little known among them. They know that truth is the exception among themselves and deplore the fact."[16] Henceforth, Ament would always be the straight-forward, stern, and forthright American — he never dressed as a Chinese as did many of his colleagues. He was confident in his dealings with Chinese, authoritative in his demands, occasionally intemperate in his language, nurturing in his relationship to his Chinese converts, but contemptuous of what he saw as a lack of manliness and courage in Chinese character. First and foremost, Ament loved to preach and did so at every opportunity, in English and steadily-improving Chinese. To his Chinese congregations, he was a preacher, organizer, protector, patron, and autocrat. William Scott Ament was on his way to becoming a general of missionaries, an admirable leader who looked to no man to do what he was not willing to do himself.

While Ament was working in the countryside his wife retired to Peking to escape the ravages of disease sweeping the famine area. Mary Ament was pregnant. Not long after the completion of the famine work the Aments suffered the first of the tragedies that would befall them in China. A daughter, Margaret, was born in November 1878 but died. The mother was much weakened by the pregnancy and also suffered recurring bouts with malaria.

Ament began again, with renewed enthusiasm, his study of Chinese and embarked on the itinerant life of an evangelist, traveling his district and preaching in halting Chinese. He made a country tour alone in January 1879, only two months after Margaret died and while his wife was still sick. He wore a long sheepskin coat and Chinese woolen boots and mittens. He carried ice skates to skim along the canals and rivers while helpers followed with his luggage in carts. He "feared nothing except the cold which is very intense." He was gloriously happy, reveling in his vitality and good health, chastising the evil he saw in the Roman Catholic competition, and boldly setting forth to expound his religion. Unfortunately, Mary was not up to the task. In July 1879, when Ament returned to Peking after a nine week trip, she was prostrate in bed. She would, thereafter, remain in Peking to be near medical treatment and sympathetic friends and Ament would live "in widowed solitude" in Paoting. The lengthy separation from his wife — it is not recorded what her opinion of his absence was— allowed Ament to steep himself in the Chinese language and the customs and character of the Chinese. He studied the most difficult of the Chinese classics, looking for gems of wisdom which would help him in his quest. "I want to be a Christian Chinaman," he wrote, "with an American education. Chinese ideas and phrases and ways of looking at things are gradually soaking into me, and I hope in good time I may draw some out by dint of hard squeezing."[17] Unencumbered by a wife he traveled for weeks to deliver his message of salvation and to hone his skills for future conquests in the name of Christ. He lived as a Chinese. "I use a little charcoal fire, pay one-tenth of a cent for hot water for my tea ... and eat the usual amount of rice and millet, cabbage, sweet potatoes, onions, garlic, and dough cut in strips."

In May 1880 the apprenticeship of Will Ament came to an end. The American Board transferred him to Peking because of the continued poor health of his wife. The change did not help Mary Ament. She returned to the United States later that same year to recover her health. A year later she came back to China. Her husband pledged that he would be "careful of her, but added fatalistically that "in China, one must hold everything lightly, as it may be taken away at any moment."[18] Mary Ament was a casualty of the missionary movement. "Consecrated to the work from infancy" she was a good student of Chinese and a charming woman, but her strength was not equal to that of her vigorous husband in those early years of their missionary work. A son, Phillip Wyett, was born to the couple in October 1882 but he sickened and in June 1883, Ament wrote of Phillip, "We had hopes for his recovery. But night before last he began to grow worse. We prevented convulsions by hot baths, but congestion of the brain could not be prevented by human means, and so the dear little soul took his flight to God." Ament's letter to his mother telling of the death of his son is anguished.

Mary Ament's health problems and the deaths of her children were not atypical. The attrition rate of missionaries was high. In Shantung province, the origin of the Boxers, Timothy Richard was the only one of seven English Baptist missionaries to last more than five years.[19] Ninety-eight Protestant missionaries arrived in Shantung in the first 20 years of missionary endeavor from the 1860s to the 1880s. Fifteen died and 43 resigned, often because of health reasons, an attrition rate of 60 percent. Ament had little problem with his health. He journeyed from the borders of Mongolia to the banks of the Yellow River in lonely missions, seeking out places in which souls might be won. In a three month period, he journeyed a thousand miles, mostly with only a Chinese servant or two with him. The peculiar attraction of China found its way into the mind of William Ament. Mary's hardiness improved with time. She recovered from the death of her second child and soon traveled with her vigorous husband on lengthy visits to the Chinese countryside.

On August 24, 1884, a daughter, Emily Hammond, was born. The following year the Aments and their daughter returned to the United States. It was a one-year furlough, the standard for missionaries after seven years abroad, but while in the United States Ament resigned from the American Board to accept a position as pastor at a Congregational Church in Medina, Ohio. Will Ament had curbed his enthusiasm for China and the missionary life to accept a pedestrian position as a pastor.

The death of the Aments' two children in China and the threat that the same might happen with Emily, the apple of her father's eye, probably influenced the Aments' decision to stay in the U.S. In Medina, a son, William Sheffield, was born in 1887. The lure of China, however, could not be quelled and in 1888, Will and Mary Ament, four-year-old Emily, one-year-old Willie, and Mary's aunt, who accompanied them to assist with housekeeping and child care, returned to Peking. Will Ament was not shy about expressing his opinion of Emily. "I only repeat the testimony of others when I say that Emily is one of the most beautiful and attractive children that one usually meets. Her golden hair hangs in ringlets over her rosy blond face.... She is the only foreign child I know that does not lose her rosy cheeks in coming to this pestilential city."[20] Emily died of diphtheria in 1893. "The dread destroyer has entered our home, and our dear and only daughter has gone to her long, long home."[21] Only William of four children was now left to the couple and Ament was not hopeful because he was "not robust and in this malarial and pestilential atmosphere the odds seem to be against him."[22]

Resentment of the country and its people not far below the level of consciousness was the probable consequence of the loss of three of their four children. It was, of course, also common for children to die of diseases in America at that time, but the risk was greater in China and the Aments may have also experienced guilt for risking their children's lives. Perhaps, they truly had the unswerving faith in God's will that enabled them to bear such emotional burdens. Both of them threw themselves into the work even more heavily after the death of Emily—but after another furlough in 1897 and 1898, Mary Ament elected to remain in the United States with her son, to care for her husband's aging mother and to ensure that Willie had "suitable associates." Will Ament would live alone in China from 1898 to 1901 without the moral compass and grounding that a sensible wife would have provided. Mary had matured to become a force in her own right, a church leader in Ohio and a missionary wife respected by others for her skill in managing a Chinese household.[23] There is not a hint of martial discord between the Aments, but whether their marriage was truly happy and intimate is impossible to say.

* * *

As the nineteenth century wore itself out, Ament was distinguished in service. He presided over the mission station in Peking and its rural churches like a patriarch of old. He spoke excellent Mandarin Chinese and acquired a modest reputation as a missionary intellectual and writer. He did not fall back on the standard missionary excuse of blaming the Chinese for missionary failures. "I think it is high time that we began to seriously meditate upon the slow progress of Christianity and throw the responsibility ... upon our poor cultivation methods and lack of spiritual earnestness ... 'It is not in our stars but in ourselves that we are underlings.'"[24]

Ament was a hard taskmaster and he had little sympathy for missionaries who enjoyed the soft life in treaty ports and foreign concessions. Charles Ewing came to visit Peking for the first time in 1895. Charles was 26 years old and had been in China seven months, studying Chinese as his main task and adjusting slowly — very slowly — to the country. Ewing says wryly of his visit to Peking, "I had the opportunity of taking a trip into the country with Mr. Ament ... I wished to see a little of the outstation work, and I was glad to seize this opportunity. It was a novel experience for me. I had never ridden a mule before, scarcely even a horse, and here I was to travel on mule back for fifty miles and back. Only once had I indulged in Chinese food and now I was cutting myself off from foreign supplies for a week."[25]

To another young missionary, on another mule-back visit to the countryside, Ament described his philosophy of religious work. "What China needs most is a great body of Christians among the common people. I know that they cannot be secured without some of us burying ourselves out of sight in this country work. I only pray for the grace to be willing to work on without the notice of men."[26] Unfortunately for Ament his work in the countryside later came to the notice of men.

Ewing also told another story of Ament. One of the complaints of the Chinese against the missionaries was their interference in legal cases involving Chinese Christians. Ament was not immune to the temptation to use his authority to help a Christian against his hostile neighbors. One of his converts was a firewood seller and his stock of wood, worth about fifteen dollars — no small sum for a Chinese peasant — was set on fire and burned one night. The convert was also told to move out of the village or his house would be burned. He appealed to Ament who spoke to the Chinese official in the village on his behalf. The official did his duty to protect Christians by putting the two men who had made the threat in jail, and convicting one of the men of burning the firewood.[27] Such interference in local affairs by missionaries was resented — as was the exemption for Christians from paying a temple tax. The missionaries debated among themselves the wisdom and ethics of using their weight to influence Chinese officials. But for a missionary on the front lines of evangelical work it was difficult not to come to the aid of a hard-won Chinese convert when he was being unfairly persecuted by the non–Christian majority.

Ament was no stranger to controversy. During his stay in the U.S. in the late 1880s he stirred up a hornet's nest with his denunciation of his home town of Owosso as having "fourteen saloons, a prevalence of harlotry and infamous women." He judged Owosso to be "the worst town in the State." The city council was enraged at the slight to its fair city and rushed to condemn the outspoken the Rev. Ament — but he would later have a street in the town named for him.[28]

Unlike many missionaries, Ament did not affect Chinese dress. He dressed as an American. He cultivated a bushy, well-trimmed mustache — showing tinges of gray — which partly covered thin lips curled down in what would appear to be arrogance combined with a hint of humor. In photos, he stares at the camera with icy eyes— blue in color, according to his biographer. His stern demeanor is that of a man of substance. No long bearded mystic was he.

* * *

Will Ament's home in Peking was the American Board Mission compound. The mission compound was about the size of an American city block circled by a tall gray brick wall. Inside, the compound was divided into interior courtyards which, after much labor, became pleasant gardens. The older buildings were Chinese with tiled roofs and curved eaves. Opening onto a busy street was a chapel and to its rear were rooms for a boys day school. Within the compound was the Bridgman School, a boarding school for girls and young women, a printing press employing twenty men, and four houses for missionaries. From the front terrace of his house, Ament enjoyed a pleasant scene of large, spreading acacia trees and flowering shrubs. Scattered around the compound were auxiliary buildings—godowns (storage sheds), stables, servants quarters, several wells, a small chapel for missionaries' devotions, and a guest house.[29]

In 1900, the missionaries living in the compound were Ament, 48 years old; Charles and Bessie Ewing, 31 and 30 years old, and their two children, Marion and Ellen, 5 and 1 years old; Mrs. John L. Mateer, 55, a recent widow; and three unmarried women: Nellie Russell, 39, Elizabeth Sheffield, 25, and Ada Haven, 50. Ada was the principal of the Bridgman School and planned to marry another missionary, a first marriage for her that would be delayed by subsequent events.

The mission compound was the spiritual oasis of the missionaries in the inhospitable world of Peking. From here the missionaries sallied forth to save China, but at the end of the day they returned to the walled compound. As one woman missionary said, "How dismal ... the ugly, dirty city full of unnamable wretchedness and pollution, a nation equally squalid and unfruitful! But love and faith and youth ignore all these. There was the lovely, quiet court of the Mission Compound, restful from the noise of the busy, evil city."[30] So impenetrable and isolated were the compounds of Peking that travelers who saw only the walls lining the alleyways spoke of Peking as a treeless city of mud and dirt; but travelers who climbed the Tartar Wall and looked down into the compounds described with enthusiasm the manicured gardens, greenery, and large trees hidden behind the walls. Peking was a city of the unknown and the mysterious.

The personal relationships of missionaries living in such isolation and close proximity to each other were often strained. Missionaries were piously complimentary about their colleagues, yet many were strong-minded, intolerant, and argumentative. Mental breakdowns were frequent, and intense ideological arguments were conducted at or just below the level of personal animosity. Clashes were common between veterans and the younger generation, theological conservatives and liberals, the outstanding and the incompetent, the men against the women, the wives versus the unmarried women, and those competent in Chinese versus those who could not or would not learn the language. Bitter quarrels simmered for years in the cramped, isolated little islands of the mission stations.

The stress of an unfriendly environment resulted in bizarre behavior in the missionary compounds. Oberlin College's attempt to conquer a whole Chinese province for Christ is instructive. The Oberlin Band of missionaries set off to Shansi province in the 1880s full of the enthusiasm and vigor that characterized their college. The mission soon dissolved into bickering and doctrinal disputes that led to bitter animosity among its members. One of the Oberlin Band diverged so far from official doctrine that he announced his rejection of the divinity of Christ. He was quickly sent home. Then, a domestic scandal nearly led to the destruction of the mission. A young wife, liberated before her time, apparently engaged in some sexual hanky panky—the missionaries were too euphemistic to say exactly what happened. Horror of horrors, it appeared that sharp-eyed Chinese servants were aware of the woman's indiscretion and spread the tale.[31]

Female missionaries outnumbered males by nearly two to one. Most male missionaries were married. Their wives were counted as assistant missionaries and a stipend was added to the male missionary's salary by virtue of him being married. Single female missionaries were almost as numerous as married male missionaries. The demographic breakdown of the missionary population in Peking in the summer of 1900 was seventy-one American missionaries. Twenty-two were men, thirty-six were women of whom fourteen were married and twenty-two unmarried, and thirteen were children.[32]

For single women a missionary's life was especially difficult. There was no refuge in family, except for letters from home, which took weeks to arrive; no relief in sex; and no recreation outside the walls of the compound. Single women missionaries had little privacy. They were frequently housed together or given a spare room in the house of a family. In response to close living, many of them developed intimate, lifetime relationships with each other, living collectively in unity — even sleeping in the same bed — in a manner the present generation would consider lesbian. Perhaps it was, but for women in that era kissing, fondling, and caressing each other was not considered incorrect, deviant, or sexual behavior.

It is difficult to answer the question why the missionaries came to China, but it is easier to understand the motivations of the women than those of the men. The men, usually university graduates, left behind abundant opportunities in the United States in exchange for an uncertain life and modest salary abroad, although the social cachet of being a missionary counted for something in proper circles. The principal motivation of women seems to have been to assist the downtrodden of their sex in foreign lands. "When the degradation and suffering of Asian women and the darkness of their future were revealed to the Western world, the conscience of Christian women was aroused." American women undertook a social gospel to supplement the male's evangelical gospel and to reach the one-half of the population that male missionaries could not reach.

The women missionaries in the nineteenth century were rarely radical or revolutionary. They saw themselves as privileged, not downtrodden, and thus were often not in sympathy with radical feminists. They mostly came from families of modest means in the farms and small towns of America and conducted themselves with an aura of piety, feminine benevolence and middle-class respectability. They treasured the concept of the family, as seen through Western eyes, in which the woman was equal in her sphere of activity and not a mere beast of burden. For opportunity, for adventure, for an alternative to marriage and family, thousands of young women chose to be missionaries. They would acquire positions of importance beyond what they were likely to attain in the United States. Women would not be able to vote until 1920 in the U.S., but they gained the vote in the consultations of the missionary stations of the American Board in 1900.[33]

Most women becoming missionaries gave up aspirations for marriage and family. "The whole women's missionary movement was built upon a celibate order of life career missionaries maintained on a subsistence level. Women missionaries were expected to serve for life without ever getting married." Should a woman missionary marry or resign during her first few years overseas, "she was required, by a signed pledge, to return her travel and outfit allowance and sometimes her salary."[34] Missionary men might see themselves as heroic Old Testament patriarchs designated by God to lead their flocks out of the wilderness; unmarried missionary women were in one way the Protestant version of Catholic nuns: self-sacrificing and subservient — and in another way the exemplars of American womanhood, feminism, and culture. Many missionary women were educated at progressive institutions such as Oberlin or Mount Holyoke, the "Protestant Nunnery." Missionaries of prestigious organizations, such as the American Board, both male and female, were members of the educational elite of the American population, only 2 percent of which had a college degree in 1900 — and the great majority of that 2 percent were men.[35]

Evidence of illicit sex among missionaries is nearly impossible to uncover due to their reticence on intimate relations. However, one has to suspect, that, given the closeness of contact in mission work and in the mission compounds, year after year, between married males and unmarried female missionaries, forbidden romances—however much repressed—must on occasion have gotten out of hand. That temptation and opportunity should be avoided was recognized. Women usually traveled in groups and chaperones were often found to ensure that the proprieties were strictly observed for meetings of missionary women and men. It was an age in which women would not even talk of being pregnant—even to themselves. During the Boxer Rebellion, missionary wife Bessie Ewing wrote in her private diary of "feeling poorly" but it is only with the birth of her child in December 1900 that one realizes she was feeling poorly because she was pregnant during the ordeal. Sex and its consequences were not topics to be discussed. Mary Bainbridge of the American Legation only hints at her condition. "Rec'd a birthday present which made me rejoice for just four weeks, then it was taken away from me and my heart has ached ever since. Don't wish any more of the kind," she added.[36]

Within their compounds the missionaries lived comfortably. They altered Chinese houses to reflect the standards of the upper middle class in the United States. "The average American sleeps in a better room than the well-to-do official of China, who erects his house with no idea whatever of sanitation, and no idea of comfort as we understand comfort."[37] The missionaries made their houses as American as they could. They removed paper windows and replaced them with glass, laid down board floors over the brick of the original, added stoves to replace smelly charcoal braziers, and built toilet facilities to American rather than Oriental standards—the end product of toilet renovations, however, still leaving the home each morning to be spread liberally on the vegetable crops the missionaries would later eat with the comprehension that something of themselves might reside on the cabbage or watermelons. Many declined to eat raw food.

The missionaries were paid modest salaries by American standards, but munificent in China. The salary for a male Methodist missionary in the mid and late 1890s varied due to years of service, marital status and children, and Chinese language fluency. A married man with less than five years service was paid $950 per year; a single man received $650—the difference being the imputed value of the work of the missionary's wife. A missionary's salary was not increased until he passed a test proving his fluency in Chinese. The top salary for a Methodist missionary was $1,200 annually for a married man and $900 per year for a single man with 25 years service. Allowances for children were $100 for each child under 21 years old, except for children over 14 in attendance at a school in the United States for which $150 was provided.[38] Given that housing was provided free and a staff of five servants could be hired for the equivalent of $16 per month, the standard of living for the Congregational, Methodist, and Presbyterian missionaries in Peking was comfortable.[39] (The value of a U.S. dollar in 1900 was about 20 times what it was in 2000, and the dollar went even further in China.[40])

* * *

For all the comforts afforded, the life of a missionary in China was difficult. The missionaries were the most visible and despised of the foreign devils and easy targets for the brickbats and insults of the Chinese. A missionary in the 1880s wrote: "We were mobbed in the *fu* [capital] city, mobbed in the district cities, mobbed in the large towns. We got so used to being pelted with mud and gravel and bits of broken pottery that things seemed strange if we escaped the regular dose.... We went out from our homes bedewed with the tears and benedictions of dear ones, and we came back plastered over, metaphorically speaking, with curses and objurgations from top to bottom. It went badly with our chapels which we rented. They were often assailed; roofs were broken up, doors were battered in, and furniture was carried off."[41]

Young missionaries studying Chinese were chagrined when their teachers—with whom they may have spent several hours a day for months and had thought, in their enthusiasm, they had cultivated the best of friendships—passed them by in the streets without a sign of recognition.[42]

For a teacher, an occupation of high status in China, to acknowledge acquaintance with a despised foreign devil was a loss of face. The highest scholarly classes, the mandarins, deigned never to notice the existence of a foreigner. Missionaries who had been in the country for decades had never been greeted by a mandarin although they might pass on the streets every day of the week.

Possibly even worse for the missionary's psyche was the lack of respect he received from his countrymen in China. In the pecking order of the foreign community they ranked lowest. The diplomats snubbed them socially. The traders and businessmen derided them as Americans gone native, Bible thumpers and street preachers, making fools of themselves for the amusement of an inferior race. The late nineteenth century may have been the great age of the Protestant missionary but hostility to the missionary existed in the home country and among his compatriots as well as among the people he had come abroad to save.

All hardships to the contrary, the tempo of missionary activity picked up in the 1880s and 1890s as Protestant Christianity acquired a fashionable idealism and the watch cry, "the evangelization of the world in this generation."[43] For the sensitive young man or woman in that imperialistic age it was more stirring than the exhortations of capitalistic economics. The earnest, well-educated, exemplary young men and women of Christianity acquired a formidable influence in Washington and London, and government was quick to listen to them. Outstanding university men and women volunteered to serve in the most backward and hostile of countries. The missionary organizations laid a heavy hand on parvenu entrepreneurs of steel and railroads to contribute a portion of their gains to the spread of Christianity. The missionaries in 1900 were confident they had the force of history and moral right on their side and that they would succeed in conquering the heathen world for the greater glory of Christ. Among all the heathen, no greater challenge existed than the Chinese and of all the missionaries, when the glorious day arrived when China became Christian, none would have a place higher in the esteem of heaven than William Scott Ament.

3

Red-Headed Devils in Peking

Edwin Hurd Conger, the United States minister to China, ginger-bearded and fifty-seven years old, was a former congressman from Iowa and a friend of President McKinley. He liked to be called "Major," his military rank from the Civil War when he marched through Georgia with General Sherman. He was slow, fussy, anxious, but conscientious and more sympathetic than most diplomats to the American missionaries. Conger was appointed minister in 1898. He had no previous experience in China.

The diplomat's wife, Sarah Pike Conger, also from Iowa, had a stronger personality. She was a devout Christian Scientist, an angel of goodness who could not bring herself to say anything bad about another human being, and a bit eccentric. Neither of the Congers was held in high esteem in diplomatic circles. Their colleagues in Peking thought them stuffy, reserved, and old-fashioned. One visitor to Peking described Sarah and the Congers' daughter, Laura, as looking "as if they had just come off the farm."[1]

Conger was much under the influence of the British minister in Peking, Sir Claude MacDonald, a younger man with a military background. MacDonald was tall, thin, splendidly mustachioed, and similarly inexpert in matters Chinese. The Americans and British in Peking had the usual love-hate relationship of the two nationalities: the Americans loved the British, and the British hated the Americans—an exaggeration, to be sure, but a reflection on the tension between the two.

Eleven countries had diplomatic representatives in Peking in 1900. The United States with its small, dingy legation and staff of four diplomats hardly counted. Those that did count, in addition to the British, were the Russians, the French, and, increasingly, the Germans. Russia was the chief rival of the British. The Russian Legation staff was large and Russian influence was increasing in northern China. The Russians had a substantial financial presence in Peking through the Russo-Chinese Bank, a growing trade with northern China, and they were the most successful foreign power in maintaining friendly relations with the Chinese. Too friendly, in the opinion of some, who suspected Russia of cultivating back door contacts with the Chinese government at the same time it was ostensibly joining with the other countries to protest Boxer depredations. If China were to be partitioned into colonies—as seemed likely in 1900—the Russians were not going to be left out. Neither were the French. The French minister was Stephen Pichon, dramatic and deceitful but well-informed, thanks to his Roman Catholic intelligence service. The French were cozy with the Russians, both striving to be in a good position to pick up the pieces of a shattered China.

The Germans were the upstarts among the Europeans. Their legation in Peking was headed by cruel, handsome, blue-eyed, aggressive, Chinese-speaking Baron Clemens von Ketteler, an ex-army officer. Ketteler was married to an American, the rich, quiet railroad heiress Maud Ledyard. Germany was just beginning to flex its muscles in Asia and the baron epitomized German vigor and insensibility. Ketteler seemed to go out of his way to stir up trouble between the China and the foreign powers.

These four — Great Britain, Russia, France and Germany — were the stars of the diplomatic show in Peking; the supporting cast was the rising sun of Japan, Italy, Spain, the Netherlands, Belgium, Austria-Hungary, and the United States.

Since the murder of Brooks, the diplomats had demanded that the Chinese government suppress the Boxers. The Chinese equivocated. While the diplomats protested, the Boxer movement came closer to Peking and grew more menacing. On May 6, the first anti-foreign incident in the city occurred. Someone hurled a stone over the wall into the Presbyterian Mission, barely missing the head of a servant within. Minister Conger sent his interpreter, Fleming D. Cheshire, to the Chinese Foreign Office, the Tsungli Yamen, to protest the incident. Cheshire complained also that anti-foreign placards were posted near the Presbyterian Mission and that Boxers were practicing their acrobatic and sword-twirling rituals in that neighborhood. If aware of that fact, the government did little to stop them and the complaint from the Americans did not stimulate the Chinese into any action.

The Boxer prairie fire in Shantung was quenched by an anti–Boxer governor. The farmers went back to their arduous task of making a living and had little time to spare for Boxer rituals. Northward, toward Peking, however, the drought continued and the farmers were anxious and under-employed. Conger wrote to Washington that "the whole country is swarming with hungry, discontented, hopeless idlers, and they ... are ready to join any organization offered."[2] The movement became bolder and more violent as it grew and spread.

Still, there was little sense of urgency in Peking. Life went on as usual. The diplomats wrote their reports and planned their summer vacations in the Western Hills and the missionaries preached their sermons and prepared for their annual spring meetings. On May 24, the British Legation hosted a costume party in honor of Queen Victoria's birthday, her last as it turned out.[3] William Ament, however, was among the ranks of the alarmed. "The Boxers are becoming a serious menace in all north China," he wrote on May 1. "A spark might stir up a mighty conflagration."[4] But Ament's concern, and that of other missionaries, notably Arthur Smith, was not sufficient to cause the missionary societies to withdraw their colleagues from the countryside.

Edwin Conger, minister of the United States to China. A former Iowa congressman, he liked to be called major, his rank during the Civil War (Smith, *Convulsion in China*, 1901).

In mid–May, Ament and William Stelle took another excursion outside Peking to assess the situation. They took the train to Cho Chou, now coming under siege by the Boxers. On their previous visit, six weeks earlier, no Boxers had been in the city. This time Ament and Stelle found Cho Chou in turmoil. In the north suburbs a company of 300 Boxers had been created and they had just returned from chopping up four Catholics in a village three miles away. Ten miles away, two Chinese Protestants had been killed and their bodies thrown in the river. Sixty-one Catholics were reported killed in a nearby country district. Ament's converts were in hiding.

The magistrate of Cho Chou, whom

Ament had known for years, sent word to the two missionaries to leave the city as soon as possible. They ignored him and later that same day called at his palace. He met them in a panic. They must leave immediately, he said, and not by the front door. He feared for his own life if the Boxers knew that he met with foreigners. The missionaries were escorted through the kitchen and stables and pushed out the back door of the palace with unseemly haste. Ament and Stelle spent the night at the Protestant chapel, revolvers by their sides, and the next morning they visited several nearby villages. They found the native Christians terrorized by the Boxers and local officials professing "unswaying faith in the most childish and incredible stories" about the supernatural powers of the Boxers.[5] Ament and Stelle returned to Peking about May 21.[6] The Chinese government had lost control of the countryside. The Boxers were intimidating Chinese officials and killing all those who opposed them.

Ament reported his observations to Conger on his return. Conger was alarmed at these new signs of Boxer violence coming ever closer to the capital. He rushed over to the Tsungli Yamen to express once again to the Chinese government the concern of the United States about the growing strength of the anti-foreign, anti–Christian movement. Conger had already sent an urgent telegram to U.S. admiral James Kempff in Yokohama on May 17. "Situation becoming serious. Request warship Taku soon as possible."[7]

A second — and even more alarming — report to the diplomatic corps was a letter to Pichon dated May 19 from Bishop Favier, the apostolic vicar at Peking. Favier, a French priest, had been in China many years, spoke fluent Mandarin, wore Chinese robes, and tied his hair in a queue, a Chinese pigtail. He was considered the best-informed European on Chinese affairs. Favier wrote: "From day to day the situation becomes more serious and threatening. In the prefecture of Paoting more than seventy Christians have been massacred; near Icheou only three days ago, three neophytes have been cut in pieces. Many villages have been pillaged and burned, a great many others have been completely abandoned. More than 2,000 Christians are fleeing, without bread, without clothing, without shelter. At Peking alone, about 400 refugees— men, women, and children — are already lodged at our house and that of the sisters; before eight days we will probably have many thousands.... From the east of us pillage and incendiarism are imminent; we are hourly receiving the most alarming news. Peking is surrounded on all sides; the 'Boxers' are daily coming nearer the capital, delayed only by the destruction which they are making of the Christians....

"Religious persecution is only one object. The real purpose is the extermination of Europeans, a purpose which is clearly set forth and written upon the banners of the 'Boxers.' ... For us here at Peking, the day is practically ended. All the city knows it; everybody is speaking of it, and a popular outbreak is manifest.... Those who, thirty years ago, were present at the Tientsin massacre are struck with the resemblance of the situation then to that of to-day; the same placards, the same threats, the same warnings, and the same blindness. Then also as to-day, the missionaries wrote and supplicated, foreseeing the horrible awakening.

"Under these circumstances Mr. Minister, I believe it my duty to ask you to kindly send at least forty or fifty marines to protect our persons and our property."[8]

Favier could not be dismissed out of hand as an alarmist. The diplomats met on May 20 to consider his request for marines to protect the Catholics and their property. Pichon proposed to bring up marine guards to Peking from the warships steaming in the Gulf of Chihli just off Taku. Sir Claude MacDonald disagreed. He wrote: "As regards my own opinion as to the danger to which Europeans in Peking are exposed, I confess that little has come to my knowledge to confirm the gloomy anticipations of the French Fathers. The demeanor of the inhabitants of the city continues to be quiet and civil toward foreigners, as far as my own experience and that of my staff is concerned, although, from the undoubted panic which exists among the native Christians, it may be assumed that the latter are being subjected to threats of violence."[9]

MacDonald prevailed — as the British usually did. The diplomats decided to address a strong diplomatic note to the Tsungli Yamen and wait five days for an acceptable reply before requesting that marines come to Peking to defend the legations.

* * *

In the category of untimely arrivals few compete with that of the Martin sisters, Dr. Emma and Elizabeth (Lizzie), Methodist missionaries newly assigned to Peking. On March 29, 1900, Emma, thirty years old, and Lizzie, age twenty-seven, departed their farm home in Otterbein, Indiana, to journey to Peking. Their fortune amounted to two hundred and fifty dollars. The two women were as green as the Midwestern grass, inseparable and complementary, Emma more aggressive and outgoing and Lizzie the homebody. On the six-day train trip to San Francisco, "we found ... that we had about as much advice we could not use as we had baggage that was useless. We could get a good meal for 40 cents; and we were ashamed to be seen eating the Grape Nuts and condensed milk we had brought along with us for we had no way of serving it." During the long train ride the elder Emma "quietly opened the car window and bidding our can of peach butter goodbye ... pitched it out the window and after it the dry buns and butter."[10] The Martin sisters pitched away their American provincialism with the peach butter while on the train to San Francisco. They kept a close eye on their limited funds. Their hotel in San Francisco cost them two dollars per night.[11]

The Martin sisters looked like missionaries with frizzy hair pulled straight back into stern buns, patterned dresses buttoned up to the neck, and serious expressions. They were spinsters and moths in the parlance of the time, but healthy and vivacious moths and they had a jolly good time on the voyage to China — perhaps too good a time for missionaries. Emma, musical and talented, had a face favored by round granny glasses and a confident demeanor; children liked Lizzie. They arrived, seasoned by their long journey, in Tientsin on May 15. Taking the train to Peking, Emma noted that, whenever the train was in the station, Chinese gathered around, pointed fingers and laughed at the two young women. The attention made her nervous.[12] A rude shock it was for the two sisters who ventured forth from Indiana to save the world for Christ.

On arrival in Peking the Martins began studying Chinese and Emma took up duties in the Methodist hospital. On their first Sunday in China, May 20, a veteran missionary, Mary Porter Gamewell, took them to a Methodist church. Attendance was down. A few months before, Sunday crowds of more than 1,000 had crowded into the church; this day only 271 Chinese attended. Chinese were afraid to attend the church — or had found a spiritual home with the anti-foreign Boxers. Emma was astonished by the Chinese students she met. "They have as much personality or individuality as any Americans I ever met. They can talk and think just as well as other young men."[13] For the Christian raised to believe that heathens were primitive and ignorant, it was an illuminating insight that Chinese might be intelligent and personable.

Emma rode horseback with Dr. George Lowry outside the walls of Peking. A Chinese grabbed her pony by the bridle and attempted to pull her off the horse. Dr. Lowry drove the man away with his riding crop. He made light of the incident, but Emma was confirmed in her opinion that the anti-foreign feeling in China was intense. Dr. Emma Martin, whose medical experience was one year of gentle internship in a Chicago hospital for women and children, would soon find herself in China attending men with bodies shattered by bullets whose last words were more often a curse than a prayer.[14]

* * *

Peking was, in 1900, a magnificent anachronism. It was a walled city — two walled cities, in fact — the northern, Inner or Tartar City, from which Han Chinese had been excluded in the

Dr. Emma and Miss Elizabeth (Lizzie) Martin. These two fledgling missionaries arrived in China a month before the siege (Mateer, *Siege Days*, 1903).

earlier and more glorious days of the Manchu dynasty, and the adjoining southern, Outer, or Chinese City. The Tartar City was fortified by walls encompassing a rough square sixteen miles in diameter and broken by nine gates. The walls enclosing the Tartar City were forty feet high. A crenellated parapet added another six feet to their height and great buttresses extended fifty feet outward from the wall at regular intervals. The walls were sixty-two feet thick at the base and forty feet thick at the top, nearly wide enough to accommodate a four-lane highway. The nine gates or *men*, breaking the Tartar wall were monumental, each a three-storied pagoda with curving roofs and green tiles. The glory of Peking was the walls and gates of the Tartar City which would stand comparison with those of Babylon, one of the seven wonders of the ancient world. Just as in ancient Babylon, the nine wooden doors of the nine massive gates were swung shut at night and the city locked tight until dawn.

The Outer or Chinese City was rectangular, abutting on the south wall of the Tartar City and possessing its own walls, thirty feet high and eleven miles in diameter, broken by seven *men*. The total circuit of the two connected cities was twenty-one miles and the area enclosed within the walls was twenty-one square miles, the same as Manhattan Island. Peking had a population of about one million.[15]

Peking's link with the world was the railroad to Tientsin, eighty miles southeast, and hence to the coast. An express train to Peking ran daily. Chinese passengers jammed their way into crowded cars, but foreigners rode in what was called the postal carriage, a lounge car furnished with wicker chairs upholstered with English cloth, the curtains on the windows an English pattern, the floor covered with an English carpet, and the car under the supervision of an Englishman. The train proceeded at the princely speed of twenty miles an hour across the north China plain.

Long before travelers reached Peking they saw the irregular outlines of the bare, brown Western Hills which rose just beyond the limits of the city. The land along the railroad track was heavily cultivated with millet (kaoliang), broom corn, and sweet potatoes — rice being a

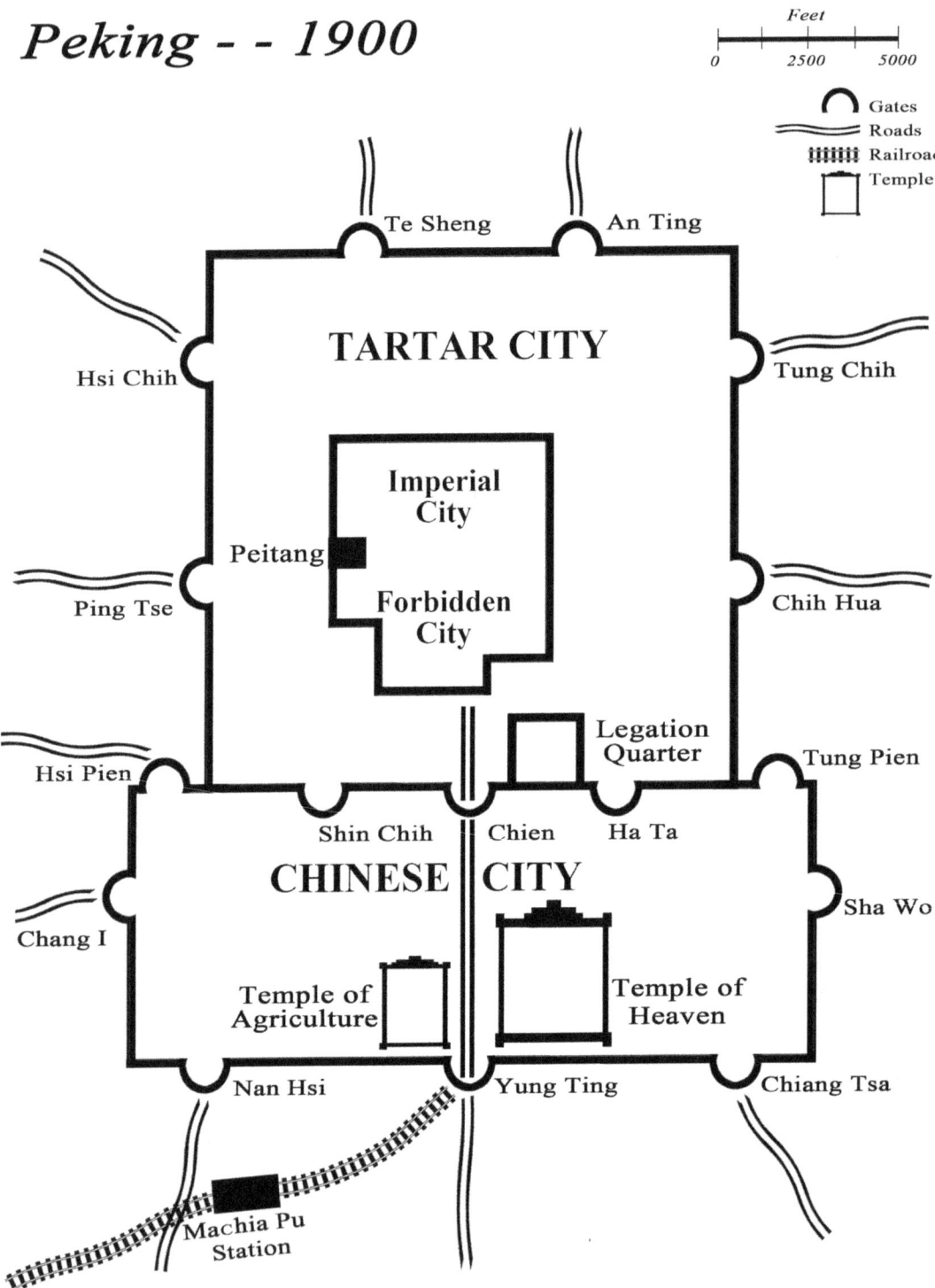

Peking—1900. Peking was a city of walls within walls. The Tartar and Chinese cities were enclosed by massive walls twenty-one miles in length and broken by sixteen gates. Peking had a population of about one million (by Kathryn Kelly-Hensley, 2008).

crop of the south and a luxury in the north. As the train neared Peking, vegetable gardens with cabbage and melons became common. The traveler caught fleeting glimpses of the walls through the trees that lined the fields and shaded gray-brick villages and whitewashed shrines and cone-shaped burial mounds in the cemeteries. The express train reached Machia Pu station just outside the southern wall of the Chinese city in early afternoon. The traveler disembarked, made arrangements for the transport of his baggage to its destination by cart, and waited in the luxurious European waiting room to board an electric trolley for a one and one-half mile ride.

Three shiny, modern trolley cars shuttled from Machia Pu to the wall. The trolley had opened for service only in 1899. A dirt track ran alongside the trolley line, the chaos of its traffic a sharp contrast to the quiet of the trolley. Mixed with horse-drawn, wooden-wheeled Peking carts—famously uncomfortable—were caravans of sardonic Bactrian camels laden with coal, plodding along untroubled by the carts, pedestrians, donkeys, herds of sheep and goats and, most noticeably, two new means of transportation. A few proud riders pedaled bicycles, steering carefully around potholes, and, here and there, was a *jinricksha*, recently introduced from Japan. The ricksha, with its fast-trotting human draft animal, was the latest word in transport for Peking. The progressive ricksha pullers, in the opinion of many, would soon capture the market for moving people, rendering obsolete the carts, the passenger wheelbarrows, and the swaying, curtained sedan chairs carried on the shoulders of four or more men.

The traveler entered the Chinese city through the Yungting gate and followed a broad, stone-paved avenue running due north. He passed tumble-down shops and houses near the gate and, then, incongruously, he was in open country with a swamp at each side of the road, a few thin sheep grazed on the scanty, salt-encrusted grass and, in the distance, straight ahead, was the Tartar Wall. The swamp gave way on his left to the Temple of Agriculture, a great park which the emperor visited annually to plow a small piece of ground in reverence to his ancestors and to ensure a bountiful crop. On his right was the even larger Temple of Heaven, its whiteness rising in stair-steps to a mighty height at two altars, one open to the sky and the other covered with a triple domed shrine of blue porcelain. To the open altar the emperor would also come once a year and prostrate himself before the Lord of Heaven. The annual visits to the Temple of Heaven and the Temple of Agriculture were among the few occasions when the emperor left his palace in the Forbidden City. On his visits, the emperor was borne on a jade palanquin by thirty-two men and followed by a retinue of hundreds of Manchu nobles, high eunuchs, the Tartar guard, and the chief ceremonial and religious mandarins of the empire. The street was covered with a layer of yellow sand so that the emperor might not be jounced in his passage. Every door of every house and shop on his route was ordered closed, a ceremonial guard post was at every intersection, and every five paces a guardsman stood with sword and whip to maintain silence among the people clustered along the edge of the road in deep obeisance, their eyes averted from the august presence. Foreigners were forbidden to view the ceremonies within the Temples of Heaven and Agriculture.[16]

It was three miles through the Chinese city to the Chienmen, the most monumental of all the gates to the Tartar City. The broad avenue leading to the Chien gate was the route of the emperor, and the only street of the Chinese city maintained in good order. The rest was narrow lanes, lined with house walls and banks of refuse and a few broader dirt roads that wound irregularly through rows of booths and shops, "so wild and wildernesslike" that a visitor was prompted to inquire of his ricksha puller whether he was indeed within the city.[17] It was like the encampment of a savage tribe, or a large caravanserai. The greatest of all the markets of the city was the covered bazaar that followed the outer line of the Tartar Wall in both directions from the Chienmen. Here one could buy the treasures of China and Central Asia, "pipes and snuff-bottles, hair pins and ornaments, the toys of the writing desk, jade bracelets and ear-rings and charms ... mandarins' belt-buckles of gold, brass, enamel and jade ... money-pouches of embroidered satin that the petticoated grandees hang in dazzling bunches from their girdles in lieu of practical, masculine pockets ... and even in this day of careful gleaning by professional buyers, the amateur sometimes finds a treasure."[18] There was food: "sausages of more than questionable integrity, tripe, portions of animals not consumed by Americans and Europeans, cakes of flour covered with sesame seeds ... shrimps and fritters of many varieties, frying in caldrons of bubbling oil."[19] In open spaces were flocks of goats and sheep and herds of donkeys and stocky, hairy Mongolian ponies. The confusion of shops, creaking carts and rickshas, caravans of camels and crowds of people mingled together in a cloud of dust and the stench of centuries. Now and then a shop owner scooped up a bucket of the sewage that flowed in irregular ditches at the margins of the streets and sprinkled it in front of his shop to keep the dust down. Peking may have been "the filthiest city in the world"[20] but it also was the "most incredible, impossible, anomalous, and surprising place in the world; the most splendid, spectacular, picturesque, and interesting city in China; a Central Asian city of the far past; a fortified capital of the thirteenth century handed down intact."[21]

Women were scarce on the streets for Chinese woman lived in seclusion, but a few were here, mincing along on bound feet like goat-hooves or peering out from the curtains of carts and sedan chairs. Mixed in with the Chinese women were long-robed Manchu women, taller and freely-walking on unbound feet, their black hair tied around elaborate, flower-decorated hairpins in elaborate coiffures extending outward like wings, the size and shape of a large soup bone.

Through the Chien gate was the Tartar City and the inner sanctum of Peking. Once through the gate the boulevard continued straight for a few hundred yards and terminated in a vast square, now called Tiananmen. Few foreigners were allowed to pass through the red doors of the Imperial City. Within all was the Forbidden City, the yellow-roofed seat of the emperor and his court, shut off, insulated, and isolated by walls of brick, protocol, and custom from its four hundred million subjects. To enter the Forbidden City was a privilege denied all but the most important citizens of the empire.

Just inside the walls of the Tartar City, between the Chien and Hata gates, was the Legation Quarter, the location of the eleven foreign legations in Peking and the other institutions associated with the Western presence. Peking had been closed to the West until 1860 — one of the few exceptions being Roman Catholic priests who had ministered to their converts *sub rosa* since the early seventeenth century — when a British and French military expedition had marched from Tientsin, defeated the Chinese armies, and captured Peking. The humiliated Chinese, forced to accept foreigners and foreign legations within the Tartar City, gave them the quarter of the city which had housed Mongols, Tibetans, Koreans, and other visitors from subsidiary kingdoms who came bearing tribute to the emperor. The British rented a *fu* or palace in the very shadow of the wall of the Imperial City to serve as a legation and the French followed suit by establishing their legation nearby in another *fu*. The palaces were of a pattern, several acres in extent, with stone lions guarding the gates, four courts and pavilions within the walls, and residences and service buildings clustered around the interior gardens and wide-paved expanses of the courts.

Now, in 1900, the Legation Quarter was also the location of the Russo-Chinese and Hong Kong and Shanghai banks, the Peking Hotel, the post office, three foreign owned stores, the headquarters of the Imperial Maritime Customs and the Peking Club, a watering hole for foreign residents. Mixed in were Chinese shops and Chinese and Manchu residences, both humble and palatial. The quarter was bisected by Legation Street running parallel with the Tartar Wall for nearly a mile from the Chien to the Hata gates. Legation Street, though wide, was hardly elegant. Having been forced to grant admittance to foreign powers in their capital, the Chinese were not about to provide any public improvements. Legation Street was a "straggling, unpaved slum of a thoroughfare, along which one occasionally sees a European picking his way between the ruts and puddles with the donkeys and camels."[22] It was a "general sewer and dumping ground for refuse of every kind ... all gutter."[23] Midway in its length, where the Russian and United States legations faced each other, Legation Street crossed a once-splendid bridge under which ran a stinking canal draining the lakes of the Imperial City. This noxious watercourse left the city through a timber-barred water gate beneath the Tartar Wall.

On Legation Street was the French Legation, "very smart in fresh paint"; the Japanese Legation, "very perky, with a European gateway"; the German, "dignified and fresh painted"; and around the corner, the British Legation, "with a massive but somewhat jail-like portal."[23] The arrival at the British Legation was recorded by Mrs. Archibald Little. "In Peking it is very pleasant to live in a ducal palace. From the moment the Embassy servant stepped forward with a fly-flap, and courteously flapped the dust off our boots, everything was charming. We never wished to go outside again to face that vile mews, with its holes, its dust, its smells.... We were surrounded by every English comfort, enjoying delightful English society! Why ever go outside the Embassy compound? Could Peking possibly have anything to show worth encountering such horrors as those of its entry, a survival from those Middle Ages so agreeable to read about, so disagreeable to live in?"[24]

The diplomats in Peking lived a sheltered existence. They were "lodged sumptuously, paid high salaries, and sustained by the certainty of promotions and rewards after a useful term at Peking.... The diplomats in exile lead a narrow, busy life among themselves, occupied with their social amusements and feuds.... They have their club, the tennis-courts of which are flooded and roofed over as a skating-rink, their spring and autumn races at a track beyond the walls, frequent garden parties and picnic teas in the open seasons, and a busy round of state dinners and balls all winter." A good life, except for the American minister, "who is crowded into small rented premises, is paid about a fourth as much as the other envoys, and, completely untrained to his career, has the cheerful certainty of being put out of office as soon as he has learned his business and another President is elected, his stay in Peking on a meager salary a sufficient incident in itself, leading to nothing further officially."[25]

Moreover, the American Legation was in an inauspicious location. The site had been occupied by the Hostel of Tributary Nations where vassals of China bringing tribute to the emperor were housed—and guarded—until they performed their ceremonial obeisance to the throne, presented and were presented gifts and were on their humble way back to their barbarous nations. The legation grounds were small, only about an acre, and contained houses for the minister, the first and second secretaries, the interpreter, and a Chinese calligrapher. At the rear of the legation, across a dirt track, loomed the Tartar Wall. Twin ramps led to the top of the wall.[26]

One other institution was prominent within the Legation Quarter: the headquarters of Imperial Maritime Customs headed by the inspector general of Customs, Irish-born Sir Robert Hart, the most important westerner in China. Imperial Maritime Customs was an institution growing out of the system of treaty ports imposed on China by the foreign powers. Hart headed an agency of the Chinese government charged with assessing duties on foreign and native goods entering or leaving the treaty ports. The management of Customs was entirely in the hands of foreigners, picked, trained, and presided over by Sir Robert, a benevolent but exacting dictator. Imperial Customs was a major source of revenue of the Chinese government.

Hart was an old China hand, arriving in the country in 1854. Among the foreign residents of Peking only the American W. A. P. Martin, who had come to China in 1850 as a missionary and was now president of the Imperial University, could claim precedence in length of residence. Sir Robert ran an organization that employed a thousand foreigners throughout China who were recruited from the finest universities of every major country. He supervised them meticulously, his tiny scrawl of reproach much-feared by those guilty of the most minor infraction.

In 1885 he had been offered — and refused — an appointment as British minister to China. Hart was resented, though not openly, by the diplomats who envied his influence, resources, and expertise.

In 1900, Hart was sixty-five years old and he had been the IG — as everyone called him — for thirty-seven years. His wife had gone back to England in 1881 and he had lived as a bachelor, alone with his band of musicians and his fabulous collections of Chinese antiques. Hart loved to entertain and his table was the best in Peking. He was "the most enchanted of sinophiles,"[27] an optimist, and a great admirer of that other old authoritarian in China, the Empress Dowager. He had undergone what *The Times* called "that strange fascination which a Chinese environment so often exercises over the European mind."[2i] But, as the century closed, he did not appear happy to William Ament. In 1898, he described himself a "poor, decayed old man" who had not seen his wife for eighteen years and had left Peking only once in twelve years. "He looks poorly and spoke sadly," Ament said. "He needs the sympathy of all lovers of China, as I believe he is a real missionary of civilization."[30]

Sir Robert Hart the exception, the foreigners of Peking and the officials of the Chinese government had little contact with each other. Once in a great while a Chinese official might deign to accept an invitation to dinner but never reciprocated the invitation. Few foreigners had ever set foot in a Chinese house, save the missionaries who visited the modest homes of their converts. Official intercourse was limited to a call at the Foreign Office, the Tsungli Yamen, by a minister upon arrival in Peking, a dreary New Year's audience, and a return visit by the thirty Chinese officials working at the Tsungli Yamen to the legations. Neither the Empress Dowager nor the emperor received foreign ministers. Social intercourse with foreigners was frowned on. Whatever business a foreign legation had with the Chinese government was transacted through the Tsungli Yamen. Most of its officials had little knowledge of foreign affairs or diplomacy.

The Tsungli Yamen was a calculated insult to the foreign powers. It was under the supervision of the Department of Inferior States and Dependencies. Rather than being located near the Imperial City as were other Chinese government offices, the Tsungli Yamen was far away in the eastern section of the city. The old palace housing the Yamen was a "dirty, dilapidated shed, that might pass muster for a cowhouse on an English gentleman's estate *if* it were cleaned and fresh painted."[31] To get there "the Ministers have always a long, slow ride in state to the shabby gateway of the forlorn old yamen, where now eleven aged, sleepy incompetents muddle with foreign affairs.... The appointment for an interview must be made beforehand, the minister and his secretaries are always kept waiting, and the inner reception-room swarms with gaping attendants during an interview." The servants come in "with their pipes and fans, tea and cake and candies" and take part in the diplomatic conversations. "An unconscionable time is always consumed in offering and arranging the tea and sweets, and to any direct questions these Celestial statesmen always answer with praises for the melon-seeds or ginger-root —'lowering buckets into a bottomless well,'" was how one British diplomat described an audience at the Yamen.[32]

The lack of social contact between Chinese and westerners was disadvantageous to both. Each had flawed insights into the politics, the character, and the objectives of the other. The walls of Peking caused a gulf of misunderstanding and ignorance between foreigner and Chinese as wide and as deep as if the two parties had been separated by an ocean rather than only a few bricks.

* * *

The walls of the Tartar City appeared a formidable defense but they were only a sham. The walls were crumbling, their facing piled up several feet against the base. The broad platform on the summit had long since become a wilderness overgrown with thorny shrubs. The massive gates to the city were a metaphor for China in 1900. Over each of the gates loomed a pagoda tower. In the towers were gun ports, designed so cannons could be mounted to defend the gate. The wooden shutters covering the gun ports were "decorated with the *painted* muzzles of large cannon ... China was ... a hollow sham, a painted gun on a wooden background."[33] The gun ports were empty of real cannons.

To avoid offending *feng shui*, Chinese were prohibited from going up on the Tartar Wall and thus they knew less about their defenses than did the foreigners who enjoyed climbing the ramps and walking on the walls to enjoy the sunset over the Western Hills. The wall, like the legations and mission compounds, was a refuge from the filth and noise of the city. A narrow path wound from one side of the wall to the other, around piles of brick and through thorn forests. On the outer side were the shops of the Chinese city; on the inner side were the wide streets and palaces of the Tartar City, the yellow-roofed Imperial City, and, at its center the Forbidden City. Within dwelt the three thousand eunuchs of the court and the young emperor, Kuang Hsu, a virtual prisoner of his aunt, Tzu Hsi, the Empress Dowager, the woman who had ruled China for thirty-nine years.

* * *

The missionary establishments in Peking in 1900 were all within the Tartar City save one Swedish missionary who resided in the fiercely anti-foreign southern or Chinese City. In the western part of the city were two British and two American organizations: the West Compound of the London Missionary Society (LMS); the Society for the Propagation of the Gospel, headed by Anglican priest Roland Allen; the Mission to the Higher Classes of Gilbert Reid; and the Alliance Mission, usually called the Douw Mission, financed and led by Matilda Douw, with a staff of four American and one Canadian teachers.

In the northern part of the Tartar City were two compounds occupied by American Presbyterians. In the east, near the Legation Quarter, was another compound of the LMS which housed a school run by Georgina Smith; the American Board mission where Will Ament lived and was the senior missionary; and the Methodist Mission, the largest in the city and the nearest to the Legation Quarter.[34] Outside the walls of Peking, 12 miles away, the American Board had a large compound in the city of Tungchou. Several missions had day and boarding schools for Chinese children: The Bridgman School of the American Board was in Peking and North China College was in Tungchou; the Methodist and Presbyterians had boarding schools as did the LMS and Miss Douw. Methodists and Presbyterians had clinics and hospitals in Peking.

The Roman Catholic Church, which counted far more members than all the Protestants combined, had four large cathedrals in Peking named for the points of the compass, the North, East, South, and West Cathedrals. The North Cathedral, the Peitang, was the most objectionable to the Chinese as it was located within the precincts of the Imperial City.

4

The Semi-Siege

Peking was a city to flee in the summer. Hot, dusty days in May continued until July when monsoon rains turned the city into a quagmire. To escape the unpleasant and unhealthy climate, men sent their wives and families to the Western Hills, fifteen miles from Peking, and joined them when they could break free from work. The British Legation and Imperial Customs built guesthouses for their employees, but most of the summer people, including missionaries, rented one of the Buddhist temples scattered around the hills. The priests welcomed the income and their religion was not offended by foreigners setting up housekeeping among the courts and pagodas nor foreign children crawling over the altars and statues—nor did missionaries find it disturbing to reside among heathen idols.

On May 28, 1900, Harriet Squiers, the wealthy wife of Herbert Squires, the American first secretary, her three small children, forty servants (!), two governesses, and a young friend visiting China, Polly Condit-Smith, were staying at a temple on the high slopes of Mount Bruce. From the temple Harriet could look out over the plain to the walls of Peking and the railroad junction town of Feng-tai, six miles south. Her husband had remained in Peking. The Chinese government provided a guard for his family in case any of the Boxers now roaming the countryside near Peking found their way into the hills. Twelve men, "ridiculous apologies for soldiers," armed with rusty spears, showed up.[1] Clara, the German governess of the Squiers—they also had a French governess—had come up from Peking the day before and reported that townspeople and farmers were participating in Boxer drills in all the villages.

This morning the two women saw a fire in Feng-tai, far below. Black smoke billowed over the town and the railroad station. The compound where foreign employees of the railroad lived was ablaze. The steel bridge crossing the river at Feng-tai was gone, its spans dropped by explosives. Also, their guards had disappeared, off to join the Boxers, so the frightened servants said. Suddenly, the two women realized they were isolated and alone. "Not a foreign man on the place to protect us," said Polly Condit-Smith, who reckoned their chances of survival as about even. Polly was 24 years old, unmarried, a Washington socialite, and a sister-in-law of Theodore Roosevelt's friend General Leonard Wood, who would become the U.S. Army's Chief of Staff.[2]

Fortunately, a knight in shining armor rescued the two fair ladies. He was Dr. George E. Morrison, thirty-eight years old, an adventurous Australian journalist who had once been a medical doctor. The two women saw him climbing up the steep, narrow trail to the temple, his armor a cloud of dust and his war horse a hairy Mongolian pony. Morrison had ventured outside Peking to investigate reports that the Boxers were at Feng-tai. He retreated hastily when he saw a mob burning the foreign settlement and the railroad station. Knowing that the two women were in the Western Hills he went to their assistance. They were happy to see him. After greeting them, Morrison made plans to defend the temple, hoping to hold off attackers with his revolver and rifle, but, if his one-man resistance proved inadequate, "to send to glory as many Chinese as possible before turning up his own toes!"[3] So said Polly, much taken with the dashing correspondent of the world's most important newspaper, *The Times* of London. Morrison was less impressed with her. He said she was "fat and gushing,"[4] but Morrison despised about everybody but himself. American women — if they had money — were all the rage among Europeans, but not Morrison. Of Harriet Squiers, rich, socially prominent, and a granddaughter of John Jacob Astor, Morrison commented that she was always late and drank too much.[5] The only woman in Peking for whom Morrison showed much respect was a British missionary named Georgina Smith who could "stare him down."[6] Despite five years in China and a reputation as an expert, Morrison didn't speak Chinese and had never tried to learn. He was brave, arrogant, conceited, imperialist, and disdainful of the Chinese, although he had a humanitarian bent and a strong belief in the White Man's Burden. Morrison was conscious also that he was both a chronicler and a participant in historical events and he strived to appear a bright, shining hero He succeeded in coming through the siege a hero; Harriet Squiers was one of its angels and Polly Condit-Smith its belle. Of the formidable Georgina Smith, we will also hear more.

Polly Condit-Smith. Politically and socially well-connected, Polly was visiting Peking and was caught up in the siege. She wrote a lively account of her experiences under her married name of Mary Hooker (Hooker, *Behind the Scenes in Peking,* 1911).

Fortunately, the mob in Feng-tai did not venture into the hills and, shortly, Herbert Squiers arrived, accompanied by a Cossack he had borrowed from the Russian Legation. With three armed men now present, the women breathed easier. The Cossack was a professional soldier, Morrison had been in many a tight spot, and Squiers had spent fourteen years in the U.S. Army, serving with General Custer's old regiment, the 7th Cavalry, and present at Wounded Knee in 1890 when the Ghost Dance movement was squelched just as the Boxers would be in 1900.[7] With night approaching, the men had the servants pack up to flee to Peking at first light. The whole party passed a nervous night but no Boxers appeared near the temple.

At six in the morning the armed men, women, children, and herd of servants departed for Peking in a caravan of carts, ponies, mules, and donkeys. Squiers' experience on the American frontier was useful. He organized the carts like a wagon train, ready to circle at the first sign of trouble. It was an eerie journey. The usually crowded countryside was empty except for long, lonely lines of camels carrying coal. The population, Polly speculated, had gone off to some rallying point for a demonstration and, as the caravan neared Peking, she worried that they would encounter the rioters from yesterday. However, the Squiers and their entourage arrived at the city without incident, and at ten-thirty in the morning the women and children were climbing out of the carts in the courtyard of the American Legation. Henceforth, Minister Conger decreed that women and children of diplomats were confined to the Legation Quarter.

* * *

Morrison was not the only knight in shining armor that day. The foreign railway employees in Feng-tai escaped to Peking, but another group of French and Belgians lived at Chang Hsin

Tien seventeen miles down the railroad. Fearing they might come under attack, Auguste Chamot, the Swiss-born manager of the Peking Hotel, his American wife, born Annie Elizabeth MacCarthy of San Francisco, four Frenchmen, and a 17-year-old, Chinese-speaking Australian named Willie Dupree sallied out of Peking with carts, spare animals, provisions, arms, and ammunition. Square-jawed Annie Chamot, 29 years old and the daughter of a real estate magnate, would become the most celebrated of the women in the siege. She knew how to use a rifle: "Annie was a good shot, having been taught, it is said, by her father in the basement of their San Francisco home."[8] The Chamots and their party met no opposition, rescued seven children, nine women, and thirteen men from Chang Hsin Tien and were back in Peking the same evening.[9] As the engineers fled with the Chamots, Boxers began looting and burning their houses.

* * *

Ament's friend William Stelle was elated by the burning of the Feng-tai station. "We are saved," he declared. "So long as the Boxers only plundered native houses and murdered converts, the Ministers did nothing; now a few yards of line have been destroyed and they *must* act."[10] He was right. Even Sir Claude MacDonald, the British minister, now agreed that the Boxers posed a danger to the foreign residents and that the measures taken by the Chinese government to repress them were inadequate. The diplomats agreed to send for soldiers from their ships hovering off the Taku banks. There was precedent for such action. Two years before, a small force of guards had come up from Taku during a period of instability within the Manchu court and protected the legations briefly before retiring again to the ships.[11]

Seventeen foreign warships were anchored off Taku, including the American flagship, the USS *Newark*. Responding to the request of the American minister, at dawn on May 29, two Marine Corps officers, forty-eight enlisted men, a U.S. Navy medical doctor and his medical assistant, and four sailors, a total of fifty-six men, disembarked their ships. The sailors brought with them a Colt machine gun and the marines were armed with rifles.[12] They crossed the treacherous banks in small craft and landed at the mouth of the Pei River. Chinese railroad authorities refused to allow them to ride the railroad from Tankgu to Tientsin. They hired tugboats and barges instead and journeyed upriver to Tientsin, passing the Taku forts guarding the mouth of the river. The marines hid behind the steel sides of the barges, anticipating that the Chinese soldiers in the forts might open fire, but the Chinese guns were silent and the marines arrived at Tientsin without incident. They were met by most of the seven hundred members of the foreign community and escorted to Temperance Hall — an incongruous place, given the reputation of the marines — for their temporary billet. Boxers also menaced Tientsin and the residents of the foreign settlements were glad to see soldiers.

In Peking the diplomats had difficulty persuading the Chinese government to permit foreign soldiers to come to Peking. The Tsungli Yamen refused to grant permission but the diplomats were no longer willing to accept Chinese assurances that they would be protected. They pressed hard and on May 30 gave the Tsungli Yamen an ultimatum. "We will give you until six o'clock tomorrow morning for a favorable answer, and if it does not come, we will bring the guards anyway."[13] The Chinese now acted quickly to save face. There was "really no necessity" for the guards "but if the foreign representatives insist on this step the Yamen will on its part interpose no obstacles."[14] MacDonald immediately cabled Tientsin and asked the marines and sailors to come quickly to Peking and he added that they should be prepared to meet resistance. A telegram came back from the troops. "Leave on special train, three hundred and fifty strong."[15] The 350 included British, Russian, French, American, Italian, and Japanese soldiers. The Germans and Austrians would send one hundred soldiers to Peking two days later. (For simplicity's sake, I will often refer to the mixture of sailors, soldiers, and marines collectively as "soldiers" or "guards.")

May 31 was a tense day as the foreign community in Peking waited for the guards to arrive. Diplomats went to the railroad terminus outside the walls at Machia Pu but they waited in vain all day until, finally, a telegram arrived. The soldiers would arrive at eight P.M. The legations urgently sent messages to the Tsungli Yamen requesting that the gates of the city, normally shut at dusk, remain open to admit the soldiers on their arrival. The Tsungli Yamen duly notified the guardian of the Chienmen to keep his gate open so the foreign military forces could enter the city. Would he obey? The diplomats also worried because the six thousand Muslim troops of General Tung Fu-hsiang were camped between the railroad terminus at Machia Pu and the walls of Peking. The Muslim soldiers from remote Kansu province were the most fierce and undisciplined unit of the Imperial Army. The smallest spark might set off a fight between them and the foreign soldiers. Unease was increasing in the streets. The American missionary Gilbert Reid reported mobs of Chinese on Legation Street and near the Chien gate. He advised his fellow missionaries to prepare to run for their lives. They should, he said, disguise themselves in Chinese clothes—Manchu dress for the women because Manchu women did not have bound feet—and, at the first sign of danger hire a cart and, with curtains drawn, drive around the streets all night. At daybreak, it might be possible to pass through one of the eastern gates and flee to Tientsin by road or river.[16]

The apprehensions of the foreign community were unfounded. The Chien gate remained open, the Kansu troops moved out of the path of the foreign soldiers, and the surly Chinese mobs remained peaceful. About 8:30 P.M. the foreign marines arrived, detrained, and marched—Americans in the van—with bayonets fixed into Peking. As the American marines entered their legation compound they were startled by a blinding flash. "When the smoke cleared away it was found that there were no casualties, only a guest of the American Minister taking a flashlight photograph."[17]

The arrival of the troops was otherwise uneventful. The residents of the Legation Quarter took late night strolls to the different legations to observe the newly arrived guards as they settled down for the night. The American marines were in a jolly mood. They were glad to be off the ships and looked forward to having a fine time and easy duty in Peking. Sarah Pike Conger commented in the metaphysical. "The moral effect upon these enraged Chinese people of having these troops here will be good."[18] Some of the missionaries were not so sanguine. The Anglican missionary Roland Allen had expected three thousand guards and thought a trainload was inadequate.[19]

Allen and the other missionaries would have been even more disturbed had they realized how lightly armed their guards were. The rapid movement from ship to shore, by barge to Tientsin, and hence by rail to Peking cost in lost equipment and light armament. The Russians inadvertently left a nine-pound cannon behind in Tientsin although they brought with them one thousand rounds of ammunition for it. The British Royal Marines had only an antiquated five-barrel 1887 model Nordenfeldt machine gun — similar to the American Gatling gun — which jammed every fourth round. The Italians brought a one-pound cannon, a useful but small piece. The Americans were the best prepared to fight. They had 8,000 rounds for their Colt light machine gun plus nearly 20,000 rounds for their rifles.[20] In anticipation of trouble they left extra clothing and equipment behind in favor of ammunition. They were already sweltering in their wool uniforms. The Austrians, when they arrived June 3, brought with them a Maxim machine gun. The Germans, Japanese, and French had nothing heavier than the rifles on their shoulders. The total guard force consisted of 450 officers and men from eight countries.[21] Morrison cast a critical eye on the British and American guards. "The British marines are nice-looking lads, cheerful and bright, and always ready and willing. The Americans were stronger and more mature, each man a sharpshooter, self-reliant and resourceful."[22] Many of the American marines had combat experience in the guerrilla war taking place in the Philippines.

Upon arrival the guards each patrolled their own legation. It was not until June 7 that the British, at the urging of the American commander, Captain John T. Myers, called a meeting and the soldiers came to an understanding for a common defense of the Legation Quarter. In Myers' words it was decided that "at the first sign of an outbreak, all the noncombatants together with all provisions should be sent to the English Legation; and that all streets leading into the Legation Quarter should at once be barricaded, no Chinese being allowed to enter without a pass. It was also agreed that we should endeavor to hold all the legations as long as possible, and as a last resort to fall back upon the English legation."[23] The Tartar Wall behind the American and German legations would also be held at all costs. "The reason for holding this Tartar Wall was obvious; first because it loomed over the Legation Quarter and second, because the water gate through it gave us means of communicating with the outer world."[24] This strategy would prevail throughout the siege.

Sir Claude MacDonald was reassured to the point of complacency by the arrival of the guards. On June 1, he telegraphed the British commander, Admiral Seymour: "No more ships wanted at Taku unless matters become more complicated which I do not think they will."[25] As a prophet Sir Claude was purblind and his optimism was quickly crushed. Matters got more complicated the next day, June 2, with reports that two British missionaries had been murdered south of Peking. And on June 4, matters got very much more complicated when the railroad to Tientsin was attacked. On that day, MacDonald and the other ministers cabled their renewed anxiety to Admiral Seymour, "Present situation at Peking is such that we may be besieged here with the railway and telegraph lines cut."[26] Conger's telegram of the same day to Washington also mentioned the possibility of a siege.[27] The diplomats were finally taking the Boxers seriously.

* * *

By late May and early June, thousands of Boxers streamed toward Peking and Tientsin. They came in groups of five or ten, forty or fifty at the most, carrying banners with their slogans: "Support the Ching! Destroy the Foreigner!" and "Fists of Righteous Harmony, carry out the Way on behalf of Heaven!" Moreover, the city people caught Boxer fervor and young men openly drilled and demonstrated. A recruit described the drill. The Boxers made him call out the name of a god nine times, then make three prostrations to produce a trance. Many of the young men shook and trembled and affirmed that the god told them to kill the foreigners and Chinese Christians, destroy the railroads and telegraph, and burn the steamships.[28]

Once in the cities the Boxers took up lodging in temples, vacant inns, or the homes of sympathizers and recruited more adherents to their cause. They operated in village groups, and lived, worshiped, and fought together, joining with other groups for a battle or ceremony, but with no unified command. A Chinese official said of them; "Tens of thousands of Boxers have come from all parts in the past few days. Most seem to be simple country folk who make their living by farming. They have neither leaders directing them nor potent weapons. They provide their own traveling expenses and eat only millet and corn. Seeking neither fame nor fortune they fight without regard for their own lives and are prepared to sacrifice themselves on the field of battle. They come together without prior agreement, a great host of only one mind. They wish only to kill foreigners and Christians and do not harm the common people. From this perspective, it seems they are fighting for righteousness."[29] The Chinese government was wary of the Boxers, but inching its way toward supporting them.

* * *

The American missionaries in Peking heard the pounding hooves of the second horse of the apocalypse. Their Chinese employees, students, and converts were deserting. Among the

Presbyterians, Bessie McCoy's Sunday school class had only two children present on May 27 and Grace Newton sent the fifty girls in her boarding school home on May 29. The women believed that a Boxer attack on their school was possible at any moment and that the girls would be safer at home. It seemed a prudent decision at the time, but it turned out a disaster. Only six of the fifty girls of the school survived the Boxers.[30]

On May 31, the four American women at the school, Newton, McCoy, Dr. Eliza Leonard, and Dr. Maud Mackey, made their plans to escape their compound if the Boxers attacked at night. Dressed as Manchu women, they planned to climb over the back wall of the Presbyterian compound, make their way down a narrow, dark lane and then light lanterns to guide their way to the Methodist Mission four miles away.[31] Being big-footed foreign women they would hope that people would take them for larger-than-average Manchus with unbound feet. The Methodist Mission, largest of all the missions and nearest to the Legation Quarter, was the safest place to take refuge. The fears of the women proved unfounded—for a few days.

Chinese seeking medical care in the formerly-crowded Presbyterian dispensary declined in numbers. The non–Christian servants of the missionaries and Chinese employees abandoned their jobs. A carter resigned. Courtenay Fenn asked him, "Why do you wish to leave? I can readily certify that you are not a Christian."

"I must not be caught here," the man answered. "The Boxers and soldiers intend to kill not only the foreigners but everyone who serves a foreigner." Fenn bid him farewell, and he had never seen an expression of greater relief on a man's face.[32] Alice Fenn and Theodora Inglis kept vigil over their children at night. The Presbyterians worried about their isolation in northern Peking.

In the midst of the efforts of the missionaries to protect themselves and their converts was also fatalism. "It seems to some of us," said Jessie Ransome, a deaconess of the Church of England, "that if we were all massacred it would be well worth while, if only it would stir up the world to take poor China in hand and govern her as she can never govern herself."[33]

* * *

Frank and Mary Porter Gamewell were veteran Methodist missionaries. They were packed and ready to leave China for a furlough in the United States. The annual regional conference of Methodist missionaries in Peking concluded June 4. The Gamewells put the conference participants on the train to Tientsin that afternoon. They planned to leave the next day, but no train came and on June 6 the Gamewells received a telegram from Tientsin: "Railroad interrupted. Other approaches unsafe. Wait."[34] The railroad was cut. By waiting a day too long to catch a train, Frank Gamewell, a modest, retiring man, would become the most unlikely hero of the siege in Peking.

The missionaries in Peking and Tientsin were lucky compared to their colleagues scattered around north China. On June 7, a last desperate message arrived in Tientsin from missionaries in Paoting, William Ament's old post. "Our position is dangerous—very.... Everything is turning from killing of Catholics to taking in both Protestants and Catholics.... Oh that God would send rain. That would make things quiet for a time. No soldiers here to amount to anything.... They frankly said that they have orders not to fire at Boxers. We have a guard of ten— ready to run at any time. We can't go out and fight—we must sit still, do our work, and if God calls us to Him, that's all. Unless definite orders come from Peking that we are to be protected at any cost or a guard of soldiers (foreign) sent *at once,* the blood must flow.... Boxers plenty here—one spark from north, south, east or west and we are gone."[35] Soon, the missionaries in Paoting would see their fears come true. They were murdered by Boxers with the collaboration, or at least the acquiescence, of the local government.

* * *

On June 8, the American missionaries—Methodists, Presbyterians, and Congregationalists— decided to gather in the Methodist Mission and to abandon the American Board and Presbyterian compounds.[36] The Methodist Mission was large, defensible, and near Legation Street. Should—heaven forbid—the walls of Peking prove inadequate to keep out the chaos of the countryside, the missionaries could flee to the American Legation, less than one mile away. The British had already told their subjects to come to their legation to sleep at night, but the American Legation was small and had no room for the seventy American missionaries in and around Peking.

The American Board was holding the annual conference of its North China Mission in Tungchou, twelve miles east. The conference was the only time in the year that the American Board missionaries in northern China, including families, got together for a week of work, worship, and socializing. It was a much anticipated event and the threat of the Boxers had not caused it to be cancelled.

William Ament noted the tension. "Everyone seems in a serious state of mind and heart and the Boxers may sweep us all out of existence." Some of Ament's colleagues seemed to be trying to encourage that prospect by fanning the flames: "The American flag is flying from the [Elwood G.] Tewksbury house in this yard. It looks a little defiant, as though we were a kingdom within China. Of course, that is one of the charges they [i.e., the Chinese] make."[37]

The conference ended June 1, the missionaries unmolested, but reports of Boxer ravages in the countryside came in daily. By June 5, even Tungchou appeared to be unsafe and several missionaries fled to Peking, among them the pregnant Bessie Ewing and her two children. Bessie's husband, Charles, was already in Peking. For Bessie, it was a harrowing ride through Boxer-infested countryside. "The rest were all to go in carts, but Ellen [her nineteen month old daughter] and I had to go in a sedan chair, and could not go by the same route. The bearers, I knew, and they were good trusty men, but I must confess that I was afraid to start on that 15 mile ride with only my baby and four Chinese for company. The bearers were given very positive orders to keep with the carts, but in many places that is almost impossible. As soon as we were fairly on our way I felt all right and as though there would be no trouble and everything was as quiet as possible. We found Peking pretty well excited and with reason. Every day brought news of fresh outrages, and refugees came in large numbers from our country church districts."[38] While Bessie and her children fled for what they imagined would be the safety of Peking, the remaining missionaries in Tungchou remained to help the Chinese Christians flooding their compound. Most of the Chinese were sent away with kind words, a little money and advice to seek safety among their families.[39] Most died in the violence which followed.

Mary Porter Gamewell. A pioneering female missionary, Mary established the first girls school in China to ban footbinding. She married Frank Gamewell, nine years her junior (Hubbard, *Under Marching Orders*, 1911).

On June 7, the missionaries still in Tungchou decided it was too dangerous to remain longer. They sent a telegram to Minister Conger, beseeching him to send an escort of marines to accompany them to Peking. Ament met with Conger to arrange for the marines but the diplomat refused to divide his small force of guards and opined that the presence of foreign soldiers on the road to Tungchou would inflame the Boxers and make the situation worse rather than better. A few marines could not protect the missionaries from a mob and, increasingly, the reports coming to the legations were of large numbers of Boxers and their sympathizers on the roads and in the towns and cities of north China.

Ament went to the rescue of the missionaries himself. He hired fifteen carts, borrowed a double-barreled shotgun from a British missionary,[40] belted on a revolver, and left Peking for Tungchou late in the afternoon accompanied by a Chinese pastor, Jen Mu Shih. None of his fellow missionaries in Peking volunteered to accompany him. The Chinese cart-drivers were reluctant but prodding with the shotgun kept them moving. The missionaries in Tungchou anticipated the arrival of marines and had prepared supper. They were surprised and frightened when Ament arrived alone at eleven P.M. He "sat down to the long table prepared for a dozen marines. Our cook ... had stayed by and made biscuits for a large company."[41]

After eating, Ament put the other missionaries and Chinese Christians to work loading up the carts with their possessions and at three in the morning he led the cart train to Peking with twenty-three Americans—five men, including missionary author Arthur Smith, eleven women, and seven children as well as one hundred Chinese helpers, students, and church members.[42] The missionaries had pangs of conscience on leaving behind hundreds of Chinese converts. The cart caravan arrived in Peking, without incident, at eight in the morning and Ament took his flock to the Methodist Mission. Thus Ament, along with Morrison and the Chamots, became one of the early heroes of the Boxer Rebellion.

Ament volunteered to return to Tungchou. To leave vacant the American Board Mission and North China College, the fruits of four decades of missionary endeavor, was to him "like deserting a sacred trust." The other missionaries talked him out of the idea. Had Ament returned he would surely have been killed. The day after the flight of the missionaries Chinese soldiers— not Boxers—looted and burned the college and mission. Seven hundred soldiers had been sent to Tungchou to protect the city from Boxers.[43] Like many elements of the Chinese Army in May and early June 1900 they hovered in uncertainty, not clear whether the Boxers were enemies or friends, but willing to take advantage of a chaotic situation to steal or destroy the foreigners' wealth.

* * *

The American missionaries, now united in the Methodist Mission, appealed to Conger for marines to guard the compound and he sent twenty of his total of fifty-six under the command of Captain Newt Hall. The Marine commander, Captain John T. "Handsome Jack" Myers, protested this division of his small force but Conger overruled him. The Americans invited the British missionaries of the London Missionary Society and their Chinese converts to join them at the Methodist compound, provided that the British Legation also sent guards and the LMS missionaries helped in the defense of the compound. On June 9, MacDonald had ordered that all British subjects must come to the legation, except for Sir Robert Hart's numerous Imperial Custom's employees. All complied, except for the formidable Miss Georgina Smith, forty-three years old, described as "little and plucky,"[44] and a veteran of 16 years in China, who remained in the East Compound of the LMS with a growing number of Chinese under her care. Georgina was a talkative and outspoken woman who loved children—being, or so she claimed, the thirteenth of a family of twenty-one all born of the same mother. She was single and, of course, childless, but outspoken adamant in deploring the "infertility of American women."[45] She would share with Ament and Elwood Tewksbury opprobrium after the siege. Most of the British missionaries abandoned their last remaining converts when they went to their legation. "Poor things," said Jesse Ransome, "they clung to me so, and some implored me to take them ... and oh it is hard to refuse them; and yet what can we do? ... The Legation is already more than packed."[46] Georgina Smith didn't abandon those in her charge, but took advantage of the American offer by sending Chinese women and children to the Methodist compound. She was surprised when they were turned away by the Americans. Dr. Lillie Saville took on the delicate task of finding out what the problem was. She went over to the Methodist compound that evening, to talk to the Americans. The Americans said that the offer to host the LMS missionaries and their converts was made contingent on British guards and LMS missionaries assisting in the defense of the compound. Neither had been forthcoming. The Methodist compound was already overcrowded, and the Americans were not inclined to take on more. Saville pleaded with the Americans and secured their agreement to permit the LMS converts to remain for the night with the promise that she would work out the problem with Sir Claude MacDonald. She then went to the British Legation, met with MacDonald and secured his agreement, or so she thought, to send 10 or 12 British marines to the Methodist compound to reinforce the American marines already there.

The next day, however, she discovered that MacDonald had not lived up to his agreement, perhaps dissuaded by Captain Strouts, the commander of his guard force. MacDonald, however, sent two men and ten rifles to the Methodists and that mollified the Americans. With the impasse resolved, Georgina Smith moved herself and more than 100 Chinese to the Methodist compound. A British missionary, Mr. Bigham, agreed also to remain at the compound to stand guard. Perhaps Bigham was persuaded by Georgina — because three years later she married him.[47] Dr. Saville, however, felt betrayed by MacDonald and relations between the two were icy, resulting in at least two public arguments between the two during the coming weeks.[48]

* * *

Theodora Ingles and the Presbyterians journeyed the four miles to the Methodist compound after dark on June 8. She packed a cart full of canned goods, cookware, mattresses, blankets, pillows and her baby's bathtub. In the slow, cumbersome cart they journeyed down narrow dark alleyways, At one point, a half-naked man rushed into the alley in front of them waving his arms and shouting curses and then running back into the dark. Her husband took his revolver out of his pocket and laid it on his knee. On a main street, two men approached and walked alongside the cart on either side. Inglis made sure they saw his pistol and they quickly departed. Almost at the Methodist compound, they drove by a group of Boxers drilling in the street, but the Boxers did not molest them.

When they neared the gate of the Methodist compound they found a long line of carts and other missionaries waiting to get in. Theodora took her baby and walked to the gate and there, "Oh, the blessed sight of the young United States marine who stood there!" It was Private Hall, a favorite of the missionary children. And inside the compound were "women and children waiting around by piles of baggage; servants running back and forth with burdens, United States marines on guard, marching slowly up and down the long walks, native convert refugees everywhere sitting about with their children, some with small hand-bundles, some swathed in bandages because of burns and cuts from revengeful Boxers; all looking most disconsolate for many had fled to Peking because their homes were laid in ruins and members of their families killed or missing."[49]

* * *

The will of the American and British missionaries came out most strongly when their Chinese schoolgirls were threatened. The missionary boarding schools in Peking and Tungchou had sent many of their students home, hoping they would be safer if they blended into the Chinese community than remained as students at Christian schools. The Presbyterians, as noted above, sent their fifty schoolgirls home. The Methodists planned to send their schoolgirls home by train but they waited too long. The Boxers tore up the track and halted railroad service. That was fortunate. Most would have been killed by the Boxers had they been sent home.[50] Mrs. Mary Smith of the LMS's West Compound closed her school, but six schoolgirls remained and they probably found their way to the Methodist Mission.[51] Some schoolchildren were orphans and had no home to return to, and others were boarding students from distant or Boxer-infested areas.

Two hundred teenaged Chinese schoolgirls took refuge with the missionaries and other Chinese Christians at the Methodist mission. Several American missionaries kept their girls together and fiercely protected them: Charlotte Jewell had 100 girls from the Methodist boarding school and Ada Haven and her colleagues had 30 girls from ABCFM's Bridgman school. Additional Chinese girls from Georgina Smith's school at the London Missionary Society's East Compound and the American Board's North China College in Tungchou were also among the refugees.[52]

Haven told of the journey from the Bridgman school to the Methodist mission with the schoolgirls. "It was expressly desired that we should not come very late, or very early (before dark), or in a great body, so as to attract notice. So, as soon as it was dark our six carts took our little band to the Methodist place. Our girls were very collected and calm, quite content to go anywhere or do anything as long as they kept with the foreigners. Arrived at the Methodist mission, we were told to go to the church. We found the Methodist girls already there.... As soon as we could we got settled for the night, spreading down our quilts between the rows of seats. We ... spread ourselves between the rows, feet to feet, or head to head, a continuous line of bodies in each row."[53] The girls and their teachers slept on the church floor; about the same number of Chinese women and their children slept in the lecture room, and eight missionary mothers and their twelve children slept on the rostrum. Men, and unmarried and childless missionary women, slept in other buildings whenever they could snatch an hour for sleep. In the compound were nearly seventy American missionaries, counting women and children, one British missionary, Georgina Smith, the twenty Marine guards, two British guards, and about eight hundred Chinese. Rifle-armed missionary men and twenty-five trusted Chinese stood guard alongside the marines.[54] Additional Chinese men were organized into squads and armed with spears.

Dr. Emma Martin — with one month of residence in China — was "sort of enjoying this.... Who would have thought I would ever have such a chance to study military tactics?" she asked. But Emma was "tired of being of girl. I wish I was a man and could carry a gun and keep guard."[55] Charlotte Jewell gave her a small revolver and she slept with it beside her, keeping the bullets in a bag hanging from her waist. Corporal Hunt oiled the pistol, gave her some instruction, and she test fired three shots "I told Lizzie," she said, "I would take care of her now that she could stay right behind me and she said she was very sure she would not want to be in front of me."[56]

The Methodist compound was about 300 yards long and 100 yards wide, surrounded by a high wall. It contained seven residences, a church, a school, and a hospital.[57] The missionaries converted the church into a fortress. It would be the last redoubt if the compound was overrun. Outside the church, they dug trenches and built barbed wire, brick and stone barricades and a watchtower. Inside, "the church was fast losing its ecclesiastical aspect. The altar was fenced around with a barricade of boxes of condensed milk, biscuit tins, baskets of household silver, etc., and the air was redolent with the smell of freshly burned coffee beans.... In this as in all provision for the welfare of the natives, the school girls, of whatever denomination, were given the place of greatest safety ... the best that could be given to the Chinese, favors that could not be given to all.[58]

The marines and the missionaries turned away many Chinese who came to the gate begging for refuge. A few were admitted, others were suspected of being Boxers; and still others who had families in Peking were told there was no room at the inn. They should seek safety with their relatives. All the Chinese in the mission had labels sewed on their clothing identifying them as Christians. At night, when the labels could not be seen, Chinese had to wear white turbans so that the marines would not mistake and shoot them for Boxers.[59] The students of a missionary school for the blind were forgotten in the rush to the Methodist Mission. The 30 boys and eight girls at the school nearly all died when the Boxers stormed the school and burned it, incinerating some of the children and capturing others.[60]

With the American predilection for hustle, the missionaries in the Methodist compound organized. They formed committees, called meetings, discussed problems, and planned the defense of the compound. Frank Gamewell took charge. He conscripted Chinese Christians for labor. It was good training for the weeks that followed. A few of the missionary women also stood guard. Others made light-weight uniforms for the marines to replace their heavy woolens. This was the period of what the missionaries called the semi-siege — the two weeks between June 8 and June 20 when they holed up for safety in the Methodist Mission compound. The semi-siege also saw the missionaries' acceptance of looting as a justifiable reaction to the threat that faced them. The missionaries got their supplies by taking what they needed from Chinese stores in their neighborhood at gunpoint."[61]

Captain Newt Hall was in charge of the 20 marines at the Methodist Mission. As compared to the dashing and handsome Captain Myers at the Legation, Hall was blunt, taciturn, and was contemptuous of civilians. Mary Porter Gamewell went to Hall one day and indicated her willingness to be of assistance. Captain Hall responded bluntly, "The most helpful thing a woman can do in a fight is to keep out of the way." He thought about his answer for a moment, facing this time-worn woman who had probably seen more dangerous situations as a missionary than had he as a soldier and plunged himself even more deeply into difficulty, "There is one thing you can do—when the firing begins you can take charge of the hysterical women and try to keep them quiet."[62] In the spirit of Christian charity, Mrs. Gamewell and the other American missionaries excused Captain Hall for his low opinion of their courage by reason of his youth and inexperience. Hall's stock with the civilians would continue to remain low.

5

Admiral See-No-More

Any residual doubts of the diplomats that Boxers were a real threat were erased June 9 when they burned the grandstand of the racecourse three miles outside Peking. This outrage struck at the marrow of the privileged foreign community. The racecourse was the symbol of class distinction in Peking and its most enthusiastic supporters included, of course, Sir Claude and Lady Ethel MacDonald. The higher orders in Peking were the diplomats, senior customs employees, respectable businessmen, prestigious scholars, and Anglican — not American — missionaries. Foreign society in Peking, an American missionary commented, "was like an English fruit tart, no lower crust." On reflection, she added, "unless we missionaries were willing to consider ourselves as such."[1]

In May the smart set celebrated its annual Spring Race Meeting with balls, theatrical performances, picnics, and tennis parties as well as the races. Now, the grandstand was gone, incinerated by the beastly Boxers and, without so much as a by your leave, they had tossed several native Christians into the flames. Fortunately, many of the diplomats had their Mongolian racing ponies stabled in the legations. In times to come, those ponies would serve an unorthodox purpose.

That afternoon a group of language students attached to the British Legation rode outside the walls to see the smoking ruin of the grandstand. A threatening crowd of Chinese surrounded them and, in escaping, one of the students, H. H. Bristol, pulled a revolver and shot a Chinese.[2] The incident didn't cause much of a commotion in the legations, except that it was the first shot fired near the capital in the war between Boxer and foreigner. The Boxers now had a martyr to whip up the citizens against the hated foreigners. A modicum of restraint would have prevented this inflammatory incident, but the arrogant foreigners in the Legation Quarter were as nervous and trigger-happy as a band of desperados in the American West.

At the news of the burning of the grandstand, MacDonald cabled Vice Admiral Sir Edward Hobart Seymour, commander-in-chief of the British Navy's China Station, that the legations needed additional guards urgently. "The situation in Peking is hourly becoming more serious" and "troops should be landed and all arrangements made for an advance on Peking at once."[3]

The next day, Sunday, June 10, more than the usual number of foreigners in Peking felt the need for spiritual nourishment. The Anglican service, the Rev. Roland Allen officiating, at the British Legation was held in the open air in front of MacDonald's house because the chapel was too small to accommodate the thronging crowd. In the afternoon came another blow to the British. Their Summer Legation and guesthouses in the Western Hills were burned to the ground and the caretakers murdered.

* * *

MacDonald anticipated that the additional troops requested of Admiral Seymour would arrive at Machia Pu on Sunday evening. His assumption was that Seymour would bivouac near the railroad station Sunday night and, next morning, June 11, his men would march into the city, leaving a strong force behind to secure the railroad station.

At four A.M. Monday the British Legation sent fifty carts with forty marines through the Chinese city to Machia Pu to escort the troops into the city. Several adventurous civilians on horseback joined the convoy which met up with carts and military escorts from the Japanese, Italian, and American Legations. All together it was an imposing procession. They were anxious that they might be fired on by Chinese troops who were rumored to have mounted a cannon on the Chien gate, but the journey through the Chinese city was without incident. They encountered only one problem: neither Seymour nor any foreign soldiers were at the railroad station. The legation guards, the civilians, and their caravan of carts and carters waited for their rescuers but, in the heat of the June day, gave up and turned sadly toward home, passing through the encampment of the red-uniformed Muslim soldiers from Kansu province of General Tung Fu-hsiang near the Temples of Heaven and Agriculture.

That same afternoon the foreign community of Peking suffered its first casualty. The chancellor of the Japanese Legation, Akira Sugiyama, decided unwisely to go alone and unarmed to the railroad station to await the arrival of Japanese soldiers. As Sugiyama passed through the Yungting gate he was seized by the soldiers of General Tung, dragged from his cart, and killed. An approving Chinese crowd witnessed the last struggles of Sugiyama. A horseman of the American Legation happened to pass by and saw the mutilated body of the top-hatted Japanese diplomat lying in the road and rode to the legation to report the incident, but neither the Japanese nor others foreigners had the fortitude to march out and attempt to recover the body. The next morning Morrison sent his servant to Yungting. He found the mutilated body of Sugiyama partially covered with dirt with one leg exposed. Several children, to the amusement of their elders, poked at the body with sticks.[4] It was said that Sugiyama's heart was cut out and sent as a trophy to General Tung. Sugiyama's death caused surprisingly little stir among the diplomats, except the Japanese. Their national pride outraged, the Japanese Legation terminated relations with China.[5]

The other legations were more preoccupied with the question: Where was Seymour? The mystery was cleared up June 13 when a courier brought a letter to the American Legation from Captain Bowman Hendry McCalla, the American naval captain accompanying Seymour. Conger sent the news over to Frank Gamewell at the Methodist Mission. "My dear Mr. Gamewell. A note just received from Captain McCalla written at 4 P.M. yesterday reports him with 1,600 men of all nationalities at Langfang [thirty five miles from Peking], pushing on as fast as they can repair the road."[6]

So, Seymour was near and repairing the railroad as he came. He should arrive in Peking in two or three days and the unpleasantness of the Boxers would end and life could go back to normal. The joy of hearing from Seymour was tempered slightly by the cutting of the last telegraph line out of Peking. The legations were now out of contact with the outside world.

* * *

William Ament was the only American missionary who refused to take refuge in the Methodist Mission.[7] Ament feared that his American Board compound, if abandoned, would be looted. He believed that no Chinese would dare trespass on the property if a foreigner were guarding it. He was both shocked and pleasantly surprised when a Chinese man, "a heathen and a stranger," came to the mission to tell him that all the foreigners in Peking were to be killed and to offer Ament asylum in his grain shop. The man had met Ament twice and liked him. This example of Chinese kindliness impressed itself on his mind.[8]

Ament's solo sojourn at the American Board Mission did not last long. On June 13 at four P.M. Charles Ewing sent him "an imperative message. There was certain information of an attack that evening."⁹ Ament hired a cart, put a few things in it, and told his servant boy to push his bicycle ahead of him in the streets. The streets were filled with excited crowds and Ament's bicycle attracted attention, but he was armed with a revolver and a repeating rifle and he reached the Methodist compound in safety. Once again, Ament was fortunate to preserve his life. A few hours later the American Board compound was in flames and the streets of Peking were littered with the burned and mutilated bodies of Chinese Christians.

* * *

That day, June 13, began calmly enough but at mid-morning an astonishing sight appeared on Legation Street. "It was nothing less than a full-fledged Boxer with his hair tied up in red cloth, red ribbons round his wrists and ankles, and a flaming red girdle tightening his loose white tunic; and, to cap all, the man was audaciously and calmly sharpening a big carver knife on his boots."⁹ He was the first Boxer seen in the Legation Quarter. The Chinese authorities had attempted to block the entrance of Boxers into the Tartar City, offering little resistance to the Boxers in the countryside but keeping them outside the walls. That was to change.

It was more than Baron Clemens von Ketteler could take. The German minister was out for his morning walk when this apparition appeared. Von Ketteler was not a peaceful man. "He tilted full at the man with his walking stick, and before he could escape had beaten a regular roll of kettle drums on his hide. Then the Boxer, after a short struggle, abandoned his knife and ran with some fleetness of foot into a neighboring lane."¹¹ Inside the cart another Boxer, a boy, was discovered and von Ketteler collared him and handed him over to the legation guards. The Germans—for no discernible reason—killed the captured boy.¹² The Boxers had another martyr to incite the people against the foreigners in the Legation Quarter. The British poured fuel on the fire when they killed several Boxers near their legation.¹³ The violence against Chinese by the foreigners had immediate consequences.

* * *

Mary Bainbridge of the American Legation remembered three nights that stood out with "terrible anxiety and dread" during the Boxer summer. This was the first of the three.¹⁴ About seven P.M.—a short time after Ament made his way to the Methodist Mission—the noise of a crowd reached Legation Street and a horde of Boxers poured into the Tartar City through the Hata gate. The Boxers raced down the street, shouting their war cry, *Sha! Sha!*, waving swords and spears, stabbing and slashing everything in their path.¹⁵ The Methodist street chapel on Hata Street was their first target and within minutes it was burning.

The Methodist Mission compound was only a few yards away down a narrow lane. Inside Luella Miner, another Oberlin alumnus and a proper schoolmarm, was in a prayer meeting with a roomful of Chinese women when someone whispered in her ear, "The Boxers are coming." Miner told the women to be ready to go to the church where they would take refuge. She went outside the building to see what was happening. The courtyard was full of smoke from the burning chapel. Luella gathered up a few personal items and rushed back to the group of Chinese women. She helped the women with their bundles and babies and escorted them into the Sunday school room in one wing of the church. The Chinese were calm and quiet. The foreign women and their children and the Chinese schoolgirls took refuge in the nave.

Outside the Methodist compound, thirty or forty Boxers ran up the narrow, crooked lane from Hata Street toward the mission. Captain Hall and eight of his marines were ready for them. They charged down the street with a rebel yell, bayonets fixed, and the Boxers and the crowd behind them fled.¹⁶ The marines held their fire. Their orders from Conger were not to discharge their rifles unless the life of a foreigner was in danger.

Frank Gamewell had worked out the defense for the Methodist Mission and every missionary knew his place. The marines were scattered throughout the compound, guarding the mo st critical defense points and reinforcing the civilian defenders. All American male missionaries were armed and had their posts. They were backed up by a few Chinese armed with rifles and more with spears. Gamewell's labor brigades rushed around the compound digging trenches and reinforcing walls. Some Chinese had never done manual labor and resisted. However, Gamewell was firm: no work, no eat, no stay. Almost all found the indignity of shouldering a shovel preferable to a short life in the hostile streets.

The mob of Boxers—repulsed in their effort to overrun the Methodist Mission—moved on to easier targets and, shortly, from the windows on the upper story of the church, Miner saw flames leaping skyward as the Boxers started fires. First burned was the nearby East compound of the London Missionary Society, the former home of Georgina Smith, and soon she saw fires at five different points in the city with a big blaze at the East Cathedral of the Catholics. The venerable priest, Father Garrigues, perished in the flames with many of his converts. Finally, Miner sadly noted that she saw "the red light hanging over our beloved American Board compound."[17]

Across Hata Street in the Legation Quarter the diplomats, soldiers, and refugees also leaped to attention at the sound of the Boxers breaking into the Tartar City. Dr. Robert Coltman, physician to the Chinese royal family, ran into the American Legation compound with glaring eyes. "An attack, an attack!" he shouted and the residents sought safe places.[18] The guards at all the legations hurriedly constructed barricades of overturned carts and piles of bricks. From the barricades, the guard posts, and the roofs of the legations the defenders watched the fires around the city and heard the booming of the big fire at the East Cathedral. The howling, running, burning Boxers stayed away from the Legation Quarter until midnight when Austrian soldiers saw a mob carrying hundreds of torches coming down the street toward their legation. The Austrians held fire until the Boxers were one hundred and fifty yards distant and then opened up with their Maxim machine gun, sweeping back and forth and up and down the street, the sound in the restricted space ear shattering. When the torches disappeared the commander called for firing to cease. Volunteers pushed to the front of the Austrian barricade, anxious to see the destruction the Maxim had wrought in the street before them. The ever-present journalist, George Morrison was among the volunteers.

At the blow of a bugle the volunteers took off helter-skelter down the street "with fixed bayonets and loaded magazines, a veritable massacre for ourselves in the dark." The charge of the volunteers "pulled up panting, swearing, and laughing. Somebody had stuck someone through the seat of the trousers, and the some one else was making a horrid noise about this trivial detail."[19] To the surprise of the volunteers they found no dead Boxers. Morrison had an explanation. The next morning he saw up the street from the Austrian machine gun that the telegraph wires thirty feet off the ground had been cut. The Austrians had fired high so high they cut the telegraph lines, and, Morrison commented sarcastically, the only persons who suffered injury were possible wayfarers two miles away. "There can be little doubt that this fiasco helped to confirm the Boxers in a belief in their invulnerability."[20]

During their charge down an empty street, a Frenchman stumbled over something and jumped back with a cry of alarm. "At his feet lay a native woman trussed tightly with ropes, with her body already half-charred and reeking with kerosene, but still alive and moaning faintly. The Boxers, inhuman brutes, had caught her, set fire to her, and then flung her on the road to light their way."[21]

The Catholic East Cathedral was now tumbled stone and charred bodies, but the North, South, and West Cathedrals still stood. Forty-three French and Italian soldiers guarded the North Cathedral of Bishop Favier, but the South and West Cathedrals had no defenders. They survived the night without attack. Early the next morning, a volunteer group, headed by the

Chinese-speaking American William N. Pethick, a Civil War veteran and secretary to China's most distinguished diplomat, Li Hung Chang, ventured out of the Legation Quarter and returned about 10 A.M., bringing back with them 150 Chinese Christians. The rescued Catholics included Father d'Addosio, an old man with a flowing white beard and a faraway look in his eye, his two Italian colleagues, a French brother, five Sisters of Charity, and twenty Chinese nuns. The good father had cheerfully predicted to the Italian minister a few days earlier that they would all meet in paradise and receive their reward for having carried God's word to the heathen. An hour after he and the others reached the safety of the Legation Quarter, Boxers fired the South Cathedral.

Notwithstanding the success of the rescue of Chinese Christians it was a provocation. "It was realized at the time," said Captain Jack Myers, "that these rescuing parties served to inflame the Boxer element more deeply against the foreigners, but it was more than flesh and blood could stand to see the terribly burned and lacerated bodies of those who escaped to our lines, and refuse to send aid to their comrades known to be still within the power of the fiendish Boxer hordes."[22]

* * *

Will Ament was also up early on June 14 and journeyed alone from the Methodist Mission to the ruins of the American Board Mission. He looked for Christians who might be hiding near the mission. He found none, but a dirty, ragged boy followed him. The boy came forward and begged Ament to take him into the Methodist Mission. He introduced himself as a Sunday school pupil. He had been apprenticed to a shopkeeper but the shopkeeper had turned him out into the streets lest the Boxers punish him for harboring a Christian convert. Through the dirt and rags Ament recognized the exhausted and starving boy and took him into the mission. The same boy was later to play a hero's role.[23]

The guards at the Methodist Mission had been up all night and they got very little sleep this Thursday. At ten o'clock in the morning thousands of Boxers in the Chinese city, on the other side of the Tartar Wall from the mission and the legations, began shouting chants and incantations. All day the twenty marines, the missionaries, and the Chinese guards remained at their posts, fearing an attack, and hearing the Boxers just over the wall with their eternal chant, *Sha, sha! Sha, sha!*[24]

That afternoon the arrogant Baron von Ketteler and his German soldiers fired from the Tartar Wall into the Boxers in the Chinese city and killed seven. Once again, foreigners had wounded or killed Chinese in the streets of Peking. Sensible diplomats such as Conger and MacDonald deplored this provocative killing, fearing it would arouse even greater anti-foreign feeling. MacDonald wrote a note to the baron suggesting mildly that it was not the wisest of actions to incite the populace when one was surrounded, cut off from the outside world, and vastly outnumbered.

At the Methodist Mission, Frank Gamewell and his Chinese workers strengthened the compound's defenses. Women boiled water and eggs and collected stacks of biscuits and cans of condensed milk and piled them in the church. Luella Miner, never known to cook and with a most unfeminine interest in politics, was more interested in the fortifications. "Our lines of defense have been extended to include all of the streets bordering on the mission property—three or four streets and alleys being under martial law—and all passersby are challenged. There are barbed wire barricades at the end of each street.... Now in the compound and adjoining streets we have barricade within barricade of barbed wire and brick, all the walls and some small buildings having been torn down to get brick."[25] Frank Gamewell was getting a heavy dose of on-the-job training in fortifications engineering. Gamewell also found three English-speaking Chinese students who volunteered to climb over the outer walls of the compound and race to the American Legation to request assistance if the Methodist Mission was attacked and in danger of being overrun.[26] One of them would surely make it.

At the legations George Morrison, the peripatetic journalist — Morrison of China, he would be called — and others were appealing to the diplomats to send out more patrols to rescue Chinese Christians who, according to refugees, were being slaughtered in the Catholic neighborhoods near the smoldering South Cathedral. But, what to do with Chinese Christians already rescued? The legations were crowded; food, water, and sanitation were serious problems. Morrison and an eccentric professor named Huberty James came up with a solution. Across the canal from the British Legation was a *fu*, a large park and palace belonging to a Prince Su. Morrison, with James as his interpreter, went over to see the prince and advised him that "it would not only be kind, but wise for him to present his palace and park to his distressed fellow citizens ... Dr. James intimated that unless he voluntarily gave up his *fu* we would take it. Prince Su was most suave and said nothing would give him greater pleasure.... He was only too glad to get as far away as possible from these legation people. The danger for his life might be very great if he were suspected, even for a moment of sympathizing with the foreigners."[27] The prince vacated his palace that same day and refugees began to occupy it.

Morrison persuaded the ministers to send out additional armed patrols and, on June 15 a morning patrol of twenty Russian soldiers and ten American marines plus volunteers went to the neighborhood of the South Cathedral. Two American civilians, old China hands Fleming Cheshire, the American legation's interpreter, and William Pethick, went with them. Pethick and Cheshire walked down the streets crying out for people to come out of their houses to be protected. At noon, the marines brought back four hundred Catholic refugees. The caravan of hungry, burned, and wounded people stopped in front of the American Legation and while Dr. Lippett, a U.S. Navy doctor, and a Russian physician tended their wounds, the women and servants of the Russian and American Legations gave them water. "Water was brought to them in bowls, pails, basins, anything our servants could lay hands on. It was pitiful to see these shaky creatures, three or four grabbing at the same bowl, others trying to drink from the spout as the water was being poured in the bowls. One woman carried in her arms a child covered with smallpox; other mothers carried children completely naked; but the most touching sight was a gray haired man of at least sixty, carrying on his back his old, crippled mother"[28] Dr. Lippet and the Russian doctor labored for hours treating the worst of the wounded and the rest were settled into Prince Su's palace, hereafter called the *Fu*. It was too late, however, for most of the Chinese Christians in Peking. Jessie Ransome learned that the Boxers had taken over the London Missionary Society compound in the west part of the Tartar City and massacred the Christians still there. She searched among the refugees at the *Fu* in vain for survivors of her converts.[29]

The diplomats were hardly pleased at this influx of Chinese Christians, spreading their defenses even thinner to guard the Chinese in the fourteen acre expanse of the *Fu*. Refugees kept coming and soon two thousand of them were crammed into the palaces, courtyards, and gardens. For *The Times* correspondent, George Morrison, saving the Chinese Christians was an obligation of his privileged race. "I should be ashamed to call myself a white man if I could not make a place of refuge for these Chinese Christians."[30]

In what looked like a favorable development, that afternoon MacDonald received from a Chinese courier a letter from Admiral Seymour. On reading it, he was less reassured: "Please believe me that we are doing our utmost to get on. Should the obstacles to progress on the railway prove insuperable, I will consider if we can march to your relief."[31] All this was too much for Sir Robert Hart — "painfully nervous and shaken," in the words of Morrison, and "an awful old funkstick"[32] according to a British doctor. Morrison, like many other residents of Peking, resented the prestige and power of Hart and had little good to say about the old man. Hart's ghost can take some satisfaction that his writings about the Boxer Rebellion are far more honest and perceptive than those of Morrison's. "I wonder at the Relief Force spending so long in the train!" said Hart. "After doing half of the journey that way, they could easily do the rest in two days across country."[33] That sentiment was common. Seymour, hailed as a savior five days before, was now Admiral See-No-More.

The murder of Sugiyama, the rush of the Boxers into the Tartar City on June 13, the firing of the South, East, and West cathedrals and the Protestant missions, the massacres of Chinese Christians, and the promise of worse to come frazzled the nerves of even the calmest and most benign of souls. Sarah Pike Conger, overcome by the events, made one of the few defiant statements of her virtuous life: "How *dare* China touch the legations?"[34]

* * *

Throughout the semi-siege, the legations maintained a nervous relationship with the Chinese government. The soldiers, sailors, and marines guarding the Legation Quarter set up barricades on all the streets and Chinese were allowed to pass the pickets only with a pass signed by a foreigner and stamped with the seal of one of the eleven legations. The British marines guarded the North Bridge crossing the odoriferous canal which carried the royal sewage out of the Forbidden City and bisected the Legation Quarter. During the day Chinese were allowed to cross the bridge — although they could not turn south into the Legation Quarter without a pass. At night, everyone coming to the bridge was halted and interrogated. Oddly enough, assisting the British soldiers were a dozen Kansu troops, glorious in their red uniforms and scarlet and black banners and well armed with Mauser rifles. The equivocal nature of the Chinese would continue: hostility one moment would contrast with periods of cooperation and friendliness.

The Tsungli Yamen continued to be conciliatory but vague. It was the policy of the government, they assured the ministers, to protect the foreign friends from any unfortunate incidents or unpleasant experiences. They was taking all appropriate measures to this end but it would be much appreciated by the government of the Celestial Personalities, his and her majesties, if the foreign friends would quit sending patrols out of the Legation Quarter to hunt Boxers. These patrols, they explained politely, irritated the populace.

The patrol most irritating to the populace took place on June 16. Thirty-five British, American, and Japanese soldiers, plus volunteers, made up the patrol. George Morrison, *The Times* correspondent, was among the volunteers. Also along was bandy-legged Lieutenant Colonel Goro Shiba, military attaché of the Japanese Legation, who would be regarded without dissent as the finest soldier in the Legation Quarter.

The patrol searched the charred ruins of the East Cathedral and the neighborhood for survivors. They found few Christians but as they were passing a Taoist temple they heard cries and entered to investigate. Within was a slaughterhouse. "Native Christians were found there, their hands tied behind their backs, awaiting execution and torture. Some had already been put to death, and their bodies were still warm and bleeding. All were shockingly mutilated. The fiendish murderers were at their incantations, burning incense before their gods, offering Christians in sacrifice to their angered deities."[35] The foreign soldiers and civilians attacked the Boxers, all of them in the red sash of their sect and armed with sword and spear. In minutes it was all over. Forty-six Boxers were dead. "I myself killed at least six,"[36] Morrison said. The patrol took the surviving Christians back to the Legation Quarter.

* * *

The fires destroying Christian properties all over Peking on June 13 and 14 were as nothing compared to the conflagration of June 16. It began at eleven A.M. in the great market of the Chinese city just outside the Chien gate. Reportedly, Boxers started the fire to burn a shop that sold foreign medicines. Before long the whole quarter was ablaze, the smoke spread like a blanket over the city and, from a vantage point on the Tartar Wall, foreigners watched flames shooting sixty feet into the air. Explosions in shops selling kerosene or fireworks sounded like heavy reports as of cannon and volleys of rifle fire. Roland Allen, the Anglican missionary, walked down the Tartar Wall to the Chien gate and conversed amiably with the Chinese soldiers stationed there while watching thousands of scurrying Chinese below try to save their valuables from the spreading fire.

At half past three a shopping arcade within the massive ramparts of the Chien gate caught fire and flames and smoke rose up through the brick tower of the gate into the wooden rafters of the high pagoda roof. Allen saw "little tongues of flames running around the ends of these rafters, leaping from one to another and licking the overhanging tiles. Soon, the great beams of Burmese teak supporting the roof, dry from six centuries of exposure, were blazing, and a great tower of flame poured out through the funnel of brick and rose hundreds of feet in the air."[37]

George Morrison noticed a small blaze not far from the Legation Quarter and the Chinese soldiers in the vicinity doing nothing to extinguish it. "The fire spread and soon the foreign soldiers were out in the streets to prevent it from spreading to the legations. The Imperial Fire Brigade "arrived with great pomp and could have furnished charming costumes for some 'extravaganza' in their get-up. They had no idea how to put a fire out, but fortunately they had some hose, which, when used in the telling places, proved most efficacious."[38] The enthusiasm of the fire brigade was dampened when a Russian soldier, mistaking the firemen for Boxers, shot and killed one of them. In recompense for this unfortunate error, the Russian soldiers, joined by a few Americans, went out of their lines to fight the fire and worked side by side with Chinese firefighters to bring it under control. The Russians also began pulling down Chinese houses near their legation to protect themselves from the flames and to create a open field of fire. The owners of the houses were evicted at gunpoint. Bertram Simpson commented icily that "barricades with loop holes have been going up on all sides, excepting near the British Legation, where the same indifference and sloth, which have so greatly contributed to this impasse, still remain undisturbed."[39]

* * *

The next day was Sunday, June 17, and the missionaries and eight hundred Chinese Christians met for religious services in the Methodist compound. An American flag flew from the roof of the church. The altar that morning was surrounded by mattresses, "cans of French butter, tins of raspberry jelly, bottles of gherkins and numerous baby cradles, while below stood a row of huge water jars filled to the brim.... Trunks of all sizes ... filled up the vestibules, lined the aisles and encumbered the platform."[40] The doors of the church were reinforced with iron plates and windows were barricaded with bricks.

Arthur Smith preached. He quoted the Ninetieth and Ninety-First Psalms to give his listeners a hopeful message. "Thou shalt not be afraid for the terror by night; nor the arrow that flieth by day; nor for the pestilence that walketh in darkness; nor for the destruction that wasteth at noonday."[41] Smith, the writer and the preacher, was soothing but every mind in the audience wandered from the promises of the Psalms to the reality of Peking. Where was Seymour?

* * *

Vice Admiral Sir Edward Hobart Seymour had problems. In fact, by this time he had forgotten about the foreigners in Peking was worried about saving his command. Seymour, the rescuer, needed rescue.

Seymour embarked from Tientsin with five trainloads of soldiers at 9:20 A.M. on June 10, the day after he received the alarming message from MacDonald asking for more troops to come to Peking immediately to guard the legations. Seymour's expedition totaled 2,078 soldiers, marines and sailors: 916 British, 445 Germans, 326 Russians, 158 French, 112 Americans, 54 Japanese, 41 Italians, and 26 Austrians.[42] The assumption of Seymour was that the Boxers had neither

The Chien Gate. The most monumental of Peking's city gates, it was burned by the Boxers, probably by accident, during the semi-siege (Coltman, *Beleaguered in Peking*, 1901).

the intelligence nor the forethought to do more than minor damage to the railroad. The diplomats in Peking expected Seymour to arrive the same day he left Tientsin. Seymour was not so optimistic but he anticipated that he could push his way through in two or three days. Seymour's chief of staff was Captain John R. Jellicoe, who would command British naval forces at the Battle of Jutland sixteen years later. The commander of the one hundred and twelve American sailors was Captain Bowman Hendry McCalla, a crusty, teetotaling old salt with abundant experience in small wars.

Admiral Seymour led his sailors and marines under his command into the interior of China without planning, intelligence, reconnaissance, communications, and logistical support. In addition, Seymour, a tidy sailor with a pointed beard and a cocked hat, had no experience with ground operations. He launched his trains like ships as self-sufficient fighting machines with the hope that he could sail into Peking effortlessly — as, in fact, the legation guards had done less than two weeks before. The difference was, of course, that a ship has freedom to go where it wishes on the wide oceans and Seymour's chugging locomotives could only follow a narrow and vulnerable railroad line.

Seymour took a risk based on necessity. His railroad armada had easy slow going its first day. The trains rolled without incident eighteen miles to Yang Tsun. The trains stopped to take on water and crossed the Pei River on a long iron bridge. The seven thousand man army of General Nieh Shi Cheng was encamped on the far side of the river, but the Chinese showed no signs of resisting the passage of the international force aboard the trains. Beyond Yang Tsun, Seymour encountered minor damage to the railroad and progress slowed but the track was repaired and by sunset the first three trains of the expedition were nearing Lofa, thirty-five miles from Tientsin with less than fifty to go to Peking. The usually teeming villages near the railroad were empty of people and animals. The weather was hot and parching by day, chilly at night, and always dusty.

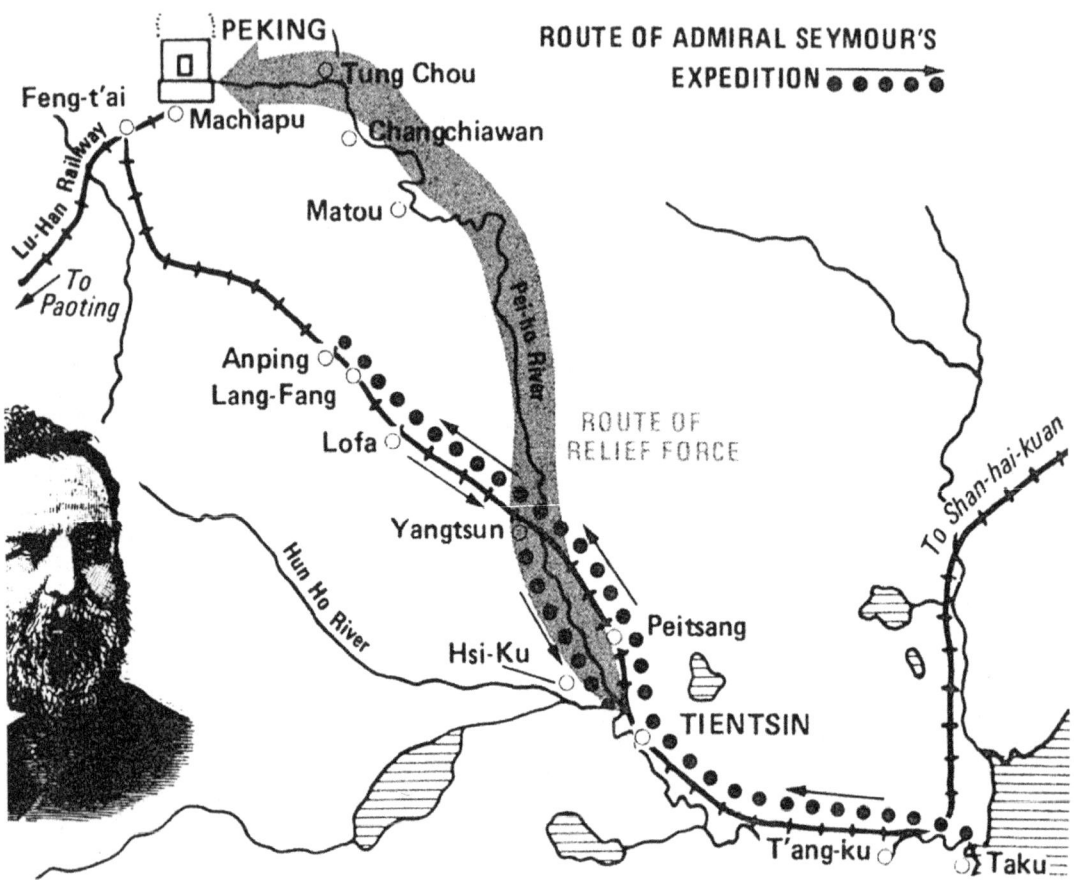

Military Operations in Northern China—1900. The routes of the Seymour Expedition and the Relief Expedition are shown (courtesy *Military Review*).

The next day McCalla led his Americans onward to Lofa station, burned by the Boxers, to repair the railroad. That afternoon, the Boxers attacked the first train. A British patrol saw a company of them, dressed in red caps, belts, and anklets, carrying red and white flags, and armed with knives and spears, sneaking up on the train through fields of millet and copses of trees. The British patrol alerted the trains and the troops poured out of the cars in confusion, some hiding under the train. McCalla formed his Americans into a skirmish line and advanced, coming across a dozen Boxers who approached slowly, pausing for incantations and kowtows. "A most picturesque group," said one officer.[43] The Americans opened fire and killed the lot of them. The British deployed on the other side of the train shot down a few more. The foreign troops suffered no casualties. Five or six wounded Boxers were recovered after the fight. They were covered with blood, almost naked and two of them were children. They "were given all the care possible"—probably the first and last time in 1900 that a foreigner, soldier or civilian, gave any care to the well-being of a wounded Boxer.[44]

Tuesday and Wednesday, June 12 and 13, were slow days of rebuilding the railroad, advancing, and fending off assaults from Boxers. On June 14, the Boxers attacked in force at ten in the morning. The Americans were repairing track, some of the other troops were washing clothes, eating, and resting. A Boxer force of several hundred men got within two hundred yards of the trains by taking cover in a village and orchard. Armed with spears and swords and waving red banners, they came toward the trains at a full run, chasing an Italian squad taken by surprise at its outpost. Down the track came the Italians, running for their lives, but five of them lost the dash and the Boxers cut them down.

The Boxers advanced in a ragged line toward the skirmish line that the foreign troops hastily formed. They were armed with spears, swords, and a few firearms and gingals—a heavy Chinese blunderbuss requiring two men to operate.

> Slowly they came on, shouting, with their swords and pikes flashing in the sun, merely to be mowed down whole ranks at a time by rifle and machine gun fire ... the leaders themselves afforded a fine example of their teaching by dancing and singing in front of their men during the attack. Without any hesitation they charged a Maxim and were literally mowed down—coming on at a jog trot and collapsing when hit. They often stopped a few yards off and went through their gesticulations for rendering themselves immune from bullet wounds. Many were shot while kow-towing towards the trains, and remained dead in that position.... Their calm regard of death was absurd ... just ahead they lay in scores, and it took several rifle bullets to finish each one unless he chanced to be killed at the first shot.... Unless quite dead they were as dangerous as vipers, and they had an objectionable habit of shamming death."[45]

The Americans counted one hundred and two Boxer dead on the field. There were no wounded, indicating that the foreign soldiers shot downed Boxers full of holes to make sure they were dead The five slow-running Italians were the only casualties of the foreign forces.[46]

Captain McCalla had a close call in this fight. Several Boxers charged his way, including a large Chinese swinging a long, two-handed sword. One of his men, an oiler on the *Newark*, tried to pull the captain toward the train and safety, but McCalla ordered him to stand and fight. At about thirty yards McCalla shot the big Chinese with his rifle, brought him down, but the man rose and came on, throwing a spear that just missed. McCalla shot him again and this time killed the Boxer.

Later the same day, hundreds of Boxers attacked a garrison at Lofa in Seymour's rear. The result was the usual slaughter. The foreign troops killed several hundred Boxers and suffered no casualties. They left Boxer bodies unburied in the hope that the rows of corpses would cast doubt on the Boxer's claims of invulnerability. The foreigners also adopted a policy of burning every village that contained Boxers. "They made wonderful blazes," said Captain Taussig.[47]

Seymour was killing Boxers, but advancing little toward his objective: Peking. The railroad in Seymour's rear was torn up by the Boxers faster than he could advance and, on June 17, he lost contact with Tientsin. He ordered McCalla to reverse course and repair track toward Tientsin to reestablish communications. He decided that the advance on Peking would be abandoned until Tientsin could be secured. Thus, a week into an expedition that intended to reach Peking in a day or two, Seymour was running in reverse, fixing track over which he had already passed. Worse news yet, the iron bridge at Yang Tsun in his rear was destroyed by the Boxers. Blocked by the downed bridge toward Tientsin and a destroyed railroad toward Peking, Seymour now controlled a forty-mile long ribbon of track across the north China plain running from nowhere to nowhere. The sailor in him must have yearned for the freedom of the seas, and in fact he considered an advance up the Pei River by boat, but the river was low from the drought and travel by boat was difficult. He thought about abandoning the trains and marching to Peking cross country, but Seymour was a sailor. He followed his maritime instincts and stayed with his ships—or rather, trains. He was now isolated, his communications to Tientsin and Peking broken, supplies running short, and menaced daily by the suicidal attacks of seemingly innumerable Boxers. The troops were hungry and the yield of foraging patrols was scanty. Had Seymour led the troops on a forced march to Peking, as many have said he should have done, they might have been destroyed or, had they arrived intact, they would have been out of food, low on ammunition, and exhausted. Seymour was right not to risk a foot expedition to Peking.

The news kept getting worse. On June 18, Boxers attacked two of the trains and one thousand men under the command of the German Captain von Usedom but, after they were driven off as usual, four or five thousand Chinese imperial soldiers renewed the attack. It was a shock to Seymour and an ominous development that Chinese soldiers had suddenly turned hostile. His expedition would now face soldiers with modern weapons rather than Boxers with only swords, spears, and clumsy gingals.

The Chinese soldiers were marginally more effective as fighting men than the Boxers. They retreated after four hundred of them were killed by the machine guns and rifles of the foreign soldiers.[48] It was an unimpressive display of Chinese arms, but they did enough damage to cause Seymour to worry about his survival. The allies lost seven killed and fifty-seven wounded in the battle and the need to care for the wounded, added to all the other problems, doomed the Seymour expedition. The gloom was deepened by a heavy rain, much needed by the farmers, and a good omen for the Boxers. The gods rewarded fighting the foreigners with a life-giving rain.[49]

Unable to advance to Peking and under attack, Seymour must retreat to Tientsin. How? The railroad was destroyed—and why, suddenly, was he attacked by Chinese imperial soldiers who had been friendly only a few days before? The answer lay with his naval colleagues on their ships in the Gulf of Chihli off Taku.

6

The Empress Dowager

On December 13, 1898, Tzu Hsi, the Empress Dowager of China, granted an audience to the wives of the foreign ministers in Peking. It was the first time she had ever entertained foreigners and probably the first time she had ever seen a foreign woman.

The audience was organized with the numbing ceremony characterizing every action of the court. For the seven diplomatic wives who would make the call on the Empress, the day began at ten in the morning. A mounted escort sent by the Tsungli Yamen went by each legation to escort the wives. Five bearers of sedan chairs carried each of the seven women. Two mounted outriders flanked each sedan chair to clear a path for its passage. Their first stop was the British Legation where waited Lady Ethel Armstrong MacDonald, wife of the British minister and the senior wife of the diplomatic corps by virtue of her length of residence in Peking. The seven women, led by Lady Ethel, set off from the Legation Quarter to a gate in the Winter Palace in the northern part of the Imperial City. En route, they were joined by Señor Cologan, the Spanish minister, dean of the diplomatic corps; four interpreters dressed in resplendent military uniforms; and another crowd of Chinese escorts. The lengthy parade—which now comprised, if the accounting of the American Sarah Pike Conger is accurate, the occupants of seventeen sedan chairs, eighty-five chair bearers, forty-two outriders, and sixty mounted escorts—continued on to the Winter Palace.

At the palace gate the train of accompaniment for the seven diplomatic wives was disbanded. Each woman was reseated in a red-upholstered court chair which was shouldered by six eunuchs. The new procession, with a fresh group of escorts, continued its glacial progress. After a short ride in their resplendent court chairs, the women arrived at another gate, dismounted again, and took seats in a railway car presented to China by France. The locomotive power for the coach was a long line of black-clad eunuchs who pushed and pulled the ladies through the Imperial City to another stop where they were met by a group of officials. After a bowl of tea the women were escorted to the throne room and there, sitting side-by-side on an elevated dais, was the emperor of China and his aunt, the Empress Dowager.

The emperor was Kuang Hsu, meaning "glorious succession." He was twenty-seven years old and in the twenty-third year of his reign. The Dowager had ruled as regent while he was a child but had gone into nominal retirement in 1889 when Kuang Hsu reached his majority and assumed rule in fact as well as in name—but with the Dowager always looking over his shoulder. Kuang Hsu made the mistake of supporting the Hundred Days Reform in 1898. Tzu Hsi returned to active life, squashed a move toward modern ideas and government, and crushed the reformers. Kuang Hsu was now a captive in the Imperial City, his jail a palace on an island called the Ocean Terrace where he lived in scantily furnished and dirty quarters, the bamboo screens and rice paper windows in tatters, his only attendants two or three insolent eunuchs. On ceremonial occasions, Kuang Hsu was brought out from his island, "robed in all the splendor of the Son of Heaven, with the great Pearl of State on his official hat and a priceless buckle of jade at his belt."[1]

After the ceremony, he would be returned to his decaying palace and would remain there, day after day, warming himself before a peasant stove emitting noxious fumes of burning charcoal.[2]

The foreign women bowed in unison before the royal pair. Interpreters presented each lady to a Manchu prince who, in turn, presented each lady to their Royal Highnesses. Lady Ethel read an address to the throne and the Dowager replied. After another bow, each woman was again escorted to the throne, bowed before the emperor, and stepped before the Dowager to curtsy. The Dowager offered her hand to each lady and, after a few words, placed a heavy gold ring set with a large pearl on the finger of each. The foreign women thanked her, backed away from the throne, took their proper place in line, bowed again in unison, and continued their backward progress away from the imperial presence.

All this bowing was followed by lunch in a banquet hall with princes and princesses of the realm, to another room where tea was served (and the ladies presumably had the opportunity to maneuver their long, heavy skirts over a small hole in the floor that served as a Chinese toilet), and, then, back to the banquet hall where they were greeted again by Tzu Hsi. The emperor had disappeared.

For Sarah Pike Conger, the frumpy, well-worn wife of the United States minister, born in a small Ohio town in 1842, it was an unforgettable moment in the splendor of a royal presence. She wrote of the Dowager: "She was bright and happy and her face glowed with good will. There was no trace of cruelty to be seen. In simple expressions she welcomed us, and her actions were full of freedom and warmth." Tzu Hsi said to this lady "with much enthusiastic earnestness 'one family; all one family.'"

The Dowager again bade them good-by and they were escorted to a theater to view a play. Tea was served (again) and then they returned one more time to the banquet hall, served tea (again) and, for a final audience, ushered into the presence of the Dowager — and served tea (again). The Dowager paid her diplomatic guests a special honor. She took a sip from her cup, then lifted the cup to the lips of each woman and said again, "One family, all one family." Another gift was distributed and then the Dowager was gone and the seven women proceeded back to the legations as they had come, a full day absorbed in this slow-paced costume drama.

Sarah Pike Conger left the Imperial City with the Dowager's words ringing in her ears. "One family, all one family." Mrs. Conger's first brush with royalty awed her and even the Boxer uprising of 1900 did not shake her affection for the Dowager. She later dedicated a book to Tzu Hsi.[3]

Tzu Hsi, the Empress Dowager of China. In 1900 she was 65 years old and had ruled China for 39 years (Conger, *Letters from China,* 1910).

* * *

The Empress Dowager of China was born November 29, 1835. She was named Yehonala and was the

Diplomatic Wives Calling on the Dowager, December 13, 1898. Lady Ethel MacDonald is the sturdy woman third from left in the front row. Sarah Pike Conger is the third woman from the left in the back row. The men in the photograph include the Spanish minister (the dean of the Diplomatic Corps) and interpreters (Conger, *Letters from China*, 1910).

daughter of a captain in the Manchu army. She was born in one of the provincial outposts where the Manchu army was posted to keep an eye on the Chinese officials administering the civil affairs of the empire. While Yehonala was still a child her father died and the family moved to Peking to live as poor relations with influential royal relatives. There she grew up in the shadow of the Imperial City. One of her childhood friends was a Manchu boy named Jung Lu who would become her political ally and probable lover for the next half century.

The Manchus had overthrown the Ming dynasty in 1644 and established their dynasty, the Ching. They were a minority people in the empire, numbering in 1900 little more than four million and ruling a population of four hundred million, the majority of their subjects Han Chinese. The Manchus were warriors and their Banner Armies numbering about 300,000 men were scattered in garrisons around China. But the Manchus had been absorbed by Chinese culture and by 1900, nearly all of them spoke Chinese, worked alongside Chinese in administering the empire, and were less an ethnic group than a military caste.[4] The Manchus expanded the Chinese empire to its greatest extent ever, but as rulers they emphasized the most conservative and inward-looking of Chinese traits. In attempting not to upset the apple cart of tradition, they let the apples rot. By the time Yehonala was growing up the odor of decay was pervasive.

Yehonala's rise to power began in 1853 when the court chose her as one of twenty-eight concubines for the Emperor Hsien Feng, a dissolute young man who had assumed the throne two years before. Yehonala, by some means—probably bribing a eunuch who attended the emperor—was quickly chosen to enjoy the great honor of being wrapped in a red rug and carried to the emperor's bed chamber and laid naked at the foot of his bed. Her charms in bed must have been exceptional because she immediately became his favorite consort. She bore his first and only child in 1855 and, shortly, she was the most powerful person in China, working her will as no woman in China had ever done. She was given the title Tzu Hsi, "maternal and auspicious," but the common people of China called her "the Old Buddha."

The Manchu court was full of intrigue, corruption, and fantasy. By custom, the emperor was the only intact male permitted to live within the walls of the Forbidden City. The court of the emperor, presided over by the Dowager, consisted of his wives, concubines, and children; two thousand female servants; one thousand guards of the outer palace; three hundred personal bodyguards; and three thousand eunuchs. The eunuchs enjoyed enormous influence with the Dowager as the purveyors of her comforts and her eyes and ears in the tortured world of plots and counter-plots among the bored and pampered residents of the palace. The custom of emasculating men to serve as palace retainers dated from antiquity. Prisoners, slaves, and criminals were the usual victims but during the Ching dynasty most of the eunuchs were volunteers who chose eunuchhood as a lucrative profession — provided they survived the surgical procedure of emasculation.

Opinions about the Empress Dowager vary. One of her biographers said: "For fifty years hers was the brain, hers the strong hand, that held in check the rising forces of disintegration; and when she died, it required no great gifts of divination to foretell the approaching doom of the Manchu."[5] Other accounts paint her character in the darkest hues or, conversely, as a simple woman swept along by events beyond her control — a leaf in the stream of history. Given the turbulence of the era in which she reigned, the impenetrability of Imperial politics, and her own secretive character, a consensus about the Empress Dowager is impossible. For better or for worse, she held the tottering empire of the Manchus together for a few final decades. In doing so, she retarded reforms which might have enabled China to meet better the onslaught of the West.

The Empress Dowager was isolated and ignorant, a harem politician with little idea of what was happening outside the walls of the Imperial City. Her suppression of reformers led to the execution or exile of her more enlightened and forward-looking advisers and ministers. What she had left in 1900 were the regressive elements of an ancient dynasty.

* * *

The Dowager was not alone in her disinterest in affairs outside her household. The inhabitants of the vast Chinese empire had a worldview scarcely more enlightened than an isolated tribe in the interior of Africa. The missionary-writer, Arthur Smith, tells the story of a Chinese fan. Everyone in China carried a fan, even — to the amusement of foreigners— soldiers marching off to battle. Some of these fans were exquisitely constructed of ivory and jewels and the silk or translucent paper stretched over the ribs was decorated with drawings or copies of well-known art works. One of the popular decorations for fans in the late nineteenth century was a map of the world. The Chinese empire occupied about four-fifths of the surface of the fabric. At the periphery were ill-defined areas called "Ocean," *Yingkuo* (England), *Fakuo* (France), and *Huihui* (Muslim lands). The Americas, Africa, Australia, and the remainder of Europe and Asia, were omitted from the Chinese map of the world, apparently because, to the artist, they were places unknown or irrelevant. China was the Middle Kingdom, the Celestial Empire, and at the periphery of the world were unimportant places known as "Ocean" and "England," which were hardly worth representing.

Smith gave another illustration of the self-centered and superior world view of the Chinese. A Chinese "of considerable ability and high scholarship" wrote a pamphlet for the edification of the scholars of his province. In the opening sentences he said that the western foreigners dwelled "in a remote, circumscribed, unproductive, and impoverished corner of the earth, which produced neither tea leaves nor rhubarb." As it was impossible for them to make a living in their overcrowded land, they came to China and were allowed by the grace of the emperor to stay and to trade. Smith commented that in this particular district the population was above two thousand to the square mile and that the people were so poor that they were "barely able by the hardest toil to keep the wolf from the door." Yet this scholar could still assert that foreigners came from an overcrowded and unproductive land "where it was impossible for them to make a living."[6]

The Chinese worldview extended to an opinion of themselves as superior to foreigners. Non-Chinese Orientals did not escape from the overweening Chinese superiority complex. They called the Japanese "yellow dwarfs" but their most colorful terms of opprobrium were applied to Europeans and Americans who were particularly uncouth in manner and strange in appearance. A missionary walking on a Peking street would hear the phrase "red-headed devils" from the mouths of infants barely able to speak.

* * *

In June 1900, the Dowager's government faced a crisis. For months, she swayed like bamboo in the wind to appease the barbarian diplomats while at the same time showing respect for the Boxers, an indigenous patriotic movement, but one which, if uncontrolled, could become dangerous not only to foreigners and Christians, but also to the Ching dynasty. With each sign of growing Boxer strength and numbers, the foreigners called on the Ching to take stronger measures to suppress them. The Dowager's government had graciously given the foreigners permission to bring foreign soldiers to Peking to guard the legations. Now, those soldiers and the diplomats had barricaded a neighborhood and dispatched armed bands to shoot down Chinese citizens as they worshiped in their temples. The final outrage was the Seymour expedition, an unauthorized invasion of Chinese territory by the military forces of eight countries—long nosed foreign devils and despised yellow dwarfs daring to set foot on Chinese soil and kill patriotic Chinese peasants.

The court of Tzu Hsi was sharply divided on the question of the Boxers. On the one side were her advisers, especially Jung Lu, who scorned the Boxers as rabble, ridiculed their claims to invulnerability, and called their supporters "absolutely crazy." Jung Lu told the empress that "one foreign soldier could kill one hundred Boxers without the least trouble."[7] On the other side was Prince Tuan, father of the heir apparent to the throne, fanatically anti-foreign and a palace politician as competent as the Dowager. Tzu Hsi swayed first one direction and then the other. Her predicament was well characterized by Sir Robert Hart. "The Court appears to be in a dilemma: if the Boxers are not suppressed, the Legations threaten to take action—if the attempt to suppress them is made, this intensely patriotic organization will be converted into an anti-dynastic movement."[8] The Dowager tried unsuccessfully to straddle the middle. As late as June 6, 1900, she declared that "Christians and Boxers both are children of the state, and the Court cares equally for both of them."[9] However, within a few days the pressure of the Boxers, virtually in control of the countryside, became irresistible. Chinese army units sided with the Boxers making suppression of the movement nearly impossible. The Boxer wave carried along the Dowager and her government. "The Ching already had become the docile and obedient slave of the foreign Powers," said one Chinese scholar, "and then it suddenly fell captive to the Boxer anti-imperialist movement."[10]

On June 9, the court came down on the side of the Boxers. The Tsungli Yamen was shaken up. Moderate and amiable Prince Ching was dismissed as president and replaced by Prince Tuan and three other Manchus. In Morrison's words, "One reasonable Chinese removed and four rabidly anti-foreign, ignorant Manchus appointed.[11] Conger reported to his government. "[Prince Tuan] is known to be malignantly antiforeign, a patron of the Boxers, and has many of them in his division of the army. His policy ... must mean continual persecution and attacks upon missionaries and their followers, destruction of their property, hindrance of trade, and constant menace and danger to all foreigners and foreign interests."[12]

It is an interesting question whether the Empress Dowager placed any faith in the Boxers' claims of invulnerability to Christian bullets. It seems that she did. She was superstitious. The unreal world of the Imperial City did not foster a sharp, clear view of reality. The archaic ceremonies, the pomp of everyday life, the astrologers and the eunuchs examining imperial excrement for auspicious omens, fortified the natural instincts of a woman who was a born gambler and sought divine intervention in the draw of the tiles.

The Empress Dowager was neither sophisticated nor worldly wise. She was an old woman who loved her robe of three thousand matched pearls, her favorite meal of eggs poached in chicken broth and strawberries and cream for desert, her cabinets of jewels and closets of silks. She wished only to enjoy the last years of her life. She could not tolerate risks to her peace of mind and the life she had made for herself, and so she would hope that the Boxers had on their side the gods and invulnerability and rid her empire of the nuisance of the West and its religion.

* * *

By June 15, the Westerners in north China were scattered like islands in a hostile sea. First, in Peking almost one thousand foreign soldiers and civilians were confined in the Legation Quarter, the Methodist Mission, and the Peitang. Second, Admiral Seymour and his 2,000 troops were somewhere between Tientsin and Peking. Third, in the foreign settlements just outside the walled city of Tientsin were 2,400 foreign soldiers, the majority Russians, and seven hundred civilians. Lastly, more than a score of naval warships were standing offshore in the Gulf of Chihli. Tientsin and the ships were in tenuous contact via the narrow, shallow, and winding Pei River and the railroad running from near the coast to Tientsin, thirty miles inland. In addition to these four concentrations several hundred missionaries were living in the smaller cities of north China in areas which the Boxer movement threatened. Those who had the possibility of doing so fled their stations. Tientsin also was undergoing an invasion of Boxers. The British Consul reported on June 15 that the walled city of Tientsin was practically in the hands of the Boxers and that Christian chapels and missions had been burned.

For the sailors in their vessels offshore, their most senior officer lost in the interior of China with more than two thousand of their shipmates, the situation had become untenable. Their lifeline to Tientsin and Admiral Seymour was the Pei River and the railroad. Should they be denied access to the river and the railroad they would be unable to assist Tientsin, to support Seymour, and to achieve the objective of their military operations, the reinforcement of the pitifully weak legation guard force in Peking and the protection of their citizens. The key to retaining communications with Tientsin were the Taku forts at the mouth of the Pei. The Chinese army had reinforced the forts and was laying mines across the mouth of the river with the likely objective of closing the river to navigation and denying the foreign naval forces access to the railroad and the river.

The Chinese had a good chance of succeeding. The four Taku forts, two on the north bank and two on the south bank, at the mouth of the two hundred-yard-wide river, were strong, squat, mud-brick structures with high walls and an armament of modern breech loading rifles and heavy rapid-firing guns made by Krupp. German engineers had advised on the construction of the forts and installed the guns. About two thousand imperial Chinese troops defended the forts. Just upstream was a shipyard. Four brand-new torpedo destroyers, made in Germany, each mounting six three-pound guns, lay alongside a wharf in the shipyard.

The allied naval commanders met June 15 and 16 on board the Russian flagship, twelve miles offshore, to consider their options. A military operation against the forts was difficult because the bigger ships of the allies could not cross the Taku banks — only seventeen feet deep at high tide — to assist in taking the forts. Only small thin-skinned gunboats and destroyers could participate in the operation. Likewise, only a limited number of sailors and marines were available for a land assault on the forts because Seymour had taken most of the men with them.

The naval officers decided to go to war with China. They knew that the Chinese government and its military forces had avoided confrontations with the foreign military forces operating in north China. They might jeopardize rather than help the precarious situation of their countrymen in Peking who would be the first and most likely targets of Chinese retaliation. However, in their minds, the necessity to maintain communication links with Tientsin took priority and on June 16 the allied naval commanders sent an ultimatum to the Chinese. They would "occupy provisionally, by consent or by force, the Taku forts."[13] The Chinese were given less than a day, until two A.M., June 17, to surrender the forts. Several officers and the French Consul called on the Chinese general commanding the Taku forts to demand surrender. The general held fast and refused.

As so often happens with military operations the original objective of the Seymour expedition — the rescue of the endangered foreigners in Peking — became lost in the welter of necessity. The naval officers planning the attack on the Taku forts forgot about the legations. That original objective now receded to the fourth order of magnitude. The Taku forts had to be taken to maintain a supply and communications link with Tientsin, so as to assure that Tientsin remained a viable base to support the Seymour expedition, so that the Seymour expedition could reach Peking to reinforce the legation guards, and, therefore and finally, so the reinforced legation guards could preserve the foreigners in Peking from harm by Boxers.

Of the eight nations with ships off Taku only the Americans declined to sign the ultimatum to the Chinese and to participate in a military operation against the forts. Admiral Kempff, the senior American naval officer present, said he did not have authority to take part in hostilities against China. A cooperative venture with the European powers and Japan in an unprovoked attack on Chinese forts qualified in Kempff's mind as a foreign entanglement. Nevertheless, the Americans would not completely avoid participation. An American gunboat, the *Monocacy*, would be near the scene of the battle to render assistance to civilians.

* * *

As always, in the Boxer uprising of 1900, civilians mixed in among the soldiers and sailors. One of them was a Mrs. James Jones who had the poor judgment to arrive by ship from Shanghai on June 15, crossing the Taku banks, noting the "splendid show" of warships assembled there, and taking the last train of the day to Tientsin at five P.M.

Her first shock was when she arrived in Tientsin to find the railroad station swarming with Russian troops. Proceeding to the British settlement, Mrs. Jones saw foreign troops on guard everywhere, armed and in battle dress. At the home where she was to stay fifty Austrian soldiers were quartered in godowns and two officers were staying in bedrooms in the house. After dinner one of the officers escorted several of the guests on a walk. Every few yards they were challenged by a sentry. Her walk was punctuated by gunshots but Mrs. Jones continued to feel quite safe and retired to bed. About midnight she was awakened and told to dress. The walled Chinese city of Tientsin was in flames and the Boxers had attacked the railroad station. She was told to remain in the house, but to be ready to respond to the tolling of the church bells, at which time the civilians were to take refuge in Gordon Hall, the center of government for the British settlement. Waiting for the bells, Mrs. Jones watched the tremendous blaze in the walled city of Tientsin, "a really grand sight," from the garden. At three A.M., she went back to bed without undressing

Captain David Beatty, later to be a fleet admiral, was second in command of the four hundred and thirty British sailors and marines in Tientsin. He established a defense along a low mud wall that ran along the outer perimeter of the British settlement. Beatty also commanded a group of civilian volunteers and these he placed "where they could do less harm than anywhere else."[14] During the day, Beatty and his men watched the Boxers in the distance moving from place to place, recruiting, worshiping, and possibly making plans for an attack. In the evening the Boxers began burning the villages surrounding the foreign settlements and the outlying missions and churches, including a Catholic cathedral. About two A.M. a Boxer mob approached the defense lines of the foreign settlements. The soldiers opened fire when the Boxers, armed only with swords, spears, and torches, were three or four hundred yards distant and knocked them down like tenpins.

Beatty had the professional military officer's contempt of civilians and he reported that "all was confusion in the settlement" where Mrs. Jones and several hundred other Westerners huddled together. The problem was the "gallant Tientsin Volunteers" who galloped up and down the street like British Paul Reveres frantically shouting, "The Boxers are on you!" blowing bugles and creating pandemonium. Finally, at 4:00 A.M. the volunteers gained access to the church and tolled the bells. Mrs. Jones, fearing that they tolled for her, was instantly awake[15] and foreign women and children poured "out of the houses in a dreadful state of excitement, anxiety and terror, some with nothing on but nightshirts and pyjamas, every woman and child in the place being in the streets at the same time."[16]

The civilians spent the rest of the night in Gordon Hall, named in honor of General Charles "Chinese" Gordon who—not a few recalled—had died in another siege, in Khartoum, fifteen years earlier. In the morning they were told that the Boxers had broken off the attack but were expected to renew it again that night. The soldiers advised the civilians to leave Tientsin and at two in the afternoon a special train took many of them from Tientsin to the coast where the women and children would board ships for friendlier climes. Unfortunately, they arrived in the midst of preparations to assault the Taku forts and Mrs. Jones, for the second time in twenty-four hours, found herself in the midst of a battle. Along with thirty-six other foreign women and children she was put on board the USS *Monocacy* to ensure her safety during the attack of foreign warships on the Taku forts.

The *Monocacy* was thirty-four years old, an obsolete, sidewheel gunboat that would have looked more at home patrolling the Mississippi than the China coast. The captain of the *Monocacy*, Commander Wise, genially greeted the women and children taking refuge on his ship, the sailors taking care not to wake the babies with outbursts of sailorly language and helping the women prepare sleeping places on the deck. Some of the women were concerned about their safety on board the *Monocacy*, which was lying in the river just upriver from three warships. Commander Wise assured them they had nothing to fear. The *Monocacy*, so said he, was in a position of absolute safety outside the line of fire. The women and children settled down on the deck confident of their security on board with the genial Commander Wise and his well-mannered crew.

The Chinese didn't wait for the foreign ultimatum to expire. At 12:50 A.M., Sunday, June 17, they opened fire on the foreign ships in the river and shells whistled over the *Monocacy* and the roar of the battle deafened the women onboard. The sailors dispelled panic among the civilians by reassuring them there was nothing to fear; but, after everyone calmed down, the composure of women, sailors, and Commander Wise was abruptly shattered when a shell from the Chinese forts smashed a lifeboat on the starboard side of the ship and sliced through the bow, coming out on the port side, injuring nobody and doing only minor damage, but causing the congenial commander to move his ship a couple of miles upriver where he reassured the passengers once again of their absolute safety on board the old *Monocacy*.

* * *

The allied navy commanders had two problems. First, only ten ships of the allied fleet could cross the shallow Taku banks and enter the river. These included three British ships, two of them modern torpedo destroyers; one old unarmored German ship; three Russian ships, only one a modern gunboat; one antique French gunboat; an old Japanese gunboat; and the *Monocacy*, a noncombatant. The second problem was that only nine hundred men could be assembled to assault the forts from the land. The allies, on paper, did not match the Chinese in either personnel or firepower.

Nevertheless, the ships moved into position on the afternoon of June 16, just as Mrs. Jones was arriving in Tangku by train and finding out that she had traveled from one battle to another. The allied ships steamed by a Chinese junk laying mines at the entrance to the river and the British torpedo destroyer *Whiting* actually collided with one of the mines, which did not explode — a portent for Chinese military fortunes in 1900. The foreign ships proceeded up the river, passing within sight of Chinese artillerymen in the forts, and disembarked the troops who would storm the Chinese forts. Just above the stations of the British *Fame* and *Whiting* was the shipyard where the four German-made Chinese torpedo destroyers lay alongside the wharf. These four ships had the firepower to defeat the allied flotilla on their own.

The allied ships were in position early in the evening, the British ships taking the precaution of shifting their moorings, on the correct assumption that the Chinese gunners had zeroed in on them earlier in the fading light. Starting at the mouth of the river and going upstream the nine ships were deployed as follows. The three British ships, the torpedo destroyers *Fame* and *Whiting* and the unarmored sloop *Algerine,* were near the mouth of the Pei, only four hundred yards from the North Fort. A mile upstream at the first bend in the river, offshore from the Northwest Fort, were the three Russian gunboats. Three or four miles farther upstream were the French, Japanese, and German warships. The *Monocacy* with its civilian passengers was still farther upstream.

When the Chinese opened fire they did so with accuracy that surprised their contemptuous enemies. Early shots hit all three Russian gunboats and one, the *Giliak,* which had proudly switched on its new-fangled device, a searchlight, drew so much fire that it had to be run aground to keep from sinking. The French and German gunboats steamed downstream, shooting as they came, and also were hit, the German commander losing a leg and the French ship catching on fire. The Japanese gunboat held her position. She was loaded with extra ammunition and provisions, and stayed a safe distance away.

The two British destroyers, the *Fame* and the *Whiting*, had the most important mission of the early hours of the battle. They held their fire and steamed unobtrusively upstream, each of them towing a whaleboat with ten men aboard. When they got to the wharf where the four Chinese torpedo destroyers were docked they darted alongside, casting off their whaleboats to assault two of the destroyers while ships' personnel leaped on board the other two.

Why these four modern ships with torpedoes in their tubes and shells in their guns were lying alongside a wharf during a battle is a mystery. Whatever the reason the British boarding parties quickly captured the ships. Their crews ran away. Roger Keyes, the commanding officer of the *Fame,* led the assault on one of the Chinese ships. He was the third British officer in China that year who, along with Jellicoe and Beatty, would become a fleet admiral. Among his later exploits was a 1918 raid on Zeebrugge which had more than a superficial resemblance to the capture of the Chinese ships at Taku in 1900.

With the Chinese torpedo destroyers out of the battle, the allied ships concentrated on the forts and the cannonading from ship to fort and vice versa proceeded without decision. The Chinese were well protected by the forts' thick adobe walls. About three A.M. allied ships stripped their crews to reinforce the shore parties on the north bank of the Pei and organized a ground attack on the upstream and most isolated of the four forts, the Northwest Fort. Two hundred Russians and Austrians led the way, followed by the main body of three hundred and eighty British and Italians. Three hundred Japanese brought up the rear. About dawn, the allies had luck. A powder magazine in the fort exploded as the ground assault began. In the confusion,

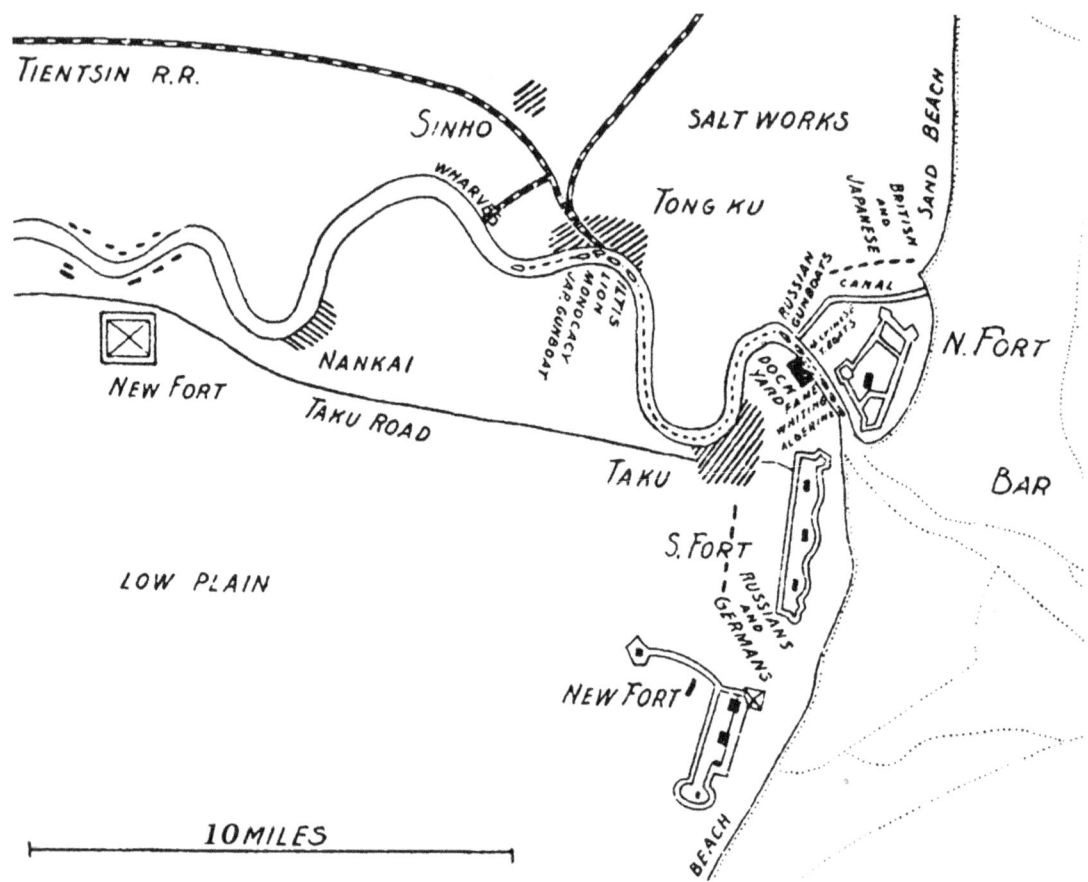

The Battle for the Taku Forts. The Taku Forts guarded the entrance to the Pei River. The foreign navies attacked the forts to ensure their access to Tientsin as a base to relieve the siege in Peking (Savage Landor, *China and the Allies,* 1901).

the Japanese, supposed to be the reserve, were the first group inside the fort and their commander, Captain Hattori, led a bayonet charge to drive the Chinese away. Hattori was killed in the charge and another Japanese sailor was shot dead in the act of raising the Rising Sun over the fort.

The Japanese having demonstrated their military prowess, the British and Italians led the assault on the North Fort, less than a mile downstream, and they soon overwhelmed the defenders. They turned the guns of the north forts on the remaining two forts on the south side of the river, which were larger and better armed than the north forts, but the Chinese by now were demoralized and another lucky shot exploded a huge powder magazine in one of the forts, filling the air with dust. Troops were ferried across the river to assault the south forts but all they needed to do was to fire a few shots at the retreating Chinese soldiers. At 6:30 in the morning the battle of the Taku forts was over. The allied forces had won — against heavy odds — a victory. The Chinese had fought bravely, but the Taku forts lasted only six hours in combat with an undermanned and outgunned allied force.

The victory was not without loss. The allies suffered about one hundred and seventy casualties of the more than 900 soldiers and sailors engaged.[17] The Chinese loss was not recorded, but some of the officers of the *Monocacy* told Mrs. Jones that "the forts were a mass of ruins, rivers of blood, with headless and armless bodies everywhere, which the blue-jackets [sailors] were gathering together and cremating in heaps."[18] Later the same morning, Mrs. Jones and her fellow refugees were bundled aboard a launch and conveyed to a merchant steamer. Mrs. Jones' adventure was over and she retired to the comforts of home in Shanghai.[19]

* * *

On June 16 the Empress Dowager took the extraordinary step of convening the Imperial Council. At noon, Manchu princes, dukes, and nobles, and Chinese and Manchu officials of the boards and ministries convened in the throne room. The emperor was hustled over from his island prison to sit beside the Dowager. The question before the council was what should be done now that the Boxers were present in Peking in large numbers and foreign troops—the Seymour Expedition—were heading toward the city. One official suggested that the Boxers be driven out of the city but he was shouted down by Prince Tuan. Another official spoke of the unreliability of the Boxers and disputed their claims to invulnerability. The Dowager interrupted him. "Perhaps their magic is not to be relied upon, but can we not rely on the hearts and minds of the people? Today China is extremely weak. We have only the people's hearts and minds to depend upon. If we cast them aside and lose the people's hearts, what can we use to sustain the country?"[20] The Dowager had spoken and her drift was in the direction of the Boxers. The council issued a decree to recruit Boxers into the army and instructed Governor Yu-Lu and General Nieh in Tientsin to oppose the advance of foreign soldiers.

The consequences of the attack on the Taku forts were not long coming. The next day the Chinese army made its first attack on Seymour's troops, and the admiral, rather than being helped by the action of his naval colleagues at Taku, had to retreat toward Tientsin. In Peking the news of the allied ultimatum to the Chinese to surrender the forts and the battle at Taku had a similar unpleasant effect. The choice before the Dowager became clear. China had to resist. The court decided to break off diplomatic relations with the foreign powers and order the diplomats to leave Peking within twenty-four hours. That afternoon, June 19, a large scarlet envelope was delivered to each of the eleven legations and to Sir Robert Hart at Imperial Customs. Sarah Pike Conger watched as her husband, the American minister, opened his envelope and, handed the diplomatic note written in Chinese, to his interpreter, Fleming Cheshire. Cheshire looked at the message and immediately said, "Let us go to the office."[21] A few minutes later Minister Conger hastened out of the legation, heading to the British Legation to confer with MacDonald.

The Chinese government, said the note, was informed that the admirals of the foreign fleets had demanded the surrender of the Taku forts. This news caused great astonishment. The demand of the foreign powers demonstrated that they wished to break off friendly relations with China. Therefore, it being a difficult manner China begged that the ministers with their families and guards depart Peking for Tientsin within twenty-four hours.

It was a thunderbolt. The diplomats had heard nothing of the demand that the Taku forts be surrendered. On the contrary, they believed that all efforts were being exerted for their rescue and that Admiral Seymour would soon arrive at Peking. Sir Claude MacDonald was outraged to learn that the admirals had placed the legations in jeopardy by a military move against Taku. Instead of rescuing the legations—as MacDonald had requested—it seemed that the sailors were off on a different military adventure. And China, instead of bowing to Western military might, was demanding—politely but firmly—that the diplomats leave Peking and travel through Boxer-infested countryside to Tientsin. Otherwise, said the note in diplomatic language, "China will find it a difficult matter to give complete protection."[22] In other words, do as the Chinese government said, or die. All eleven ministers received identical notes and their deliberations continued into the evening. Outside, in the streets and compounds of the Legation Quarter, foreigners met in little buzzing groups to discuss the Chinese ultimatum. The non-diplomats were almost unanimous in opposition to undertaking a journey to Tientsin under the dubious protection of the Chinese government. The consensus opinion was "if to stay meant probable massacre, to go meant certain destruction."[23]

In the ministers' meeting the champion of that view was Baron Clemens von Ketteler, the German minister. The baron argued fiercely that the foreigners should defy the Chinese government and remain in the legations until a military expedition reached them with sufficient force to guarantee that they could depart in safety. The opposing view — that they should comply with the Chinese demand — was argued by Stephen Pichon, the gloomy and dramatic French minister, and Edwin Conger, who had more faith in the good will of the Chinese government than his cynical colleagues. The remaining eight ministers were equivocal, listening to the arguments without committing themselves. MacDonald, who as British minister could sway the group his way, kept his own counsel.

Conger wrote a letter to Frank Gamewell at the Methodist Mission that evening.

> My Dear Mr. Gamewell: The Chinese government has notified us that the Admirals at Taku have notified the Viceroy that they will take possession of the Taku forts.... This they consider a declaration of war by all the Powers ... and ask us to leave Peking in twenty-four hours. We have replied that we know nothing of this, but if the Chinese desire to act upon such information and declare war themselves, that, of course, we will go as soon as they will furnish us the necessary transportation and send reliable escorts to take us all (of course including our nationals) to Tientsin.
>
> If we had a thousand men here and any knowledge of where other troops were, we might then refuse to go, but under the circumstances there is only one thing to do. It is bound to take us some time to get ready to start, and in the meantime something may happen.... Sincerely yours, E.H. Conger[24]

7

The Assassination of the Baron

Conger's letter telling the missionaries that the foreigners must leave Peking caused a moral dilemma. If the missionaries left, what would happen to the eight hundred Chinese Christians in the Methodist Mission? In addition, two thousand mostly Catholic Chinese were in the *Fu*, although the Protestants did not worry themselves much about the Catholics. Conger and the other ministers would not take responsibility for the Chinese. Were the Chinese Christians to be abandoned to the mercies of the Boxers with the surety that they would be killed? If the diplomats left Peking, should the missionaries refuse to leave and stay to face a certain death at the sides of their converts? Or should they leave behind their hard-won Christians and save themselves? Would it be martyrdom or flight?

The missionaries called a meeting that night, June 19, at nine p.m. Only men attended, and only those one-half of the men who were not on guard.[1] Will Ament was probably not at the meeting or he would have had something to say about it — and the decision taken by the missionaries might have been different.

Arthur Smith, who would have been expected to write the fullest account of the meeting, was evasive: "It was resolved to write the Minister a letter pointing out the practical difficulties of leaving Peking under the conditions mentioned, as well as the probable consequences for those who did so, and also the certain massacre of the Christians necessarily abandoned."[2] The letter pleaded: "For the sake of these, your fellow Christians, we ask you to delay your departure by every pretext possible.... We appeal to you in the name of Humanity and Christianity not to abandon them."[3] As an afterthought Smith wrote in his book that the Protestants "would not abandon" their Chinese Christians — but his account of the meeting indicates that the sentiment leaned the other direction.[4]

The moral question is inescapable: would the missionaries have fled Peking and abandoned the Chinese Christians? Will Ament says no. The one sentence he wrote on the subject was, "We all refused to leave our people and resolved to share our fate together."[5] Dr. Emma Martin said that "Mrs. Jewell and others would not have gone and left the school girls and Christians behind"—but Emma, a newcomer, had no real insight. The other accounts are different. Emma Smith says that when her husband, Arthur, told her they must leave the Methodist compound he also reminded her not to "leave the disconsolate Christians without a word of cheer." She ran over to the area where they were and "told them we were ordered to go" and that if they stayed it would only "make the destruction of the Chinese Christians more speedy. I emphasized once more the watch-word which all those weeks I had been drilling into them, 'I will never leave thee or forsake thee.'"[6] The "I" in this sentence apparently applies to God rather than Mr. and Mrs. Smith who packed their trunks quickly after her benediction and prepared to leave. The British missionary, Georgina Smith told her Chinese to fast that noon "and get close to God, that he may deliver us."[7] Abbie Chapin asked the rhetorical question, "Should we stay and be massacred with them, or make a final attempt to save our lives for further work?"[8]

Other women commented in the same vein. "Aunt Mary" Andrews, 60 years old and 32 years in China, rationalized, "We are facing the dreadful possibility of being obliged to leave all those dear native Christians to massacre or something worse." She continues, "To die with them would be easy, as compared to leaving them to their fate.... They [the Chinese Christians] felt our danger in going was as great as theirs in staying."[9] Mary Porter Gamewell said, "The missionaries expected to meet death outside the city gates. To stay contrary to orders would involve the Chinese Christians in certain death." Suddenly, it seems that the independent-minded American missionaries were obligated to obey orders from their government. She added, "We could not think of taking the Chinese with us." The missionary women called together the Chinese schoolgirls. "Money sufficient to support one for two or three months was given to each girl, and they were told how they were to be scattered among the families of the Methodist Mission's Chinese neighbors."[10] If any missionary spoke up strongly in favor of remaining with the Chinese Christians to defend and die with them rather than leaving them to their fate that fact was not recorded.

It appears that the missionaries, always quick to celebrate a Chinese Christian who died rather than recant Christianity, looked into their hearts and did not find the courage to stand with their converts if they had the opportunity to leave Peking without them. Some, however, might have refused to leave the Chinese. Will Ament would likely have been one. Perhaps others. But most missionaries stared martyrdom in the face and declined to accept the honor. Delay was their anguished advice to Minister Conger.

The missionaries should not be judged too harshly for their failure to stand with their Chinese converts. Most of the missionary men had wives and children and it seems that, no matter how dedicated a person may be, his first priority will always be the safety of his spouse and children.[11] Will Ament's wife and son were in the United States. He could afford to be braver than other men who were trying to protect their families. Missionary women might also be forgiven their lapse in conviction to stand in solidarity with their Chinese converts. In that era women were told what to do and most of them, single or married, accepted the decisions of men. But it is disappointing that most of the missionaries were apparently willing to abandon their Chinese Christians and to justify themselves with transparent rationalizations.

* * *

Three-quarters of a mile away, in the Legation Quarter, the diplomats were coming to the same conclusion as the missionaries: delay. The ministers sent a message to the Tsungli Yamen requesting a meeting the following morning, June 20, at nine o'clock. "The Foreign Ministers have received with great astonishment the note which the Tsungli Yamen has sent them dated today," the message said.

> They know absolutely nothing of that which the note contains upon the subject of what may have taken place at the Forts of Taku. The Foreign Ministers can only accept the declarations and the demand which the Yamen makes for them to leave Peking. It is utterly impossible to arrange for this departure in the short time of twenty-four hours. The Chinese government must understand that there are a great number of women and children here, and that is it a very numerous procession that must be provided for.
> The Tsungli Yamen tells us that it will furnish safeguards en route. The Foreign Ministers desire to know in what these safeguards will consist, understanding that the country is full of rebels ... the Foreign Ministers desire that these detachments should be quickly advised so that they may join us and all depart together.
> The Foreign Ministers must demand besides the necessary means of transport — carts, boats, and provisions and also be accompanied by some of the Ministers of the Tsungli Yamen.
> For the purpose of arranging all these questions the members of the Diplomatic Corps request to be received by Prince Ching and Prince Tuan tomorrow — Wednesday — at 9 o'clock A.M.[12]

It was a message crafted to gain time, but in the American Legation preparations were made to leave Peking. Conger ordered a hundred carts to transport Americans and their possessions. To Polly Condit-Smith it looked very much "as if we were all to start out to our deaths the following morning." Nevertheless, the amusing Miss Condit-Smith could still think of trivial matters. She wondered whether to fill the small handbag allowed for personal luggage with a warm coat or six clean blouses. She does not say what she decided, but six clean blouses seems most likely.[13]

Several men protested vigorously the inclination of the ministers to accept the Chinese demand for departure from Peking. Chief among them was Dr. George Ernest Morrison, who led a group of citizens who met with the ministers. He expressed his views in blistering words. "If you men vote to leave Peking tomorrow, the death of every man, woman, and child in this huge unprotected convoy will be on your heads, and your names will go through history and be known forever as the wickedest, weakest, and most pusillanimous cowards who ever lived."[14]

Morrison of China was overstating his case. A siege offered a better opportunity to be a hero than being slaughtered on the road to Tientsin. In the meantime, equivocation was the only course of action the diplomats had.

* * *

The diplomats met the next morning, June 20, at seven o'clock at the French Legation, their sedan chairs, guides, and squads of marine guards ready to accompany them on a group visit to the Tsungli Yamen, but no reply had been received to their request of the previous night for a meeting. While the ministers waited, their compatriots prepared both to leave and to stay. The British marines strengthened the barricade at the gate of the legation and set up their five-barreled Nordenfeldt machine gun to command the lane and canal running in front of the gate. A British diplomat dashed about in his shirtsleeves, his head tied up in a cowboy handkerchief, collecting fodder for the horses in the stables. Another diplomat hauled coal into the legation. Auguste Chamot and Fargo Squiers, the fifteen year old son of the American first secretary, cruised the streets of the Legation Quarter in a cart collecting provisions and taking them to the Peking Hotel where the Chamots and a select group of refugees were living. The three foreign-owned stores in the Legation Quarter were stripped of everything useful and Chinese merchants could only smile and cooperate with the foreigners who trooped into their stores, laid their arms on the counter, and demanded to carry away grain or other commodities, promise of payment being made with a hand-written chit. Most of the collected goods were taken to the British Legation. As the largest and most defensible of the legations the foreigners would assemble there if talk came to fight. Over the course of the morning mountains of strangely mixed goods were deposited in the pavilions, gardens, and tennis court of the legation. The military officers, the Austrian naval Captain von Thomann presiding, met to make their plans for departure if the diplomats decided on that course — or defense if the diplomats and circumstances dictated otherwise.

At the Methodist Mission it was a time of waiting. The women gathered in the courtyard to depart for the American Legation at a moment's notice. Bessie Ewing, three months pregnant, her two small daughters clinging to her, felt pushed and pulled about. "First we were told we could take all we could carry for baggage, next that nothing could go except what the ladies could carry, next that the ladies and children were to go first and the gentlemen and the marines would wait until all baggage and provisions had been sent over. With all these conflicting orders it was hard to pack for flight. I could not do much except attend upon Ellen [her nineteen-month-old daughter]. Her morning lunch is at ten and not knowing when or how she would get another meal I felt this was very important."[15]

Mary Porter Gamewell was "tired almost beyond the possibility of thinking" as she stood in the courtyard and watched Bessie Ewing and the other mothers feed their children and make rolls of clothing to be slung over young shoulders.[16] Luella Miner, unattached and independent, stood guard at the girls school, ready to sound the alarm if any threat appeared, but at ten o'clock Ament sent word to her to pack a handbag and get ready to go to the American Legation.[17]

A flustered Emma and Lizzie Martin sorted through their trunks to decide what to take with them. They left many photos behind, including that of a man who had once meant much to Emma, "as we could neither eat nor wear them." They wore as many clothes as they could and were told they should take bedding. Emma stuffed a brightly colored laundry bag with a lace-trimmed pillow and extra pairs of shoes for both her and Lizzie. She forgot her Bible. Emma left her trunk open; Lizzie, more orderly, locked hers and put the key in her pocket. Outside, in the courtyard, a Chinese servant offered to carry the bundle and her telescope bag.[18]

As the women and children milled around the courtyard in the hot sun of a Peking morning, still unanswered was the moral question of the Chinese converts. Would the missionaries, if ordered to go to the American Legation, leave behind the Chinese Christians, mostly women and children, virtually defenseless, virtually all survivors of families ripped asunder and decimated by the Boxers? However, Conger had said that "something might occur" to prevent the foreigners from leaving Peking. It did.

* * *

At nine thirty the diplomats had waited more than two hours for a response from the Tsungli Yamen. The debate raged. Should they go to the Yamen and wait to meet with Chinese officials or should they wait at the legations? Finally, an impatient Baron Clemens von Ketteler said that he would go by himself. If necessary, he would cool his heels at the Yamen waiting for an audience. He had books and cigars if he had to wait.

The other diplomats were uncomfortable with the volatile German going alone. He would be in danger, they asserted. Ketteler responded that the Chinese were not likely to assault a diplomat en route to an audience at the Tsungli Yamen. Probably more important in the mind of the diplomats was that Ketteler would protest forcefully the Chinese decision to expel the foreigners from Peking. The other diplomats were not at all certain they wished to antagonize the Chinese by digging in their heels and refusing to leave. They preferred to temporize, to seek additional information, to await new developments—while preparing to leave Peking if that seemed the safest course of action. Ketteler was likely, in their opinion, to make things worse with his intemperate language and threats of German retaliation. None of the diplomats, however, volunteered to accompany him.

The baron could not be dissuaded and he and his interpreter, Heinrich Cordes, departed for the Yamen shortly before 10 A.M. The two men two men left the Legation Quarter in sedan chairs, Ketteler in front. Both chairs were covered with scarlet and green cloth to denote the official status of the travelers. The baron left behind an escort of four German soldiers, fearing that their presence on the streets of Peking might cause a riot. He took as protection only two unarmed mounted outriders—*mafus*—one riding in advance of the sedan chairs and the other behind to clear away any riff-raff who might impede the passage of the personage in the leading sedan chair. Neither Ketteler nor Cordes was armed, another oddity as Ketteler usually carried a pistol.[19]

The German minister was on Hata Street, passing a police station when a Manchu soldier suddenly stepped forward to within a yard of his chair, pointed his rifle and fired. Cordes, three paces back, shouted "Halt," and in that same moment the chair bearers dropped the chairs and fled in terror. Several shots rang out and Cordes was hit in the thigh. He ran down the street, turned into a narrow alley, rifle shots ringing out behind him. Looking back, he saw no sign of life in Ketteler's chair. Two men with spears chased him, but gave up the chase. Cordes, a descendant of Portuguese traders, dragged himself through a maze of narrow alleyways, dripping blood, while Chinese crowds watched impassively, ignoring his plea for directions to the Methodist Mission, the nearest place of refuge. Finally, a Chinese man, a humble peddler, pointed him down an alleyway and he reached a barricade in front of the Methodist Mission and fell in a faint.[20]

The Chinese students at the barricade carried the wounded interpreter inside the mission and he told his tale quickly before sinking into unconsciousness due to loss of blood. It seemed unlikely that Cordes would live. The bullet had passed through both thighs. It was a miracle he remained conscious long enough for a race through the back streets of Peking to the mission.

The legations were already aware of the baron's death. The *mafus* had galloped back to the Legation Quarter with the news. A squad of German marines was sent out to recover the body, but

Hata Street. A photograph taken from the Tartar Wall. Legation Street came in from the left; the Methodist mission (not visible) was to the right. Baron von Ketteler was assassinated beyond where Hata makes a gentle curve. The American Board mission and Will Ament's palace were left of Hata Street near the top of the photograph (Ricalton, *China through the Stereoscope*, 1901).

they turned back after a few blocks, afraid that Chinese soldiers might cut them off from the Legation Quarter. It devolved upon Sarah Pike Conger to give the news of the baron's death to his wife, the tall, stately, refined, blond American heiress, formerly Maud Ledyard from Detroit.[21] The baroness, already in mourning for her brother killed in the Philippines, panicked, running wildly through the corridors of the German Legation. Only after a message was sent that all foreigners were to congregate in the British Legation was Mrs. Conger able to get her to pack a few things and go with her. Lady Ethel MacDonald, more sternly practical than the metaphysical Mrs. Conger, took Baroness Ketteler in hand and settled her down in a room of the MacDonald residence.

The baron was dead. A debate still continues whether he was a victim of random violence or assassinated at the order of some faction in the Chinese government. The second alternative is more likely. It is difficult to believe that a humble Manchu soldier, standing by the edge of the road, would — in an offhand and unplanned manner — kill a high official passing by in a sedan chair. The baron, bluff, aggressive, cruel, and arrogant had infuriated the Chinese for the last time. He was murdered. Whether the other diplomats would also have been murdered had they appeared on the streets is unknowable — but it seems unlikely that the Chinese would have been bold enough to assassinate all of them at this point in the Boxer Rebellion.[22]

The diplomats immediately abandoned all thought of leaving Peking. If the German minister could be assassinated, the remaining ten ministers would not trust their security to the protection of the Chinese government for an eighty mile journey to Tientsin. They would stay in the legations and defend themselves.

* * *

When the wounded interpreter staggered into the Methodist Mission with the news that Baron von Ketteler had been assassinated, near panic broke out. Marine captain Newt Hall sent a runner to the American Legation requesting permission to abandon the Methodist Mission and take refuge in the Legation Quarter. Minister Conger responded with an order for the twenty marines and the missionaries to come to the American Legation. A missionary was sent to the legation to ask, "What shall I do with our Chinese Christians?"

Conger replied, "Bring them. I do not know how they will be fed, but it is sure death to them if they are left behind. Bring them."[23] In the course of the night, he had changed his mind. The American government would extend its protection to the Chinese Christians.

The missionaries were relieved. They dodged the moral bullet. The Chinese would not be abandoned. The missionaries organized themselves for the mile-long walk to the legation. One woman took as her hand baggage a halter for a non-existent horse, a hot water bottle, and a quilt.[24] The missionaries left the Methodist Mission in a long line. Elwood Tewksbury led. He enjoined a Manchu captain at the Hata Gate to guard the premises of the Methodist Mission against looting. Next came the twenty American marines, preceding and flanking a column of American women and children; following them was a squad of German marines, bearing the unconscious dragoman, Cordes, on a litter. The schoolgirls were next, and then the mass of Chinese converts, the refugees and survivors of forty years of Protestant mission work. Lastly came the American male missionaries as a rear guard, armed and ready. Legation Street was nearly deserted, and a hush seemed to have fallen on the city as the missionaries marched like Israelites fleeing Egypt in the shadow of the great, gray Tartar Wall. A few Chinese spectators watched without emotion and a thousand Chinese soldiers looked on from the top of the wall. Bessie Ewing, feeling poorly, struggled to carry her daughter. Two single missionaries, Nellie Russell and Elizabeth Sheffield, helped her with the children and carried the small bag that contained the Ewings' worldly possessions.

The missionary caravan plodded through the heat and dust, through the Italian barricade blocking the street, across the canal, and into the compound of the American Legation. The Chinese were led north to the palace and park of Prince Su, the *Fu*, where they would join the Catholic survivors already residing there. Prince Su hurriedly left his palace, leaving half his harem and much of his treasure behind.

Harriet Squiers, rescued by Morrison a little more than three weeks ago in the Western Hills, paid her debt to good fortune by opening her doors to the milling crowd of American missionaries. While her husband, Herbert, was junior to Edwin Conger in the American Legation, socially the Squiers were paramount. They were a rich, congenial, and attractive couple. Herbert Squiers was clean shaven, a ruggedly handsome man of fashion who wore new-fangled Arrow shirt collars. Harriet was rich. She served the missionaries a lunch of sardines, scrambled eggs, crackers, and tea, and generously invited them to take what they needed from the Squiers' store of food. "A happy mothers' congress" invaded the storehouse and carried off cases of condensed milk and staple groceries.

However, the missionaries were not to stay in the American Legation. The diplomats decided that all foreign non-combatants would take refuge in the British Legation. After lunch, the missionaries marched the short distance alongside the canal to the legation. Within, all was a flurry of grand confusion as refugees streamed in. The British diplomats abandoned their houses to the polyglot invaders of their compound. The British assigned the American missionaries the chapel as their living quarters. The chapel seated fifty people for services; most of the seventy American missionaries would find a place to live and sleep among the pews and on the altar.

While the missionaries arranged their belongings in the chapel, Will Ament went back to the Methodist Mission to recover some of the useful things left behind. None of the other missionaries was bold enough to accompany him, so he walked alone down the quiet streets to the mission compound, climbed over the wall to gain entrance, and found several Manchu soldiers inside. The soldiers "were as scared as I was" but Ament reassured them, crossed their palms with silver, and got them to help him collect a few things. He found his bicycle and rode it back to the British Legation.[25] He assured the other missionaries that the streets were safe and got ten missionaries and a hundred Chinese to return with him to the mission. The looters had been at work, but Ament and the other men salvaged canned goods and trunks of clothing and personal items. Lizzie Martin's trunk was saved as was Emma Martin's Bible.

The twenty-four hours granted to the diplomats to leave Peking expired at four P.M. on June 20. The foreign community hastened to ensure that it was safely within the British Legation before four. Last to arrive were Sir Robert Hart and his Customs employees, thirty-one of them, plus family members and servants. Hart and his employees had planned to remain at Customs headquarters and defend it, but, about two P.M., the Austrians, whose legation was next door, abandoned their exposed position and retired to the more centrally located and secure French Legation.

The Austrians had been frightened by a flourish of trumpets and a parade of Chinese soldiers in front of their position. Without bothering to tell anyone they left their defenses and retreated to the French Legation. The French and Austrian soldiers immediately got into a row. The Austrian retreat would force the French to rebuild and strengthen their own defenses and the worn-out French soldiers wearily began to load carts with bricks and stones to fortify the alleyways and houses within their share of the defense perimeter.

Sir Robert Hart and his tribe of Customs employees came in "at the double, very angry, and cursing the Austrians for a retreat which was only discovered by them by chance." Hart, broken in appearance, the best-known foreigner in all of China, had saved nothing from his palace home. He carried a mattress and a pillow. He spread his mattress on the veranda of the British Legation and insisted that he would stay there with the men under his command. "What is good enough for my men, is good enough for me," he said. He was persuaded to occupy a small room in the MacDonalds' residence.[26] His diary, a record of forty-six years in China, was rescued by one of his employees and brought to the legations.

George Morrison was also furious at the Austrians because his home was nearby. Morrison was determined to save his book collection — already becoming famous. He rushed to the house, packed up the books, and hauled them back to the British Legation where Lady MacDonald let him store them in a room where he would sleep, ringed by stacks of books reaching to the ceiling. Although fearing for his books, Morrison was elated at the prospect of a siege. "A siege does not occur to any individual but once in a lifetime," he said. "Our lives are marked by few landmarks. Let us, while we will, have a siege that will be recorded in history."[27] Morrison was a conscious hero, reminiscent of those ancient Greeks who saw fighting and dying heroically as their route to immortality. It was a romantic age, those years before the machine gun on the Western Front destroyed the image of glorious war.

As the hour of four approached, the British Legation was a babel of confusion and activity.

> The Legation students had a quarter of an hour given them to clear out of their rooms and make up their beds in their mess-room, and then their quarters were occupied by a mixed multitude of French people, storekeepers, and Japanese women from the Legation — nice clean people with jolly little dolls for babies.... The Russians went into the Second Secretary's house, the Americans [diplomats] into

the Doctor's, the French into that of Mr. Tours, who moved into the Minister's house. The First Secretary's house, already occupied by [British] missionaries, received fresh inmates, and its south verandah had beds for six men. The stable-house was full of Norwegians.... The old Escort Quarters, of late occupied by students, were given up to the Customs people. In the Minister's house was a mixed multitude of men and women, amongst whom were the Baroness von Ketteler and any others of the refugees who were in special trouble or need; the ballroom affording sleeping accommodation for a goodly number of ladies, and others were packed into smaller rooms. The two great Ting-rhs [pavilions] in front of the house were crowded. In the first were encamped the military officials; in the second a multitude of French and Chinese Sisters, some French brothers and priests, and a few other French people surrounded with boxes, packages, and a perfect medley of goods. Boxes, bundles, packing-cases, were scattered everywhere in heaps. The place resembled nothing so much as the deck of an ocean liner just going out of dock, only that it was on a much larger scale, and order had to be reduced out of chaos not by a band of well-trained sailors who knew exactly where everything was to go, but by the passengers each for himself.

Such an incongruous collection of people it was; all languages, races, and tongues, struggling and striving to arrange their property in something like usable order — many sitting disconsolately in corners or grouped in parties equally disconsolate! Some had brought in practically nothing, some were quite helpless, some were fearful and anxious. The poor French and Chinese sisters, who had never done anything outside the regular routine of their house, were distraught and had to be tended like children; no food, no bedding, no idea what they were to do, hungry and tired, but calm and resigned.[28]

While the civilians wrestled with their goods, the legation guards and a few civilian volunteers stood at their posts and waited. At the British legation, "a small group of men gathered on the lawn, watch in hand, to await the expected moment.... Five minutes more, three minutes more, two minutes more, and then firing was heard to the east."

Sergeant Murphy of the Royal Marine Light Infantry marched up to his commander, Captain B.M. Strouts, who was among the men standing on the lawn. He saluted and said, "Firing has commenced, sir." It was 4:00 P.M., June 20, 1900.[29]

The siege of the legations had begun. It would be a battle between five hundred armed foreigners and ten thousand Chinese — the estimate by the besieged of the number of Chinese soldiers and Boxers surrounding the legations.[30] It was never clear that the Dowager's government intended it to be a siege, nor a war of extermination against the foreigners inside the Legation Quarter. The Boxers had unwittingly accomplished the underlying goal of all terrorists and revolutionaries by confusing and frightening a government into making stupid decisions that would lead to chaos. The foreigners in the Legation Quarter were equally blinded by fear and ignorance. In retrospect, Sir Robert Hart and Sarah Pike Conger were the only people in the Legation Quarter to have an insightful and sympathetic appreciation of China and the Chinese.

* * *

The first foreigner killed during the siege was Huberty James, the British professor who helped George Morrison commandeer the *Fu* as a refuge for Chinese Christians. Frank Gamewell saw James in the *Fu* an hour before the siege began. James expressed confidence — even though the deadline to leave the city was soon to expire — that the Chinese government would protect the foreigners. He said he had been assured by Prince Su there would be no attack on the legations.

James began his return to the British Legation about the time that gunfire began. He left the *Fu* and crossed the north bridge over the canal — outside the defense lines of the British Legation — and walked alongside the canal toward the legation gate. At the same time, three hundred Chinese soldiers also crossed the canal. One of them saw James walking alone and made a prisoner of him. He was marched off with the column of soldiers. Shots were heard soon afterwards.

8

In the British Legation

The Mongolian pony is a hardy little beast, surviving the sub-zero temperatures and dust storms of the Gobi. Genghis Khan and his Golden Horde rode all the way to the gates of Vienna on Mongol ponies. The Mongols drank their blood, obtained by opening a vein in the neck, and their liquor was fermented mare's milk. They were as hard on their ponies as they were on their enemies and they were very hard men indeed. The Mongolian pony, undersized, pot-bellied, and hairy, has no expectation of good will from his human masters and he shows none himself.

Not the least element of confusion at the British Legation on the late afternoon of June 20 — scattered rifle shots cracking — were the ponies. Some were aristocrats, competitors in the spring race meeting at the late, lamented Peking racetrack. Others were the riding ponies of diplomats. Many were humble beasts of burden, snatched at the last moment off the streets by foraging foreigners and led away to the British Legation. One hundred and fifty ponies, a few mules and donkeys, a small herd of sheep, a milk cow, and a pack of barking dogs were inside the six-acre compound of the legation. The ponies were tied in strings all over the grounds, their restlessness and high-strung hostility aggravated by milling crowds of soldiers, diplomats, missionaries, crying children, Chinese servants, lines of carts hauling provisions, and the desperate clutter and chaos of people torn loose from their moorings.

A British diplomat, Herbert Dering, was the master of equines and he was seen that afternoon, shirt-sleeved and sweating, tearing around the compound after one or another of his refractory brutes. Even tied, they were a noisy lot, bellowing and fighting, snorting, kicking, and complaining of insufficient water and inadequate fodder. Dering tied many of them up near his former house, now occupied by more than a score of British refugees. The people in the house were kept awake all night by the neighing ponies. Next morning, Sir Claude MacDonald, the angular British diplomat with the elongated mustaches, made one of his first executive decisions of the siege. The ponies must go. Dering drove those belonging to the Russians over to their legation and another herd was turned loose in the *Fu* to graze in Prince Su's flower gardens. The remaining ponies were confined to the stables in a corner of the Legation compound where they would contribute least to the pandemonium.

Pandemonium was the right word to describe the scene at the British Legation. The walled compound was rectangular, approximately 800 feet north to south and 350 feet wide, dotted with trees, flower gardens, residences, offices, a chapel, a bell tower, and a monumental front gate. It normally housed about 50 British plus servants. Now, in a single day, hundreds of civilians had descended on the legation, hauling their possessions in carts or on their backs or the backs of their Chinese servants. A census of foreigners in the legation quarter, not including the legation guards, counted 473 people: 245 men, 149 women, and 79 children. Four hundred and fourteen civilians were to live at the British Legation and 59 chose to hole up elsewhere in the Legation Quarter, most notably the Chamots and their friends who stayed in the Peking

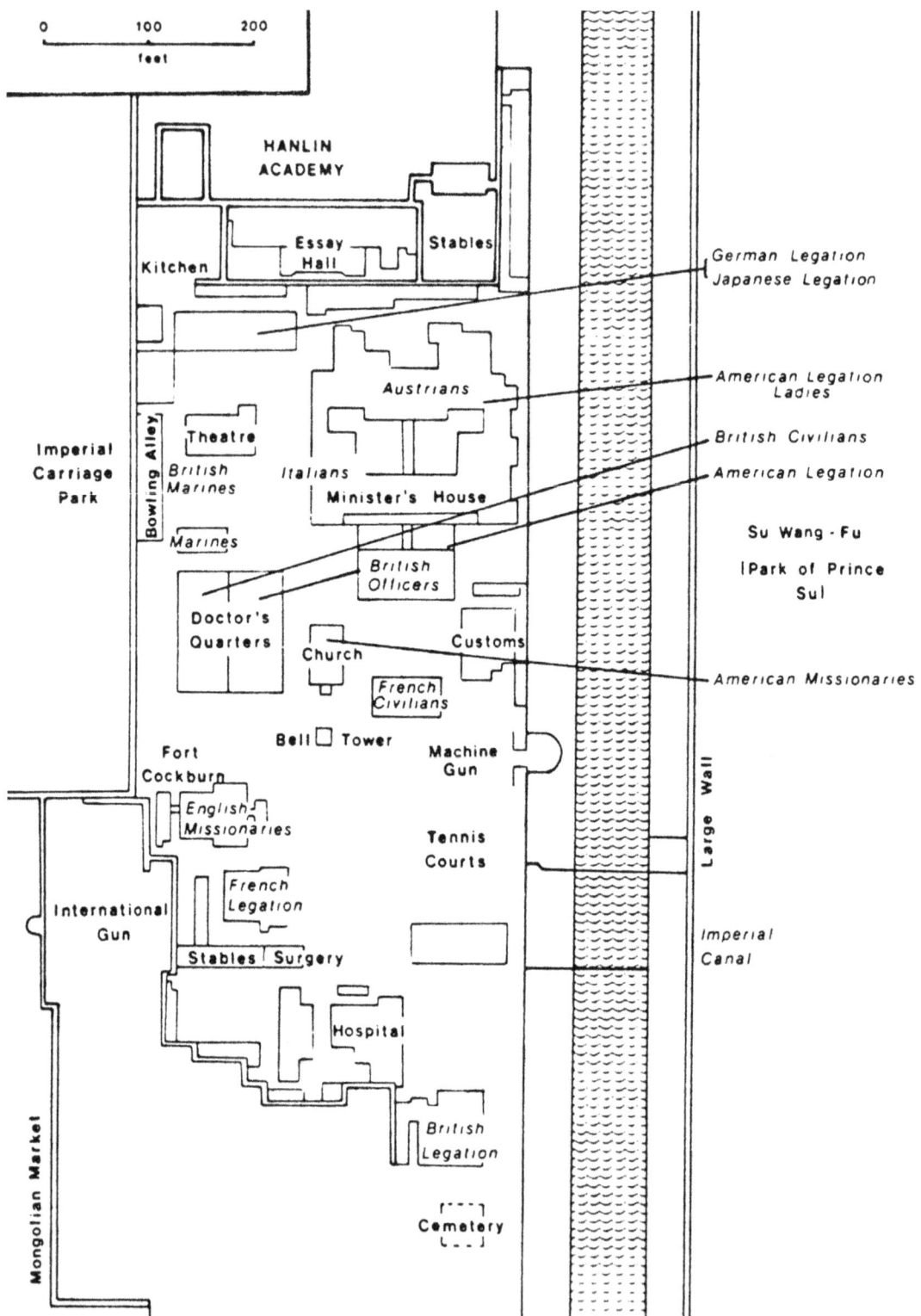

The British Legation. More than four hundred civilians crowded into the houses and buildings of the legation. British marines and civilian volunteers, including the dubious Carving-Knife Brigade, defended the legation (Smith, *Convulsion in China*, 1901).

Hotel and enjoyed the enormous wine cellar of the hotel. It was the most cosmopolitan body since the Tower of Babel, comprising nineteen nationalities: American, Austrian, Belgian, Boer, British, Chinese, Danish, Dutch, French, Finn, German, Italian, Japanese, Norwegian, Portuguese, Russian, Spanish, Swedish, and Swiss.[1] This list does not include sub-species of British nationality: English, Irish, Scots, Welsh, Canadian, and Australian, nor Eurasians. The Chinese refugees totaled at least 2,800, mostly housed in the *Fu*, 1,700 Catholics, 800 Protestants, and about 350 non–Christian Chinese, mostly servants, who remained in the legations with their employers, finding shelter under the eaves of the buildings.[2] A few Chinese, neither Christian nor employees, who lived in the Legation Quarter were trapped in their homes and would pass the siege as semi-captives.

The strength of the legation guards was 20 officers and 389 men of eight nationalities:

	Officers	*Men*
British	3	79
Russian	2	79
U.S.	3	53
German	1	51
French	2	45
Austrian	7	30
Italian	1	28
Japanese	1	24[3]

Each nationality of guards was headquartered in its own legation — except the Austrians who had abandoned their legation and joined the French. The Italians would also soon abandon their legation and collaborate with the Japanese. Each nationality held a section of the defense line adjacent to its legation. The British Legation was to be the last redoubt of the defense, the ultimate stronghold to which the soldiers of the legation guards would retreat if — under desperate pressure — they were unable to hold the outer lines of defenses.

These were the besieged in the Legation Quarter: 892 foreigners and 2,800 Chinese. At the Peitang cathedral, less than two miles away, on the other side of the Imperial City, were 31 French and 12 Italian officers and men, 13 French priests, 20 twenty nuns, and 3,200 Catholic converts.[4]

It is fortunate that the Chinese were no better prepared to undertake a siege than the foreigners were to resist. For the first couple of days the combat was desultory: a few Chinese snipers and an occasional outburst of heavy fire, a faint-hearted rush forward and retreat after a fusillade from the attacked. The French and the Japanese saw most of the action. A three-inch gun fired at the Japanese positions in the *Fu* but mostly missed, the shells passing harmlessly over the Legation Quarter. Frontal assault was not a tactic favored by the Chinese. They liked to stand back at a distance and fire in the direction of the Legation Quarter. They would also use fire as a weapon.

* * *

The foreigners in the Legation Quarter had no anticipation that they were in for a long siege. Admiral Seymour was surely just over the horizon. Minister Conger said that he thought the besieged could hold out ten days — that being the longest period he could contemplate surviving without being relieved.[5] There was normality amidst the clutter of the British Legation. The British minister, Sir Claude MacDonald, appeared after dark, "smoking a cigarette reminiscent of his Egyptian campaign, and clad in orthodox evening dress."[6] Many of the other diplomats dressed for dinner and retired early to their improvised beds. An alarm in the middle of the night found many of them sleeping peacefully. "In his nice pyjamas under a mosquito net was found a sleek official of the London Board of Works, who wanted to know what was meant by waking him up in the middle of the night."[7] Meanwhile, the guards at the barricades, already exhausted by three weeks of increasing tension, stood their positions, two hours on and four hours off, but the four hours off were more often than not taken up with the sundry chores of soldiers or interrupted by an alarm calling them back to the barricades.

The American missionaries ate a picnic supper that first evening. The missionaries divided themselves into shifts and established a schedule; it was impossible to prepare enough food for all seventy at the same time. Breakfast was six to nine, each of the three churches— Methodist, Presbyterian, and Congregational — having one hour to feed its people. Prayers followed, "then an hour for cleaning, and dinner from half-past eleven to half-past two. Supper begins at 4 and keeps up until 7, and then people begin to retire. We are not allowed lights in the evening, except a candle for a short time, as the enemy could easily locate us; and as we must rise so early, we try to get to bed early."[8]

The missionaries went to bed in the chapel, the space allotted for each less than the proverbial six feet by three. "We did not dare disrobe lest we should have to flee for our lives. The night was warm, the babies were cross, and the rest is better imagined than told." [9] One of the fears of the women was that they would be slaughtered in their nightdresses and so they kept their clothes on to sleep, the better to meet death while modestly clothed. William Ament went over to the American Legation and slept on a couch but later he and several other men swept out the garret of the chapel and made their beds there, tucked in under the roof, but exposed to the nightly serenade of bullets and shells.

* * *

When he rose the next morning, Sir Claude MacDonald must have looked around his compound in dismay. People camped everywhere; assorted supplies and equipment were piled up on the tennis courts and around the bell tower. The Mongolian ponies furiously neighed, children wailed, and Chinese servants argued with each other for space to care for their masters. An occasional bullet whistled overhead.

Order was needed and Sir Claude MacDonald applied to Arthur Smith — the prose laureate of the American missionaries in China —"for information as to whom among them he could depend upon for assistance in the innumerable matters requiring immediate and ceaseless attention." Smith told Sir Claude that, during the semi-siege at the Methodist Mission, the missionaries had formed committees "covering every need and that if it were desired thoroughly competent men could be summoned within five minutes, who had already had considerable experience in their respective duties."[10] Within an hour, MacDonald had turned over the management of the legation to more than a dozen committees headed mostly by American missionaries.

The captain of the missionaries was the American Board's Elwood Gardner Tewksbury, thirty-five years old, chairman of the General Committee of Public Comfort. It was Tewksbury, "indefatigable and versatile ... whose tireless energy never appeared to flag,"[11] who coordinated the care and feeding of foreign civilians and Chinese Christians. The sardonic Bertram Simpson said "no one has yet fathomed" the purpose of the General Committee.[12] Tewksbury was more admired than liked, a rising star of missionaries, a former student leader at Harvard and a young disciple of the guiding light of the Protestant missionary movement, John R. Mott. The missionaries treasured the Ivy-Leaguers among their ranks who gave the movement a touch of class and an elegant contrast to the sallow faces and nasal voices of the Oberlin band and their kindred from the Midwest.

Tewksbury was one of a new breed of missionaries with purposeful confidence — and perhaps a measure of un–Christian arrogance — that they would soon bring Christianity and Western civilization to China. They were men of ambition, substance, and culture, politely respectful of the accomplishments of older missionaries such as Ament, but, among themselves, in the spirit of Christian introspection, they perceived too much of the black-garbed, long-winded air of the revival meeting in the older men. New blood—well educated, sophisticated young men and new ideas—was needed to overcome what had been, it must be admitted in the pious spirit of Christian honesty, a sparse and disappointing harvest of souls. Humility was not a virtue of the Reverend Tewksbury.

Tewksbury, like William Ament, would see his reputation tarnished and he would never attain the high honor and esteem in the missionary ranks he so desired. He was, in the words of an experienced colleague, "a man of great executive ability, and must be at work doing large and stirring things, and must have a leading hand in what he has any hand in. He is not careful in using money, but is most conscientious in his purposes.... How wisely he would deal with Christians engaged in earning money and in business relations I do not feel certain."[13] In the careful prose of the missionaries those comments amounted to condemnation.

MacDonald's most important appointment was Frank Gamewell as chief of staff of the Committee for Fortifications. Mac-

Sir Claude MacDonald. The British minister to China had a military background and was the commander of the defense of the legations (Smith, *Convulsion in China*, 1901).

Donald, however, must have wondered about Gamewell. The Methodist missionary was stringy, unprepossessing, and shy, hardly seeming the man who could lead disorganized foreigners and frightened Chinese to construct defensive works and hold off an assault by Chinese soldiers and Boxers. But Gamewell, as MacDonald would learn, was made of whipcord. He would be the indispensable man who made the difference between life and death.

Francis D. Gamewell was born in Camden, South Carolina, in 1857, the son of an inventor. He saw war first-hand when Sherman's all conquering army passed through Camden with terrible carnage. After the Civil War—opportunities in the South gone with the wind—the Gamewells moved north to New Jersey. The young Frank Gamewell aspired to be a civil engineer. He enrolled at Renssalaer Polytechnic Institute, but an injury interrupted his studies. He returned to school at Cornell, but an illness felled him and prevented him from completing the course. After two failed attempts to become an engineer, Gamewell yielded to what seemed divine will and became a missionary instead. In October 1881 he arrived in Peking. Shortly, he married Mary Porter. She was thirty-three, distinguished by eleven years in China, and he was only twenty-four. She had been the first missionary of the Methodist Women's Foreign Missionary Society assigned to China and a pioneer in the anti-foot binding movement. Her school, opened in 1872, required that its female students have unbound feet.[14] Somehow—doubtless from a respectable physical distance—romance blossomed between the soft-spoken southerner and the matronly Miss Porter. It was a whirlwind courtship and marriage between two ill-matched people, but the Gamewells apparently were a happy couple. They never had any children.

Gamewell's missionary career was unremarkable. In the 1890s he accepted a position as professor of chemistry at the Imperial University and occupied his spare time building a new Methodist church, the largest and finest Protestant church in Peking. As an evangelist Gamewell was mediocre; as a builder he was talented. The religious said that Frank Gamewell was a gift of God to the defenders of the Legation Quarter.[15]

Gamewell wasted no time. Immediately after talking to Sir Claude MacDonald, he hopped on his rickety bicycle and undertook a tour of inspection of the British Legation. Little had been done — despite three weeks of growing tension and semi-siege. A low earth rampart had been thrown up to protect the Nordenfeldt machine gun at the front gate of the legation and a crew was cutting down the trees along the canal to give the machine gun more play plus strengthening the rampart to protect the gunners. A few Chinese snipers fired at the Chinese coolies cutting down trees. No sandbags were in place. A few days before the British officer Captain Halliday had started to improvise barriers by filling dry-goods boxes with earth, but "he had been so laughed at and snubbed by Captains Strouts and Wray that he had given up the attempt." The British marines were scornful of fighting from behind barricades — that is, until the first of their number was killed a day later.[16]

To the British, the Continentals, and the Japanese fortification seemed déclassé, the sort of thing an American would worry about. With a tradition of Indian wars and the bloody Civil War, the Americans had less élan and compunction about taking cover. Gamewell, no doubt, still had uncomfortable dreams about the day when he, a boy of seven, had seen Sherman's brutal army descend on Camden, burn its business district, and carry off everything of value.

Gamewell's first order was for sandbags, thousands of them, and every piece of spare cloth and sewing machine in the legation were to be devoted to their production. So hungry were the inhabitants of the legation for a man of decision that stringy little Frank Gamewell got what he wanted. The American missionary women ransacked the Legation Quarter for sewing machines, set them up in front of the chapel, and commenced a production line for sandbags. One woman would measure, another would cut, another fold, a fourth feed the cloth into the machine, a fifth woman would sew, and, finally, a sixth woman would cut the thread and stack the bags in piles. In less than four minutes each group of women could produce a sandbag, as many as two thousand a day, forty to fifty thousand during the siege. A mixed assortment of people joined the sandbag brigade. One day Sarah Pike Conger, wife of the American minister, stood in a hole holding bags open while a Russian priest scooped up dirt with a porcelain kettle to fill them. Even Luella Miner, the missionary teacher, who never once in her twelve years in China had been seen to rattle a pot, whisk a broom, or thread a needle, was soon engaged.

Finding enough cloth for sandbags was a problem but Lady Ethel MacDonald donated the luxurious curtains from her residence and, soon, expensive cloth — damasks, embroidered tapestries, silk, and satins — was cut into pieces, sewed, and filled with dirt. The optimists among the besieged complained about the waste. Surely, Admiral Seymour would be knocking at the gates of Peking in a day or two and all this furious activity was unnecessary. A dispute broke out about the size of the sandbags. A soldier complained they were too small. The ladies made them bigger. Another soldier said the bigger bags were too heavy to carry. Gamewell resolved the problem. He took a piece of paper and scribbled on it that all sandbags were to be thirty-four inches long by seventeen inches wide without exception and he posted the instruction, saying, "'No matter who tells you to make them different, make them just according to these measurements' and then, with a polite 'good morning,' he instantly vanished."[17]

Gamewell needed scores of workers every day, and the missionaries formed committees to organize the Chinese Christians into coolie forces to labor on fortifications. The Protestant Chinese were already accustomed to the missionaries as hard and unforgiving taskmaskers and

Frank Gamewell and the "Fighting Parsons" of the Fortification Committee. Left to right, standing: Charles Ewing, Gamewell, Charles Killie, William Stelle, Joseph Stonehouse (British), and Franklin Chapin. Above is Sgt. Murphy, Royal Marines. Killie was the photographer who fit himself into the photograph (Smith, *Convulsion in China*, 1901).

the Catholics found they had to work to eat. The missionaries "know just how to manage these coolies" said one woman, "who have to do a certain amount of work before they get their meal-tickets. It was hard at first to make them work but they soon learned that their own life depended upon obedience."[18] Gamewell had absolute authority to draft Chinese workers where he could. One morning the elderly Spanish minister had to beg hot water from the Congers to mix with his gruel because his servant had been set to work on fortifications.[19]

There were complaints. The phlegmatic British said there was a "little too much system in the system of committees" and Bertram Simpson had, as usual, an irreverent — though grudgingly favorable — remark.

> It is the Yankee missionary who has invaded and taken charge of the British Legation; it is the Yankee missionary who is doing all the work there and getting all the credit. Beginning with the fortifications committee, there is an extraordinary man named G[amewell], who is doing everything — absolutely everything.... G[amewell] is the man of the hour, and will brook no interference. Already the British Legation, which at the commencement of the siege was utterly undefended by any entrenchments or sandbags, is rapidly being hustled into order by the masterful hand of this missionary. Coolies are evolved from the converts of all classes, who, although they protest that they are unaccustomed to manual work, are merely given shovels and picks, sandbags and bricks, and resolutely told to commence and learn. Already the discontented in the outer lines are sending for him and asking him to do this and that, and the hard-worked man always finds time for everything. It is a wonder.
>
> And behind this one man fortifications committee there are many other committees now. There is a general committee...; a fuel committee; a sanitary committee; nothing but committees, all noisily talking and quite safe in the British Legation. Out of the noise and chatter the American missionary emerges, sometimes odorous and unpleasant to look upon, but whose excuse for not shouldering a rifle and volunteering for the front is written on his tired face.[20]

The sardonic Simpson also commented: "crowds of vigorous men, belonging to the junior ranks of the Legations' staff and to numbers of other institutions are skulking, or getting themselves placed on committees so as to escape [military] duty."[21] (Simpson's own contributions as an armed volunteer in the defense did not attract favorable or unfavorable comment by other chroniclers of the siege.)

Most of the American male missionaries served on at least one committee. The important food supply committee was chaired by the Rev. H. E. King, a Methodist. Vice-chairmen had responsibility for mutton and horsemeat. Presbyterian Courtenay Fenn, in addition to milling flour for bread, also was the printer for the daily food ticket that allowed Chinese workers to eat at the legation. The Rev. W. T. Hobart, a Methodist, headed the Committee for Native Labor and Food Supplies, organizing and feeding Chinese workmen and other Chinese residing within the British Legation. Ament's friend William Stelle registered Chinese labor. The Rev. George D. Davis, also a Methodist, measured the water level in the wells every morning and evening. It was adequate: three feet deep at night and five feet in the morning as two feet of water seeped in overnight.[22] The two most distinguished missionaries, W.A.P. Martin (an ex-missionary) and Arthur Smith held the most menial of jobs: watchmen at the North Gate to check the passes of Chinese workers passing through the gate between the *Fu* and the British Legation.[23] Will Ament was chairman — and the only member — of the Committee for Confiscated Goods.[24]

Every task was organized by the missionaries. An Englishman was in charge of a laundry. He appeared at the tennis court every afternoon at five to receive dirty clothes and deliver clean clothes. His efforts were appreciated but received few compliments. The laundry was "not very good, little attempt at ironing being made."[25] There was even a shoe repair committee, headed by Stelle. The committees customarily held their meetings at the tennis court or in the leafy shade of the Bell Tower. Leaves shot from the trees overhead often fell down among them.

Most of the actual labor was done by Chinese workers drafted, sometimes by force, from the Chinese Christians and servants sheltered within the Legation Quarter. Each Chinese worker had an identification badge sewed onto his sleeve which indicated his hours of work and task.[26] First choice for workmen in the British Legation were the Protestant converts who were fed better than the Catholics residing in the *Fu*, although the deficiency in food was blamed on Roman Catholic priests who didn't look after their people in the gathering and distribution of food.[27]

Missionary women were not, of course, members of any formal committees. They organized themselves. Each of the three denominations — Congregational, Presbyterian, and

Methodist — had committees for cooks, food supplies, and housekeeping.[28] Most of all the women sewed sandbags, nearly all the time, plus making bandages and washing sheets for the hospital.

* * *

Across the canal from the British Legation, Lt. Col. Shiba organized the defense of the *Fu* with his Japanese soldiers and volunteers and a work force drawn from Chinese Catholics. While Gamewell and Shiba were building defenses, the soldiers were bickering among themselves. Captain von Thomann, the Austrian, by virtue of his rank and the strength of his voice, was recognized, more or less, as the commanding officer of all the legation guards. Von Thomann had been vacationing in Peking at the beginning of the Boxer troubles. He was the commanding officer of the Austrian cruiser *Zenta*. His reign would be brief.

The first crisis of the siege occurred at nine A.M. on June 22. Bertram Simpson told the story.

> Without a word of explanation, Captain T[homann], the Austrian commander, suddenly ordered all the French, Italians, and Austrians to fall back on the British Legation, sending word meanwhile to the Japanese and the Germans to follow his example.... The result was that for ten minutes armed men of all nationalities poured into the British Legation, until every rifle-bearing effective was standing there, all jabbering in a mass, and not knowing what it was all about. The Americans, who had established themselves on the Tartar Wall as the main point in the western defense, guessed they were not going to be left there cut off from salvation by a failure to remember their existence; and presently they, too, ran in, openly swearing at their officers ... the Americans are not going to be forgotten — we soon found that out.[29]

It was one of those inexplicable panics that sweep through armies, "a veritable stampede," Morrison wrote, "a panic that might have been fraught with the gravest disaster."[30] Three-quarters of the defenses had been abandoned with hardly a shot being fired. Von Thomann seemed to be the guilty party. He had had been told by somebody that the American Legation was being abandoned. Concluding that the defenses in that quarter were crumbling, he ordered the other legation guards to retreat to the British Legation. The panicky retreat of the legation guards was a golden opportunity for the Chinese soldiers to march in unopposed and capture every legation except the British and to occupy the *Fu* and dispose of the Chinese Christians there. The German contingent was the only one with the military presence to undertake a fighting withdrawal rather than a headlong flight, and German resistance discouraged Chinese troops from advancing down Legation Street. The Germans had a man killed in the confusion and the Italian Legation was occupied by the Chinese and burned. That the Chinese were not able to take better advantage of the abandonment of the defenses was a stroke of great good fortune.

At the British Legation, while the soldiers stood in their ranks, the ministers met urgently in a circle around MacDonald. Von Thomann, as commander, must go, they all agreed. By military protocol, the next most senior officer present was Lt. Col. Shiba, but, despite the respect given him, he was an Asian and not even the Japanese Minister had any thought that one of his countrymen could command Europeans. The Americans, bumptious colonials, were almost equally unacceptable as leaders—barring the reincarnation of Robert E. Lee—as were the backward Russians. The Germans were surly and uncooperative; the French were irritating. Only one man could unite and rule over this uneasy coalition. Sir Claude MacDonald stood at the center of the ring of diplomats, tall, straight, and angular, his military posture reminding his fellows that he had until recently been an officer in a highland regiment. The French and Russian ministers leaped forward to offer the command to MacDonald and the other diplomats acquiesced.

MacDonald's first order as commander-in-chief was for the legation guards of the eight nationalities to reoccupy their abandoned defenses. All did so, flushing a few Chinese soldiers out of the French and German Legations, but no attempt was made to retake the Italian Legation. Henceforth, the Italians would take up a position on the right of the Japanese, helping hold the *Fu*. Von Thomann was in disgrace and, in the weeks to come, exposed himself recklessly at the barricades. He was killed on July 8. MacDonald's appointment did not meet with universal acclaim. A Russian lieutenant described it as "unpleasant" although necessary.[31] The American marines despised MacDonald.

* * *

The next crisis came that same afternoon, June 22. The British Legation had two points most vulnerable to attack. The first was the north wall bordering the Hanlin Academy, China's national library, and the second was the southwestern wall bordered by a maze of Chinese houses and shops pushed up against the legation wall. The Chinese chose to attack first from the southwest and their weapon was fire.

Chinese soldiers set the fire at five in the afternoon and, with a good wind from the west, it threatened to burn the legation compound. "A huge column of smoke went up into the air, and in its centre forked tongues of flame burst out," said Polly Condit-Smith. "It seemed impossible that this enormous fire — one so large or so near I have never before seen in my life — would not in an hour or so completely burn us up."[32]

The ringing of the bell turned out the civilian population and the struggle began. The lack of preparation to fight fires was soon apparent. The largest of the two fire engines in the legation refused to work and many of the leather water buckets leaked. A bucket brigade of men and women stretched from the nearest well to the fire and water was passed from hand to hand with a collection of hastily collected utensils. "Pails, jars, foot-tubs, small bathtubs, teapots ... most of which started from the well only partly filled, and by reduplicated jerking from the hand to hand of excited men and women often arrived at their distant destination practically empty."[33]

At the head of the bucket brigade men stood on ladders and threw water on the flames just over the wall. Every fifteen minutes they were relieved, scorched and burned, and gasping for breath in the terrible heat. Chinese riflemen from nearby roofs directed a stream of bullets toward the legation and the firefighters. British marines took up positions on roofs and picked off Chinese foolish enough to expose themselves. A British marine was killed, the first British loss during the siege. The fire was beaten back after two hours of frantic work. Civilians had passed — just barely — their first test at survival. Sterner challenges were to come. Polly Condit-Smith commented wryly, "Peking had never seen such unanimity of her foreign residents."[34]

The stress took a toll. Dr. George Lowry's Chinese hospital assistant hung himself. The Conger's adult daughter, Laura, who suffered from a nervous ailment, wept convulsively and threw herself into her father's arms. And Sarah Pike Conger, the wife of the American minister, gave a startling demonstration of mind over matter. Ethel MacDonald, Polly, and Mrs. Conger were in a room where a baby was sleeping in a crib when a bullet came slicing through the headpiece of the crib, missing the baby's head by an inch. The mother snatched up the baby and the women all fled together to a safer part of the house.

Mrs. Conger assured the frightened women that "it was ourselves, and not the times, which were troublous and out of tune, and insisted that while there was an appearance of warlike hostilities, it was really in our own brains. Going further, she assured us that there was no bullet entering the room; it was again but our receptive minds which falsely lead us to believe such to be the case." After these comments to her open-mouthed audience Mrs. Conger departed, and the other women, astonished by this extraordinary statements, forgot all about the "very material bullet which had driven us from the room."[35]

* * *

After their narrow escape from fire, the besieged were thoroughly frightened and they worked through the night to improve the security of the British Legation. A crew of volunteers went over the wall in the area of the fire and pulled down Chinese houses, notching and weakening the wooden pillars supporting the brick walls and tile roofs, attaching ropes and pulling the whole building down with a crash. Chinese carpenters improvised buckets by fixing handles on three gallon cans. MacDonald, still in his first day of command of the defense, called together the diplomatic ministers, his British officers and the fortification committee and they worried together about the threat of fire from the Hanlin Academy, adjacent to the north wall of the British Legation.

The Hanlin Academy was the greatest repository of ancient learning in the world. The academy was a large compound with more than twenty halls of learning around the customary four courtyards, each with its inner gates, gardens dotted with huge old trees, lotus ponds, and gazebos. The nearest of the Hanlin buildings to the British Legation was less than fifteen feet from the common wall they shared. The greatest treasure of the Hanlin was the one and only copy of the Yung Lo Ta Tien, the Great Encyclopedia, compiled in the fifteenth century. This immense work of 22,000 volumes contained 366,992,000 Chinese characters, compared to only thirty million words in the *Encyclopædia Britannica*.[36] The volumes of the Great Encyclopedia were stored in camphor-wood boxes "bound in yellow silk pasted on the board covers, each book nineteen and one-half inches long, twelve wide, and about an inch in thickness, having a strip of bright-coloured silk pasted on one cover with the four characters of its title."[37]

As the foremost atrocity against scholarship during the Boxer Rebellion, the issue of who was responsible for burning the Hanlin arouses passions. The event happened quickly and in great confusion and no one person had a complete picture of what was going on. According to Polly Condit-Smith, after the first near-disaster from fire the fortification committee, headed by Frank Gamewell, recommended to the diplomats that the Hanlin be burned down to deny the Chinese the possibility of using it as a torch against the legations or as cover during an armed attack. The ministers unanimously disapproved this recommendation. Although the diplomats decided against burning the Hanlin, they authorized a reconnaissance patrol. At dusk a group of fifteen men — ten British marines, three Customs volunteers, and Captains Poole and Strouts climbed over the wall. Poole recorded that he was "the first European [ever] to enter the Hanlin."[38] The patrol explored the premises and found the Hanlin unoccupied. They returned and reported their findings.

The next morning, June 23, MacDonald ordered Captain Poole to return and occupy the Hanlin. Poole and seventeen men, including the ever-present George Morrison, bludgeoned a small hole through the wall and entered. "Some buildings which endangered our position particularly were pulled down," said Nigel Oliphant. "They were full of valuable books and archives, many of which were destroyed or spoilt. A few were saved, so as to show the Yamen that we had only destroyed the place for safety's sake, and not for spite."[39] Morrison, well aware of the opprobrium that might be called down on the foreigners for destroying venerable books, does not mention that the foreign soldiers pulled buildings down as a precautionary measure and thus began the destruction of the Hanlin. In the first and most influential account of the siege, he places full blame for the destruction on the Chinese, as do most other accounts.[40] Poole's patrol got into a small battle with Chinese soldiers who overnight had occupied the large temple at the entrance to the Hanlin. According to Poole, the Chinese set fire to the temple and the blaze spread to several nearby buildings. The Chinese soldiers took up positions in one of the halls and peppered the British Legation with rifle fire.

The fire continued to spread toward the British Legation, assisted by a stiff north wind, and about 11:30 A.M., when the American missionaries had just sat down to lunch, the alarm bell was rung, and the tired foreigners responded once again to a fire threatening their survival. British marines rushed into the Hanlin. "They had to clamor over obstacles, through tightly jammed doors, under falling beams, occasionally halting to volley heavily until they had cleared all the ground around the Hanlin, and found perhaps half a ton of empty brass cartridge cases left by the enemy who had discreetly flown."[41]

The civilians poured into the Hanlin behind the marines. "Every available man was set to work passing buckets of water from the nearest wells, working the small fire-engines, and cutting down trees with much labour and not a little risk of being crushed beneath the trunks or other falling walls. These huge old trees were one of the most efficient means of spreading the flames.... One of the large halls standing nearest to the legation had to be pulled down for our own safety. It was a difficult and dangerous undertaking, for the building was lofty, with large and solid posts, and roof-timbers."[42] The firefighters steadily lost ground as the whole compound of the Hanlin erupted into a blazing inferno, the fire fed by centuries old timbers, manuscripts, and thousands of wood blocks used for printing.

Just as it seemed that the British Legation could not be saved, the wind shifted from north to west — the missionaries declared it a miracle — and the advance of the fire slowed. The firefighters took no chances that the wind might shift again. They cleared the Hanlin of flammable material and destroyed the buildings nearest the British Legation. One of the buildings was the repository for the Great Encyclopedia. Without a pause for contemplation, the firefighters and the marines emptied the building of its ancient manuscripts. They carried the volumes of the encyclopedia into the courtyard and dumped them on the ground. Some books were thrown into a lotus pond to prevent their catching fire; others were soaked by fire hoses and bucket brigades. A few people snatched up volumes of the encyclopedia as souvenirs.

Thus perished, in an afternoon, the greatest literary work of the oldest living civilization on earth. Volumes of the encyclopedia later turned up in good numbers around the world. Among the foreign soldiers and firefighters apparently many paused in their work for looting. A building that survived the blaze was burned on June 28 by the British and another was incorporated into the defense.[43]

* * *

Chroniclers of the siege put the entire blame for the destruction of the Hanlin on the Chinese. In reality, the foreigners deserve at least an equal share of the blame. It fit, however, into the mindset of the foreigners that the destruction of the Hanlin portended a China that was imploding upon itself—a society bent on suicide. Arthur Smith titled his book *China in Convulsion*. Some Chinese believed the same. The American consul in Tientsin, J. W. Ragsdale, reported to Washington on June 14. "Peking authorities have concluded that their government is about to disappear from the Galaxy of Nations but before doing so are determined upon committing an outrage unparalleled for centuries. In the event they are unable to hold Peking, they contemplate the sacrifice of every foreigner within the city walls."[44] Ragsdale's source for this Wagnerian scenario was a U.S.-educated Chinese.

Far from being a suicidal last stand, the Chinese during the early days of the siege were as indecisive and confused as the frightened foreigners. The two factions in the Chinese court, that of Jung Lu which favored co-existence with the foreigners and Prince Tuan who fantasized that the Boxers and the Chinese army could sweep the foreigners out of China, continued their arguments. The Empress Dowager yielded to first one, then the other.

Jung Lu, the ostensible commander of the Chinese army, and his faction were still in the minority in Peking. He described the situation in a telegram to the governors of the southern provinces. "Half of the entourage of Their Majesties and the princes belong to the Boxer societies, as do the majority of Manchu and Chinese troops. They [the Boxers] swarm in the streets of the capital like locusts, several tens of thousands of them, and it is extremely difficult to reestablish order."[45] Jung Lu's faction was not helped by the receipt of what seemed good news from the fighting front. On June 21, the court received an upbeat report from Yu-Lu, the governor in Tientsin. In the fighting at Taku, he said, foreign gunboats had been hit and the cooperation between Boxers and Chinese soldiers had been excellent. Yu Lu forgot to mention one small detail: the foreigners had captured the Taku forts.[46]

Based on this misleading report of Chinese military success, the Dowager's government took two major steps on June 21. First, it issued orders that Boxers be enlisted in the army and appointed three high officials to deal with Boxer affairs. Secondly, it published what has been called a "declaration of war on the world." It was not really a declaration of war, but rather an acknowledgment, sent to the governors of the provinces of the empire, that a state of war existed between the foreign powers and China.

The most infamous of the decrees emanating from the Forbidden City during these confused days was a June 23 decree from the Empress Dowager to the Imperial Council. "The work now undertaken by Tung Fu-hsiang," it read, "should be completed as soon as possible, so that troops can be spared and sent to Tientsin for defense."[47]

The scholar Chester Tan points out that the character (shi) translated as "work" is unusually vague and imprecise. Usually, Tan says, a decree "would at least name specifically the matter in question, if it did not spend a few words to explain its nature." Tung was the commanding general of the troops assaulting the legations and the "matter in question" or "work" referred to would seem to be the extermination of the foreigners within. With this decree, the Dowager is covering her tracks. Kill the foreigners, she said, make certain there are no survivors to tell the tale, but don't leave a paper trail to point the finger of blame at the court. If and when the day of reckoning arrived, the massacre of the foreigners could be blamed on the Boxers. Unfortunately, for the Dowager and her court, the foreigners in the Legation Quarter were a difficult lot to massacre.

The intentions of the government of the Empress Dowager toward the Legations and the Peitang never became clear and consistent. The efforts to kill the besieged foreigners over the next few weeks were sporadic, ineffectual and interspersed with attempts at reconciliation. In the contest between China and the West in 1900, the Dowager's policy was to drift along with events and, as the defeat of China became probable, to seek leniency from the foreigners rather than to go down fighting to the last bullet.[48] She and her dynasty would in fact survive the events of 1900. The treatment of China would not be lenient, but the Dowager and most of her Manchu advisors would escape punishment. On a positive note for China, the Boxer Rebellion in 1900 forestalled the partition of China by the Western powers, although it did so at the cost of bankrupting the country and subjecting it to even more foreign meddling than in the past.[49]

* * *

Mary Porter Gamewell recalled the tragedy of days before. She saw the Baroness von Ketteler in the gray of early morning, standing at her window in the MacDonalds' residence, white and grief stricken. One day, the baroness wrapped her black robes around her, stepped forward, clasped hands with Mrs. Gamewell, and said, "I am so alone." She "looked only a girl."[50]

9

Herbert Hoover and Smedley Butler

While the Westerners in Peking fended off Chinese soldiers and Boxers, Tientsin would have its own siege. Admiral Seymour, who had passed so confidently through Tientsin en route to Peking, found that the Boxers and the Chinese army could muster sufficient force to repel his 2,000 man army.

One of the Americans living in Tientsin was Herbert Hoover, a future president of the United States. Hoover was twenty-five years old in 1900, the son of a Quaker blacksmith in West Branch, Iowa. He was an honest, blunt-spoken, plain-dressing, and self-reliant man of affairs. Had he not later become the unfortunate president who presided over the beginning of the Great Depression he would be best recalled as a brilliant administrator of international relief programs saving millions of lives in the aftermath of World War I.

Fame was far in the future and when Hoover and his new wife, Lou, arrived in Tientsin in 1899, he was only a young mining engineer. Hoover had a mustache like a Mexican bandit and he already had a reputation, gained in Australia, as a man who could find gold. He was hired as the chief enginer of the China Engineering and Mining Company at a munificent salary of $12,500 a year. Hoover embarked on a series of exploratory trips to mines north of the Great Wall in the wild deserts of Mongolia.

Hoover planned a fast first trip to the gold mines: saddle ponies for himself, an interpreter, and another foreign engineer, two or three pack mules, a servant, and a cook. For food, they would live off the land, buying what villagers had to sell them. His Chinese employers were horrified. Hoover must travel with the dignity commensurate with his position. An expedition was assembled which included one hundred mules; half a dozen carts; a company of 100 Chinese cavalry; twenty officers, including a general; a herd of servants and grooms; an interpreter and his staff; and dozens of other Chinese bringing up the rear, each with his assigned place in the caravan, but whose purpose Hoover never learned, except for the cook. The expedition finally departed "banners flying, making a cavalcade of some 200 animals with advance heralds and rear guards." In this cumbersome caravan Hoover proceeded slowly — very slowly — to the gold mines.

The caravan journeyed to Mongolia. At night they stopped at inns. Most travelers in China merely endured the filth and insects of a Chinese inn. Hoover, the engineer, did something about it. He put his army of Chinese to work cleaning up and battled the nightly invasion of bedbugs by setting the legs of cots into pans of water. He had some success although he suspected that "the spiders collaborated with the bugs by building bridges for them."

Hoover was both fascinated and frustrated during his first Chinese expedition. He was appalled at the working conditions in the mines. The workers were paid the equivalent of twelve cents per day and crawled through tunnels less than three feet high and three feet wide and five hundred feet underground. The mine managers spent their time thieving, never descending into the mines because underground work was only for coolies.

On another trip Hoover inspected the dikes on the Yellow River. A superstition said that when the Yellow River broke out of its banks and changed course it portended the fall of a dynasty. In fact, the Yellow River had changed course in 1870, but the Manchu dynasty had not fallen yet; one old woman in Peking kept it alive. However, Hoover sagely concluded that the superstition had a foundation in fact. The dikes holding back the water required a million cubic yards of earth per mile and an enormous commitment of labor each and every year.[1] A young and virile Chinese dynasty planted willow trees to hold the dikes together and conscripted peasants for construction and maintenance. By the time of Hoover's visit the peasants had cut the willows for firewood and local officials had stolen the money given them to repair the dikes. Hoover predicted that the time of the Manchus was nearly over.

Hoover also got a taste of missionary life. He arrived in Kalgan at the Great Wall on a Christmas Eve with the temperature

Herbert Hoover in 1900. The dashing young mining engineer lived in Tientsin with his wife, Lou (Herbert Hoover Presidential Library Museum).

below zero. He called on the American missionaries in the town and ate dinner with them. The missionaries were in a moral quandary. Many years ago during a famine, they had purchased several children from starving families and raised them as Christians. Two of these children had grown up and married and still lived in the mission compound. The wife had given birth to several girls, but no boys and, in disgust at her inability to bear a son, she drowned her newest arrival, a daughter. What should the missionaries do? Hoover suggested they consult with the local magistrate, but the missionaries feared that if they brought the matter to the attention of Chinese authorities the woman would be charged with infanticide and executed. Hoover left with the missionaries still debating the problem.

Herbert and Lou Hoover were visiting Peking in May 1900 and narrowly missed being caught there in the siege. Lou became seriously ill with a sinus stoppage, aggravated by the all-pervasive dust of the capital, and the Hoovers quickly took a train out of Peking on May 11 to return to Tientsin where better medical care was available.[2] Thus, a future president and his wife providentially escaped from becoming participants in the siege of the legations. The Hoovers, however, were to have an exciting time in Tientsin.[3]

* * *

Most of the one million population of Tientsin lived in the walled city on the south bank of the Pei River, thirty miles inland from the Gulf of Chihli. The foreign settlements of Tientsin were east of the walled city. Tientsin was a treaty port where China had given the foreign powers tracts of land for businesses and homes. Tientsin had Japanese, French, British, German, and Russian settlements. The Americans had no settlement of their own but a consulate was in the British settlement. All of Tientsin — the walled city, several villages, the foreign settlements, the railroad station, a military fort, and several miles of the Pei River — was encircled by the mud wall, a defensive work about ten feet high and ten feet broad on top.

Herbert and Lou Hoover lived in a comfortable two-story house near the edge of the British settlement on Racecourse Road. They employed fifteen servants. Lou, an elegant brunet, owned a string of horses, collected porcelain, entertained the best people in the foreign society of Tientsin, and studied Chinese two or three hours a day. Her husband was much less apt at the language but, for the rest of their lives, the Hoovers conversed *sotto voce* in Chinese on occasions when they didn't want their conversation understood.

Life in the foreign settlements of Tientsin lacked the exotic appeal of Peking, but it was clean and healthy and the Chinese who lived or worked within the settlements were subject to foreign laws and foreign customs. One could live there and never come into contact with a Chinese, except servants and shopkeepers. Life in the settlements was an artificial existence — a piece of England, France or Germany set down in China.

* * *

Thousands of Boxers descended upon Tientsin. On June 13, the American consul reported to Washington that Boxers had taken over most of the walled city. As in Peking, they set about burning foreign-owned businesses and missionary compounds. Chinese Christians fled to the foreign settlements. The foreign population of the settlements was four hundred men and three hundred women and children. Recently arrived soldiers totaled 2,400, 1,700 of whom were Russians — among them squadrons of mounted, scourging Cossacks. Tientsin was surrounded by Chinese armies and more than 20,000 Boxers. As in Peking, the foreign residents prepared for a siege by foraging for supplies. In one bit of derring-do, an assistant of Hoover spotted a herd of dairy cows on the plain outside the settlement, rounded them up, and drove them to the Hoovers' house. Lou Hoover took over management of the herd but the Hoovers' domestic capabilities diminished when all but two of their servants deserted them, either to join the Boxers or to break away from association with foreigners to avoid Boxer reprisals.

In the early morning hours of June 17, the residents of Tientsin heard the distant booming of the artillery duel between the allied ships and the Chinese forts at Taku. Hoover, among others, thought that the allied attack on the Taku forts was insane. He later told the press that the "allied fleets did the very thing ... to unite all the factions of the natives in opposition to us."[4] Twenty-nine-year-old Commander David Beatty of the Royal Navy was somber as he listened to the guns at Taku. "There was no knowing what we were to go through in the next month."[5] They were to go through a lot.

The siege of Tientsin began later that same day, at one P.M., Sunday afternoon, June 17. The Chinese fired a cannon at the foreign settlements. The projectile landed in the river. The next day, the marines and sailors of the Seymour expedition, forty miles up the railroad from Tientsin, were attacked by the Chinese army. Seymour was unaware of the allied attack at Taku and could only speculate why the Chinese army had suddenly turned hostile.

When the Chinese army fired the first official shot of the siege, Beatty was already preparing to attack with two hundred soldiers a Chinese military college just across the river from the foreign settlements. The military college was defended by two hundred young cadets who had four Krupp guns, sufficient to flatten the foreign settlement. Its elimination as a threat was essential.

The soldiers crossed the river in sampans and steamboats and stormed the college. In twenty minutes of heavy fighting it was all over. Fifty cadets were dead. The foreign troops had five men killed and nine wounded. Beatty ordered the college burned, and he and his men retired to the settlements, bloodied but victorious in their first encounter with Chinese soldiers, albeit their opposition had been eighteen-year-old cadets.

During the next two days Beatty, a handsome, dashing fellow who wore his cap rakishly tilted, participated in some of the most desperate struggles of the Boxer Uprising as the Chinese army belied its reputation and mounted a well-organized assault on the railroad station and a fierce bombardment of the foreign settlements of Tientsin. Beatty was wounded twice in his left arm and wrist within twenty minutes on June 19, but after two days in the hospital he was up again and leading his British sailors and marines.

* * *

The senior military officer in Tientsin was a Russian, Colonel Wogack. The other foreign soldiers in Tientsin accepted Wogack's leadership, but the British insisted on their independence with Captain Bayly in command and Beatty as his second. Colonel Wogack had the good sense to ask Herbert Hoover to mobilize his engineers and take charge of fortifying the settlements. Hoover quickly rounded up a thousand Chinese Christians and ransacked the godowns along the Pei River for sacks of sugar, peanuts, and rice to use as building blocks of barricades. The settlement area was one mile long and a quarter-mile wide. Hoover designed a defense and put the Chinese to work carrying sacks of grain and sugar and piling them up in walls to shield the settlement's defenders.

The Hoovers abandoned their house at the edge of the settlement because it was exposed to Chinese rifle and artillery fire from the other side of the mud wall. They, their dairy herd, and other American families moved in with Edward Drew, the American commissioner of Customs. Unfortunately, the Drew house had a magnetic attraction for shell and shot. Chinese artillerymen fired at nearby godowns, trying to set them on fire, but they frequently hit the house instead.

Hoover's hastily-constricted barricades helped the settlement's defenders beat off Boxer and Chinese army attacks on June 18 and June 19. The Russians held the railroad station — with help from Beatty and his British marines and sailors — but it was of little avail. Tientsin was cut off. Since the rumble of guns on June 17 announcing the battle for the Taku forts, Tientsin had been without communication with the sailors at the mouth of the Pei. Seymour was somewhere up the railroad toward Peking, location and situation unknown. Somewhere down the river were foreign gunboats — if they had not been beaten by the Chinese at Taku. But the foreigners in Tientsin on June 19 were as isolated and alone as were the legations in Peking.

* * *

Reinforcements were on the way, including American marines. Two Americans in the Boxer Rebellion became famous in the future. The first was, of course, Herbert Hoover. The second was Smedley Darlington Butler. Butler, like Hoover, was of Quaker birth although a less Quaker-like person can hardly be imagined. He was a marine, one of only two U.S. marines ever to be awarded two Congressional Medals of Honor — the other being Private Daniel J. Daly, who was at the legations in Peking. That Butler was the son of a congressman did not harm his career, and by the 1920s he was a general and a certain choice for commandant of the Marine Corps — if he could keep his mouth shut, which he could not.[6] In the 1930s he was a political gadfly and quirky stump speaker, claiming on one occasion to have uncovered a plot to assassinate President Roosevelt. His friend, the explorer Roy Chapman Andrews, said of him that he "was a hundred horse-power motor in a [Model T] Ford chassis. His tremendous nervous energy simply burned up his frail body. It gave him devastating headaches and nervous indigestion."[7] Butler acquired nicknames like he did medals. He was the "fighting hell-devil marine," the "fighting devil of the devil dogs," the "stormy petrel" of the Marine Corps, and, mostly, he was "old gimlet eye," the name referring to the clear, icy stare he fixed on subordinates when he gave an order.

Like Hoover, Butler's fame was in the future. In 1900 he was an eighteen year old first lieutenant—the youngest of his rank in the Marine Corps. He ran away from home to join the marines at 16 and was stationed in the Philippines when the call came that marines were needed in China. Butler arrived in China on June 19, a member of a contingent of one hundred and thirty-one marines under the command of Major Littleton W.T. Waller, no slouch at the devil-dog business himself and a man who gave offense to nearly everyone he met.[8] Waller's orders were to rescue the beleaguered foreign defenders of the settlements at Tientsin to make it possible to rescue Seymour, whose objective had been to rescue the legations in Peking—only it was impossible to say now whether Seymour and the legations still existed. All that the allied forces knew of Tientsin was that a lot of noise from artillery was coming from that direction.

The marines found an antediluvian railroad engine at Tangku and got it working and shoved off into the unknown toward Tientsin on June 19 at noon. It was a desperate enterprise. None of them had ever been in China; they had no maps. Waller told them fifty-thousand Chinese were attacking Tientsin. The marines—all one hundred and thirty-one of them—were going to relieve the place. Shortly, they came across a column of four hundred Russian soldiers marching toward Tientsin. The Russians "were carrying their fat, puffing colonel ... because his feet had become so sore that he could no longer limp along in his big boots."[9] The marines offered the Russians a ride and together the two nationalities proceeded slowly up the railroad, repairing track as they advanced. Butler noted, as did many other observers, the extraordinary strength and hardiness of the Russian soldier. Two Russians could do the work of four Americans. By nightfall the Russians and Americans had gone as far as they could by train. A bridge across a river was down in front of them. They were now on foot. They waited one day for reinforcements and when nobody arrived, they decided to advance on Tientsin. Butler said Waller persuaded the Russian colonel to make the advance; other sources said Waller reluctantly consented to join the Russians.[10] Whichever version is correct, it was a foolhardy plan, but at 2:00 A.M. on June 21 the Russians and Americans began what they calculated was a four hour march to Tientsin.

They made it to within sight of the roofs of the city when they were attacked by 2,000 Chinese troops and pinned down. The American marines had four men killed and nine wounded, the first American fatalities of the Boxer Rebellion. In the face of overwhelming odds, Waller ordered a retreat. The 400 Russians had already retreated in unseemly haste, shouting as they dashed by that they would reunite with Americans back where they had started their day's adventure.

The retreat had begun when Butler realized that one of his men, Private Carter, was missing. He was last seen lying in a ditch on the battlefield. Butler went back for Carter along with Lt. Harding and four enlisted men. They found the private in a mud puddle near the destroyed railroad track, moaning in agony, his leg shattered by a rifle bullet. Butler, Harding, and two of the enlisted men bandaged up the wounded man; the two officers made a chair out of their arms and two enlisted men took his feet and they began a walk to the rear. The other two marines stood fast with their rifles to cover the retreat. Nearly surrounded by Chinese, who milled around nearby, Butler and his colleagues carried the wounded Private Carter out of the battle area. Ringed on three sides, outnumbered an infinity, Butler attributed their survival to the superstitious awe the Chinese soldiers had of foreigners. "Lucky for us they believed in magic."[11] After four hours of carrying Carter, menaced at all times, Butler and his men caught up with the main American force.

Heroics aside, their first encounter with the Chinese was a defeat. The Russians and the

Americans were sufficiently humbled to await reinforcements which began arriving that same day. Six hundred British troops, six hundred additional Russians, and small numbers of Germans, Italians, and Japanese followed the railroad tracks from Tangku. The next day, the allied force, now more than 2,000 men, advanced again toward Tientsin. Butler and the American marines were hardly recovered from their ordeal of the day before. Butler said: "Half-blinded by a terrific North China dust storm, we plugged on. I had a howling toothache. I also had barber's itch, aggravated by the sand particles which lashed across my face like scorpions. I felt like hell. I sat down on the railroad track so damned tired that I didn't care how many Boxers shot me full of holes. A good-natured Russian soldier insisted on pulling off my shoes and greasing my feet with bacon fat. The heels were rubbed raw."[12]

Dinner that night for Butler and his American platoon was a chicken "which had walked entirely too far in its life." Butler chewed on a drumstick while British officers one hundred yards away enjoyed a banquet served on white tablecloths with proper silver and linen napkins. At bedtime the marines retired to a cluster of filthy mud huts along the railroad. At 2:30 A.M. on June 23 Major Waller woke them up to begin the day and the hungry, bedbug-infested marines joined their well-rested British colleagues and other allies for the march on Tientsin.

The Chinese soldiers and Boxers who had repulsed the Americans and Russians two days before had disappeared except for a few snipers. About noon the American marines were across the river from the foreign settlement of Tientsin. The river was jammed with logs. They used the logs to fashion a makeshift pontoon bridge, crossed the river, and marched unopposed into the settlement. One of the besieged residents met them with bottles of beer. The marines broke off the top of the bottles with their bayonets, drank the beer, cleaned up a bit, unfurled their American flag, and marched down Victoria Road through the British settlement. Hoover watched the approach of the marines from the roof of a warehouse and he said, "I do not remember a more satisfying musical performance than the bugles of the American Marines entering the settlement playing 'There'll Be a Hot Time in the Old Town Tonight.'"[13]

"I've marched in many parades since then," Butler said. "I've heard crowds cheer in a way to set marine blood a-tingling. But the whole-hearted enthusiasm of our Tientsin reception has never been equaled."[14] The marines were billeted in a godown filled with cotton and rice. Butler, still a growing boy, raced off to Watson's store and bought all the jam he could carry and stuffed himself with hardtack and jam and settled down for a good sleep. The siege of Tientsin was relieved — temporarily.

* * *

The Hoovers were busy. Herbert, in addition to supervising a crew of Chinese strengthening the defenses of the foreign settlement, took on the task of providing drinking water to the besieged. A municipal waterworks was just outside the barricaded area and Hoover, with a guard of British sailors, ventured outside the lines each evening to purify water in the boilers of the plant. In the morning he transported the boiled water back to the settlement in municipal street-sprinkling carts. A canal ran by the waterworks and Boxer corpses floated on the water near the intake for the boilers. The British guard, recalling the British beef bouillon named Boveril, christened the purified water — they claimed it was flavored by decomposing bodies— as Boxeril.

Hoover also took responsibility for the care and feeding of six hundred Chinese who had taken refuge in the compound of the mining company which employed him. These were Chinese with close ties to foreigners who were not willing to risk execution at the hands of Boxers. Among them was Hoover's Chinese boss. Hoover distributed rice and purified water every morning to the Chinese.

However, hysteria among the besieged foreigners mounted as the Chinese attack intensified.

The panicky foreigners feared an enemy from within, and some believed that Hoover's Chinese were communicating with the enemy outside the barricades by means of pigeons with whistles tied to their tails. The rumor was also spread that some of the stray bullets flying around the settlement were fired by Chinese within the settlement. Hoover was sitting down to dinner one day, totally exhausted after a hard day's work, when a messenger came and told him that all six hundred Chinese living at the mining company headquarters had been arrested and were being tried, sentenced, and executed by Captain Bayly, a British bulldog who regularly ran afoul of Americans and all other civilians. Hoover rushed to the site on his bicycle "to find a so-called trial going on under torch-lights with Bailey [sic] a pompous judge and various hysterical wharf-rats testifying to things that could never have taken place."[15] Several of the Chinese had already been executed. Hoover tried to stop the trials, but Bayly ordered him to leave. He jumped on his bicycle and rode to Russian headquarters to find Colonel Wogack. Wogack and a platoon of Russian soldiers returned to the scene with Hoover and persuaded the British captain to stop the drumhead trials. Hoover and other like-minded foreigners were later able to secure the release of the Chinese.

Hoover's protection of the Chinese earned him the antipathy of many of his countrymen. He also came to the assistance of Chinese on another occasion. One evening, a big shell exploded in the compound across the street, the home of an American educated Chinese, Tung Shaoyi. Hoover and one of his American engineers rushed to the scene. Tung's wife and a baby were dead, but the men gathered up several surviving children, and carried and led them from the wreckage to the safety of the Hoover house. This story has an interesting postscript. "Some eighteen years afterward, when I was War Food Administrator in Washington, Mrs. Hoover and I received an invitation to dine at the Chinese legation. While I was taking the Minister's wife out to the dining room, Mrs. Koo said in perfect English, "I have met you before. I am Tung Shaoyi's daughter whom you carried across the street during the siege of Tientsin.""[16]

Lou Hoover worked as hard as her husband. She managed the dairy herd, with the help of two foreigners and several Chinese women. She worked in the understaffed hospital — two doctors and one nurse — and spent long hours there, commuting by bicycle and riding close to the walls of buildings to avoid bullets. One day, a rifle bullet punctured a tire on her bicycle. She carried a revolver and was dubbed the "Captain of the Guard," because every day on returning from the hospital she organized the night watch for the compound where the Hoovers lived. She stood watch herself. Many of the foreign women and men in Tientsin were not so bold and enterprising. About three hundred lived in the basement of Gordon Hall.

The Hoovers were not the only foreigners in Tientsin who took on the problems of helping the Chinese survive. Edmund Cousins, the agent for Jardine, Matheson & Company, took in all the Chinese Christians in the city and fed them for two weeks. "When some one told him it would hurt his business he said, 'My business is to care for God's people.' ... He even took milk around to the babies and several have kept the condensed milk tins as souvenirs of his personal kindness. He welcomed all missionaries to his private table and made the siege for us a pleasant memory in many respects."[17]

* * *

As Smedley Butler and the allied force advanced on Tientsin from the coast, Admiral Seymour was at Yangtsun eighteen miles up the rail line from Tientsin, contemplating a downed bridge over the Pei River. His trains were as useless as beached ships. He was unable to retreat to Tientsin by rail. The downed bridge prevented that. An advance to Peking by rail was also impossible. The railroad was torn up. He was surrounded by more thousands of fanatic Boxers than he had bullets. Most recently, and most seriously, the Chinese army had attacked his multi-national force and inflicted serious casualties on him. Seymour ordered a retreat to Tientsin.

Common sense seemed to dictate that the sailors of the expedition cross the Pei River on boats and walk eighteen miles back to Tientsin following the railroad track, the shortest and most direct route. However, Seymour and his officers and men were sailors, unaccustomed to fighting on land. Walking was an unfamiliar form of transportation and they had the added complication of transporting more than fifty wounded men. Seymour decided, therefore, to follow the thirty-mile winding course of the river to Tientsin.[18] It was an odd decision by the sailors to take a long route along a heavily populated riverbank when they could have followed the railroad through open country.

Seymour and his commanders made their plans with a distant background rumble of Chinese artillery pounding the settlements of Tientsin. All northern China was in eruption and Seymour's 2,000 men, a powerful force only a week ago, now seemed more like a pitiful band of lost sailors. Seymour confiscated four junks and several sampans to carry his wounded and began his retreat at four P.M. on June 19. The sailors quickly discovered differences between navigating a ship at sea and a junk in a river. They frequently ran the boats aground in the narrow, winding, gray river and, in five hours of travel on the first day, the foreign troops and Chinese boats advanced only three miles.[19] In addition to the men's unfamiliarity with navigating Chinese rivers, villages every half-mile along the river concealed groups of Boxers and, approaching each, the advance guard had to deploy, form a firing line, and advance to clear the village.

On June 20, the flotilla continued down the river and the sailors spent the day on land overrunning and burning one Boxer-infested village after another. June 21 was an even heavier day of fighting. Two Americans were killed, the American Captain McCalla was struck by a spent bullet, and Seymour's chief of staff, John Jellicoe, was wounded. Jellicoe had been rallying British and French sailors to advance on a village when he was hit in the left side of the chest, the shot turning him half around. "I thought my left arm was gone," he wrote later. A British gunner helped him to shelter and cut away his uniform around the wound. The doctor came to bandage the wound and told Jellicoe he would die. Jellicoe wrote a will on a piece of paper and gave it to a sailor. The chaplain came along shortly afterwards to give solace to Jellicoe during his last few minutes of life. Jellicoe confounded them all by living and even continued to write in his diary.[20]

Captain Bowman McCalla, pugnacious by nature, was the American hero of the retreat. The American sailors ate their last ration on June 21. Thereafter, they lived off chickens and vegetables rounded up in captured villages, and, on one occasion, a soup made of mule bones. McCalla was always near the front of his advancing column, mounted on his white mule and urging his men forward. "We must push on, we must push on," was his constant advice to the more leisurely British and Europeans.[21] A bullet passed through his hat, another hit his sword scabbard, and a piece of shrapnel struck his foot.

By the afternoon of June 22, Seymour's expedition was at the point of collapse. Ammunition was down to less than 10 rounds per man—except for the Americans who customarily packed plenty of ammunition. "There was no thought of surrender," said Lieutenant Wurtzbaugh of the U.S. Navy; "the intention was to fight to the last with the bayonet."[22] It might have come to that on June 23 except that Seymour had a stroke of luck. His men discovered a Chinese fort just across the river from them. This was the Hsiku arsenal and the Chinese army—which had thousands of troops in the vicinity—made the monumental blunder of leaving the arsenal poorly defended. Seymour ordered an assault on the arsenal and, after a short, bloody fight, the Chinese defenders fled.[23]

The arsenal was the answer to every soldier's prayer. "Here was enough artillery for an army. There were stacks and stacks of modern rifles—Winchesters, Mausers, and Manlichers; and hundreds of thousands of rounds of ammunition. There were field guns and siege guns by the score. There were magazines containing immense stocks of both black and smokeless powder.

That this place was so easily taken seemed a miracle. It was our salvation."[24] Not the least of the needed stores was rice and several vegetable gardens.

The Chinese perceived their error in losing the arsenal and attempted to dislodge the foreigners, keeping up a fierce bombardment. A dust storm added to the misery of both attacked and attacker. "Our spirits were not very high," said one of Seymour's British officers. "Every morning hurried burials with bullets flying over the common grave; every day renewed fears for our friends in Peking and Tientsin; every night the same forlorn expectation of a returning messenger who never came."[25] They were only six miles from the foreign settlements of Tientsin. Finally, on June 24, a Chinese servant got through to the settlements with a plea for rescue from the admiral.

The soldiers in Tientsin organized a relief expedition of two thousand men to rescue Seymour. Butler and his marine colleagues joined as did a contingent of British, including the dashing Commander Beatty who, arm in sling, rode a prancing white horse and defied the Chinese gunners' attempts to hit him. The relief column reached the arsenal, almost unopposed, at noon on June 25. Butler recalls his reception by Captain McCalla. After the greeting, the captain said, "'I have a sore back. Wonder what's the matter with it?' When we pulled up his coat and shirt, we discovered that he had been peppered with buckshot. Several pieces of lead were still sticking into him."[26]

The next day Seymour's wounded sailors were loaded into carts and the whole expedition walked to the foreign settlements. The Chinese did not contest their passage. The wife of the Anglican bishop, Mrs. Scott — who had fled Peking only to end up trapped in Tientsin — saw the troops coming in. "I shall never forget to my dying day, the long string of dusty travel-worn soldiers, who for a fortnight had been living on quarter rations, and fighting every day; officers almost unrecognizable with a fortnight's beard and layers of dust, but so glad to get back and have a handshake; while the men were met by kind ladies with *pails* of tea which the poor fellows drank as they had never drunk before — some bursting into tears— like children. Alas, the saddest part was the long line of stretchers with their poor motionless figures inside, which turned into the Hospital gate."[27]

For all the scorn called down on the Boxers and the Chinese Imperial Army, they had defeated a Western army. Seymour's retreat showed that allied armies could not march around China without consequence and that the Chinese were not to be taken lightly. Seymour's casualty list was sixty-two killed and 232 wounded. By nationality the casualties were:

	Killed	Wounded
British	27	97
German	12	62
Russian	10	27
American	4	28
French	1	12
Italian	5	3
Japanese	2	3
Austrian	1	0
Total	62	232[28]

Nobody knew any news from the legations in Peking. Seymour had been too busy saving his command to worry about them.

* * *

A chronicle of the march of armies does not describe the impact of the war on the rural population in warring areas. Foreign troops were careless in distinguishing between combatants and non-combatants. One observer said of the Russians, "Against Asiatics they are probably the most successful troops in the world, for they do not hesitate to apply in warfare the daring tactics and Tartar mobility of Genghis, or in pacification the 'root and branch' policy and merciless justice of Cromwell."[29]

The Chinese soldiers and Boxers were hardly any less brutal to their own people. The peasant had always been the victim of passing armies. The Boxers executed anyone who disagreed with them. One eye witness described the Pei River near Tientsin. "There were many corpses floating in the river. Some were without heads; others were missing limbs. The bodies of women often had their nipples cut off and their genitalia mutilated.... There were also bodies in the shallow areas by the banks, with flocks of crows pecking away at them. The smell was so bad we had to cover our noses the whole day. Still, no one came out to collect the bodies for burial. People said that they were all Christians who had been killed by the Boxers and the populace dared not get involved."[30]

The common people were in the crossfire, mistaken for combatants or shot for sport. The village women often drowned themselves to avoid falling into the hands of the foreign devils. Admiral Seymour himself recounted one incident. "We had just taken a village, when a Chinese woman threw herself into a well to escape.... The Germans saw this happen ... they fished the woman out alive; then [came] to ask me what to do with her. She was young and good-looking, but, of course, dripping wet and nearly dead with fright; but she had preferred death to captivity."[31] Her fate is not recorded.

The worst massacre of Chinese took place at the mouth of the Pei River. For days every military and civilian ship which entered the mouth of the river saw blue clad bodies floating out to sea with the tide. These were the remains of the three hundred Chinese employees of the Taku Tug and Lighter Company. In ordinary times, the Chinese workers lived on board an old ship anchored in the shallow waters off the river's mouth. Their job was to unload cargo from large ships into lighters. After the fall of the Taku forts, the Chinese workers had no ships to unload and they decided to go ashore. Unfortunately, they steered too close to a Russian-occupied fort. The Russians opened fire, sank the ship, and kept on firing until all three hundred of the Chinese were dead.[32]

The journalists who followed the soldiers described the ravages of war. Alfred Henry Savage Landor was one of them, a representative figure of the eccentric and not altogether scrupulous British who wrote fat, luxurious volumes of their exotic adventures.

> The trip up the Pei river was at no time a pleasant one between the uninteresting, flat, muddy banks, something in colour between a ghastly raw sienna and a dirty gray. To the lack of beauty in the scenery was now added the profusion of dead bodies, swollen to double their normal proportions, and in a state of advanced decomposition, which were floating down the river or had stuck in the mud close to the banks. Dogs were tearing away at them, fighting among themselves over the human meal. It was not a pretty sight, and made some people quite sick....
>
> All the way up to Tientsin one saw squads of Cossacks riding their ponies with characteristic long-stirruped saddles, and they seemed to take special delight in setting villages on fire.... As we steamed up the river, high columns of black smoke rose everywhere, on the right bank of the stream especially, whole villages flaring up, set in flames by the Chinese or the Allies. It was a sight of heartbreaking desolation.[33]

George Lynch, another British journalist, traveled from Tangku to Tientsin by train. "Here one got the first touch of that feeling which intensified as we advanced — a palpable breath of blasting desolation that seemed to have passed over the land. It was a strange feeling passing through what had evidently been a densely populated country, but that was now the scene of tenantless houses, often roofless, frequently with charred walls, empty doors and windows, that gave them a skull-like appearance to the imagination."[34]

1900 was a very hard year for the residents of northern China. The invading foreigners saw no reason to observe any laws or customs of war in dealing with heathens. Take no prisoners was the rule; shoot first and ask questions later was the practice.

10

A Tour of the Defenses

Early in the siege 23-year-old ne'er do well Bertram Lenox Simpson toured the front lines of the Legation Quarter. He began at the British Legation, the northwest corner of the defense. To its west was the Imperial Carriage Park, a large, open, grassy area; to the north was the Hanlin Academy, now reduced to ashes. In those directions the defenders of the legation faced burned and open ground giving them good fields of fire and visibility.

Simpson, moving clockwise, crept out of the British Legation through a gap in the wall and crossed the stinking canal, shielded behind a low, hastily-constructed barricade. He passed through another gap cut in a fifteen-foot-high wall and into the *Fu*, the northeast corner of the defense. The *Fu* was a nightmare, one thousand feet north to south and seven hundred feet east to west, filled with courtyards, large and small buildings, pavilions, gazebos, statuary, artificial lakes and hills, manicured gardens, large trees, and all broken into squares by walls.

The *Fu* was the domain of the Japanese Lt. Col. Goro Shiba. Here, amidst the tile roofs of a Chinese palace, Simpson was close enough to Chinese soldiers to hear them talking. Peering through a loophole, he saw bricks moving fifty or sixty yards away as the Chinese, under cover, built barricades "gradually surrounding us in a vise which may yet crush us to death." Shiba's little army to defend the *Fu* consisted of twenty-five Japanese sailors plus 26 Japanese volunteers and 26 Chinese Christians for a total of seventy-seven effectives, although casualties were heavy and the number of men available for duty never approached that total.[1] The Japanese held a thousand feet of the defense lines, their meager numbers divided into widely-spaced posts of three or four men. Japanese soldiers were on duty two hours, followed by four hours rest, day and night. The Japanese were "plucky little fellows"—the most disciplined, best humored, and most efficient of all the legation guards.[2] The Japanese, having begun to emulate the West and modernize their feudal country only thirty years before, had learned many of the virtues of the Christian countries; without yet having adopted many of the vices.

Shiba controlled the defense with a map decorated with green, blue, and red spots, constantly updated to show the distribution of his forces and their strength and fighting abilities. Simpson said, "I could not tear myself away from this quarter. It was so orderly."[3] Colonel Shiba was, along with Frank Gamewell, the indispensable man in the siege. "One felt the better of it for the rest of the day after meeting Colonel Shiba," said one woman.[4] He was 41 years old, the son of a samurai, and had many years experience in China.[5]

The Japanese fought in nerve-wracking close quarters. All day long, they played a game of wits with Chinese riflemen a few yards away. The Japanese drew the fire of the Chinese toward an empty loophole or section of the wall, located the source of the firing, and then a Japanese rifleman popped up above the barricade for an instant and snapped off a shot at the Chinese. As marksmen, however, the Japanese were indifferent. Despite the skill of the defense, the Japanese were being forced to give way. The Chinese advanced with extreme care, zigzagging barricades across open areas, bringing men ever closer to the Japanese lines until, finally, with their soldiers only a few feet apart, Chinese numbers would prevail.

Beyond the Japanese positions was the Italian sector of the *Fu* commanded by Lt. Paolini, whose legation had been burned and abandoned. Simpson found Paolini sitting behind a little hillock eating bread and bologna while bullets clipped leaves off trees above his head. Paolini was a brave man, in the estimation of Simpson, but, in contrast to the active Japanese defense, his sailors were "lying comfortably on their stomachs completely out of sight, and wildly volleying far too often." Their ammunition was running low. Simpson's reflection on the Italians reflected customary British opinions. The Japanese were admired as plucky and competent; the Continentals were considered lazy and lacking in courage; the Russians were savages; Americans had the virtues of being good shots and speaking English, but were unreliable and undisciplined.

Two thousand Chinese Christians collected in the ornamental gardens surrounding the artificial lakes behind the Japanese and Italian defense lines in the *Fu*. The able bodied men among them were conscripted for barricade building and the daytime population of the *Fu* was the very young and the very old. The schoolgirls were "sitting on the ground in their sober blue coats and trousers, peacefully combing each other's hair, or working on sandbags." Japanese civilians circulated among the Chinese handing out little knick-knacks to the children, meticulously keeping records, and organizing work gangs. Contrary to their later history as brutal conquerors, the Japanese were almost unanimously benign, sensible, and practical during the siege, the best behaved and disciplined of all the foreigners.

From the Italian position, Simpson threaded his way through alleyways and past "precariously feeble" French and Austrian positions. Here, over several hundred feet of convoluted, smoldering urban terrain the most desperate fighting of the early days of the siege took place. The French and Austrians lost half a dozen men, due, in Simpson's view, to an excess of élan and an absence of common sense. The French Legation was the center of the defense, held by 78 French and Austrians and nineteen volunteers, although like the Japanese the numbers available for duty were quickly reduced by casualties. The most critical post was the barricade across Legation Street facing east toward the Hata Gate. The Chinese lines were only fifty feet from the French barricades and, 20 feet away, houses sheltered Chinese arsonists and snipers. In the French sector, Simpson moved slowly, very slowly, never exposing as much as an elbow. The Chinese were advancing, a brick at a time, building walls toward the French lines. The French also feared that Chinese sappers were digging tunnels beneath their positions. Lt. Darcy, the French commander, doubted that the French and Austrians could hold their positions in the face of a determined Chinese rush forward.

Among the volunteers serving at the French Legation was Dr. Arthur von Rosthorn, an Austrian diplomat, who with his wife occupied a room in the battered legation compound. Paula von Rosthorn, Annie Chamot, and Mme. d'Arc (whose first name is unknown: Joan, perhaps?) at the Peking Hotel were the only women who passed the siege outside the relative safety of the British Legation.

The Germans were next. Their lines ran from their legation southward to the top of the Tartar Wall. Of all the defenses, the Tartar Wall was most crucial to hold, for it loomed up over the quarter, forty feet from ground to parapet, forty feet wide on top. If the Chinese could capture the wall, they would dominate the Legation Quarter. The Germans did not welcome visitors to their defense lines and mixed little with the other foreign soldiers. They seemed to suffer from that famous German paranoia. Their minister had been killed; everyone was at fault; nobody could be trusted. For all the vaunted German military expertise, Simpson thought their lines on the Tartar Wall were "indifferently barricaded." The German mood was angry and "dangerous for everyone" and their men "recklessly desperate," taking unnecessary risks and casualties.[6]

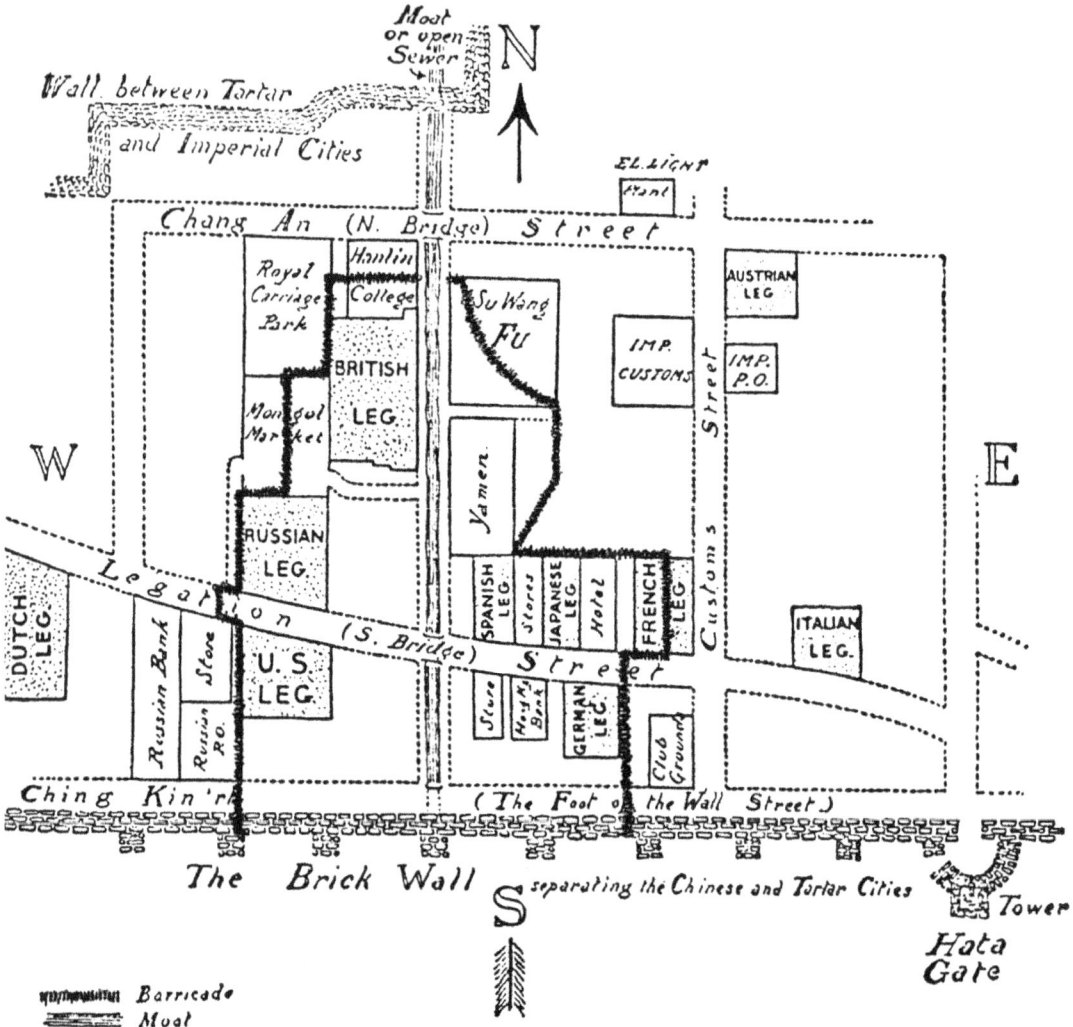

PLAN OF THE BESIEGED LEGATION QUARTER.

The Defenses of the Legation Quarter. Four hundred foreign soldiers and one hundred and fifty civilian volunteers held off the Chinese army and the Boxers with walls and barricades encircling most of the Legation Quarter. Most civilians took refuge in the British Legation but Auguste and Annie Chamot and their friends remained in the Peking Hotel (Mateer, *Siege Days*, 1903).

The Germans on the Tartar Wall faced the Hata Gate, six hundred yards down the wall to the east. They received cannon fire from the towers over the gate. A three-inch Krupp gun was firing this morning at the Germans, but the Chinese were firing too high and the shells passed overhead and landed in the Imperial City beyond the Legation Quarter. Four hundred yards behind the German positions on the wall, Simpson saw American marines in their distinctive slouch hats and khaki uniforms lying on the ground and facing the enemy's fire from the other direction.

To get from the German to the American position on the wall required a complex and dangerous journey. A simple walk on top of the wall was suicidal. Instead, Simpson edged down a ramp from the wall, passed through the German Legation, crossed Legation Street into the French lines, and went through a hole in the back wall of the French Legation into the compound of the Peking Hotel. Auguste and Annie Chamot, Mme. d'Arc, and a group of well-to-do guests endured the siege at the hotel comfortably, if one could ignore the constant pounding of artillery striking the upper floor and rifle bullets ricocheting through the halls.[7]

Like Gamewell and Shiba, Chamot thrived in the difficult conditions of the siege. "This fellow C[hamot] is an original, who knows how to make his Chinese slave with the greatest industry and sets them an admirable example himself.... Everyone is at work quite peacefully, milling wheat, washing rice, slaughtering animals, barricading windows—doing everything in fact at once."[8] Chamot kept a bakery going throughout the siege and delivered the loaves every morning, rain or shine, shell and shot falling all around the cart, to customers in the British Legation and to the Chinese in the *Fu*. His guests were a lively group of Belgian and French civilians who ate well and drank deeply from the hotel's excellent wine cellar. Amidst the gaiety and imbibing was always the thought that a thin line of French and Austrian sailors a few dozen yards away might break at any moment and a horde of Chinese overrun the hotel. The hotel had its own roster of military watches, and Annie Chamot stood guard along with the men.

The careful walk west on Legation Street from the Peking Hotel to the Russian and American legations was through a wasteland of abandoned shops and homes that, as time went on, were honeycombed by Chinese artillery fire. After a dangerous, unshielded crossing of the canal bisecting the Legation Quarter, Simpson reached the Russian barricades. A V-shaped Russian barricade blocked Legation Street. Simpson commented that the Russian and American legations were thoroughly barricaded and sandbagged; but the Russians at the barricade were idle, most of the soldiers sleeping while one stood guard. Bullets had been few at this corner of the defense. The main threat was fire. The Russians had the foresight to clear many of the houses near their legation before the siege. On June 23, the Chinese had fired the Russo-Chinese Bank just down the street, burning up $80,000 in cash that someone had left behind when the bank was abandoned. From the Russian and American legations to the Chien Gate, five hundred yards to the west, the homes and shops of the city were smoldering ruins.

Simpson reached the American position on the Tartar Wall by climbing one of the twin ramps leading to the top. The marines were mutinously silent, lying behind their barricades and peering down the wall at the Chinese gun emplacements at the burned ruin of the tower of the Chien Gate. The marines did not like it on the wall, isolated from the rest of the world, under fire from all four directions, out of touch with what was going on. They were angry that people were living in safety at the British Legation while they lay in the hot sun every day. Everyone, they said, every able-bodied man, should take his turn at the defenses.

The Americans were the best shots of all the foreign troops. Their marksmen were called upon to root out troublesome snipers. Sir Robert Hart said that "the Americans were stronger and more mature [than the British], each man a sharpshooter, self-reliant and resourceful."[9] Unlike the other nationalities, most of the Americans had combat experience in a nasty war in the Philippines—but they were also Americans. The old-school British found their discipline deplorable. "The lack of discipline among these Americans is astounding."[10] They showed no respect for their betters—even Sir Claude MacDonald was not immune to their profane, abusive barking and growling. They drank on duty and they got in drunken brawls with the Russian soldiers with whom when sober they were on the best of terms. The Americans seemed always in a state of near panic, forecasting disaster and raining down maledictions from their perch above the Legation Quarter. "Curious people these Americans!" said one British language student. "The American captain kept on sending in messages to the effect that the barricade on the wall was untenable. However, they still managed to hold out."[11]

The marines, in Simpson's view, had a disastrous habit of abandoning their positions on the slightest pretext. He tells of a council of war on June 24 called by MacDonald and composed of all the officers commanding detachments to deal with the American complaints. MacDonald himself did not attend — apparently wishing to avoid the indignity of being a target of American brickbats. The consensus opinion of the officers was that the American position was "well fortified, easy to retain, and absolutely essential to hold."[12] The Americans were shamed into a more reliable performance.

A command problem plagued the marines. Three officers and fifty-three enlisted men were in the contingent. One of the officers was a naval surgeon, Dr. Lippett; the two combat officers were Captains John T. Myers and Newt H. Hall. Myers was a dashing officer from Georgia, the son of the quartermaster general of the Confederate Army and a poet of scurrilous verse. He boasted a splendid and bushy mustache. Newt Hall was a Texan, dour and sour, little inclined to pay attention to the suggestions of civilians and the chatter of the diplomats. Moreover, he lacked the dash and spirit of an inspirational military leader. Hall remained in the legation supervising the less hazardous posts of the marines while Myers spent day after day on the wall. The most eloquent testimony about Hall is the silence about him in the accounts of the siege. Myers is praised, other marines are praised; Hall is barely mentioned — and then frequently in the negative. "They say ... there is internal trouble in the American contingent and that one of the officers is hated."

Simpson, however, said that the Americans had superior intelligence and were unrivaled as sharpshooters. "You only have to see these mutinous marines at work for five minutes as snipers to be convinced of that."[13] The greatest danger to the marines were snipers who looked for an exposed arm or leg or an eye peering out of a three-inch square loophole. They learned to use mirrors as periscopes to see out a loophole without exposing themselves. In the tradition of American squirrel hunters, they worked in pairs to pot Chinese snipers, one man with binoculars, the other with a rifle.[14]

Simpson completed his circular tour by climbing down the ramp, going through the American Legation and across Legation Street behind the Russian barricade. The barricade across Legation Street was eight feet thick — three feet of bricks and rubble and five feet of earth — designed to withstand cannon fire.[15] Simpson passed through the Russian Legation, and back into the British Legation through a hole cut in the wall. He was much depressed at what he had seen: the undermanned barricades, the lack of cooperation among the different nationalities, and the inequity of the burden of defense.

The British Legation was the most heavily fortified and defended part of the defense. Respect for the quality of the British was not universal. Arthur Smith said that both officers and men were "young and without the smallest experience of the kind of warfare in which they were now to engage."[16] A look at the royal marines enabled one "to comprehend something of the reasons for the [British] disasters in the contemporary South African campaign." Sir Robert Hart was more discreet in his appraisal. "The British Marines were nice-looking lads, cheerful and bright, and always ready and willing."[17] With their own legation not under heavy attack after the attempts to burn them out early in the siege, the British functioned as a mobile reserve and strike force to assist other nationalities under more pressure than their own.

Gamewell constructed several strong points on the west and north walls of the legation. He barricaded Fort Cockburn with walls seven feet thick and 12 feet tall with a gun platform embedded near the top of the barricade. Despite the doubts of many military officers, Gamewell had absolute authority to build the fortifications he deemed necessary — and those were invariably very strong. High walls kept the civilians in the legation mostly safe, although the Chinese peppered the second stories and roofs of buildings with bullets and cannon shot. The 82 British marines were augmented by 92 volunteers, one half of them British, the other half of many nationalities, including three Americans: the missionaries Will Ament and Bill Stelle and the excitable Dr. Robert Coltman.[18] Five American missionaries, including Frank Gamewell, and one British missionary, Joseph Stonehouse, comprised the Fighting Parsons of the fortification staff.

The volunteers stood guard and fought alongside the legation guards as common soldiers. A British army officer, Captain F. G. Poole, who had been living in Peking to study Chinese, took charge of the volunteers. The best were often sent to the *Fu* or the Tartar Wall to reinforce the Japanese and Americans, the less capable stood guard in the legation. All the volunteers not on duty assembled at the Bell Tower when the alarm was sounded, which often happened several times a day.

Morrison made sardonic remarks about the quality of some of the volunteers.

> There was also an irregular force of 50 gentlemen of many nationalities, who did garrison guard duty in the British Legation and were most useful. They were known, from the gentleman who enrolled them, as "Thornhill's Roughs," and they bore themselves as the legitimate successors on foot of Roosevelt's Roughriders. Armed with a variety of weapons, from an elephant rifle to the fusil de chasse with a picture of the Grand Prix, to all of which carving knives had been lashed as bayonets, they were known as the "Carving Knife Brigade." They were formidable alike to friend and foe. For, all unaccustomed as they were to the military art — the most experienced of them was he who had once witnessed the trooping of the color in St. James's Park — they had a habit of carrying the knife horizontally over the shoulder, so that when they swung quickly around the blade swept into the throat of the man behind.[19]

These, then, were the defenders of the Legation Quarter. They protected an irregular area of 50 acres, 1,500 feet east to west and nearly 2,000 feet north to south.[20] The outer perimeter of fortifications measured 2,176 yards — more than one mile — at the end of the siege.[21] The defenders were gathered into small groups at strong points, leaving long sections of the defense perimeter empty and vulnerable to a Chinese rush on the barricades.

The arms and ammunition of the defenders were as scarce as their numbers. Three machine guns and a popgun one-pound Italian cannon were their heaviest. Ammunition was limited. The Japanese marines arrived with only one hundred rounds per man; the Americans, the best supplied of all, had three hundred rounds per marine. Every nationality had different calibers of rifles and ammunition was not interchangeable. Arms and ammunition taken from dead Chinese soldiers were an important supplement to their diminishing supply. In the beginning some of the legation guards wasted ammunition with useless volleys, but as the siege went on they became adept at making every shot count. Sir Robert Hart said, "It was sometimes curious to note the silence and stillness of the Legation, not a shot replying to the furious fusillade kept up by the Chinese from their secure hiding-places on the neighboring roofs and behind the loopholes in their barricades."[22]

Simpson cited two major problems. First, none of the legation guards trusted the other nationalities to stand firm and not abandon their ground. The guards were always looking over their shoulders, afraid that the Chinese might break through some other sector of the defense and be on their backs with no warning. Secondly, Simpson commented on the inequity of the fighting. The British Legation was "full of able bodied men doing nothing — whereas on the outer lines of the other Legations many men are so dead with sleep that they can hardly sit awake two hours."[23]

* * *

Opposing the 550 soldiers and volunteers defending the Legation Quarter were the Kansu soldiers of Tung Fu-hsiang on the west and the forces of Dowager-friend Jung Lu on the east. The besieged believed that 10,000 Chinese soldiers and an indeterminate number of Boxers surrounded them. Certainly that number of soldiers was in and around Peking. But, the Boxers played little role in the assault on the legations — and, in fact, they were a fading movement. As Sir Claude had predicted they dissolved with the first good rains of the summer, leaving the reluctant Chinese army to face the foreigners.

Chinese artillery, which was moved around during the siege, consisted of four guns on the wall of the Imperial City near the British Legation, two pieces at the Chienmen, one at the Hatamen, and one at the foot of the ramp near the Hatamen. Some of these artillery pieces were old, firing solid shot; others were new Krupp guns—rifled, breech-loading, fast firing and accurate cannons made by the famous German armaments company in one-inch, two-inch, and 3-inch calibers.[24] The foreigners countered the short-range artillery and gingals with rifle sharpshooters who, with good success, picked off the gunners. The Krupp guns could be fired with less exposure and greater distances—but they fired high and most shells passed harmlessly over the Legation Quarter.

The religious found the survival of the foreigners in the legations a miracle. An American military officer writing of the siege after the fact stated, "I seek in vain some military reason for the failure of the Chinese to exterminate the foreigners."[25] Fortunately, coordination was not a word in the Chinese vocabulary. Two armies and a diminishing number of Boxer irregulars ringed the Legation Quarter and there seems to have been no cooperation among them at all. Missionary author Arthur Smith summed up Chinese military performance in Peking succinctly.

> There were occasions ... when it would have been easy by a strong, swift movement on the part of the numerous Chinese troops to have annihilated the whole body of foreigners ... but the opportunity was not seized ... though the attacks were fierce and murderous, the Chinese soldiers did not expose themselves. Upon unnumbered occasions, had they been ready to make a sacrifice of a few hundred lives, they could have extinguished the defense in an hour. Yet they lost five or ten times as many men by sharpshooting as they would have done in a rush. The artillery was badly served with poor shells, and the firing was inconstant and often wild ... when the siege was over countless new Krupp guns were discovered which might have been employed simultaneously with deadly effect. Some of them had never even been set up.[26]

Some speculated that the Chinese overestimated the number of defenders in the Legation Quarter, thus accounting for their caution. Yet the Chinese knew that the number of guards reaching the Legation Quarter numbered only four hundred and presumably they also knew by observing their arrival that the guards had little more equipment, guns, and ammunition than they could carry on their backs.[27]

* * *

The military situation on June 24, the fifth day of the siege, was far from bright. Twice, the civilians and soldiers at the British Legation had narrowly avoided being burned; the Japanese in the *Fu* were pushed back, and the Germans and Americans on the Tartar Wall had only a precarious hold on their critical perch. Moreover, for the first time, an artillery shell landed within the walls of the British Legation and caused a momentary panic.

The Chinese attacked in the *Fu*, their soldiers throwing fireballs of petroleum over the walls to set fire to the buildings. Soon, the main pavilion of the palace was burning. Fearing that the *Fu* would fall, all the Chinese Christians there were evacuated and resettled in empty houses between the British and Russian Legations.[28] Later, when the danger decreased, they were sent back. While the fire at the *Fu* was raging, the Chinese made their third attempt in three days to incinerate the British Legation. They set a house afire just outside the stable gate of the legation at its southwestern corner. The wooden gate caught fire and Chinese soldiers fired at the burning gate with small arms fire to discourage firefighters. "For a time," said Arthur Smith, "the danger was as great and the confusion even greater than yesterday" [when the Hanlin Academy was burned].[29] The Chinese also employed a new tactic of throwing hot bricks over the wall on the people fighting the fire. It was war at close quarters.

The British sortied to drive the Chinese further away. Two groups of marines, led by Captains Strouts and Halliday, led squads out of the legation grounds and attacked the Chinese from the rear, setting counter-fires to burn out the Chinese soldiers near the walls of the legation. During this sortie Captain Lewis Halliday, the best of the British officers, was wounded and narrowly survived, and he kept on surviving until 1965 — one of the last living combatants of the siege of the legations. Halliday led five marines outside the defense lines and, coming down an alley, his patrol ran into a group of five Boxers. The Boxers fired at point blank range, killing one enlisted man and hitting Halliday in his left shoulder, piercing a lung. Halliday fired back with his pistol and killed four of the Boxers. Only a misfire prevented him from killing the fifth, who quickly fled around a corner. Halliday made it back to the British Legation unassisted and was helped to the hospital. He was out of action for the remainder of the siege.[30]

* * *

An odd twist of Chinese policy came on June 25. At four in the afternoon, after a day of continuous rifle fire and shelling, trumpets sounded all up and down the lines of the Chinese troops ringing the Legation Quarter. The firing died away. In the sudden silence of a hot afternoon, a British guard reported that a man had posted a placard on the North Bridge across the canal bisecting the Legation Quarter. The sinologues in the British Legation rushed to the post with binoculars and telescopes and copied the message. Sir Robert Hart proclaimed that the message read: "In accordance with the Imperial Commands to protect the Ministers, firing will cease immediately and a despatch will be delivered at the Imperial canal-bridge."[31]

Something important was afoot. The ministers wrote a reply on a message board telling the Chinese that the dispatch would be received. However, no volunteer was found with the courage to take the reply to the North Bridge, three hundred yards from the fortified gate of the British Legation. Finally, a Chinese volunteered — or was volunteered. He was dressed up in top hat and tails, given a small white flag to wave in one hand and the message-board to carry in the other.

The Chinese messenger was not happy. He proceeded slowly down the road toward the North Bridge, encouraged by the shouts of his masters who were tucked in safely behind the barricades. When the messenger reached the North Bridge his diminishing supply of courage ran out. He tossed the message board down and dashed back to the legation. Nothing could induce him or anyone else to venture out and place the message in a position where it could be read.

What happened next is unclear. Several mandarins and soldiers appeared on the bridge with the apparent purpose of a parley with the foreigners. Somebody — the Italians and Japanese in the *Fu* were blamed — fired at them and they took flight. The Chinese made no further efforts to talk, although a few Chinese soldiers and foreigners — the American missionary Elwood Tewksbury among them — left their barricades and chatted amiably between the lines. For a few hours the Legation Quarter was in suspense, speculating on the meaning of the Chinese cease-fire. At midnight, the speculation ended. The Chinese opened fire, the siege resumed, and, whatever the purpose of the Chinese initiative, it became irrelevant.

This curious incident was an attempt by Jung Lu to communicate with the foreigners in the Legation Quarter. He later complained:

> After the death of the German Minister, the British Minister had Prince Su driven out of his palace and ordered thousands of Christian converts to live there. The various legations were united and daily fired their rifles and guns, killing innumerable officials and people.
>
> It was therefore impossible for the Headquarters Army and Tung Fu-hsiang's troops not to defend their positions and make counterattacks.... On June 25 I had a notice written in big characters saying that in accordance with the Imperial decree we will protect the legations, that shooting is forbidden, and that we should communicate with each other. [The Legations] not only paid no attention, but [opened fire].... The difficulty is that there is no way to communicate with [the foreigners].[32]

Jung Lu's statement should not be taken at face value. Like the Empress Dowager, he was covering his tracks, first, because he had no faith in the magic by which the Boxers promised to kill the foreigners and, secondly, he knew that the West would come to rescue its citizens in Peking. He anticipated a searing defeat and he wanted to limit the culpability of his country — and himself — as much as possible. So, he fought when he had to, and moderated the anti-foreign stance of the government when he could. The foreigners in the Legation Quarter gave him no help. The terrified, trigger-happy soldiers and civilians were so convinced of the nefarious designs of the Chinese that it was impossible to reach them.

* * *

That night, the temporary truce broken and the bullets flying over the Legation Quarter, Polly Condit-Smith told another of her stories about Sarah Pike Conger, the earnest Christian Scientist whose good-hearted but old-fashioned standards of morality tickled the sophisticated Miss Condit-Smith. In the midst of this furious fusillade Mrs. Conger came into Polly's room where she was lying on her mattress on the floor in her nightdress. Said Mrs. Conger, "Do you wish to be found undressed when the end comes?"

Polly, the niece of a justice of the Supreme Court, answered that "it made very little difference whether I was massacred in a pink silk dressing-gown ... or whether I was in a golf skirt and shirt waist that I was in the habit of wearing during the day hours of this charming picnic.... I had come to the conclusion that, as it was absolutely of no benefit to anyone my being dressed during these attacks, I was going to stay in bed unless something terrible happened, when I should don my dressing-gown and, with a pink bow of ribbon at my throat, await my massacre."[33]

Mrs. Conger was not amused.

* * *

Gunner's Mate Joseph Mitchell, U.S. Navy, like Frank Gamewell, was a tinker and a mechanic. In his spare hours between watches, Mitchell and a British sailor, Armorour's Mate J. T. Thomas, tried to build a cannon from brass piping lashed with copper wire. That project failed, but a Chinese worker rooting around in a shop on Legation Street found the barrel of an old cannon and brought it to Mitchell and Thomas.

The two sailors tied the gun barrel to a ricksha carriage. They recovered the Russian 9-pound shells thrown down a well at the beginning of the siege and refilled them with German powder. They rammed a bag of nails down the barrel and the rig was ready for a test. Mitchell, the co-inventor, had the honor of testing the cannon. He expected to die when he shot it, but "the result was magnificent; there was a deafening din, the gun turned head over heels, the ricksha wheels went to pieces, and the whole was mixed up in glorious confusion; but it had not burst."[34]

The test firing a success, the home-made cannon was refitted to a gun carriage owned by the Italians and a timber placed to control the recoil which sent the barrel backward about as far and fast as it launched the projectile forward. Dr. Emma Martin described shooting the cannon. Mitchell "lights the fuse and then runs to get out of the way. He risks his life every time he fires it off."[35] It was a rough looking thing but the next day, July 8, Mitchell fired a cannon ball at a post on the wall of the Imperial City. The shot demolished a troublesome part of the wall, sent up a cloud of brick and dust, and scattered the Chinese riflemen. "The noise of the explosion was so much greater than anything the Chinese had heard coming from our lines that five sentries incautiously put their heads above the Imperial Wall to ascertain what was going on, and were promptly shot down by our guards."[36]

The old gun had no sights and it took ten minutes to reload, but it could send a cannon ball through three house walls. The cannon was moved after nearly every shot, both to confuse the Chinese and to protect the shooter who had to expose himself to fire it. Even a hint of its

Betsy — the Homemade Cannon. American sailor Joseph Mitchell and British sailor J. T. Thomas built the cannon and were brave enough to fire it. It was also called "The International" due to the multi-national origin of its components (Smith, *Convulsion in China,* 1901).

appearance sent Chinese soldiers scurrying away from their barricades. Wonders were attributed to the cannon but sound and fury were probably its major impacts. The Chinese speculated: what other deadly weapons did the red-headed devils conceal behind their walls?

Mitchell's cannon was officially named "The International." It was an English barrel, tied to an Italian gun carriage with Chinese rope. It used Russian shells refilled with German powder and was fired by an American gunner using a Japanese fuse. The Americans called it "Betsy" and their name won out in the end. After the siege Minister Conger sent Betsy to the Smithsonian Institution in Washington.

* * *

There were two sieges in Peking, the much-storied siege of the legations and the lesser-known, but more grueling, siege of the Peitang, the North Cathedral of the Roman Catholic Church. Only three miles separated the Legation Quarter and the Peitang, but each fought its own little war of survival with no more communication than if they had been separated by an ocean.

To the Chinese the Peitang was the most hated symbol of the foreign barbarians in Peking. The cathedral was within the precincts of the Imperial City. Its three towers rose fifty feet above low Chinese houses, and, without doubt, their height interrupted the passage of *feng shui,* thereby angering the gods. The twenty-acre walled compound included the cathedral, palaces for the two bishops, Monsignors Favier and Jarlin, apartments for Marist fathers and nuns, a large orphanage — the Catholics adopted rather than converted most of their members — a school, museum, and a hospital, plus godowns, servants quarters, courtyards, guest quarters, pavilions, and gardens.

Bishop Favier had been among the first to call attention to the menace of the Boxers and to suggest that soldiers were needed to protect foreigners, the legations, the missionaries, and their converts. When legation guards arrived on May 31, Favier had persuaded the French minister to send a contingent of thirty French sailors and one officer, Ensign Paul Henry, to the Peitang to guard the cathedral and its residents. On June 5, the French marines were reinforced by eleven Italian sailors and one officer, Ensign Olivieri. The Peitang, thus, had forty-three guards to defend it — one-tenth of the number guarding the Legation Quarter.

When the Boxers burst into the Tartar City they burned the East, South, and West cathedrals on June 13, 14, and 15. The Catholic survivors took refuge in the Peitang and the Legation Quarter and Favier soon had to feed and protect 14 foreign priests, 14 foreign nuns, 43 French and Italian marines, and 3,420 Chinese Christians, of whom about 1,000 were men and the remainder women and children. The refugees in the Peitang had neither sufficient food nor arms. Favier summed up the situation. "At one pound per person per day, we have food for more than a month. As armament, we have forty rifles of the marines, seven or eight of all types in the hands of the Chinese, some miserable sabers, and 500 lances, or better said, 500 long poles tipped with iron. That is all. The perimeter we defend is exactly 1,360 meters."[37]

For the Peitang the siege began on June 15.

> At seven P.M. we hear the Boxers in the south, east, and the west. At 7:30 come their horrible cries. We are certain to be attacked. The sisters and all their children go to the cathedral to take refuge with 1,800 women and children already there. They are all panic-stricken.
>
> At 7:45 the Boxers arrive from the south. Their leader, on horseback, is a monk. Before him is an immense red flag, circled by young Boxers raising their incantations and dressed in red. They burn incense and make prostrations in the street and, then, advance in close ranks. The marines behind our great door allow them to approach to within 200 meters, and then fire heavy salvos into their ranks. Forty-seven of the so-called "invulnerables" fall and the rest are put to flight. The marines sortie out and capture 5 sabers and a lance.

On June 21, a Christian sneaked into the Peitang bearing a dramatic message from French Minister Pichon in the Legation Quarter. "The French Legation and other ministers have taken refuge in the British Legation. The minister of Germany is dead and his interpreter is wounded. The Austrian Legation is evacuated and in flames. The project to evacuate Peitang is abandoned. We prepare ourselves for the last extremity, but still we have hope." This would be the last message the Peitang would receive from the outside world for nearly two months.

The next day, at 6:30 in the morning, the Chinese Imperial Army opened fire with its cannons, the beginning of an artillery barrage at the Peitang which continued for many days. Five hundred and thirty shells were fired at the Peitang on June 22 and 360 were fired on June 23. The cross on the highest tower of the cathedral was blown away on June 25 "amidst the wild cries of delight 'Ho, ho, ho!' of the Boxers and soldiers outside."[38] The Chinese had assuaged *feng shui*. A hated foreign symbol was destroyed.

On June 27, a mob of Boxers, apparently believing that the artillery barrage had eliminated the Catholics' will to resist, advanced toward the main gate of the cathedral. One of them carried a huge red flag. The result was the same as their first attempt to storm the Peitang. The French and Italian marines opened fire, almost every shot leaving a Boxer dead or wounded; the survivors ran away, and the marines sallied into the street to collect the arms left behind by the fleeing Boxers. Chinese soldiers, sheltered behind walls, did not take part in the assault but directed a heavy, but inaccurate, fire at the foreigners. A few hours later, at 11 P.M., the Boxers were back and, under cover of darkness, crept up to the walls of the Peitang and hurled incendiary bombs and flaming spears. Water pumps, manned by Chinese Catholics, quickly doused the fires.

After the two failed attacks on the Peitang on June 15 and June 27, the Chinese kept their distance. The French and the Italian guards were able to hold off the Boxers and the Chinese army with an expenditure of one or two shots per rifle per day. In the first month of the siege only three foreign sailors were killed, casualties much lighter than at the Legation Quarter.

Bishop Favier and the Peitang. The Peitang (North Cathedral) was located within the Imperial City of Peking; 3,400 Chinese Christians took refuge within the cathedral and were protected by 43 French and Italian guards and a few priests and nuns under the leadership of the bishop (Savage Landor, *China and the Allies,* 1901).

At the Legation Quarter old veterans of war were amazed at their survival. "Had we been fighting such people as the Zulus or Dervishes," said one, "we should have been polished off in two or three days."[39] It is even more amazing that the Peitang survived. The Chinese could have sent a thousand soldiers forward to attack a sector of the Peitang defense guarded by fewer than a dozen French and Italian marines. But they preferred to wait, harass, starve the defenders out, and tunnel under them.

The great differences between the siege at the Peitang and the Legation Quarter were leadership, disease, and food. The Peitang had the undivided leadership of Bishop Favier. Smallpox broke out among the Chinese Catholics and for a time was killing them at the rate of fifteen per day. The epidemic was brought under control after more than one hundred children and many adults died. The defenders of the Peitang had little food. Monsignor Favier rationed his meager supplies, giving preference to the European soldiers. The Chinese ate dahlia and canna lily roots, day lily tubers from the flower gardens, and leaves from the trees, boiling all together into a gruel to augment the pittance that Favier gave them from his food stocks.

For the inhabitants of the isolated Peitang, the greatest threat to their survival would come late in the siege.

11

The Tartar Wall

A British diplomat came across a pamphlet written by Charles George Gordon for the Chinese during the military campaigns against the Taipings in the 1860s. Gordon acquired the moniker "Chinese" Gordon and later was called "Pasha" Gordon and, still later, he died in the siege of Khartoum and became Gordon of Khartoum, one of the great eccentric British heroes of the Victorian era. Gordon advised the Chinese how to conduct war. "He strongly recommended them never to show themselves in an open attack, but to gradually wear out their enemy by constant firing at night, so that the men could get no rest. It would be very interesting to know if it is in pursuance of this advice that the Chinese favor us with their erratic and annoying fusillades."[1]

The Chinese tried to wear down the enemy in the legations with sound and fury. They fired cannons, rifles, and antique gingals. (A gingal was a blunderbuss, ten feet long, requiring two men to operate, and firing a shell five inches long weighing about four ounces.)[2] Their marksmanship was atrocious. The Chinese rifleman rarely exposed himself to aim his rifle, but rather held it over the top of his barricade or wall, pointed it in the direction of the legations, and fired. The Chinese set off strings of firecrackers, blew trumpets and clanged gongs, shouted, blustered, and feinted. They aimed to keep the foreigners awake, alert, and on guard twenty-four hours a day and their fusillades killed eighteen legation guards during the first week of the siege. Moreover, the nightly serenade kept the inhabitants of the Legation Quarter in a state of anxiety. "From June 20 to July 17 we had daily and nightly attacks. Sometimes they lasted for three and four hours, and at other times only a half hour; sometimes on all sides, and again only on one side. The night attacks came between midnight and 2 A.M. Major Conger said some of them, for furious firing, exceeded anything he experienced in the Civil War. One night we had a terrible thunder shower, and all the time we had a furious general attack. The soldiers on the wall said it seemed as though all hell had broken loose."[3]

For all the noise of the fusillades, the greatest threat to the legations was a methodical Chinese advance toward their barricades. The Chinese built "movable barricades, behind which they would advance, dismantling, pushing forward and rebuilding." As the Chinese moved closer and closer, the threat became greater and the intensity of the attacks increased. Nigel Oliphant, one of the coolest of the defenders, could say on June 25, "We are by no means hard pressed yet." The next day he was less sanguine: "I think we shall be in a tight hole if the troops don't come in a week." By July 1 he was resigned. "Even now things seem to the most hopeful of us to be getting worse and worse, and it is hard to say what may happen. Of course, we never admit even to each other what we really think, far less to the women."[4] Morrison shared his pessimism. On June 28, he wrote, "Daily the cordon is drawing closer. Our two vital points are the City [Tartar] wall and the *Fu*. One third of the *Fu* has today become Chinese."[5]

Chinese artillery mostly made noise rather than causing damage. "One of the many mysteries of the siege was the ineffectiveness of the Chinese artillery. Usually the guns were over-elevated and most of the shells would whistle harmlessly over their targets. Barrages were seldom prolonged and rarely, if ever, followed up by a determined infantry assault."[6] One reason for the ineffectiveness of Chinese artillery was that, whenever it was put in forward positions, legation sharpshooters picked off the gun crews. Safer for the Chinese was to keep their big guns out of sniper range at the Chien Gate or behind the wall of the Imperial palace. Indecision marked the Chinese strategy. They never seem to have made up their minds whether they should kill the foreigners in the legations or not.

On June 24 Sir Robert Hart sent a Chinese courier with a message for his countrymen. The courier delivered the message in Tientsin on June 29. It read, "Foreign community besieged in the Legations. Situation desperate. MAKE HASTE!!"[7] This was the last the outside world was to hear from the legations for nearly a month.

* * *

Only belatedly did the Chinese and the foreigners realize that the Tartar Wall looming up out the back door of the American Legation was their key to victory—and survival. Captain Myers described the wall. "This solid structure was 45 feet high, 50 feet wide on the bottom, and 40 feet wide at the top.... On the top of this wall, on the sides were parapets, that outside being high and crenellated, and inside low. Every 100 yards a bastion juts out toward the Chinese city, the first houses of which are distant about 300 yards. On the inside two double ramps give access to the top of the wall, the one being directly in the rear of the United States Legation and the other in the rear of the German Legation."[8] The wall was crucial because it overlooked the Legation Quarter. If the Chinese occupied the wall, the American, German, and Russian Legations were little more than 100 yards away and could be rendered uninhabitable by riflemen and artillery firing down on them from above. The British Legation was 350 yards distant and the Chinese would be able to fire with impunity upon its inhabitants and make movement very hazardous. If the Chinese took the wall, the besieged might be bombarded into extinction. The foreigners had no avenue of retreat.

It was several days into the siege before the defenders took positions on the wall. During the first two days Chinese soldiers had full run of the wall, but they used it only to pass back and forth from the Hata to the Chien gates. Not until June 22 did the Germans establish a post on the wall at the top of the ramp behind their legation. On June 24, the Americans and the Germans made their claim to permanence on the wall—the Germans advancing east toward the Hata and west to the Chien gates to push the Chinese back.[9] That night top priority was given to strengthening the German position and establishing an American position on the wall. Under cover of darkness seventy Chinese Christians, supervised by diplomat Fleming Cheshire, began the work. Cheshire, who ate meals at the Squiers' table whenever he could, was one of Polly Condit-Smith's favorites. He christened himself "Major General of the Corpses." Among his duties on the wall every night were to dispose of dead Chinese soldiers. "The number of corpses that accumulate is astounding," he told Polly. Bodies were thrown off the wall into the Chinese city. No quarter was given. "On this, as on all other occasions no prisoners were taken, all the wounded being either bayoneted, or thrown over the city wall."[10]

The respective barricades of the Germans and Americans were separated by four hundred yards of empty wall swept by Chinese rifle and artillery fire. To walk down the wall from the German to the American posts was suicidal; bullets came from all directions. Chinese workers built barricades in front of and behind the American and German positions and at each edge of the wall to protect them from bullets and artillery. They lived in a box.

The Americans and the Germans were unhappy at their claustrophobic posts. They were isolated. All other guards had second lines of defense to which they could withdraw if hard pressed, plus relatively comfortable and safe rear areas to rest between duty tours at the barricades.

The wall had no second line of defenses or rear areas. Reinforcement or relief was difficult during the day because the access ramps to the top of the wall were under constant fire from Chinese snipers. The soldiers on the wall had no safe avenue of retreat. To reach their legations, they had to go down the exposed ramp, cross a road, and run through open areas, all the time coming under rifle fire from nearby houses. They were in danger of being cut off and isolated from their base without a source of food, water, and ammunition. The imaginative marines had plenty of time to conjure up just such a scenario. "Handsome Jack" Myers expressed his opinion in a penciled note written to Minister Edmund Conger. "It is slow sure death to remain here.... The men all feel that they are in a trap and simply await the hour of execution."[11]

Neither the Americans nor the Germans put all their forces on the wall. The Americans had also to guard their access route to and from the wall and prevent the American Legation from falling into the hands of the Chinese. Their usual deployment consisted of 15 men on the wall, six or seven in a trench connecting the wall with the American Legation, twenty resting within the legation, and seven or eight at a barricade across Legation Street. Each post was doubled — allowing one man to sleep while another stood watch except on the wall on which five posts of three men each were established.[12] The Russians, whose defense lines were relatively quiet, frequently helped out. Duty on the ground beneath the wall was not without hazards. On June 29, Naval Surgeon Lippett was wounded badly in the thigh while talking to Minister Conger in the American Legation. His place was taken by a missionary, Dr. George Lowry.

The threat of being trapped on the wall contributed to command problems among the American marines. The marine commander, Captain Myers was popular and conscientious and had a good relationship with Sir Claude MacDonald, the commander in chief. His second in command, Captain Newt Hall, was not popular and had strained relationships with MacDonald, Minister Conger, and First Secretary Herbert Squiers. Myers mostly stayed on the wall; Hall commanded the marines around the American Legation.

The fortifications on the wall took place none too soon. On June 27, the Chinese army made its first and last attempt to overrun the American defenses. Captain Myers reported:

> A sentry noticed that the Chinese were apparently breaching their barricades, then about 300 yards distant. The field glasses soon showed a number of Chinese issuing from the breach and running along the wall toward us. This movement was made in silence without firing, as they evidently hoped to catch us napping in the heat of the afternoon. We got ready for them and when they were some 100 yards away rose on the banquette and fired over the top of the barricade. They broke and ran back, and not until the last of them had squirmed and wiggled through the tall grass to the safety of their barricades was our fire returned. A few remained lying between the barricades, and their presence, dead, was very disagreeable.[13]

After the failure of their direct assault, Chinese tactics on the wall thereafter consisted of firing artillery at the British Legation from the Chien Gate, 700 yards away, while their soldiers inched forward at night, building barricades as they came until they were within brick-throwing distance of the Americans.

The most serious threat to the survival of the legations came June 30 on the Tartar Wall. The Legation Quarter had been drenched by the first heavy thunderstorm of the summer. As the rain died down and dawn broke, the Chinese shelled the German defense lines with a Krupp cannon. By the end of the day four German marines were dead and six men, four Germans and two English, wounded. The next morning eight Germans and three British soldiers on the wall were surprised by Chinese soldiers who sneaked up one of the ramps from the city below. The German corporal in charge of the barricades ordered a retreat and the soldiers fled down the adjoining ramp, abandoning their positions. The Chinese now occupied the German barricades.

Four hundred yards to the west, the American marines saw the Chinese climb over the barricades into the empty German positions. Captain Myers was in charge of the Americans and had been unrelieved on the wall for six days. The American marines had the opinion, expressed by Captain Newt Hall, that "the position is untenable," and they reacted as if it were. Myers and fifteen marines rushed down the ramp and took refuge in the American Legation.[14]

Suddenly, the Tartar Wall, the most critical line of the defense, was empty of legation guards. The Germans and the Americans had abandoned their posts. To dominate the wall, the Chinese had only to occupy the empty American barricades. It didn't happen. The Chinese soldiers who captured the German barricades belonged to Jung Lu. Their orders had been to drive the Germans from the wall and having done so, they rested. The Chinese soldiers facing the Americans were the Kansu troops of General Tung. They were hidden behind their barricades—probably sleeping after another night of noisemaking to keep the foreigners awake. They never noticed that the Americans had fled.

It was a disastrous turn. A quick conference was held at the British Legation. Conger ordered the Americans to retake their positions and MacDonald sent British and Russians to reinforce them. Captain Myers led a force of fourteen Americans, ten Russians, and ten British up the ramp and reoccupied the former American position without opposition. The Chinese soldiers a few yards away never knew that the American barricades had been empty for an hour. The Germans also tried to retake their barricade on the wall but failed, losing another man in the attempt.

The Americans had returned to the wall but they held only a few yards. The diplomats finally addressed their complaints about their exposed position. Their purchase must be both strengthened and expanded. The call went out for sandbags. Frank Gamewell was sick with fatigue and laryngitis but, voiceless, he organized a sandbag brigade. The missionaries cancelled church services that Sabbath.[15] Two thousand sandbags were needed plus Chinese workers and foreign supervisors. A ditch was dug across the road between the American Legation and the wall and a line of sandbags erected to protect the ditch. By walking in the ditch behind the sandbags a soldier could reach the wall without coming under fire. On the ramp itself Gamewell's crew erected zigzag barricades to reduce exposure to Chinese rifle fire from north, east, and west. Most of the work had to be done at night. The missionary Courtenay Fenn described building barricades on the wall at night.

> There was something very weird and awesome to the civilian in night work on the city wall. At times there would be a terrific and almost incessant fusillade for hours, rendering work even behind the barricades unsafe, and one could only crouch or lie in the best protected spots. At times, while we were at work strengthening the exposed side of the fortifications, protected only by the darkness, a magnificent rocket would suddenly shoot up from the Imperial Palace, brilliantly illuminating the entire city for a moment and forcing us to stand absolutely still, lest we become a visible mark for the sharpshooters.[16]

It was tense for the women who sewed sandbags all day and waited all night. One Chinese Christian was killed and six wounded working on the fortifications. "What a fearful Sabbath!" one woman said. "God keep us this night. Mr. [Arthur] Smith and three others went over to keep the Christians company at work all night building barricades with our men, bullets whistling around them. We are anxious for our men tonight."[17]

Mary Bainbridge, wife of the American diplomat, described an incident in the clash between the practical and the spiritual among the missionaries. One of the missionary women — it was probably Emma Smith, wife of Arthur — who Mary described as a religious fanatic and faith healer — said to several women sewing sandbags, "Now ladies, let us lay aside our work and go inside to have a few prayers. I think it will strengthen the courage of our boys on the wall." All of the sewing women went inside to pray except for Mary, and missionary wives, Katharine Lowry and Louisa Scott Killie.

Emma Smith asked them, "Come. Aren't you going in to pray?"

Chinese Barricades on the Tartar Wall. This photograph looks east toward the Hata Gate. The foreigners had to construct much stronger barricades to defend themselves from artillery (Savage Landor, *China and the Allies*, 1901).

Mary answered that she "could pray and sew at the same time and wouldn't give much for a person who could not, and that while bullets were flying over our heads by the thousand, that sand bags would be of more use just now in saving the lives of our boys on the wall in their awful position than prayers." Mary, Katharine, and Louisa continued sewing while the other missionary women prayed.[18]

The next day, July 1, Conger ordered an exhausted Captain Myers to turn over his command to Hall and leave the wall. Myers had been on the wall for a week and this prompted Conger's decision. However, in putting Hall in charge on the wall, Conger showed his lack of confidence in the captain. Conger told Hall that he would court-martial him "if you leave before you are absolutely driven out."[19]

The British expressed concern about the steadfastness of the American marines.[20] A British volunteer said, "The American Captain kept on sending in messages to the effect that the barricade on the wall was untenable. However, they still managed to hold out. Curious people these Americans!"[21] British doubts about the bravery of American and other nationalities were exaggerated. Suffice it to say in response that the British Legation guards suffered a lower rate of casualties during the siege than any other nationality and that their duty was the most agreeable, being mostly in the British Legation in which the comforts of hot meals, hospital facilities, and shelter were most readily available. In general, the British guards endured a lesser challenge and less strain than other nationalities, save the Russians. British officers and civilian volunteers, including the Australian journalist George Morrison, however, were to be among the boldest of the defenders. American civilians, mostly missionaries, distinguished themselves for efficiency and hard work rather than bravery under fire.

* * *

The Americans missionaries, fearing that the *Fu* would be lost, evacuated the Chinese Protestants, leaving the Catholics behind, and installed them in abandoned houses between the

British and Russian legations. For the rest of the siege most of the Protestants would remain outside the *Fu*, living in better conditions near the foreigners in the British Legation. The Chinese schoolgirls were relocated to one of the houses on June 29. Only one schoolgirl was killed during the siege. She was hit by pieces of a bursting artillery shell in the *Fu* and bled to death.[22] The principal danger to the girls was not Chinese bullets but Russian soldiers.

The Russian soldiers at the barricade across Legation Street soon discovered the school girls nearby, but several elderly Chinese men and women chaperoning the girls prevented the soldiers from entering the compound. The Russians conjured up a little drama to gain admittance. One night, in the midst of the usual fusillade from the Chinese, the Russians simulated a fierce battle and a noisy retreat — giving the impression that Boxers were pursuing them directly toward the house of the schoolgirls. The elderly Chinese chaperones fled in panic — as the Russians had hoped — leaving the girls unprotected. The Russians entered the compound, laid their guns aside, and prepared to slake their carnal desires with an abundance of young and innocent Chinese schoolgirls. But a patrol came over from the British Legation to investigate the strange events in that quarter and stopped the Russian orgy, before — or almost before — it began. Delicacy prevented an investigation into whether any of the girls had been raped.

The American missionaries were infuriated. The female missionaries in 1900 were advanced for their time, willing to assert that women — even Chinese girls — had the right to be considered something more than chattels to be bought, sold, and raped at will. There are intimations that this was not the only incident in the siege in which foreign men raped or attempted to rape Chinese Christian women. The Russians were blamed for most such incidents. Sir Claude posted a notice on the bell tower declaring the schoolgirls compound off-limits and warning of severe penalties for violators.

* * *

The most popular parlor game of the besieged was an endless debate about the day their rescuers would come. The only fact the foreigners knew was that the Taku forts had been attacked about June 17. Inferring that the foreign navies were successful at Taku, the time needed for an army of rescuers to advance to Peking was endlessly argued, and the consensus was that the earliest the relief force could arrive was June 28. When that day passed, the Americans became quite sure that foreign troops were to arrive in Peking to help celebrate the glorious day of independence, July 4.

The speculations concerning the day of deliverance were magnified by the appearance at night of strange lights in the sky which the defenders took to be the rockets and searchlights of advancing allied columns. The first sighting of mysterious lights came on June 24 when both American and German sentries reported rockets in the west. Two nights later the respected Colonel Shiba reported that he had seen a Japanese rocket in the north. On June 29, a sentry at the British Legation saw a "steady beam of light moving laterally in the south." It was surely a searchlight. The Anglican Roland Allen commented sardonically that, based on the different directions of the reported lights, it appeared "that the Allies were trying to take Peking as the Israelites took Jericho, by walking around it."[23]

On June 30, searchlight-seeing reached epidemic proportions. British marines said they had seen a searchlight only five or six miles away. After the searchlight was seen again the next night, they identified it with the Royal Navy ship, the *Terrible,* it being unexplained how a naval vessel was navigating its way across the north China plain. MacDonald thought the incident worthy of a bulletin he posted on the bell tower.

"Last night between 10 P.M. and 2 A.M. an electric flashlight was seen on south-east horizon; the appropriate distance is from twenty-five to thirty miles. The flashes were regular, and occurred at intervals of about a second, with a pause of from five to ten minutes between each forty or fifty flashes."[24] The desperate foreigners in the Legation Quarter grasped at far-fetched speculations and incorporated them into their fantasies. Had they not been able to conjure up hope from the most tenuous of favorable omens, they would never have been able to face one day after the other.

In the midst of the tension were amusing episodes. One day a Chinese civilian walked up to the gatehouse between the British Legation and the *Fu* and asked the foreign guards to change a dollar. The guards collected their coins in their pockets and were able to give him ninety cents for his dollar. He departed happily, to complete the business transaction in which he was engaged, apparently unconscious that a war was going on.[25]

* * *

The Chinese sensed victory on the wall. They had driven the Germans away. The American now had to defend themselves from attack in both directions. Moreover, the Americans, presumably Captain Myers, had made an amateurish error in placing their barricade on the wall. The ramps leading to the top of the Tartar Wall came in pairs, angled up like the arms of the letter A and thirty yards apart where they reached the top. The Americans had placed their fortifications at the top of one ramp and left the other one of the pair in Chinese hands. Thus, the Chinese could, at hazard, supply and reinforce their position from below.

A second error was even more serious. The Tartar Wall was strengthened at hundred-yard intervals by bastions extending out from the wall toward the Chinese city. The Americans had built their barricades across the width of the Wall at the edge of a protruding bastion, leaving the bastion itself outside their lines. By occupying the bastion, the Chinese could take a position from which they enfiladed the American barricades. They saw their opportunity and built a wall of brick "like the vicious tail of a scorpion" to control the bastion. At the end of their scorpion wall—a few yards from the American barricade—they constructed a tower to look over and dominate the American position. From their loopholes the American marines watched helplessly as Chinese soldiers built up the tower brick by brick. By the evening of July 2, it was fifteen feet high and eight or nine feet thick and so close to the American barricade that the Chinese threw stones from the tower into the American lines. Shortly, when the tower was raised a few more feet the Chinese would be able to look over and into the American lines. The Americans would have no choices but to die or retreat from the wall.

Captain Myers came back to the wall about seven P.M. that night to take charge after a day of rest. Apparently, Hall, disgruntled by the preemptory orders received from Conger, had not seen fit to inform anyone of this imminent and immediate threat. Myers immediately communicated the problem to Squiers and Conger who met with MacDonald.[26] They agreed that the Americans had to throw the Chinese back and take control of the bastion. Herbert Squiers devised a plan to oust the Chinese. Squiers—who had the dubious distinction of having been a cavalry officer at Wounded Knee ten years before—visualized that the Chinese, if attacked at night, would fire their rifles straight ahead into the darkness. A dash by foreign troops single file down the rims of the wall might be accomplished without loss and, once the foreigners climbed over the Chinese barricades, it would be a hand-to-hand fight at close quarters. The foreign soldiers with bayonets and pistols could win that fight.

Squiers ran to the foot of the Tartar Wall and shouted to Captain Myers. "Captain Myers," Squiers called, "is an assault on the Chinese barricade feasible?"

"I think not. We could not get over," was Myers' reply.

Squiers gave a quick summary of his plan. "If I explain to Sir Claude MacDonald and Major Conger and they approve, will you try it?" shouted Squiers.

A dubious Myers responded, "Yes, if I have orders."[27]

Squiers got approval from Conger and MacDonald and secured from MacDonald a heavy reinforcement of British and Russian marines for the attempt. Twenty-six British, fifteen Russians, and fifteen Americans would take part in the operation. Nigel Oliphant, a civilian volunteer, was one of the British participants. The jumping-off hour was set for two o'clock.

Myers, "cool headed and capable," called his men together and talked to them just before they assaulted the Chinese.[28] His speech and the reactions to it illustrated that British and Americans are truly two peoples separated by a common language. Oliphant said Myers made an interesting speech "because it was so utterly unlike what a British officer would have said under similar circumstances."[29] Rather than exuding confidence, Oliphant recalled, Myers began by saying they were about to embark on a desperate enterprise he had advised against. Orders being given, they must accomplish the mission or lose every man in the attempt. He described the plan to the men and then invited anyone who wished to back out. One of the American marines said he had a sore arm and begged off. The British "marines were by no means happy after Myers' gloomy speech, and showed no violent alacrity in lining up in the front rank of those who were to vault over the barricade."[30]

To the contrary, an American described Myers' speech as a "remarkable harrangue.... The Americans and English must have been moved beyond expression by this appeal."[31] W.A.P. Martin recorded the speech as inspirational. "Men, we must take that place at all costs or be driven off the wall! Once off the wall, the legations will lie at the mercy of the Chinese, and we, with all the women and children, will be butchered. This is our opportunity. I expect every man to do his duty. We cannot stop to pick up any who may be wounded until we return. If I fall, Sergeant Murphy of the British marines succeeds to command; if he falls Corporal Hunt of the American marines succeeds him. Now, when I give command, spring over the barricade, and follow me."[32]

The gloomy British, the inspired Americans, and the uncomprehending Russians followed Myers over the top of their barricade. Once over the top, Myers and the British ran down the south rim of the wall, to deal with the tower and the scorpion's tail leading to it. The Russians ran to along the north edge of the wall to the Chinese-controlled ramp. Myers found a small hole in the Chinese barricade and led his men through. He tripped over a Chinese spear and slashed his leg.

The Chinese fired through their loopholes at the empty American barricade as the Americans and British moved carefully behind the Chinese barricade in the dark. A bullet from nowhere killed Turner, the best marksman of the American marines, and Nigel Oliphant shot a Chinese soldier who had crept up within two yards of him. Inexplicably — a word that is always applicable to Chinese military strategy and tactics in 1900 — the tower was empty and the Americans and British simply crept down the back side of the barricade and potted Chinese as they went, bayoneting several who were sleeping in tents.

When the sleepy Chinese soldiers realized foreign troops were among them they broke and ran, taking refuge behind another barricade one hundred yards further west. The operation was over and a success. The British counted fifteen Chinese bodies; the Americans counted thirty-six. The truth was probably in between. Two American marines were killed, one British and one Russian were wounded. "Handsome Jack" Myers' wound appeared minor but he went down to the American Legation for treatment. The wound became infected and he caught typhoid fever and never returned to duty during the siege.

The Chinese barricade was now occupied by the Americans, British, and Russians. Captain Percy Smith, a retired British army officer visiting Peking when the siege began, took command temporarily. Forty Chinese workers were sent up to the top of the wall to reinforce the newly-won barricades.

The chroniclers of the siege are universal in extolling this event. "This was the most momentous and stirring episode of the siege," said an American.[33] Another said it was "a struggle ...

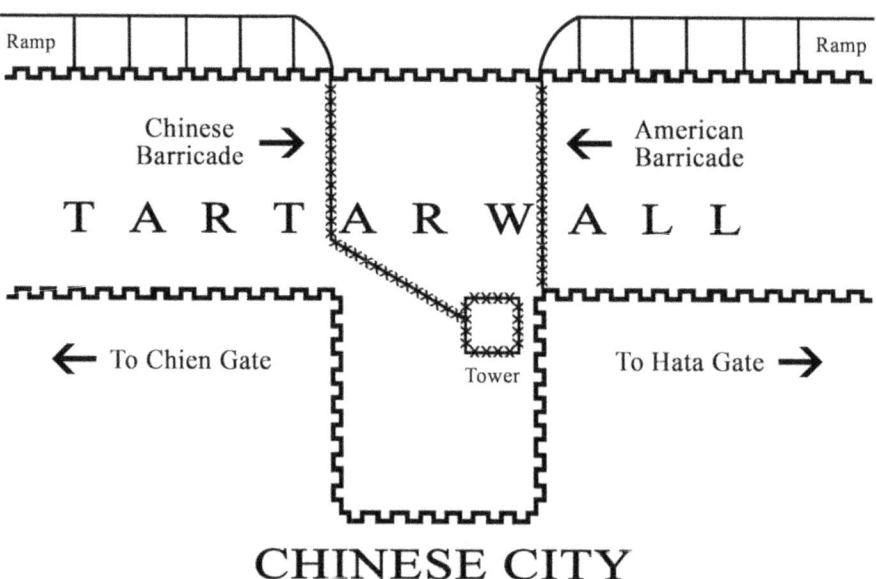

The Night Attack on the Tartar Wall — July 3. American Captain John T. Myers led the attack to storm the Chinese barricades on the Tartar Wall. The tower under construction as shown on the map threatened to enfilade the American position and force the American marines to abandon their vital positions on the wall (by Kathryn Kelly-Hensley, 2008).

which more than any other was the pivot of our destiny."[34] The British were also laudatory. The storming of the Chinese barricade gave the defenders a position on the Tartar Wall which they held without difficulty for the remainder of the siege. It also gave the besieged a psychological uplift, shaken as they were by heavy losses and the glacial but steady progress of the Chinese in strangling all other sectors of the defense. The Chinese, on their part, gave up their attempts to capture the wall and merely occupied their barricades on the wall for the remainder of the siege. As always, Chinese strategy seemed self-defeating. They could have easily advanced from the old German barricade toward the rear of the Americans and caused all manner of trouble by flanking the German and French legations. They didn't. They stayed put, although keeping up a steady fire at the foreigners.

* * *

The legations sent dozens of Chinese out of the Legation Quarter to spy out the situation in Peking or to carry messages to the allied troops whom they still believed to be en route from Tientsin. Most of the messengers were never seen again. At night, July 4, Will Ament's street urchin, the fifteen year old boy Ament had taken in after the American Board Mission was burned, was lowered on a rope off the Tartar Wall into the Chinese city. He was disguised as a beggar and he carried a message from Sir Claude MacDonald. The message was wrapped in oiled paper, placed in the bottom of his begging bowl and covered with gruel. It read:

Since June 20th we have been besieged by Imperial troops who have four or five guns—one quick-firing, a 1-inch, a 2–3 inch, and two throwing 14 lb. shells—chiefly used at barricades. The enemy are enterprising but cowardly. Chinese Government, if any, doing nothing to put this down; all their positions very close to ours [the positions were then described]. We can hold out, if enemy go on as at present, say ten days; if they attack in earnest, four or five. Haste absolutely necessary, if you want to avoid a horrible massacre. Entrance probably easy; enemy hold gates of city; canal sluices afford easy entrance. We have lost forty killed.[35]

* * *

The *Fu* was nearly destroyed, its buildings and walls burned and bombarded, its gardens stripped of vegetation by the hungry, diseased Chinese Catholics. One American-educated Chinese doctor attended to the Catholics in *Fu*; most of the foreign priests took idle refuge in the British Legation. The Protestants cared for their own, but gave little attention to the Catholics. Finally, a committee—for every task a committee was created—visited the *Fu* on July 7 and found "its sanitary condition unspeakable." Scarlet fever and smallpox had broken out among the Chinese. The committee concluded that it was "difficult to know what to do" and little was done.[36] Many of the besieged foreigners feared an epidemic of disease spreading from the Chinese in the *Fu* as much as they feared death by Chinese bullets. Nobody bothered to keep count of Chinese Christians who died of bullets or disease during the siege.

It seems to have occurred to none of the foreign participants in the siege of the legations that the 2,800 Chinese sharing their experience might be treated as equals. The Chinese refugees were registered, organized, and their movements controlled. They were fed only if they worked. Scholars, students, merchants, native preachers, and peasants were all lumped together as a single group, handed shovels, and assigned to work gangs. The hospital did not admit Chinese—even those wounded in the line of duty—and foreign doctors concerned themselves with the health of the Chinese only to the extent of preventing disease which might spread to the foreign community. The food given to Chinese was the leavings of the foreigners. Chinese workers were cuffed and beaten at the will of their foreign supervisors. They preferred to work for the Japanese who did not beat them and politely bowed when requesting a service.[37]

It fell mostly to Methodist missionary W. T. Hobart and William B. Stelle, always described as "kindly," to organize the Chinese workers for the defense.[38] Claude MacDonald called the Committee on Native Labor "most important" and its leadership capable.[39] They made lists of all able-bodied Chinese and assigned them tasks. The priority was fortifications and even the domestic servants of the foreigners were required to work two hours a day building barricades—a substantial inconvenience to the great ladies of the Legation Quarter. Only the "scavengers" who cleaned up and disposed of the bodies of horses, dogs, and Chinese soldiers and Boxers were exempt from fortification work. The missionary women sewed "hands off" labels on their clothing.

Chinese were permitted to eat from communal food stocks only when they could show a meal ticket, signed by their foreign supervisor certifying that they had completed their assigned tasks for the day. The kitchen for Chinese workers was in the open air of the British Legation, adjoining the slaughter house. Several large iron kettles on open fires boiled wheat and rice and meat that the foreigners found inedible. Food was carried to workers in isolated or exposed positions. Chinese Protestant families housed on Legation Street were given a daily ration of food and they cooked it themselves. The Chinese ration was rough brown rice and boiled wheat and millet, probably only a little less in quality and quantity to what most of them were used to, but inferior to the pancakes and syrup, horse stews, and looted chickens and eggs of the foreigners.

The Chinese Catholics who lived in the *Fu* had a much harder time of it. There were accusations, probably well-founded, that some Catholics starved to death. Courtenay Fenn, an

American missionary on the Food Supply Committee, denied any starvation. The problem with the Catholics was that they were "not properly looked after by their priests, either in the gathering or the distribution of their food. Had it not been for the brave but not too scrupulous M. Chamot ... they would have suffered terribly. Under his direction they provided themselves with a large amount of grain, of their consumption of which, however, there was no sufficient supervision; so that, having gorged at the beginning, they came to want at the end, and our Protestant supplies had to contribute to their necessity."[40] By the end of the siege the Chinese in the *Fu* were fed "a mixture of a little grain, chopped straw, and other fodder, which made a coarse and revolting kind of bread. Beside that they had the entrails and heads of the ponies killed for the foreigners and a few dogs."[41]

* * *

The glorious Fourth of July passed without rescue and despite the victory on the Tartar Wall, the situation of the trapped foreigners in the Legation Quarter deteriorated. On July 6, an American civilian, the missionary Gilbert Reid, was shot in the leg while crossing the south bridge over the canal. Reid was one of a clan of forward thinking missionaries, the creator of the Mission to the Higher Classes. He asserted that the old method of converting each of four hundred million Chinese one by one would never succeed. Rather, he devoted his efforts to gaining influence among the upper classes of China on the theory that if the rich and powerful admired and emulated Western civilization they would also accept Christianity. Where the rich led, the poor would follow. Will Ament disagreed.

Whatever the merits of his thought, Reid was the one American missionary in the siege who appears to have been useless. His missionary colleagues noted the occasion of his wound in passing but even Arthur Smith forwent any expression of great distress. The Anglican Roland Allen said of him. "His was one of the cases in which temporary disablement was a real blessing to the man. He was not strong, and had suffered considerably from strain and the strangeness of the siege diet. A few weeks of enforced rest in the hospital not only mended his leg but his constitution. It was a great pleasure to be able to assure his wife, as soon as his wound had been examined, that the shot was one of the most fortunate things that had happened to them since the troubles began, and with true American shrewdness she understood and acknowledged the truth of the saying."[42] A soldier said he was probably looting when he was wounded.[43]

12

The Conquest of Tientsin

In early July, the allied forces held the foreign settlements of Tientsin, the railroad station and the thin line of damaged railroad track and navigable river to the coast. They were beset on three sides by the Chinese Imperial Army and Boxers. Chinese artillery pounded the foreign settlements.

Fresh troops arrived almost daily from the coast to strengthen the defenses. Mutual suspicions ran high among the so-called allies. The British and Japanese were suspicious of Russian designs to take over northern China; the French were congenitally suspicious of everyone; the Americans were concerned with maintaining their independence from European cabals; and the Germans were their usual prickly selves. Councils of war took place almost daily, but action to break the Chinese hold on Tientsin and open the way to Peking was slow in coming.

Roger Keyes, the twenty-eight-year-old commanding officer of HMS *Fame,* expressed his outrage at the inactivity.

> Naturally one thought that with about 10,000 troops there [in Tientsin], and reinforcements continually arriving, they would have no further trouble; but, to everyone's consternation and surprise, things got worse and worse, and Tientsin was practically besieged again. The Russians were safely bivouacked on the opposite side of the river, secure from shell fire, and would do nothing. The Japs did not like to take the initiative for fear of giving offence — but when they did do anything they did splendidly, as did our men, but they were hardly ever allowed to. The French troops, disciplinary battalions from Indo-China, are simply the scum of the French army and quite disgraceful. The American and German Naval Brigades, who are splendid, only had very few men and could do nothing. Consequently the Chinese shelled the Settlement every day for some hours....When one thinks that at Tientsin there were more European troops than there were all over India in the Mutiny, and that they allowed themselves to be practically shut up by a few thousand Chinamen, and prevented from marching 80 miles to the relief of Peking in such desperate straits— well, it is simply too sickening, and I can't express what one naturally feels about it.[1]

For the civilians locked up inside the settlements the Chinese artillery barrage mostly damaged buildings. The cellars and basements typical of Tientsin houses afforded protection and most of the Chinese shells were defective, landing with a dull thud, not an explosion. On July 5 most of the civilian men, women, and children were evacuated by tug downriver to Taku and hence by ship to Japan. Herbert and Lou Hoover stayed, Herbert's entreaties to his young wife notwithstanding. Lou Hoover and six or seven other women tended to the wounded in the hospital.

The Hoovers, as the number of foreign troops in the city increased, moved back to their house on Racecourse Road at the edge of the settlements. They played host to several of that new, romantic breed of reporter, the foreign correspondent. Frederick Palmer, an acquaintance of the Hoovers, arrived in Tientsin on June 28 and others soon followed, the Hoovers providing a place on the floor to sleep for a dozen or more. Their guests, however, had to forage for their own food.

Among the foreign correspondents was an unlikely choice for the rough-and-ready profession of war reporter — the California poet Joaquin Miller, the "Sweet Singer of the Sierras." Miller was sixty-one years old and he had little notion where he was and what he was supposed to do. The Hearst papers had told him to go to Peking and he was determined to do so. He hired a rickshaw and made ready to depart, deaf to the arguments that Tientsin was still surrounded by Chinese armies. Lou Hoover resolved the situation by bribing the rickshaw driver to desert his client and Miller, foiled, gave up and settled down to enjoy the hospitality of the Hoovers.

The correspondent Palmer wrote vignettes of the Hoovers. Herbert ignored the shells and bullets falling all around him "coursing the streets at the double quick — nervously jingling coins or keys in his pocket and seeming to be chewing nuts without shucking them — on his errands to protect the property and employees for which he was responsible."[2] Lou Henry Hoover was a picture of coolness and seemed to enjoy the battle raging around her. One day a shell burst at the foot of the stairs in the Hoover house. Nearby, Lou Hoover fanned away the dust and continued playing a game of solitaire. As the military buildup continued, Hoover's services as fortification engineer and labor organizer were no longer crucial to the defense but he stayed in Tientsin to tend to business interests and to protect his Chinese associates from the likes of the English bulldog, Captain Bayly.

When the disorganized Western and Japanese military forces finally got themselves together to attack the walled city of Tientsin on July 13, the American marines asked Hoover to accompany them as a guide. He had ridden his horse around the Tientsin region and was familiar with the terrain.[3] The attack on the walled city of Tientsin would be the bloodiest battle of the Boxer War.

* * *

Lt. Smedley Butler and the marines were among the allied soldiers who would attack Tientsin. Butler described his little group of 130 marines as a glorious outfit. The men looked like tramps, with hardly enough clothes to cover themselves and none of the fancy paraphernalia — swords, dress uniforms, and the like — of other foreign soldiers. They got dead drunk every payday and caused Butler endless problems. The old soldiers in the unit, Butler recalled, took good care of their young officers and taught them the tricks of the trade. They carried his pack when he was tired and shared stolen food with him.[4]

The military challenge for the allies was formidable. Tientsin was one mile square, surrounded by a wall more than twenty feet high and sixteen feet thick. Four gates pierced the wall at each of the compass points. The Chinese had artillery in the city and the Black Fort northeast of the city wall and more Chinese gun positions and infantry dug in across the river east of the city and west in a swampy area on the flank of an allied advance. The mud-hut villages on the plain surrounding the walled city provided cover for Boxer irregulars.

The allied plan was for the Russians and a few Germans, 2,500 men, to advance the evening of July 12 on the opposite bank of the river from Tientsin. The next morning they would capture several batteries of Chinese artillery, cross the river, and attack the East Gate of the city. The other allies — Japanese, British, French, and American forces totaling 4,000 — would attack from the south and storm the South Gate. Both forces would be supported by naval artillery mounted on the mud wall adjoining the foreign settlements and, a new innovation, a telephone link between gunners and observers would help direct the guns.

It was the kind of plan that would lead a few years later to the slaughter of millions in World War I. The allied soldiers would attack a well-armed foe occupying fortified positions. To overrun the position they would have to advance more than a mile under fire across open terrain with little cover. The Chinese would have done the Western world an enormous favor

Boxer Prisoners in Tientsin. The fate of captured Boxers was execution — which probably took place shortly after this photograph was taken (Ricalton, *China through the Stereoscope*, 1901).

by demonstrating the idiocy of such operations. Several Maxim machine guns, of which the Chinese possessed many, mounted in well-concealed positions could have swept the field and demonstrated to the allies the futility of an old-fashioned infantry assault against fast-firing modern weapons. Alas, the Europeans of the nineteenth century would not have their military tactics disproven by battles with the untrained soldiers of Asian and African armies. When they employed those same tactics against each other in World War I the consequences were catastrophic.

The allied soldiers, sailors, and marines left the foreign settlement at three A.M. on July 13 and looped south and west, sheltered from Chinese artillery by the ten-foot high mud wall surrounding the environs of Tientsin. The attacking force totaled 1,500 Japanese, 900 French, 900 Americans, and 800 British. The French contingent was comprised primarily of Tonkinese from North Vietnam, the ancestors of the Viet Minh and the Viet Cong. The British consisted of 500 Royal Welch Fusiliers and 300 sailors under Commander Beatty. The Americans were 550 soldiers

The Mud Wall. The Tientsin region was circled by a mud wall about 10 feet high. This photograph shows an American soldier giving water to a wounded colleague during the heavy fighting at Tientsin on July 13, 1900. Japanese soldiers are dressed in white and a British marine with a high-domed helmet is in the background (Ricalton, *China through the Stereoscope*, 1901).

of the Ninth Infantry led by Colonel Emerson H. Liscum and 350 marines led by Colonel Robert L. Meade. Herbert Hoover was with the marines.

At 5:30 A.M. British naval artillery opened fire on the walls of Tientsin. A few minutes into the bombardment a shell detonated a Chinese powder magazine near the Black Fort sending a "column of smoke and men going up a thousand or more feet in the air, and the shock being felt a mile and a half away."[5] Russian troops 500 yards away were knocked off their feet and the Russian commander was thrown off his horse and injured by falling debris.

At 6:30 A.M. the allies began the attack. The Japanese passed through a gap in the mud wall, and formed up into companies under cover of some mud huts. The U.S. Ninth Infantry followed the Japanese. To their left the American marines and the Royal Welch Fusiliers passed through another gap in the mud wall. To their right the French came through another gap.

The scene that greeted the allied soldiers this damp July morning was daunting. A mile away, straight down a narrow causeway, was the objective, the massive gate in the south wall of Tientsin. From the battlements atop the wall came the flash of cannon, machine gun, gingal, and rifle fire aimed out over the plain. On either side of the causeway were muddy fields interspaced with broad expanses of water. The Chinese had flooded the plain and the water in some of the pools was eight feet deep. The plain was crisscrossed by canals and dikes and dotted with cemeteries, rice paddies, and villages of mud huts. The allies would be thankful for the cover afforded by the dikes and gravestones. Colonel Daggett's judgment was that "had a formidable enemy defended the Chinese position, the attacking column would have been annihilated."[6]

The order of battle was the American marines on the far left with the Royal Welch Fusiliers and British sailors to their right. Next in line came the Japanese, who were to advance down the causeway to the gate, supported by the French. The American Ninth Infantry ended up on the right wing of the allied advance. The Ninth ran into a buzz saw. It came under heavy fire from Chinese in a village of mud huts, and artillery shells poured in from the walls of the city. The American soldiers advanced in short rushes toward the mud huts until they found their progress blocked by a canal. The soldiers took what shelter they found behind dikes and in the pools of water dotting the landscape. Chinese artillery only seventy-five yards across the canal poured shells in on them; rifle fire flashed out of a fortified flour mill three hundred yards away, and, from across the river, both artillery and small arms were directed at them out of loop-holed houses and gun emplacements. The Americans were pinned down, unable to advance with a canal in front of them and unable to fall back without exposing themselves to a rain of shot and shell. Colonel Liscum took his color bearer and tried to find a way across the canal. The color bearer was hit while crossing a dike. Liscum picked up the flag. He was shot in the abdomen and died shortly afterwards.

The Americans laid low for the next twelve hours, some of them standing in water up to their shoulders and others lying in ditches with only their heads above the water, until they could withdraw under cover of darkness. The American consul J. W. Ragsdale visited the battlefield carrying bottles of water and "stimulants" to the soldiers. Ragsdale said, "The shelling was far more terrific than any I experienced during the Civil War, and I served under General Sherman."[7] General Dorward sent a British naval company to reinforce the Americans where they lay and to help evacuate their wounded.

The 350 marines on the left of the allied attack, including in their number the civilian guide, Herbert Hoover, had nearly as hard a time of it as the army. The marines, along with the British sailors and Royal Welch Fusiliers, advanced in skirmish lines toward the walled city. Herbert Hoover described the advance. "We came under sharp fire from the Chinese located on its old walls. We were out in the open plains with little cover except Chinese graves. I was completely scared, especially when some of the marines next to me were hit. I was unarmed and I could scarcely make my feet move forward. I asked the officer I was accompanying if I could have a rifle. He produced one from a wounded marine, and at once I experienced a curious psychological change for I was no longer scared, although I never fired a shot. I can recommend that men carry weapons when they go into battle—it is a great comfort."[8]

Butler also tells the story. "The whole country was flooded. The Chinese had diverted the water from the canals into the open space between the two walls. We struggled through this filthy swamp, with bullets splashing and whining around us. The low mud walls of the rice patties provided some slight protection. We crouched behind them, firing furiously, slipping, sliding, and stumbling from one to another." The marines bogged down about eight hundred yards short of the walls of Tientsin and dug in behind grave mounds and canal dikes. Butler and his half-company sortied to prevent Chinese soldiers from going around the marines' flank. Private Partridge was wounded. The marines drove the Chinese away and, withdrawing, Butler and two others picked up the wounded Partridge to carry him away. Butler "felt a burning sensation in his right thigh" and thought at first that Partridge had kicked him. Then, he realized he was wounded. He bandaged his wound and took refuge behind a grave mound.

Butler soon found himself alone and isolated from the main body of marines. With a hand from Lt. Leonard, Butler was able to withdraw by creeping from grave mound to grave mound and eventually reach shelter behind the mud wall. There, he found another marine officer who had been wounded in the opposite leg and the two of them linked arms and hobbled back on their two good legs to the hospital in the British settlement. Butler's wound wasn't serious and while he waited through the rest of the day for treatment he helped dress the wounds of other soldiers brought into the hospital. That afternoon, the Lt. Leonard who had rescued him was brought to the hospital with a shattered arm which had to be amputated. Leonard, mustered out of the marines on disability, subsequently became an outstanding lawyer. Thirty-one years later, when Butler was court-martialed for injudicious remarks about an Italian leader named Mussolini, Leonard was his defense lawyer.[9] Herbert Hoover was president at the time.

The correspondent Frederick Palmer described the battlefield at noon from his vantage point sitting, back against the mud wall, beneath field artillery manned by turbaned Sikh gunners. Between his position and the city wall of Tientsin he saw American marines and British sailors in their blue jackets clustered behind grave mounds, as many as twenty behind two very large graves. Nobody moved. The officers were not standing up or moving around. Spouts of dust marked where Chinese bullets struck. At a gap between the blue of the marines and the British sailors were the Welsh fusiliers dressed in khaki and nearly invisible. It was a new-fangled idea that soldiers should blend into their surroundings rather than stand out.

Two hundred dead and wounded lay in rows behind the wall. The allies had quit trying to evacuate wounded from the battlefield. Every attempt to rescue a wounded soldier cost additional casualties. A doctor was shot in the arm. Ammunition bearers, orderlies, and messengers from the battle lines were hit in front of Palmer's eyes. "As I watched first one man and then another tumble in the advance this morning, it was hard to believe that the fallen would not rise and walk off the stage when the curtain fell."[10]

None of the foreign soldiers had reason to be happy as the day wound down. The assault on the south gate had been a bloody failure. The military leaders debated that night whether it would be better for the allies to stick to their positions for another day of fighting or accept defeat and withdraw to the foreign settlements.

There was no news from the Russians and Germans attacking the eastern gate of the city. Later, it was discovered that they had little more success than the other allies. Advancing on the opposite bank of the river from Tientsin and the Black Fort, the Russians and Germans captured a large battery of Chinese artillery with only light casualties. However, the Chinese in the Black Fort stopped their advance and they had been unable to cross the river to assault the eastern gate as had been the plan.

The Japanese held the center of the allied lines all day, and had taken a higher number of casualties than any other nationality. Japanese stoicism and steadiness under fire became legendary during the Boxer Rebellion, the only criticism of them being their poor marksmanship and an inclination toward sacrificing their lives in battle rather than the more practical approach of the Americans and British of living to fight another day.

The British general Dorward was the coordinator of the allied attack on the South Gate of Tientsin, but the Japanese general Fukushima was the backbone. Fukushima settled the question as to whether the allies should withdraw or continue the fight. Faced with a proposal by General Dorward to retire from the battlefield, the Japanese general said, "If I give an order at

Tientsin Vicinity

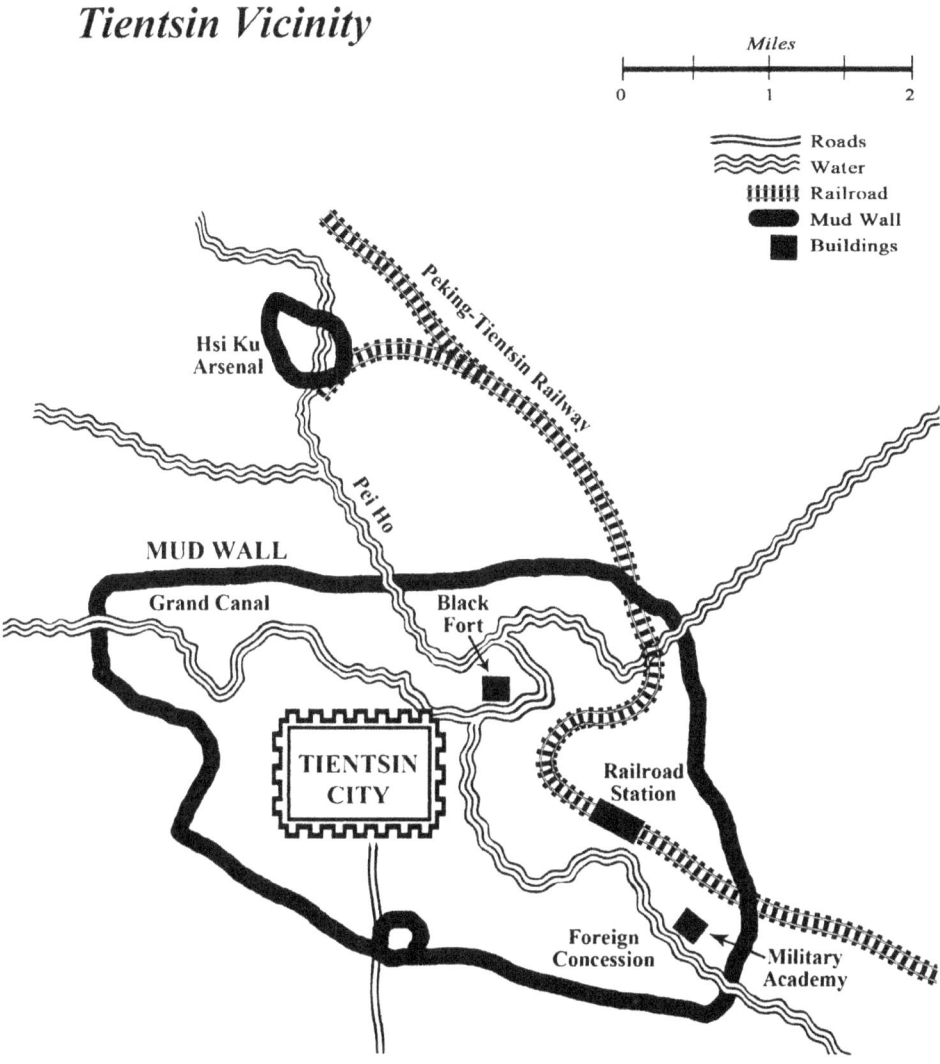

Tientsin and Vicinity. Tientsin consisted of a walled Chinese city and several foreign settlements along the river. A mud wall about ten feet tall circled the area. The Americans, British, and Japanese attacked the south gate of the walled city on July 13 (by Kathryn Kelly-Hensley, 2008).

all, it will be to go still further."[11] Under cover of darkness, the Japanese continued their advance on the South Gate, now battered by the big twelve-pound guns of HMS *Terrible* firing from the mud wall.

The end of the Battle of Tientsin was anti-climactic. Chinese soldiers had fought successfully on July 13. They had stopped the advance of the allies toward the South Gate a long rifle shot away and they kept the Russians from crossing the Pei River to threaten the East Gate. They had suffered losses from the heavy artillery of the allies, but the gates to the city stood firm, the wall chipped but solid—capable of withstanding many more days of bombardment. The allies were hurting. A few more hours of stiff resistance and their will to continue the assault would have wilted. Tientsin could have held out.

The Chinese seized defeat from the jaws of victory. During the night the defenders of Tientsin evaporated, fleeing the city via the north and west gates. Palmer expressed the European view: "Our Oriental enemy could not stand the stream of shell fire from the British lyddites and twelve-pounders and the field guns. They could not see that we were beaten if they held out a little longer ... they cannot assume the character and initiative or the adaptability of the martial peoples." By "martial peoples" Palmer meant "white" plus the Japanese who in 1900 achieved the status of honorary whites.[12]

At three A.M., July 14, the Japanese reached the South Gate of Tientsin. A demolition unit set an explosive charge to blow up the gate. The first attempt failed when a Chinese bullet cut the wire from the explosive to the detonator. A Japanese lieutenant raced up to the gate, lit a fuse on the charge with a match, and blew himself and the South Gate into very small pieces. The sacrifice was unnecessary. A second gate was behind the first, but, rather than blow it up, Japanese soldiers simply scaled the wall and opened the gate from the inside. Only a few Chinese soldiers and Boxers remained to contest the conquest.

The Japanese, followed by the British, French, and Americans, poured into the city, happily shooting any Chinese they saw. The Russians and Germans—once they learned the city was taken—came in through the East Gate. The Battle of Tientsin was over. The road to Peking was open.

* * *

A long-winded American missionary expressed the view of the enlightened West on the Boxer Rebellion. "The Great Powers will have an opportunity that has seldom occurred in the history of the world to exhibit the superiority of Christian civilization, in loftiness of moral purpose and an exalted spirit of unselfishness, starting China upon an era of reform and progress that will be a blessing to all nations, and cause future generations of Chinese to remember with gratitude the benefactors."[13]

The benefactors of Christian civilization were very much on display in Tientsin on July 14, after Japanese soldiers scaled the wall and opened the South Gate of the city to foreign soldiers. Tientsin was a mass of miserable humanity. Headless bodies floated in the canals outside the city gates. Heads, hung by their pigtails, decorated walls, the grisly trophies of Boxer executions of Chinese suspected of sympathy with foreign ways. Inside the city, amidst the ruins of smoldering houses, were hundreds of bodies, some killed by allied artillery, others long dead, their rotting corpses the food of gaunt pigs and starving dogs. Tientsin was ablaze in a hundred places; smoky, sodden air hung over the city like a shroud. "The walls of the city," said one writer, "on the day it was occupied, surrounded a square mile of such filth, ruin, and death, such turmoil and pillage as history could hardly duplicate."[14]

With "a loftiness of moral purpose and an exalted spirit of unselfishness," the conquerors of Tientsin proceeded to loot the city. They were assisted by Chinese and civilians from the foreign settlements who were knowledgeable of the best places to find treasure. "The whole city is filled with an indiscriminate mob of Chinese and soldiers of all nationalities, who are breaking open stores and smashing chests and safes and rushing hither and thither with their arms filled with silks, furs, jewelry, silver bars, and money.... Fires have been started throughout the city and men are fighting in the streets over loot. Revolvers have been drawn and threats of shooting are not uncommon. The Chinamen sometimes offer a show of resistance against being plundered, and in these cases are shot."[15]

The aftermath in Tientsin was a premonition of what would happen later in Peking. "Many commanders turned their men loose. Soldiers of all nations joined in the orgy," said American marine Lieutenant Wise. "Men of the allies staggered through the streets, arms and backs piled high with silks, furs and brocades, with gold and silver and jewels." The American leaders issued orders not to loot but before the order it was "help yourself" in the words of Lt. Wise. He and several friends collected silver and sold it though a banker. Wise's share came to five thousand

Tientsin after the victory. In this photograph, taken from the canal in the French Concession, the shelling damage to the buildings is visible. A dead Chinese is in the water (Ricalton, *China through the Stereoscope*, 1901).

dollars. "Although my men were too busy to take serious part in the looting the first day or two," continued Wise, "they soon made up for lost time." The Chinese population suffered the ravages of the foreign armies. "The allied soldiers piled up the Chinese dead in heaps with wood and cremated them to keep the place from becoming a pesthole."[16]

Tientsin also witnessed the beginning of problems in the relationships of the missionaries and their saviors, the soldiers. The ever-practical American missionaries wished to charge rent to the military for buildings expropriated for military use, but as George Wilder said, "We have secured no rent from the Army for our buildings. When they go in they agree to pay rent.

When they leave they object to it on the ground that they are here to protect us and ought not to be charged rent."[17] Problems between the military and the missionaries would continue.

* * *

The butcher bill for the foreign soldiers at Tientsin was substantial. Colonel Meade of the U.S. Marines reported casualties as follows:

U.S.: 24 killed, 98 wounded, 1 missing
British: 17 killed, 87 wounded
Japanese: 320 killed and wounded
French: 13 killed, 50 wounded
Russians and Germans: 140 killed and wounded.
Total: 750 killed, wounded, and missing.[18]

13

The Darkest Days

July 13, in the words of Sir Claude MacDonald, was "the most harassing day for the defense during the whole siege."[1] Stephen Pichon, the gloomy French minister, decided that his oft-repeated prediction of "today we die" would be fulfilled and he performed that most emotional and solemn last rite of a diplomat: he burned his official papers. The Peking wind came up and scraps of the burning paper blew around the British Legation. Madame Pichon chased down the burning bits of paper, stamped them out, and carried them back to the fire to be re-burned.

Pichon was astute. Before the day was out the Legation Quarter would face a new terror. The trouble began at four P.M. in the *Fu* when the Chinese bombarded the Japanese and Italian barricades and drove them back to their eighth and next to last line of defense. Three-fourths of the *Fu* was now in Chinese hands. An Italian marine was killed and Frank Norris, the British missionary working on fortifications, was hit in the neck by a piece of shell. Norris walked to the hospital, had the wound dressed, and fell into an exhausted sleep. In a day or two he was back on duty.

Unlike most Chinese military enterprises this one had the appearance of being coordinated. While the fighting at the *Fu* still raged, about six P.M. the ground shook like the roll of a giant earthquake and the sound of two tremendous explosions came from the French Legation. Two wounded French marines were carried to the hospital. Two mines, they said, had exploded beneath the French Legation.

The French had been warned. Two days earlier they had captured eighteen Chinese soldiers and one of them had said that a mine was being dug under their legation. The French ingested this bit of information without doing anything about it. A corporal executed the prisoners with his bayonet as he didn't want to waste bullets.

The first of the mines exploded beneath a fortified house with Lt. Darcy, the French commander, the Austrian diplomat Dr. von Rosthorn and four French marines inside. Two of the marines disappeared—only a foot was found belonging to one of them. Von Rosthorn was buried in the rubble of the explosion but, a moment later, the second mine exploded nearby and he was magically lifted from the ruins and deposited, shaken but unhurt, on solid ground again. The others were pulled out of the rubble, "the colour of death and bleeding badly" but not seriously wounded.[2]

A Chinese attack followed the explosion of the mines. The garrison in the French Legation—twenty Austrians, twenty-nine French marines, and nine civilian volunteers on duty—fell back to their last line of defense. What remained of the French Legation went up in flames and, soon, the Chinese raised banners over the ruins of the residence of the French minister. Simultaneously, the Chinese attacked the Germans on the other side of Legation Street. The Germans had only thirty-two men to meet the attack. The Chinese broke through the wall of the Peking Club but, as they were crossing the tennis court, the Germans charged with bayonets. The Chinese broke and raced away in panic. Many of them retreated in the wrong direction, along the base of the Tartar Wall toward the American positions. The Americans fired on the Chinese from the wall and mounted their own bayonet charge and drove back the Chinese to the tender mercies of the Germans. The sharp-shooting Americans killed thirty Chinese and the Germans eighteen.

At day's end the foreigners had suffered five killed and nine wounded. Most of the French Legation was lost; the Japanese and the Italians in the *Fu* had their backs to the wall, and the shelling of the British Legation was heavier than usual. Reinforcements were sent to the French and Germans. A Chinese labor brigade in the *Fu* worked desperately all night to strengthen the barricades. They heard Chinese soldiers doing the same only a few yards away. The foreigners drove the Chinese workers as never before to pile earth, bricks, and sandbags atop the barricades. At four A.M. they quit. "They fell asleep the minute they ceased work. They dropped like stones, and became at once insensible even to blows. Exhortations, threats, entreaties, warnings were in vain. It was plain that they could not stand on their feet any longer."[3]

Mines were a new worry. If a mine could be exploded under the French Legation, why not under the British Legation with its women and children, busy missionaries, skulking men, and diplomats? Frank Gamewell had foreseen the possibility of mines but the demand for barricade building was such that he had neither the men nor the time to devote the effort to digging counter-mines—trenches ten to twelve feet deep just above the thirteen-feet water table along the borders of the defense line of the British Legation.[4]

Moreover, in preparation for the last extremity at the British Legation, Gamewell had put Chinese workers to work building bombproof shelters. They dug trenches six feet deep and covered them with a roof of timbers and boards and from two to four feet of sandbags or earth. In the last extremity the women and children would take refuge in the bomb shelters. The women shuddered at the thought of having to crowd into these dank and dark cellars. For Gamewell, it was another duty piled on his narrow shoulders.

* * *

Bastille Day dawned, wet and miserable, the fires in the *Fu* and the French Legation still smoldering. The French, all feared, could not hold the remnant of their legation more than another day or two. If the French retreated, the German Legation would be flanked and the Germans would also have to withdraw. The gunners rolled "Betsy" over to the French Legation to blast away at Chinese positions.

At noon came a surprise. A Chinese spy returned. Boxers had arrested him and found he carried a message to the foreign armies the besieged still hoped were just over the horizon. Eighty blows with a bamboo rod loosened the spy's tongue, but, instead of beheading him, they took him to Chinese army headquarters. There, he was given a letter to Sir Claude MacDonald and sent back to the Legation Quarter under a white flag of truce.

Prince Ching and Others to Sir Claude MacDonald, British Minister:
In the last ten days the soldiers and militia have been fighting, and there has been no communication between us, to our great anxiety. Some time ago we hung up a board expressing our intentions, but no answer has been received and contrary to expectation the foreign soldiers made renewed attacks, causing alarm and suspicion among soldiers and people. Yesterday the troops captured a convert named Jin Sixi and learned from him that all the foreign ministers were well, which caused us great satisfaction....
We now request your Excellencies to take first your families and the various members of your staffs, and leave your legations in detachments. We should select trustworthy officers to give close and strict protection, and you should temporarily reside in the Tsungli Yamen, pending future arrangements for your return home, in order to preserve friendly relations from beginning to end. But at the time of leaving the legations there must not on any account whatever be taken any single armed foreign soldier, in order to prevent doubt and fear on the part of the troops and people, leading to untoward incidents.

A counter-mine in the Hanlin. The only surviving building of the Hanlin Academy was incorporated into the British Legation defenses. The trench is a counter-mine, ten feet deep, to prevent the Chinese from tunneling under the legation (Smith, *Convulsion in China*, 1901).

> If your Excellency is willing to show this confidence we beg you communicate with all the foreign Ministers in Peking, tomorrow at noon being the limit of time, and to let the original messenger deliver your reply in order that we may settle in advance the day for escorting you out of the legation. This is the only way of preserving relations that we have been able to devise in the face of innumerable difficulties.
>
> If no reply is received by the time fixed, even our affection will not enable us to help you. Compliments.
>
> (signed) Prince Ching and Others[5]

The letter caused a sensation. The savants of the Legation Quarter had a new subject to debate, the mysterious searchlights no longer seen and mathematical computations of the date of arrival of a relief expedition having paled. Was the letter genuine? Prince Ching was known to be a moderate. Was this an attempt to lure the ministers out of the Legation Quarter to be massacred and thereby finish the job begun with the killing of Baron von Ketteler?

The next day, July 15, the ministers answered the letter. MacDonald summarized the response with a bulletin posted on the bell tower. "A reply has been sent today, declining, on the part of the foreign representatives, the invitation to proceed to the Tsungli Yamen, and pointing out that no attacks have been made by our troops, who are only defending the lives and property of foreigners against the attacks of Chinese government troops. The reply concludes with a statement that if the Chinese government wishes to negotiate, they should send a responsible official with a white flag."[6]

About three in the afternoon the Chinese sent the besieged "a shower of bullets and a liberal supply of shell, probably to assist in 'preserving friendly relations intact,' and as a proof of their deep and abiding affection for the Foreign Ministers."[7] That evening, a Chinese language student, Henry Warren, was hit in the jaw by a shell. He was treated and seemed to be all right when a piece of bone slipped down his throat. Dr. Velde, the German surgeon, did a tracheotomy, but to no avail. Warren died of shock and loss of blood.

* * *

The wall had been mostly quiet since Jack Myers had captured the Chinese barricades on July 3 and been wounded. The Chinese now kept their distance. Captain Newt Hall was in charge and the marines had pushed forward to build a barricade about 200 yards to the east of the bastion that Myers had taken. Captain Hall was less admired than Myers. He had gotten off on the wrong foot with the missionaries by disparaging the bravery of women. Dr. Emma Martin was to accuse him in her diary of "cowardice and drink" although one suspects that her knowledge was second- or third-hand.[8] He also ran into difficulty with the diplomats at the American Legation. The Congers apparently got angry when marines resting at the American Legation didn't stand up and salute the ladies when they paid a visit.[9] Hall was no diplomat. He thought rest was more important for his men than obeisances to meddling civilians. Morrison, never generous with other people, also criticized Hall on July 10. "Today on the Wall there were 13 men under Captain Hall," he said. "He is never put on the Wall, his men having no confidence in his judgment. He has no control over his men."[10]

Hall fell out most seriously with First Secretary Herbert Squiers and his fashionable wife and associates. Trouble between the civilians and Captain Hall broke out on July 15. Squiers wanted the marines to build a new barrier farther east to command the Water Gate beneath the wall. Although a noxious canal flowed under the gate, the diplomats rightly perceived that Water Gate would be the easiest access for the relieving force — if and when it arrived in Peking. Hall resisted. He objected to the marines expanding their advanced and exposed position. He was pleased that the Chinese soldiers were now keeping their distance — about 200 yards — down the wall westwards rather than butting heads at brick-throwing distance with the Americans. To change the status quo might provoke the Chinese holding the former German positions 400 hundred yards to the east.

Hall started work on the advanced barrier, but Squiers insisted that he build the barricade farther east toward the Chinese position. Hall demurred, demanding that Squiers undertake the dangerous journey to the top of the wall to show him exactly where he wanted the barrier placed. Squiers did so, Hall yielded and that night he and Private Daniel Joseph Daly went forward to reconnoiter the position. Hall and Daily were to be joined by a group of 23 Chinese workers carrying sandbags and supervised by two marines and a Dutch diplomat, W. J. von Dhuysberg. When the workers didn't arrive, Hall went back to look for them, leaving Daly alone at the advanced position. Private Daly stayed there for a lonely hour or two. When Hall found the workers and their supervisors, he sent them out to join Daly and undertake the work of building the new barrier. Private Upham wrote that the marines were "in a regular trap" but fortunately the Chinese didn't advance on the three men and 23 Chinese building the barricade.[11] Hall stayed at the rear of the marines' position while sending additional marines forward to the advanced barrier.[12] Daly received the first of his two Congressional Medals of Honor for his solo stay on the wall, the only marine except Smedley Butler to receive two. He would later be famous for his exhortation to his colleagues under fire in World War I, "Come on, you sons of bitches, do you want to live forever?"

An American marine was killed that morning and the funeral was that afternoon at 2:30 P.M. in the Russian Legation, the American Legation considered too dangerous for funerals. The legation staff and many missionaries attended. "We gathered what flowers there were to be found and some green leaves to strew over the graves of all ... the rain was falling softly down on our umbrellas and the tears silently rolling down most of our faces. I stood at the foot the grave and ... looked down upon the form of the poor boy lying on the cold ground dressed in his blue clothes and an American flag wrapped around his lifeless body ... Dr. Wherry took charge of the services after Mr. Conger had made a few remarks.... [I] never dreamed it would be my lot to be in the midst of battle, or drop a tear over an American Marine's grave in far off China."[13]

Hall was criticized for leaving Private Daly alone on the wall and not being at the front with his marines. Dhuysberg, who was enamored of the Conger's niece, Mary Pierce, probably gave an unflattering account of Hall's actions on the wall to the Squierses and Congers.[14]

* * *

Captain B. M. Strouts, MacDonald's chief of staff, ate breakfast at the Squiers' mess on July 16. Strouts was a small man, cool, self-reliant, and thirty years old, the eldest of the British marines. He was going over to the *Fu* that morning. The handful of surviving Japanese soldiers and volunteers were exhausted. They were to be replaced by British marines and rested a full twenty-four hours. Strouts would inspect the defenses at the *Fu* and make arrangements with Lt. Col. Shiba for the Japanese to be relieved.

"Are you up for the *Fu*?" Strouts asked Morrison, the Australian journalist. Morrison was. He had the sense of destiny and a reporter's instinct that made him a very brave man. The two men crossed the canal to the *Fu* behind a barricade and there met up with Lt. Colonel Shiba. They began their tour of the defenses. One spot in the *Fu* was most dangerous. From the Italian guard post to the Japanese lines the way led behind a low range of artificial hillocks, little decorative bumps in the gardens of the *Fu*. On their side of the hillocks the Chinese had built high barricades with a clear view of this piece of open ground. Several men had been wounded here; three ponies had been killed in one night; and the wall facing the Chinese barricades was pockmarked with bullet holes. It was standard practice to race across the open area behind the hillocks on the double.

This morning, Strouts didn't make it. Morrison recalled:

> I heard some shots, how many I cannot tell, but I think three, and felt a cut in my right thigh. At the same moment, "My God" said Strouts, and he fell over into the arms of Shiba, who was on the left. Then I jumped forward and with Shiba dragged Strouts out of fire, though shots were still coming whizzing by us; and then he lay down while Shiba ran off for the surgeon. In the meantime I tried to slip my handkerchief round his thigh and stepped out to find a twig with which to use it as a tourniquet. But the result was not good. I could see the fracture and the bone projecting against his trousers. Then Nakagawa [the Japanese doctor] came up and we two tried to staunch the bleeding by compressing the external iliac. The body was soaked in blood, but the poor fellow was conscious and asked me where I was hit. I said mine was unimportant. Then I fainted.
>
> In a little while the stretcher bearers came up and the Captain was carried away. Then I started to walk, but was getting faint and was carried into the Legation, Caetini [an Italian officer] coming with me. Then it was found that another bullet had splintered and some the fragments struck me. [Dr.] Poole cut this out and while he did so I fainted again and then vomited, the pain being intense, though I have no reason to think it was one half as great as other pain I have suffered. In the ward Strouts was brought in. He was dying. He said nothing, but by and by he gave a few sobs of pain, then his breath came quickly, and then he sank away into his death.[15]

Polly Condit-Smith was walking to the hospital with a pot of coffee for the doctors and nurses when Captain Strouts was carried in on a stretcher. "It was especially shocking to me to see him thus," she said, "as he had breakfasted with us at seven o'clock, and had seemed tired

George Morrison. The correspondent of the *Times* affected Chinese dress in this photograph taken with his household staff. Morrison's account of the siege was the first published and the most influential (George Ernest Morrison, *An Australian in China,* 1902).

from his constant work, but hopeful and in good spirits. His arm was hanging limp, the hands and fingers stiff with agony. It seemed but a moment before that I had passed him at breakfast a cup of black coffee, to receive which he had held out that strong, slim hand, with the signet ring on the little finger, and now it was all so changed. In less than two hours the hand was again being held, but in his death throes.... Poor Captain Strouts, with a cut artery in his thigh, only lived four hours, and died while asleep. He was so very, very tired."[16]

For Dr. Emma Martin this was the darkest day of the siege. "It was drizzling and everything was wet and sticky and dirty and smelled so bad and the flies were terrible." She stood outside the hospital and watched Strouts, Morrison, and about 20 marines go through a hole in the wall of the British Legation to cross into the *Fu.* And about an hour later she was there when the marines carried in the wounded Strouts and Morrison. Strouts, she said, was the best officer left of the British and Americans. Halliday had been wounded; Myers had been wounded and Captain Hall of the U.S. Marines and Captain Wray of the British marines were both despised "for cowardice and drink habits."[17] Morrison's wound was not serious. The correspondent for *The Times* spent the rest of the siege lying on his stomach and writing an account of the events for his newspaper.

The student Warren and Captain Strouts were buried in a single grave that evening at six P.M. in the cemetery of the British Legation. The community turned out for the ceremony — diplomats, missionaries, ladies, children, and all the British marines who were not on duty. Six officers bore Strout's coffin and eight students carried Warren's. Several shells burst overhead as the mourners followed the coffins to the grave.

The funeral procession had just begun when American minister Edwin Conger was called away. A messenger from "Prince Ching and others" was at the front gate of the British Legation. He bore another letter urging the foreign ministers to come to the Tsungli Yamen where they could be protected. It expressed surprise that the foreigners had continued to fire on Chinese soldiers and reiterated the desire of "Prince Ching" to protect the legations. Curiously, attached to the letter was a telegram for Conger. The telegram consisted of several groups of meaningless letters with no indication of the sender or the addressee. Conger sat down with the other Americans of his legation to try to make some sense of it. It was a State Department cipher and, looking in his codebook, Conger found the key. A few minutes of work and he deciphered the message. It read: "Communicate tidings bearer."

This was perplexing. The first communication with the outside world in a month was three ambiguous words. Who was bearer? How were tidings to be communicated? Was the telegram an elaborate fraud?

Conger didn't know the answers but he drafted a reply to the three-word inquiry in the same cipher as it was received. "For one month we have been besieged in British Legation under continued shot and shell from Chinese troops. Quick relief only can prevent general massacre."[18] He sent his reply back to the Tsungli Yamen, requesting that that it be transmitted to Washington and asking for a copy of the original cablegram.

The next day the Chinese cleared up the mystery. The telegram had been sent by the Chinese minister in Washington in response to an inquiry from the secretary of state concerning Conger's well-being. The Chinese minister had assured the secretary of state that Conger was indeed well and under the protection of the Chinese government, although, as the esteemed Secretary Hay was aware, a mob of ragamuffins called Boxers had created a serious problem of insecurity in the capital. As proof, Minister Wu promised to see to the delivery of a coded message from the secretary to Minister Conger. The Chinese government promised to transmit Conger's coded reply to Minister Wu who would pass it along to the secretary of state. However, it would be four days before Conger's short, grim message arrived in Washington. The Boxers had cut the telegraph lines and the Chinese government communicated with the outside world by pony courier to Shantung two hundred miles south, where the telegraph was still operating.

Conger's correspondence with the Tsungli Yamen was only one of several exchanges of letters taking place on July 16 and 17. The Chinese government had become garrulous. At the same time, all up and down the defense lines, the firing slowly died down and, by and by, an absolute silence reigned over the Legation Quarter. An armistice had begun.

For the foreigners, it was just in time. Fifty-seven men had been killed and eighty-seven seriously wounded. One-third of the legation guard force was dead or wounded. All three of the British officers were dead or wounded; two of the three American officers were wounded. Twenty of twenty-five Japanese, twenty-two of fifty-two German, and fourteen of twenty-nine Italian marines were dead or wounded. Fourteen civilians had been killed or wounded.

The legation defenders were on the ropes. A plausible explanation for such a timely event comes from defender Lancelot Giles. "There had been suspicions that the war against the Legations had not been carried out in a whole-hearted manner. Casualties on the foreign side were high and disturbing, but when compared to the number of rounds fired by the Chinese they were incomprehensibly low. It almost seemed, at times, as if the Imperial soldiers at least were merely putting up a show of attack and seemed content to make things uncomfortable for foreigners, which fitted in with the defenders' theory that Jung Lu, the Army Commander, was not anti-foreign, but were being forced to act as if he were."[19]

* * *

Sir Claude MacDonald did not know it but the very day the armistice began in Peking *The Times* of London published his obituary. It was not very flattering. On July 16, *The New York*

Times headline screamed an account of the massacre of the besieged in Peking: "Details of the Peking Tragedy Foreigners All Slain After a Last Heroic Stand SHOT THEIR WOMEN FIRST They Had Formed a Square Round them and the Children HEADS CARRIED ON RIFLES."[20]

Every newspaper added a few details of its own to freshen up the information for its readers. The New York *Tribune* trotted out another truism of the Imperialistic Age: it was the duty of white men to shoot their women and children rather than let them fall into the hands of the rapacious heathen. "One thing is certain," said the *Tribune*, "the white men died at the post of duty and honor, and it is a matter of congratulation in the awful circumstances that the white women and children died at the hands of their loved ones."[21]

The news united the bickering and jealous foreign powers. "Vengeance no man desires. Justice all men must demand.... A cooperative force must be collected at the mouth of the Pei River from all the nations whose envoys have been murdered. This force must be strong enough to sweep all before it. In it the United States must be represented, not for vengeance, an unchristian and unworthy desire, but for justice — inexorable justice; delayed it may be and slow, but which, when it smites, will smite without respect of persons from Prince Tuan to the most ignorant rioter known to have shared in this fell, foul work."[22]

In London a memorial service was scheduled for victims of the massacre in Peking on July 23. Then, from Washington, came the news of Conger's telegram: The British cancelled the memorial service at the last minute. The fate of the foreigners was in limbo. They were still alive.

* * *

The Empress Dowager and her court were having no easy time of it. Boxers roamed the streets of the capital and they had left their austerity and purity of purpose in the countryside. In the city the Boxers killed, burned, and looted at will and nobody was immune to their depredations. High Manchu and Chinese officials were assaulted, forced to humble themselves, and robbed. The dead littering the streets of Peking were so numerous that the Imperial armies were put to work hauling bodies away from the city. Chinese fled the capital from fear of the Boxers. "When the Boxers first came, they claimed that they had supernatural power, that they were invulnerable to guns and swords, and that they were capable of burning the foreign houses and exterminating the foreigners as easily as turning over a hand. Now they are different: first they evade by artifice, then they retreat and make no advance. Only the army of Tung Fu-hsiang has attacked with all effort day and night."[23]

The Dowager didn't get any help from the other regions of China. To the contrary, the governors of the southern provinces chose to interpret the imperial decrees as they saw fit. On June 20, the day the siege began, the governors of the south urged the court in Peking to suppress the Boxers. Later, the southern governors openly met with foreign consuls and worked out procedures to ensure that the Boxer Uprising did not spread. The power of the Manchu dynasty was tenuous outside its north China heartland. The southern governors ignored its dictates.

14

Life Under Siege

The American and British chroniclers of the siege were quick to point fingers at the deficiencies of other nationalities, especially the Europeans who appeared languid and excitable in turn. "There was a marked and an impressive contrast," remarked Arthur Smith, "between the conduct of the representatives of the Anglo-Saxons, and that of many of the Continentals, who for the most part sat at ease on their shady verandas, chatting, smoking cigarettes and sipping wine, apparently trusting for their salvation to fate; while their more energetic comrades threw off their coats, plunging into the whirl of work and the tug of toil with the joy of battle."[1]

Smith was unfair. The most worthless foreigner in the siege was the Anglo-Saxon Sir Edmund Trewlawny Backhouse, a gifted linguist working with the monolingual Morrison. Backhouse would become one of the most notorious frauds of the 20th century. Even his own relatives had little good to say about him. "I doubt whether he was much help to anyone, as I heard that he had managed to shoot his own sergeant-major."[2] Officially a military volunteer, Backhouse complained of an injury and avoided exposure to danger.

Harriet Squiers, the wealthy wife of the American first secretary, was admirable. Her three small children, two excitable governesses, a maid, and Polly Condit-Smith occupied two rooms in one of the homes of the British Legation. The two women and the maid slept in one room on a mattress which they rolled up in the daytime to use as a seat. They had several trunks and a mountain of canned food piled up around the walls. The room was damp and "all night the fleas and cockroaches that appear would horrify anyone." They donated their mosquito nets and mattresses to the hospital for use by the wounded men. They slept on a straw-stuffed bag and "unless one lies in a pool of bug powder there is no such thing as sound sleep."[3] The room overlooked the crowded and filthy servants' quarters and the smell of a broken sewer wafted into the room. Mrs. Squiers' three children slept in cribs in the other room and the governesses slept in the hall. Herbert Squiers slept at the American Legation along with the other three American diplomats. Polly Condit-Smith took up smoking cigarettes to counter evil smells and repel insects.

Their accommodations were less than luxurious but Harriet Squires had a bottomless stock of food. One day, her enterprising cook went outside the defense lines and procured a dozen baby chickens. Some were kept in a basket and raised as food for sick children. The others were served at a little party to which Sir Robert Hart and others from the social set of the Legation Quarter were invited. The menu included celery soup and anchovy toast as appetizers, broiled baby chicken as the *pièce de résistance*, green peas, fried potatoes, bean salad, and plenty of coffee. A quart or two of champagne and wine from the Squierses' bountiful wine cellar was served at all meals; liquor was more palatable and safer than the water supply. The Squierses had a banquet every meal. Most of the besieged ate horsemeat, rice, and little else.

The inhabitants of the Legation Quarter divided themselves into messes for eating: Lady MacDonald's mess, the American missionary mess, the Customs mess, etc. The Squiers' mess was the most amusing. Its members included Dr. Velde, an excellent and self-important German surgeon; Dr. George Morrison, the journalist, "as dirty, happy, and healthy a hero as one could find anywhere";[4] Fleming Cheshire and William Pethick, two old China hands who did yeoman work fortifying the Tartar Wall; Fargo Squiers, the fourteen-year-old son of Herbert Squiers by a previous marriage; the children and their governesses; and, of course, the amiable Miss Condit-Smith and her maid. Harriet Squiers invited, as part of her duty, missionaries to lunch and her more intimate friends to dinner, many of them like Sir Robert Hart once so lofty and now so sadly in need of a good meal. So generous was Harriet that she was called Lady Bountiful.

Other than inspiring young men to deeds of valor, Polly Condit-Smith's principal contribution was to serve morning coffee. She was roused every day by a knock on the door at six A.M. Outside would be two or three men just coming off night duty. Polly told them to come back in half an hour, found and woke up the cook who slept under the eaves of the house, and got cooking the porridge, biscuits, and coffee for breakfast. In the meantime, Harriet and Polly would take sponge baths, tidy up their wrinkled clothing, roll up their straw mattress and put it in a corner, and arrange their table for breakfast. They had only four chairs so latecomers had to sit on trunks. Napkins were placed, a few green leaves—shot off a tree by Chinese bullets—decorated the table and finally breakfast would be announced. One cup of coffee per person was the rule.

Nearly every day Frank Gamewell, head of the fortifications committee, appeared for breakfast. He was "the mildest of men ... a stooping figure, very quiet, and rarely speaks to us, and, when he does speak, never about what he is doing.... His working hours are so continuous, and everybody calling for him from every quarter, that he did not believe he could keep on if it were not for the hour's rest and good hot breakfast that he gets daily in Mrs. Squier's rooms." Gamewell spent his days "superintending the filling of sand-bags, the tearing down of houses adjoining our walls that might serve as cover for the enemy, the building of barricades and strengthening of walls from the timbers and bricks so obtained, making loopholes at the proper places for firing through."[6] Gamewell also dropped by Lady Ethel MacDonald's ballroom late at night when it was full of women in repose. He would chat through the door with the women, giving them an optimistic account of the military situation and reassuring them that there was nothing to fear. Frank Gamewell was enjoying the admiration of his missionary sisters, the elegant Mrs. Squires, and the high-spirited Miss Condit-Smith.

After breakfast Polly took a pot of coffee to the hospital to share it with the nurses and doctors and every night until midnight the Squireses' mess kept a pot of coffee hot for men coming off duty who were often wet, usually grimy, always exhausted. The two women also kept a zinc-lined box full of boiled rice water, the only remedy for the most common affliction during the siege: diarrhea. Men and women came by and helped themselves to a bottle as necessary.

The American missionaries lived in less splendor. Most of them had lost all their possessions except what they carried in their hands to the British Legation. A few missionary men went around the British Legation barefooted to save their only pair of shoes.[7] The chapel was the missionaries' base for living, eating, and sleeping. It was crowded but safe from shells and shot. Several single women, to escape the continual sound of crying children, went over to the MacDonald's house to sleep on the ballroom floor. "But, oh, how loud the bullets were! They cracked, cracked and crashed against the sides of the wall and the house."[8] Luella Miner was taking a nap in the ballroom one afternoon when a cannon ball took a piece out of the roof and showered tile down on the floor and the ten women resting there. Another cannon ball ruined Lady Ethel's lunch by blasting through the wall of her dining room and covering everything with plaster.

Most of the refugees in the Legation Quarter survived on the daily ration of communal food. Starvation was not a danger. Within the Legation Quarter several grain shops filled with thousands of bushels of white and brown rice and wheat were looted. Methodist Courtenay Fenn supervised the milling of the grain and Elwood Tewksbury, in addition to being chairman of the General Committee, supervised a bakery producing 300 loaves of bread per day. Fifteen mules in the Legation Quarter were appropriated to grind grain, most of them later serving the besieged as steaks and stews. Looting also produced an abundance of spices, pickles, candy, and liquor but a shortage of condensed milk and other foods for babies. Six foreign babies died during the siege. Their deaths were attributed to inadequate and unsuitable food.[9]

The much-admired Chamots also baked 300 loaves of bread every day.[10] The bread was coarse, a sour brown loaf made of crudely ground wheat and millet. Every day the Chamots loaded a cart with bread and delivered it to the British Legation. Their route was via Legation Street where Gilbert Reid had been wounded. Annie Chamot sat in the cart, rifle in hand, Monsieur Chamot on the shafts, guiding the mule, the two of them untroubled by the bullets and shells passing a few feet over their heads.

Horse meat was a major item on the missionaries' menu. "The race horses made good soup, while the fatter and lazier beasts furnished prime roasts and steaks.... The better the [racing] record the tougher the steaks."[11] The only milk cow in the Legation Quarter was cared for by Baron de Pokotilov, manager of the Russo-Chinese Bank, who hobbled around on a crutch and spent all day following his charge, ensuring that in her search for grass the lonely milk cow did not venture into harm's way. The milk produced was rationed out, spoonful by spoonful, to young children.

The Russians were the most equivocal nationality in the siege. Their soldiers and sailors were barbarous, but Russians of all social classes were warm-hearted and hard-working. It is hard to imagine Sir Robert Hart or any of the ministers, even the plebian Edwin Conger, tending a cow. But the exalted Baron de Pokotilov did so without complaint and gave the task as much devotion as he had formerly given to earning money in his bank. The American and Russian marines got along famously — when they were sober. The Russians hated the British. The Japanese and the British hated the Russians. The Americans liked everyone — except uppity British who called them "my man" and patted them on the shoulder.

Bertram Simpson told an amusing story about the eternal Russian search for sex. A Russian student made an appointment for a liaison with a young Japanese servant girl. That night, in the dark he sneaked into the women's quarters and felt his way down a corridor to a door he thought was the right one. Suddenly, from the dark room, came a voice in French. "Monsieur, do you want something? I would be pleased to give you what you want if you will stay at the door."

It was the voice of the wife of a diplomat and the Russian student saw his life flash before his eyes. These were the days when a husband killed — out of duty and honor — a man caught trifling with his wife. The startled Russian recovered and replied. "A thousand thanks, madame. I am only looking for grease for my gun."[12] The phrase "grease for my gun" became immortal among the young men of the siege.

Tastes differed. Harriet Squiers and her elegant messmates ate their meat out of cans and did not claim their daily ration of one-half pound per person of horsemeat. Many of the American missionaries, on the other hand, pronounced horse as good as beef. The missionaries donated their small stock of canned hams to the American marines who deserved, in their opinion, the best food the Legation Quarter could offer.

Horse meat was on the menu at the British Legation for the first time June 25. The ornamental rock garden in front of the theater was dug up and hollowed out and large kettles were set up to boil the horse meat. It was called "French roast beef" and served curried with rice. The bones and the table scraps were saved by missionary women to give to the Chinese Christians.

The Bulletin Board and Bell Tower. A peaceful scene photographed during the siege in the British Legation. The American missionaries were housed in the pagoda-roofed chapel in the right background. The Bulletin Board was the assembly place for the besieged (Smith, *Convulsion in China,* 1901).

Mary Porter Gamewell gives the recipe for cooking horse. "Cut in steaks, cover with hot water, and simmer for three hours; then brown in fat and add spice."[13] The menu at the American missionary mess on June 28 was as follows:

> BREAKFAST
> Porridge of ground wheat
> Steak
> Wheat Bread and Butter
> DINNER
> Soup
> Stew with brown flour dumplings
> Crackers and jam
> SUPPER
> Brown rice pancakes and syrup
> Bread, no butter[14]

The syrup and butter ran out shortly. The most popular item on the menu was pancakes. The recipe: "Left-over rice and left-over millet porridge were mixed with water and salt; a very small portion of flour, from our one bag of white flour, was added to help hold the mixture together, and baking powder made it rise. This combination, cooked on griddles prepared with drippings from horse meat or mule meat, returned from the kitchen in the shape of griddle-cakes each the size of a tea-plate — very light, very brown, very beautiful."[15] Eating rice was considered difficult by many of the besieged, especially those recently arrived from the U.S. who could not stomach the stuff.[16]

The worst plague of the Legation Quarter was flies. They covered the "ceiling of the chapel so completely that one could not see the ceiling for the flies. A gentleman coming into the chapel one night did something to disturb the flies that were roosting on the ceiling. He says that the buzzing of the flies was so loud and pervading that he could not hear the artillery booming outside."[17] The missionaries ate their meals with a Chinese servant pulling a punkah, a fan suspended from the ceiling, sweeping it over the dining tables and shooing the flies away. Although harmony prevailed among the American missionaries — or so they said — the Chinese punkah-pullers split along denominational lines. The Methodists and Presbyterians refused to shoo flies for the Congregationalists.

The besieged were lucky in the matter of water. Eight wells were inside the British Legation and five of them supplied cold and clean water. Although the conventional wisdom was that all water in Peking should be boiled before drinking, many people drank the water just as it came from the wells. At mealtimes, people were asked if they wished boiled or unboiled water. Nobody thought to keep a record whether those persons drinking unboiled water were more likely to suffer from diarrhea or typhoid fever.

The missionaries committed crimes in the name of nourishment. Alice Fenn had a sick child who could not keep any food down. Mrs. Fenn wanted an egg white to mix with water for the girl to drink and shamed her husband by telling him that another father had brought in an egg for his daughter. "I pointed out ... that if it were possible to loot one, we should thankfully use the only means that Providence allowed us of securing one."[18] The Reverend Fenn was uncomfortable with her theological reasoning, but, nevertheless, he went out and shortly came back with an egg in his pocket.

The peccadilloes of the missionaries were minor compared to the enormity of a crime by Polly Condit-Smith and one of her admirers, the near-sighted Belgian minister. One quiet evening the two of them were walking past the bungalow in the British Legation where Russian civilians were living. Knobel, who was always hungry, saw several fat hens nesting in the branches of trees. The two continued their walk. Nobody was around. Everyone had taken advantage of the quiet to get some sleep before the nightly fusillade.

Temptation conquered diplomatic propriety. On nearing the Russian bungalow again, Knobel turned to Polly and whispered. "If you will watch, I will get a chicken." Polly wrote:

> It flashed through my mind that at home, if clever darkies could not steal chickens without making a racket, I did not see how Knobel, who has probably never in his life come nearer to one than to pay his steward's bills, could expect to be successful. However, there was no time to argue. Knobel had left me standing in the road, watching his figure disappear in the darkness. A rustle, a slight squawk, and my Minister friend was by me again, with a squirming bundle under his coat. We ran, as if the Boxers were after us, straight to the Chinese courtyard, where we found our fat cook.... [He] was obviously delighted to receive our stolen booty — "All lighty. Me flixy good dinner to-mollow," and winked comprehendingly as he saw that Knobel had been holding Miss Chicken's neck so tightly she could not utter a sound. With a sign of relief, Knobel turned her over to the cook, and with another but deeper sign of anticipation of tomorrow's dinner, he stealthily started by a roundabout way to return to his quarters.[19]

* * *

The disharmony between the American marines on the wall and the diplomats in the legation continued. The marines suspected Herbert Squiers of maintaining his own elegant mess while feeding them poorly. Private Upham said that Squiers "put himself in charge of our stores at the beginning of the siege, and although we took enough canned fruit and vegetables and hams over to the general store house in the British Legation, he will not draw any for us although his own table is well supplied. We can get no satisfaction from Sir Claude as Mr. Squiers was appointed his Aide-de-camp [sic] after Captain Strouts was killed."

Nor did MacDonald escape the wrath of the marines. "Whenever Sir Claude or Squiers comes on the wall they get a very chilly deal from the men; they are frequent visitors there now that there is no danger. When the firing was going on they shunned the wall like poison. Sir Claude sent up orders by Captain Wray for us to fire on any Chinese exposing themselves. I told Captain Wray that Sir Claude's orders 'didn't go' on the wall; even Captain Hall when giving any orders was careful not [to] mention Sir Claude's name in connection with them for he knew how dearly we loved him." One can conjure up an amusing picture of a status-conscious British officer being told "Sir Claude's orders don't go on the wall" by an impertinent American private.

A food fight of comical proportions broke out when somebody stole Herbert Squiers' turkey on the dark, rainy night of July 27. Squiers had been saving the turkey for a rainy day and when it disappeared "he got out a search warrant for it." Alas for Squiers, the missing fowl was never found. The finger of suspicion for filching the turkey pointed at the American marines—who took the charge of thievery with merriment.[20]

* * *

Many men and women folded under the stress. Bertram Simpson wrote of the soldiers in mid–July. "Now all the fighting line is becoming openly discontented.... Discipline is becoming bad, too, and sailors and volunteers off duty are looting the few foreign stores enclosed in our lines. Everything is being taken, and the native Christians, finding this out, have been pouring in in bands when the firing ceases and wrecking everything they cannot carry away.... A German marine killed one and several have been dangerously wounded.... Our casualty list is now well into the second hundred, and as the line of defenders thins, the men are becoming more savage. In addition to looting, there have been a number of attempts on the native girl converts, which have been hushed up.... Ugly signs are everywhere, and the position becomes from day to day less enviable."[21]

Polly Condit-Smith commented about the civilians. "People who, before the siege began, seemed to have reasonable intelligence, and, if one had thought about such a thing, looked as if they would show up pretty well if they were put to it, have now gone to pieces entirely, lacking apparently the desire even to appear courageous. The men often make some trifling ailment an excuse to shirk all work for the common defense, and spend their time groaning over the situation, and becoming more hateful daily to the men and women upon whom the real responsibilities of the siege are resting; while the women who have collapsed simply spend their hours, day and night, behind the nearest closed door, and await each fresh attack to indulge in new hysterical scenes.

"I can honestly say there are more men to the bad than women.... Several people have already lost their minds."[22]

The most notorious of those who lost their minds was the Norwegian missionary Nostegarde—although he was probably crazy before the siege. He was a well-known character in Peking, a self-appointed missionary who made his living horse-trading. "He was subject to violent fits of anger, and always had a complaint against first one and then another. His manner was so extraordinary that only two opinions prevailed concerning him. One was that he was a wicked character, not to be trusted in any way, another that he was insane and therefore irresponsible."[23]

Nostegarde—the American marines called him "nasty guy"—began the siege by preaching a sermon in English to the uncomprehending French guards manning their barricades. Removed to the British Legation, he was a pest. While Captain Myers was marshalling his forces for the all-important assault on the Chinese barricades on July 3, the Norwegian turned up and caused a ruckus and had to be dragged away. Later he was locked in a room at the stable and placed under the care of the irascible Scottish missionary Dr. Dudgeon. Nostegarde wailed prayers and maledictions from his stable room — disturbing the British marines who slept in a room nearby. So loud was Nostegarde that, amidst the "demoniacal howls" of the Chinese attackers, he was heard shouting that the day of God's judgment was at hand. It is unlikely that Dudgeon's therapy would win the endorsement of psychiatrists, but he had an admirable scale of priorities. Dudgeon silenced Nostegarde with a few well placed cuffs to the head and shoulders.

The young American missionary William Stelle was disturbed by the doctor's forthright methods and asked if he could exercise "the persuasive force of kindness" to rehabilitate — or at least silence — Nostegarde. One evening, when Nostegarde started shouting, Stelle went to his cell room to begin his therapy of kindness. He was talking to Nostegarde when Dr. Dudgeon rushed into the dark room and, mistaking Stelle for the Norwegian, beat a tattoo of blows on Stelle, shouting, "I'll teach you to pray aloud. Didn't I tell you to keep quiet? I'll teach you to pray aloud."

Herbert G. Squiers. The rich, handsome American diplomat was chief of staff to MacDonald. He was a former cavalry officer (Coltman, *Beleaguered in Peking*, 1901).

Stelle ducked and dodged and, finally, unable to maintain his reverently mien, broke into laughter, while Nostegarde, "the real culprit, silenced by astonishment, knelt with clasped hands, in the attitude of a plaster image of little Samuel, and stared with wide eyes at the performance of which he was supposed to have the part of victim."[24] For that moment, at least, Nostegarde was silenced by astonishment.

Nostegarde later escaped from the Legation Quarter. The besieged assumed — many with relief — that the Chinese killed him, but he turned up again three days later, unharmed and unfazed. From a Chinese spy, the foreigners heard that he had been picked up in the streets — ragged, dirty, hatless, and coatless, and taken to Jung Lu's headquarters. He was fed and questioned and he gave the Chinese his assessment of the situation in the Legation Quarter, including telling the Chinese that they were firing too high and their shots and shells were doing little damage. His return was attributed to the superstitious awe the Chinese had for the insane. Some of the besieged wanted to shoot him as a traitor — or a nuisance.

* * *

The responsibilities of William Ament during the siege contained the germ of what was later to lead him into the murky waters of justice and revenge. He stood guard regularly at the British Legation. We don't know whether he ever fired a rifle in defense of the legations. A comment in the eulogy at his funeral, however, rings true. "In the siege he was scornful of bullets and was impatient of what he considered excessive caution against personal exposure."[25]

Within the boundaries of the Legation Quarter were dozens of Chinese-owned stores and residences. The owners had fled before the siege, leaving their property behind. Thus, the besieged had, ready at hand, a vast supply of goods of every kind for the taking, including the most abundant of commodities during the siege — liquor, champagne being the most abundant.

Pilfering quickly became a problem and the General Committee, impassioned with order and organization, sought to check pillage and ensure a wise use of resources. Will Ament, a man of stern principle, was the one-man Committee for Confiscated Goods.

"When the Chinese living in the Legation Quarter fled or were forced out by the foreign guards at the beginning of the siege, they left their things in their homes," and, according to one missionary woman, "it comes within the rules of war that we can take possession of the necessities of life. There were homes deserted where furniture and clothing, bedding, etc. were found, things much needed by those who had lost almost everything. Of course some one (Dr. Ament) was appointed to receive such things and deal out to needy ones."[26]

The more valuable items Ament acquired were turned over to Sir Claude MacDonald for an auction to benefit British soldiers; the less valuable were given to needy persons among the besieged, especially the Chinese in the *Fu*. Ament thus continued his pre-siege role as benefactor of the Chinese in a powerfully paternalistic position. The tennis court served as his base of operations. He displayed items for distribution and disposed of them in "equitable ways." This included a "booth for agate ware, one for Chinese clothes and trunks, one for tinned stores and later eggs, one for cigars (for the English and the Continentals, not patronized by our American missionaries)."[27]

Ament's work was both useful and necessary. Without him the scramble for confiscated goods by the Chinese and foreigners might have deteriorated into chaos. Discipline and obedience by the Chinese were essential to the survival of the legations. The missionaries were the instruments of discipline imposed in the name of Christianity — but it would have been wise for Ament to have paused in his labors for a moment of reflection. His life work was evangelism — a humble preacher of the gospel of Christ to the heathen. If, during the extraordinary times of the siege, he became as a moneychanger in the temple, he might have prayed to regain his moral equilibrium by a focus on less worldly tasks once he had guided his flocks through the valley of the shadow of death. He did not easily relinquish the power he attained during the siege.

15

Not Massacred Yet

The fall of Tientsin to foreign armies on July 14 stimulated the conciliatory attitude of the Chinese government toward the foreigners in the Legation Quarter. The Dowager and her advisors had little doubt that the day of reckoning was drawing nigh. The foreign armies would soon begin their inexorable march to Peking, and it would take more than Boxer magic to stop them. The Boxers, in fact, were missing in action, faded into the countryside from which they rose. It was time to dazzle the barbarians in the Legation Quarter with kindness and conciliation. With luck, when the foreign armies neared Peking, the unfortunate events of the last month would be forgotten and the red-headed barbarians and yellow dwarfs could be placated with a few trinkets from the treasury and the heads of a few insignificant officials.

The Chinese underestimated the vindictive resolve of their Western opponents. The foreigners in the Legation Quarter were bloodied but unbeaten, pleased to accept a respite in hostilities but placing no faith in Chinese promises. The Chinese had always enjoyed the respect and awe of both friends and enemies of the Celestial Empire. China had been conquered before, but absorbed barbarians as it had the Manchus. Now, the Chinese—self-satisfied and superior—realized that to this new species of barbarian, the Western Christian, China was a heathen, inferior, uncivilized nation of no great consequence. The Christians lived in China not to enjoy the benefits of its civilization, but to take advantage of its weakness. The once-mighty fall hardest. The humiliation of China was to endure for a hundred years as China lurched around the political spectrum searching for its lost equilibrium.

When diplomats and military commanders met at the British Legation on the quiet morning of July 17, their agenda was not the cease-fire but preparation for renewed fighting. Captain Strouts having been buried the previous day, they selected Herbert Squiers, the urbane, wealthy American diplomat and former cavalry officer, as chief of staff to Sir Claude MacDonald.

MacDonald and his new chief of staff toured the defenses on the Tartar Wall. Since the July 3 sortie of Handsome Jack Myers—whose spear wound refused to heal and who was still in the hospital—the Americans, and their Russian and British reinforcements, had taken control of two hundred yards of wall. Most importantly, the Americans had extended their fortifications eastward to control the wall over the water gate, a barred, semi-circular opening, fifteen feet high and a little wider, at the bottom of the Tartar Wall. The water gate allowed the passage out of the Tartar City of the drainage canal bisecting the Legation Quarter. It was through the water gate that the messengers to the outside world came and went and it would afford foreign soldiers—if and when they arrived—their easiest entrance to the Legation Quarter. The Chinese still occupied barricades on the Tartar Wall but they kept a respectful distance from the American barricades. The Chinese had made no attempts to advance their lines since July 3.

While MacDonald and Squiers were inspecting the defenses a Chinese commander hailed them and advanced down the wall with a white flag. He requested to remove the bodies of dead

Chinese soldiers rotting in the sun. MacDonald readily agreed; the smell of the dead men was overpowering. While Chinese soldiers were carrying away the bodies, the Chinese commander chatted with MacDonald and Squiers through an interpreter. He offered to take a letter to Jung Lu from MacDonald proposing a truce. MacDonald hurriedly composed a letter. MacDonald said the foreigners would not fire unless fired upon — provided that the Chinese not build any new barricades to advance on the foreign lines.

MacDonald's letter cemented the cease-fire and for several days scarcely a shot was fired in anger. The siege of the legations became an armed and wary standoff, but Frank Gamewell, his assistants — the "fighting parsons" — and Chinese labor crews continued their unceasing work on the barricades. The focus now was on counter-mines, ditches parallel to the defense lines of the British Legation to intercept attempts by the Chinese to dig tunnels and blow the foreigners up from beneath.

The diplomats sent letters back and forth. The Chinese said that the foreigners should place themselves under the protection of the Chinese government for escort from Peking to Tientsin. The foreigners — having no faith whatsoever in Chinese assurances of protection — equivocated and delayed, becoming more and more confident that some fine day the long-expected armies of their nations would appear in Peking to rescue them.

* * *

No cease-fire occurred at the Peitang, three miles from the Legation Quarter. Boxers and Chinese soldiers were determined to kill the hated Catholics. They ringed the cathedral and directed a stream of artillery fire at the handful of foreign soldiers and sailors, foreign priests and nuns, and more than three thousand Chinese Catholics within. On July 18, slow-burrowing Chinese duplicated their action at the French Legation five days before. They detonated an underground mine at the northwest corner of the Peitang, killing 28 people, including a French priest.

The hardships grew more terrible with each day. A nun tore up her letters to use as cigarette papers for the soldiers. The tobacco used for cigarettes was the dried leaves of a pear tree. The nuns did their best to take care of some five hundred orphans under their care, marching them from one safe haven to another. To the Italian nun, Sister Vincenza, was entrusted the care of sixty-six infants. She carried them around in an open umbrella, six at a time, swinging the umbrella in a vain effort to comfort the starving children. There was no food for the motherless foundlings and day after day and one after one they died. By the end of the siege, Sister Vincenza's brood of sixty-six was dead. Not a single infant survived.

The nuns themselves had little to eat but they did not complain. They longed for bread. "If ever I come out of this furnace, I will take my fill of bread. Only of bread!"

While Providence did not provide for the nuns and the babies, it was kinder to the fighting men. Vincenza recounted "the miracle of the yellow hen." She said: "Poor Signor Olivieri [the Italian commander] was in bed with a quinsy. And one of the Marist fathers was dying. We had no food that either of them could eat: not a thing! But the divine Providence came to our help. A yellow hen flew over the wall into our garden. The sailors caught it, and we made some chicken broth. With this we fed Signor Olivieri for two days."[1] Lt. Olivieri, twenty-two years old, survived to command the French and Italian guards.

On July 30, Lt. Paul Henry, commander of the French guards, was killed. Henry had rushed to the north wall with two of his French sailors to defend against what looked like a Chinese infantry attack. Henry and one of the sailors took a place at the wall. A bullet nicked the sailor's shoulder and deflected into Henry's throat, cutting an artery. Blood ran down the front of his uniform. Another bullet hit Henry in the side. He staggered away, then collapsed. One of his men took him into his arms. "Seeing blood on his tunic, they opened his collar. Then a jet of blood spurted from the wound.... He made a sign that he wanted to speak ... but no sound came.... His head fell inert."[2] A Chinese priest appeared and administered the Last Rites.

Henry was buried in the garden of the Peitang. Unlike the secular buildings of the Legation Quarter, all of which, except the building once occupied by the Italian Legation, are no more. The Peitang still exists. It is now the Beijing Thirty-Ninth Middle School, one of the most monumental schools in China.[3] The Catholics' foothold in the Imperial City — like most Christian influence in China — was erased during the communist era. China, in the end, it seems, absorbs all.

* * *

The initial provisions for a hospital in the Legation Quarter were modest. Dr. Wordsworth Poole of the British Legation and Dr. Carl Velde of the German Legation, both military surgeons, moved the furniture and books out of two rooms of the British chancery and set up an operating room with two tables and a hospital ward. The doctors had four beds and seven camp cots to accommodate their patients. Within three days the casualties overflowed the two rooms. They expanded to five wards, each adequate for 10 patients, in rooms in the chancery and neighboring houses, including a ward for officers and civilians in Sir Claude MacDonald's residence. For an overflow, three mattresses serving as hospital beds for five men were put in the hallways.[4]

Fortunately, in addition to the two military surgeons, the legations counted a large number of medical personnel, including at least eighteen doctors, but few nurses. With doctors in abundance, the critical need was for nurses. Anglican deaconess Jessie Ransome, forty-three years old, managed the hospital. She took leadership by virtue of her Church of England affiliation and religious title. The head of the nursing staff was Marian Lambert, also British and with the Church of England. Fuller, first name unknown, the steward from the British ship *Orlando*, was a tower of strength in the hospital. Five female missionary doctors, Americans Anna Gloss, Eliza Leonard, Maud Mackey, the recently-arrived Emma Martin, and British Lillie Saville volunteered to serve as the nursing staff. Feminists may deplore the second class status of the female doctors, but the surgeons had experience treating wounded soldiers and none of the women doctors did. American missionaries Abbie Chapin and Nellie Russell and Canadian Annie Gowans headed the hospital kitchen and provided, by all accounts, healthful meals for wounded men. A large number of volunteers, including several of the great ladies of the Legation Quarter, rendered admirable service.

Medical supplies were scarce. "It was a great mercy that two great essentials were on hand, antiseptics and. trained women as nurses.... All hearts were controlled by one desire, to give every possible help and comfort to the brave men who were giving their lives in the defense of men, women, and children unknown to them. All rejoiced together when the wounds were slight or when the desperately ill began to recover. All hearts ached with sympathy for the weary sufferers who wore out the siege week after week on beds of pain."[5] Sarah Pike Conger, always angelic if slightly batty, collected bandages, cloth, and linen for the use in the hospital. One day, Dr. Emma Martin was feeling sorry for herself but Mrs. Conger cheered her up by complimenting her work in Peking with the wounded soldiers. Emma dried her tears and accepted God's will and Mrs. Conger's blessing.[6]

Emma's comments reveal some of the inner workings of the hospital. Drs. Saville and Gloss were "to work during the day time for neither of them are very strong and I was so well and strong that they put me on as night nurse with Dr. Leonard."[7] One suspects also that the surgeons preferred to work with the more experienced Gloss and Saville during the day when most surgeries were performed. Emma had a taste of things to come the first night she worked alone in the hospital. She was to watch the wounded Captain Halliday carefully for signs of hemorrhage and to sit with the German soldier who had a fatal wound. The doctors could do no more for the German and their orders were they were not to be disturbed. The blond-haired German soldier — hardly more than a boy — died at dawn.

That was only the beginning. A wounded Russian was brought in soon afterwards with a bullet wound in the chest. The doctors operated on him successfully, but they had no more than finished than six American marines showed up at the hospital carrying one of their own shot through the head. The American, vomiting and dripping blood, died before the doctors could attempt to do anything for him. Turning away from the dead American, they found the Russian hemorrhaging. Back on the operating table his bandages were removed and the wound repacked. The Russian breathed in and out through the wound making a terrible sucking sound. Emma felt like crying, but she kept her composure through this marathon of fatal and near fatal wounds."[8] The American marine Martin described was probably Private C. B. King, the first of the Americans killed. The Russian apparently survived, a team of women including Polly Condit-Smith hovering over him to shoo away the flies that tried to congregate on his blood-soaked chest.[9]

Dr. Emma Martin, the Indiana farm girl, spent long, hot nights in the halls of the siege hospital, picking her way around sandbag barricades and among the pallets on the floor, her only light a tiny lantern shielded on three sides, breathing the acrid smell of gunpowder, and surrounded by men haunted by pain and fear. "They used to say that the blind beggars of Peking," said Dr. Anna Gloss, "could find their way from street to street by their nose, each alley and lane having an odor of its own. I have my doubts about that, but one thing I can say from experience — that in going around ... in the dark one could thus locate the hospital; an odor of carbolic acid and other disinfectants from the sheets hung out to dry proclaiming the place."[10] The hospitals of the time were characterized by the penetrating odor of the antiseptic phenol or carbolic acid, discovered by a Dr. Lister, and best known in later times — in diluted form — as a mouthwash honoring the name of its discoverer. The antiseptic of choice, carbolic, was in short supply and used near the end of the siege only for sterilizing instruments.

Military medicine had advanced since the American Civil War when principles of sterilization were hardly known and amputation was the remedy for a wound causing a broken bone. In the Civil War 30 percent of amputees died, mostly of infection, and nearly 20 percent of all wounded men died of their wounds. In the siege hospital only about 10 percent of wounded men died. Of 181 patients, mostly wounded soldiers, treated during the siege only fourteen would die of complications to their wounds in the siege hospital: three from dysentery, two from tetanus, and nine from wounds too serious to treat successfully. A few more patients died of wounds after the siege was over. Not a single person died of infection, a remarkable statistic. As was true later in the twentieth century a wounded soldier who lived long enough to get to a hospital had an excellent chance of survival.[11]

The success of the siege hospital treating wounded men was due to the quality and quantity of medical personnel. By the end of the siege the hospital was down to its last thermometer, last hypodermic needle, and last bottle of chloroform. Nurses fabricated dressings of ladies' "dainties"— linen underwear — and washed, sterilized, and reused them. Chinese assistants washed blood-soaked mattresses and put them back in service. American missionaries sewed hospital clothing, pillows, and sheets from the most colorful and expensive of Chinese fabrics — anything not appropriated by Frank Gamewell for sandbags.

The doctors and nurses worked under trying conditions. "I shall never forget one Sunday after the fighting began," wrote Janet McKillican, a Canadian. "I was in the hospital, and wounded were being carried in, while the smoke and ashes nearly blinded us. The bullets flew everywhere, knocking down plaster and bits of tile. A shell struck the ground near the hospital, where horses were tied under the trees, and killed one ... by night we often had to go into a room in total darkness and carefully grope our way among the beds on the floor, trying to be careful not to stumble over broken limbs and battered heads, doing what we could do for these poor suffering men — most of them mere boys."[12]

The nurses saw the fighting men with their emotional guard down. Outside, the men affected a casual optimism and good humor to bolster their resolve and to preserve the courage of the women — whose gentle natures, according to the chivalry of the day, would have been sorely tried had they been told the grim reality of the military situation. But in the hospital the wounded men dropped their pretenses. "The men were brave, patient, uncomplaining, but rarely hopeful. Other people might talk and plan for the coming of the troops; not so the hospital. The wounded lamented, being deprived of their guns, spoke more often of the fear of falling unarmed into the hands of the Chinese, who seemed like demons to them."[13] Again and again, the nurses had to restrain wounded men who tried to rise and go forth to fight, hallucinating that Boxer hordes were storming the legations. The noise of the Chinese fusillades was often so loud that nurses and patients shouted to hear each other.

The hospital was a place of blood, men screaming in pain, heat, dust, and flies. It was too much for Paula von Rosthorn, wife of the Austrian diplomat who, along with Annie Chamot, was one of the two women who carried a rifle and served on the defense lines. Brave though she was, Paula fainted dead away one day from the smell of blood, the heat, and the sight of a dying soldier.[14]

Emma Martin recorded frustrations in the hospital. Of Jessie Ransome, she said, "We have an English Deaconess as Hospital Supt. and she goes around with her keys and scissors jingling from her belt with no more executive ability than a chicken."[15] Emma was also critical of the male doctors — especially when a second patient was dying of tetanus. The male doctors were careless about sanitation. The tetanus patient slept on three different mattresses, which were washed and reused. So were the sheets and bed linens. Emma worried about catching tetanus or another communicable disease from her patients. The sheets the patients slept on were often soaked with blood and pus and she never wiped her hands on the towels. Moreover, Dr. Poole was careless with needles, giving injections to patient after patient with the same hypodermic. She commented however, that the nurses were careful with sanitation.[16] Emma also complained in her diary about the regime of male leadership. "We nurses were never allowed to do any dressings except when a surgeon was present, even when the dressing was neglected for days because the surgeons were too busy."[17]

Emma described the strain in her unpublished diary. "I fear I am a demoralized missionary. Spending many nights in the ball room [sleeping] and much of my time in the billiard room (set aside for the night nurses) sewing on Sunday (sandbags) sitting up all night with young men (in the hospital) sometimes too busy and tired to comb my hair daily or read my bible and pray as I should."[18] Publicly, the missionary chroniclers of the siege never expressed doubts in their faith; privately many of them must have had similar sentiments.

Emma was fond of the British hospital steward, Fuller, whose wife was in England. The two talked during the long dark nights. Their relationship verged on romance — the missionary doctor and the married sailor. Moreover, Emma attracted the American steward, a young sailor named Stanley. And William Stelle, the young missionary, spent time with the Martin sisters. "Mr. Stelle is the only bachelor [missionary] here to about 28 spinsters," she said. "Still he does remarkably well in showing no preferences."[19] (He would later marry the loveliest of the missionary spinsters, Elizabeth Sheffield.)

* * *

Another group of medical personnel concerned themselves with public health. Conventional wisdom had it that foreigners took their lives in their hands if they tried to live out a summer in Peking. Nearly all foreigners — including the missionaries — usually passed the hot months of summer at rented temples in the Western Hills or at the new beach resort of Peitaiho. However, in 1900, despite close confinement, danger, and poor food nine hundred foreigners lived through the Peking summer. The number of foreign deaths during the siege not related to wounds or complications of wounds was only eight. Six of the dead were young children for whom proper food was impossible to obtain. The other two were Russian soldiers who were notoriously unsanitary in their habits.

The "summer disease"—dysentery—was the most serious health problem. For Bessie Ewing, pregnant, sick, caring for two small children, it was a time of unremitting misery. Her daughter Ellen clung to her in terror and suffered terribly from the heat. Charles Ewing cut the little girl's long golden hair because it got soaking wet from sweat during the hot nights. Bessie got cankers in her mouth and could not chew the coarse rice served at every meal. The doctors put her on a liquid diet and she nearly starved. Ellen got running sores on her shoulder, cheeks, and in her hair and moaned "baby hurt, baby hurt, mamma put on medicine."[20] But no medicine cured the sores or the dysentery and, soon, the girl was too weak to stand and could only cry for her mother.

Theodora Inglis lost her baby on July 22. "It was a sad Sabbath morning. We watched by her little bed quietly and just as the clock finished striking the noon hour, her little spirit took its flight. One of the missionary men made a casket of pine boards and the ladies covered it with white flannel and lined it with some white silk which the ladies found. We found some white flowers and with a few green leaves tied them with some satin ribbon Mrs. Conger sent over. I put a little pink rose in her left hand and as we looked at the form lying there so quietly, while bullets were flying over our heads outside, could not feel that it was all for the best. Just as the sun went down we laid the little lamb beside the brave soldier boys who had given their lives in trying to defend hers."[21]

* * *

William Ament's boy — the fifteen-year-old Sunday school pupil he had taken in from the streets — brought the first news from the outside world. Disguised as a beggar, he was lowered over the Tartar Wall on a rope July 4, carried a message to British authorities or allied armies, wherever they might be, describing the plight of the besieged. He returned to the Legation Quarter on July 28 by slipping through the bars of the water gate at night.

The boy, named Liu Wuyuan, told of his journey to an admiring audience. He had his first problem before he even reached the bottom of the wall: the begging bowl in which he had hidden MacDonald's letter struck against a brick and broke. Liu tore a small piece of cloth off his tattered clothes and wrapped it together with the message around his finger as a bandage. Under cover of darkness he made his way down the moat along the wall to the burned Chien gate where he spent the night. The next morning he walked through the Chinese City and into the open countryside. Boxers stopped and searched him, but his disguise was convincing and he was released, the message still safely concealed in the bandage around his finger. On foot, and relying on the charity of poor country women, he made his way toward Tientsin. The foreigners at the Legation Quarter had anticipated that he would find foreign troops advancing on Peking at no great distance. He found only farms and villages, half empty of men who had gone off to join the Boxers.

Halfway to Tientsin, he stopped at a farmhouse to ask for food. The farmer put him to work, holding him a virtual prisoner for eight days. Liu's problem was to escape without arousing suspicion. A beggar boy should have been reveling in his fortune to have a job, food, and a place to stay. On the eighth day Liu shammed illness and the farmer turned him out of his house and bade him depart, quickly, lest his illness spread. Finally, on July 18, he reached Tientsin and found foreign soldiers, but it was July 21 before he managed to slip through the foreign military defenses to deliver his message to the British Consul. The next day, the consul, W. R. Carles, gave him a message for MacDonald and the boy left Tientsin on the return journey, the letter sewn into the collar of his coat. On July 27, he arrived back in Peking, and that night crawled along the moat to the water gate and entered the Legation Quarter unseen, his dangerous journey successfully completed.[22]

Never was the arrival of a messenger greeted with more enthusiasm. The last news the besieged foreigners had from their countrymen was a note June 15 from Admiral Seymour telling them he was forty miles from Peking. Sir Claude MacDonald's hands must have trembled with excitement as he unfolded the tiny piece of paper to read the response to his plea for rescue. He was profoundly disappointed. The letter read:

> Yours of the 4th July. 24,000 troops have now landed and 19,000 here [Tientsin]. General Gaselee expected Taku tomorrow. Russians hold Peitsang. Tientsin city is under foreign government, and Boxer power has exploded. Plenty of troops on the way if you can hold out in food. Almost all ladies have left Tientsin.
>
> W.R. Carles[23]

MacDonald and his diplomatic colleagues went purple with rage. How could the British Consul write such a casual and vague message? Carles had not even speculated on what most concerned them: the date they would be rescued. Rather it seemed that the foreign troops felt little urgency to reach Peking and rescue their citizens. The letter exploded hope in the legations that rescue was only a few days away. It was a devastating disappointment to learn that foreign armies had not even begun their march to Peking. Carles' letter was a low point. "Had not the arrival of the messenger been witnessed by numbers of people," Sir Claude MacDonald wrote, "it is more than probable that no notice of the contents of the letter would have been posted on the Bell Tower."[24]

The public was not pleased. George Morrison, wounded ten days before, was his usual caustic self. "Men read this communication and then moved away to express their feeling beyond hearing of the ladies. It was amusing to witness the petulance with which the British were forced to admit that this somewhat incoherent production was really written by a Consul still in the British service."[25] To Polly Condit-Smith, Carles' letter was "the worse news of the siege.... This was all very disheartening; but we realize more than ever before how long we still may be besieged, and the consequent economy of stores which should be practiced, and there is talk of commandeering all private food-supplies." She added, "Most people now feel that no reasonable Foreign Office should take two months to get a military relief party ready."[26]

Poor abused Mr. Carles was not quite as inane as he appeared to the residents of the Legation Quarter. "How should we have felt had Mr. Carles told us the truth?" asked Roland Allen. "The foreign military officers at Tientsin were feuding; foreign troops were slow in arriving, Chinese resistance to the Seymour expedition and at Tientsin had discouraged many military experts, who now believed that a hundred thousand troops might be necessary to advance successfully to Peking. Other military experts asserted that large-scale movements of foreign troops was impossible until the end of the rainy season—late August or September. Had Mr. Carles told the legations that an attempt to rescue them might be delayed another month or more the result would have been despair. Wrath and disappointment, with ignorance, were better than wrath and despair. We abused Mr. Carles roundly then; we know how to thank him now."[27]

* * *

The truce between the Chinese army and the foreigners in the Legation Quarter continued, with sporadic outbreaks of shooting, until August 4. The Chinese objective was to persuade the foreigners to accept the protection of the Chinese government and leave Peking with an escort for Tientsin. The foreigners had no faith in Chinese promises. Each day survived meant one less to wait for rescue. Pointless communication flowed back and forth between the Tsungli Yamen and the diplomats.

The truce enabled a flourishing black market in eggs. Those sick with dysentery could keep nothing on their stomach except egg whites. The Chinese surrounding the Legation Quarter quickly learned that eggs would bring a premium price of four cents each. With the cease-fire in force, they sold eggs to the besieged. On July 20, the General Committee headed by Elwood Tewksbury acquired 300 eggs and distributed them to the sick and children. Bessie Ewing got three. "What a Godsend these eggs are to us. Ellen was almost wild over hers. I am allowed to buy three a day, but only children or sick persons have permission to eat these luxuries."[28] The egg trade continued until July 31 when, it was noted with indignation, "The French have distinguished themselves this morning by shooting a nice peaceful Chinaman who was coming to sell us eggs."[29] The killing of an egg seller understandably discouraged his fellows and eggs again became an unattainable luxury.

Melons were another great luxury for the besieged. The Emperor and the Empress Dowager, as an expression of good will, sent three cartloads of melons to the Legations on July 20 and more along with other delicacies on July 27. The receipt of the melons put the foreigners in a moral dilemma. Should they refuse them? Might the melons be poisoned? Was it a sign of weakness to accept the melons? A deputation of women sent a memorandum to one of the diplomatic ministers arguing against the acceptance of "such treacherous bounty." Ada Haven was one of the anti-melon missionaries. "I am so anxious that the whole business should be finished up thoroughly, and the whole rotten structure of the present [Chinese] government be razed to the ground, that I am quite glad to have the siege continue till such time as the troops can come in sufficient numbers to accomplish the business properly. So when watermelons came in the other day, sent by the crafty Foreign office in the name of the Emperor, I would not take a bite."[30] She later relented by eating pickled watermelon rinds.

Folk of lesser moral purity enjoyed the succulent melons. "Men formed melon clubs and had solemn meetings in the morning for the discussion of these delicacies with true Epicurean precaution. The luscious gourd was allowed its proper season to cool in the well; then, brought forth with care, it was duly scooped and seasoned with claret. It was a most superb performance and quite unworthy of the tragic style of a serious and protracted siege. But men did not then want a dramatic famine, they wanted fruit."[31]

The cessation of hostilities also led to the resumption of a community life. Lacking the deafening roar of the nightly fusillade, a quartet of Americans serenaded the wounded soldiers in the hospital. The concert became so popular that the quartet moved to the Bell Tower to sing popular songs to a delighted audience. Soon, representatives of all the countries competed in rendering patriotic songs, national anthems, and hymns. The Russians were the best singers. The wife of Baron Pokotilov — the director of the Russo-Chinese Bank and the tender of the one lonely milk cow — was a former opera singer. Her interpretations of the Russian national anthem pierced the quiet of the night like a banshee shriek. The Chinese soldiers, it was said, fired off a volley at the sound of her voice.

On July 25, came another of the letters from "Prince Ching and others." This one reported that telegrams had been received from foreign governments inquiring as to the welfare of their citizens. The Chinese government, the letter stated, would be pleased to forward simple replies to these inquiries. A British marine suggested an appropriate reply. "Not massacred yet."[32]

16

Marching to Peking

At 3:00 P.M. on August 4, the allied expeditionary force left the foreign settlements of Tientsin and headed for Peking. The British, Americans, and Japanese marched up the west bank of the Pei River, the Russians and French up the east bank. Finally, the allied armies were on the way to rescue their citizens.

The British army numbered 3,000, mostly colonial troops from India—turbaned Sikhs, Punjabis, and Rajputs and the colorful Bengal Lancers—led by British officers. British sailors wrestled with 12-pound naval guns taken off HMS *Terrible* and mounted on wheels for the march. Three hundred British marines and three hundred Welch Fusiliers—the Fusiliers wearing a ribbon commemorating their service at the battle of Bunker Hill—comprised the British element of the ground forces. One hundred Chinese recruited for the First (and only) Chinese Regiment marched under British command.

The British commander was General Alfred Gaselee, an amiable and efficient officer of the Indian Army. At the general's side was his naval aide-de-camp, Roger Keyes. Lieutenant Keyes had schemed—to the fury of his superior, Admiral Seymour—to liberate himself from boring transport work with the navy to join the march to Peking. Keyes, the sailor, outfitted himself with a Chinese pony he bought for fifty dollars. The pony "had a perpetual readiness to jump off at full gallop, and the staff quickly named him 'the Torpedo.'"[1] Keyes didn't have much in the way of duties so he roamed up and down the allied columns.

Marching with the British and Indian soldiers were a thousand Chinese coolies. The British rounded them up in Tientsin and impressed them into service at a wage of three meals a day. The coolies carried the baggage of the soldiers, plus tents, camp equipment, water, fuel, and other essential items. The Chinese marched shirtless in the burning sun, straw sandals on their feet and bamboo poles suspended over their shoulders bearing their loads.

The Americans followed the British up the narrow track. Major General Adna R. Chaffee was the American commander. He was an old soldier, bluff and blunt, with thirty-nine years in the army, twenty-five years of which he spent on the western frontier chasing Geronimo and other hostile Indians. He respected Indians, but hated missionaries and marines—which did not bode well for the devil dogs, including eighteen-year-old Smedley Butler, recently promoted to captain and still recovering from a leg wound. To Butler, however, Chaffee "was magnificent. Just my idea of the way a general should look. He sat very straight on his powerfully built American horse. With everyone else in khaki, his blue coat made him look even more impressive."[2]

Chaffee had 2,000 soldiers from the army's Ninth and Fourteenth infantry regiments and a battery of field artillery, plus 500 marines who, reflecting General Chaffee's views on marines, brought up the rear and ate dust. The Americans had an easy-going, casual step. They dressed in khaki, although many men doffed their jackets to survive the hot days in their blue wool undershirts. They were a slouchy lot with unadorned uniforms worn in an as-you-please manner—soft caps bent into every shape and angle, shirts open at the neck, sleeves rolled up and flapping in the wind, and belts and leggings worn at the pleasure of the individual. A British officer described the Americans as "a magnificent body of men—few under 5' 10"—but they have not much discipline."³ The Americans also had Chinese coolies in their ranks, although—unlike the British—the Americans paid their employees a munificent ten cents a day. Most of the American baggage, however, was carried in big four-mule team army wagons hauling up to 4,000 pounds each. The American mule team drivers were the terrors of the road, sliding around the curves with breathtaking speed and disdain for safety.

Nothing illustrated the difference between the British and the Americans better than their respective messes. A British officer asked an American correspondent to dinner one evening. They ate inside a spacious dining tent with chairs and a camp table covered with cloth. Ice-cold Manhattan cocktails began the evening and dinner was six courses, two kinds of wine, coffee, and cigars, all served by Indian servants. By contrast, an American officer's dinner consisted of bacon, hardtack, potatoes, and black coffee eaten on upturned ammunition boxes. "The American officer prides himself upon the fact that he lives exactly as do the men in the ranks. Between the fare of the British army officer and that of the private there is no similarity whatsoever."⁴

The Japanese, with 8,000 men, on this first day brought up the rear of the allied column. Chinese coolies carried their equipment. The Japanese also had small carts, each drawn by a single horse—usually a stallion. They were not proficient at horse handling. A furious, plunging stallion broken loose from his cart frequently disrupted the neatness of the Japanese ranks. The Japanese soldiers wore white twill uniforms which were too tight for comfort. A bull's-eye design inscribed their white hats, drawing fire from Chinese riflemen. Other foreign soldiers scorned the Japanese uniforms, pointing out the impossibility of keeping them clean in the field. Impossible or not, the Japanese kept their uniforms tidy. In imitation of the Westerners, the Japanese wore—to their discomfort—heavy combat boots. At times, their soldiers would violate proprieties by removing their boots to march barefooted.

Major General Adna R. Chaffee. Commander of U.S. China Relief Expedition in China in 1900 (William Gardner Bell, *Commanding Generals and Chiefs of Staff 1775–2005*, Center for Military History).

Russia's 4,300 soldiers marched up the eastern bank of the Pei River. The white uniforms of the Russian soldiers quickly took on the color of their surroundings. The Russian soldiers were the least encumbered of the allies. They had carts pulled by Mongolian ponies but the soldiers carried most of their own supplies. Each soldier carried a blanket rolled up around a haversack, a soup can, and a wooden canteen. The Russian soldier ate soup and black bread three times a day. Americans thought the soup was good, but the sour bread seemed made "of equal parts of bran, sand, and sawdust."⁵ The Russians got bad marks from observers, "The Russians are an awful lot—no discipline—they are simply hordes of men—know little about their rifles—loot everything and everywhere — shoot everybody — they shoot all day long any defenseless Chinese. They are nothing more than savages and the Cossacks rather worse."[6]

Eight hundred French soldiers marched with the Russians, but their presence was symbolic as they had no supply train. Their transport consisted of a few carts and the staple commodity they hauled was casks of claret. It was a regular sight to see French soldiers off the edge of the road huddled around an overturned cart trying to rescue — or drink — the wine pouring out of a broken cask.[7]

Roger Keyes said the French troops were "disciplinary battalions from Indochina" and "simply the scum of the French army and quite disgraceful."[8] A German commander said, "The French are in universal disrepute — even the Russians do not want to have anything to do with them." The Americans would say of the French, "I guess they get cold feet when the guns pop!"[9] Most of the French enlisted men were Tonkinese — tough little men, even smaller than the Japanese, from what was later called North Vietnam. They were dressed in worn blue uniforms with white sun helmets.

The lack of French manpower, supply, and transport did not inhibit the French commander, General Frey, from attempting to play a leading role. The French had nothing to contribute but claret — and most of it was spilled. The French fell behind in the march, never coming near the sound of gunfire until they managed to catch up with the allies just in time to make a dubious contribution to the assault on Peking.

Scattered among the other nationalities were a few Germans, Austrians, and Italian soldiers. The Germans, for all their martial ardor and belligerent speeches, had still not managed to put together an expeditionary force. The Germans returned to Tientsin after a couple of days on the road after they tired of living on the charity of the other armies. Larger numbers of both French and Germans were on the way, however, and they later would play a major role in the occupation of Peking.

Between the Japanese, Americans, and British on the west side of the river and the Russians and French on the east was a flotilla of junks carrying supplies and wending its slow way up the muddy gray river. An American marine, Lt. Wirt McCreary, weary of snail-like progress following the convoy, crafted an admiral's flag out of an old blue shirt and flew it over his junk, asserting his right of way on the river. He kept pace with the column of marching Americans and kept them well supplied with the bacon they ate every meal. McCreary's deception was not discovered until his junk collided with another junk bearing a real Japanese admiral.[10]

Up and down the columns of marching troops were war correspondents. Two Americans, weighty Oscar King Davis and Herbert Hoover's friend Frederick Palmer, shared a cartload of supplies and worked together, one staying with the Americans, the other roving near the action at the head of the allied column. Palmer carried a bottle of Bass ale with him, "the last on the shelf of the Tientsin store for which he had paid two dollars." It was for William Bainbridge, one of the American diplomats besieged in Peking. Despite the hunger and the thirst of the long march, Palmer guarded his bottle of ale, "grimly, devoutly stubborn" to save it for Bainbridge. "What nectar it would be to him as, unshaven, palsied, hollow-eyed, he emerged from a dugout to greet the relief column!"[11]

* * *

The first objective of the allied armies was Peitsang, six miles beyond Tientsin, where Japanese scouts reported fortified Chinese positions. The columns of allied troops slept on the ground and ate cold food their first night on the road. At 3 the next morning, August 5, they were up to attack the Chinese positions. The plan was for the Japanese to turn the right flank of the Chinese by capturing an artillery battery on an embankment and assault the nearby trenches. The Russians and the French on the opposite side of the river would attack the left flank of the Chinese positions. The British and Americans would operate in the center, putting pressure on the Chinese to prevent them from reinforcing their flanks.

In fact, the battle was fought entirely by the Japanese. The Russians and French bogged down in marshes and never got near their objective, although the Russian artillery did some damage. The Americans got lost and never found the battlefield. The British bombarded the Chinese positions and were bombarded in return, with one man killed and twenty-five wounded.

The Japanese infantry, under General Fukushima, attacked alone up and down the allied front on the west side of the river. They were splendid, in the eyes of the beholders, advancing in a compact mass through tall fields of millet and corn, machine gun, rifle, and artillery fire pouring in on them from the Chinese trenches, their medical corps ranging the battlefield scooping up the dead and wounded as soon as they fell. The Chinese broke, but retreated in good order. Japanese cavalry chased them and captured eight guns.

By 8:30 A.M. the battle was over. The Japanese suffered heavy casualties: sixty dead and two hundred and forty wounded. As in the battle for Tientsin, Japanese ardor carried the day. Their troops advanced against strong positions and took them when soldiers of the other allies would likely have paused for reflection. Moreover, the Japanese showed an amazing sense of timing and location. Their units arrived where and when they were supposed to and achieved their objectives according to plan. The bogged-down Russians, the belated British, and the befuddled Americans would have required hours, possibly a day or two more, to have won the Battle of Peitsang.

The Japanese had a problem with their tactics—and it would haunt them in later wars. Their much-praised organization on the battlefield was achieved by advancing in close order ranks, men shoulder to shoulder and easy targets for machine guns, riflemen, and artillery. The Japanese never learned the dictum of General Patton: a soldier doesn't win a battle by sacrificing his life for his country; he wins battles by making the fellow on the other side sacrifice his life for his country. Chinese casualties in this battle were probably less than the Japanese. Few bodies were found in the Chinese trenches.

The next day it was the turn of the Americans to take punishment. The allied armies bivouacked at Peitsang for the night and at four A.M. began the advance to the next town on the road to Peking, Yang Tsun, ten miles away. The Americans and British, crossed over to the east bank of the river, and set out with the Americans leading, followed by the Russians and French while the Japanese brought up the rear. Bengal Lancers and Russian Cossacks scouted the terrain in front of the advancing columns. They reported a heavy concentration of Chinese soldiers at Yang Tsun occupying fortifications behind a high railroad embankment and between the embankment and the river.

What followed was less a battle than an ordeal. The Allies deployed five thousand yards from the Chinese positions, Russians on the left near the river, British in the center, and Americans on the right along both sides of the railroad embankment. The American Fourteenth Infantry, mixed in with British-led Sikh and Punjabi companies, led the attack with the Ninth Infantry covering its flank.

It was eleven A.M. before the allied troops were in position to attack. They advanced through tall fields of millet and muddy fields. The sun scorched them. The soldiers charged through the heat, their canteens empty. "There were no wells or streams of water in the country over which the advance was made. The men were famishing with thirst. They fell by scores with heat exhaustion."[12] The Royal Welch Fusiliers started the day with two hundred men. Half of them collapsed of heat exhaustion and twenty-nine were treated for sunstroke. When they located a well or a puddle the soldiers crowded around and fought for a drink.

Lt. Frederick M. Wise told the story of the battle: "The plain in front of us was a furnace. Dust rose in thick clouds. There was no air to breathe. That heavy heat and dust left us choking.

As we started forward there was a crash of sound at our rear. Our own artillery, firing over our heads was covering our advance."

Wise and the marines advanced rapidly more than a mile with the sun beating down on their heads, the men staggering and collapsing from sunstroke and heat exhaustion — a few dying. Bullets whizzed over their heads, but, as usual, the Chinese were shooting too high. Finally, the marines got within rifle range and they deployed in the dust and heat to fire a volley at the Chinese defense lines. They advanced and fired again. The Chinese were shooting back, but not a marine was hit. Another volley, another advance, and then they were near the Chinese earthworks and the Chinese soldiers broke and ran.

The marines climbed onto the earthwork defenses. Nobody was behind them. Chinese soldiers fled across the plain. The marines collapsed into the meager shade of the earthworks. They were exhausted. At Yang Tsun, the heat had been a more formidable opponent than the Chinese.[13]

For the American Fourteenth Infantry and its commander, Colonel A.S. Daggett, the heartbreak of the day came after the regiment, outpacing the British, overran the Chinese positions. General Gaselee, the British commander, did not see American soldiers enter a small village. He directed British and Russian artillery fire on the village and killed four American soldiers and wounded eleven others.

The Americans frantically sent out messengers to tell the British and Russians to stop the shelling, but several collapsed in the heat. Finally, they located several British soldiers sheltering behind the railroad embankment. One of them, Private Joseph Jackson of the Royal Welch Fusiliers, stood on top of the railroad embankment, under fire from both sides, and signaled the allied artillery to halt the bombardment.

The battle of Yang Tsun was over. The Chinese army retired in good order from the battlefield, abandoning a strong position after putting up little fight and suffering few casualties. The Americans had nine killed and sixty-four wounded, but fifteen more of the wounded would die within a few days. The British had six killed and thirty-eight wounded. The Russians reported casualties of seven dead and twenty wounded.[14]

The road to Peking was open. The Chinese army had scattered, its two strongest positions, Peitsang and Yang Tsun, overrun in two days.

* * *

After a day's rest, the allied armies renewed their advance. The Japanese moved out first at four o'clock August 8 crossing the river on a bridge of boats, following the road and the river leading north to Tungchou, thirty five miles away in a straight line — although nothing in China was a straight line. From Tungchou it was only twelve miles to Peking. The Russians followed the Japanese. Next came the Americans, the Ninth and Fourteen Infantry leading and the marines, including the limping Smedley Butler, in their dust. The British came last. The French remained in Yang Tsun to garrison the town and protect the route.

It was a trek nobody would forget. The road — narrow and dusty — twisted through fields of *kaoling*, Chinese millet, the tall, tasseled stalks rising ten feet tall and cutting off any flow of air. Clouds of mosquitoes ascended as the troops passed. No shade broke the heat. The noonday sun beat down and men collapsed. The dust kicked up by the eight-mile long column choked the soldiers. The road looped away from the river and water was scarce. What could be found was covered with green scum. The soldiers discarded their loot. "Our line of march was plainly marked by silk robes, rich furs and chunks of solid silver," commented Lieutenant Wise.[15]

The veteran foreign correspondent Frederick Palmer said it was "the most wearing campaign I ever knew. It wore this white man down to skin and bones. It dropped me on my face but, fortunately, in a shady place, so I was saved from the serious consequences of sunstroke....

Any man, white, brown or yellow, who went through that march to the end, is entitled to be called majestic."[16]

The Japanese had the easiest time of it. They bore the brunt of the fighting along the route, but there wasn't much. They got an early start every day. They regulated the speed of the advance, deploying to chase away groups of Chinese soldiers and civilians who looked as it they might be Boxer sympathizers. When they outran their transport, the Japanese soldiers found a shady spot and rested until their horse carts caught up with them. The soldiers of other nations behind them had to wait in the sun until the Japanese were ready to move forward. By midday, the Japanese completed their day's work, found a good place to camp, a watermelon field to harvest, and were washing themselves and their clothes in the nearby river or at a village well.

The Russians following the Japanese turned a darker shade of dust every day. They were a hardy lot, lightly burdened, ready to eat, drink, and kill anything. They were "physically, by far, the sturdiest soldiers of the allies."[17] Even so, Russian soldiers collapsed in the heat, their men joining a polyglot army of stragglers who trailed after the main column, motivated to stay close by the knowledge that lurking Chinese were not gentle with captured allied troops. Smedley Butler saw two Japanese soldiers nailed to a door, their eyes and tongues cut out.[18]

Bringing up the rear, the Americans and the British trudged through the heat and the dust, playing a game of hurry-up and wait, strung out or compressed like the bellows of an accordion. They drank the putrid water left behind by the Japanese and Russians. The Indian troops bore the heat better than their lighter skinned colleagues. Lt. Keyes, like most British officers frugal in his praise of Americans, said, "The Americans, who were just ahead of us, were far worse off than we were, thanks to the silly felt hat they wear, and the route was strewn with their heavy kit, which many had thrown off, and men were lying by the roadside beat to the world."[19] The British had a long-term fixation on the notion that a proper man wore a tope in the midday sun.

Stragglers, revived in the cool of the evening, struggled into camp all night long or caught a ride in a field ambulance or the big American wagons following the column. The American Fourteenth Infantry had four field ambulances "reserved for the severest cases, but forty could have been filled."[20] Played out soldiers and marines were left behind. A regiment of American marines numbering 511 officers and men left Tientsin August 4. Only 281 reached Peking. Their battle casualties were one man wounded; the rest were felled by the heat. Newly promoted Captain Smedley Butler was among the survivors. His wounded leg gave him pain and one day he nearly collapsed but he clung to the horse of a mounted officer and "managed to worry through."[21]

Lieutenant Harllee described the four-day trudge from Peitsang to Tungchou.

> We marched through corn fields where the corn was higher than a horseman's head and the heat was stifling. The halts for rest gave us no relief because the sunshine beat down upon us. The men cast away their rolls and some their haversacks and then lay down and died along the road. Both sides were lined with men in convulsions and foaming at the mouth and of all nationalities mixed up together. The Indian soldiers also died along the way. Every short distance dead Chinamen with bayonet holes through them and all swollen up had to be stepped over. Some were beheaded and their heads suspended from cornstalks by their pigtails. All Chinese stragglers were killed, by the bayonet if practicable, and the Russians chopped their heads off. Some Russians fell into the hands of the Chinese and were butchered.
>
> Burning villages lit up the skies at night all along the road. What couldn't be used by troops was destroyed. We did all our camping in corn fields and for over a week I was never under the shade of a tree.[22]

The Chinese committed their share of atrocities; the Japanese and the Russians added their contribution. The journalist Palmer saw Japanese soldiers kick a Chinese soldier to death. To the Japanese, a soldier who surrendered was worst than a beast. Women were, as usual in war, the victims of the worst atrocities. "One needs not to be puritanical or hysterical to condemn the wholesale ravishing, sometimes to death, of terrified females between the ages of six to sixty by clodhopping brutish soldiers, who misrepresent alike Christianity and civilization."[23] Many women committed suicide by throwing themselves down wells or drowning themselves in the river.

The British and Americans—although not innocent of killing Chinese of all ages and sexes—took the practical approach of impressing Chinese males to work pulling transport junks up the Pei River or carrying supplies in the columns. The Russians also soon learned that a live Chinese was more useful than a dead one. They snatched up any Chinese they found and saddled him with their packs. The Russians found a couple of camels and loaded them down with field packs like umbrellas hanging on a coat rack.

The twice-defeated Chinese army lost any desire to contest the passage of the foreign armies. The Japanese cleared and burned villages as they advanced, driving the Chinese before them with artillery salvos, and marking their passage with Chinese bodies and heads—many of whom appeared to be non-combatants.[24] The Bengal Lancers,

A Chinese family sits down to lunch. The war damage to this modest house near Tientsin is visible (Ricalton, *China through the Stereoscope,* 1901).

scouting at the head of the column, encountered Chinese cavalry and drove them away after a brief skirmish. The British found and exploded a Chinese powder magazine so large the ground shook three miles away.

* * *

On August 10, messages from the advancing army were smuggled into the Legation Quarter. General Gaselee, the British commander, was brief: "Strong force of allies advancing. Twice defeated enemy. Keep up your spirits."[25] The Japanese deputy commander, General Fukushima, was more specific. "Unless some unforeseen event takes place, the allied forces will ... arrive at Peking on the 13th or 14th."[26]

Joy! The besieged were elated but reflection caused apprehension. Would the Chinese make a last-minute attack to eradicate the foreigners in the Legation Quarter? Frank Gamewell kept on working. The thought that their ordeal might be over perked up Polly Condit-Smith. She had cracks in the veneer of her courage. "The shrill cries of 'Sha! sha! sha!' (Kill! kill! kill!) and the constant blowing of trumpets is enough to account for our continued nightmares. While awake the brain can be somewhat controlled, but the real horror of our situation follows us even in our sleep. On awaking, one wishes one were asleep again, as the heat is something awful. The very worst weather of the year is upon us: the rain is almost incessant, and everything is sticky and muggy. Of course, this continual downpour is very hard on the soldiers, making everything a mass of mud, and the long, nightly attacks keep them out in the wet for hours. The flies, mosquitoes, and fleas are pests that still continue."[27]

The Chinese Christians in the *Fu*, mostly Catholics, were starving. A delegation of Protestants went to the *Fu* to devise a plan to relieve the hardship. The daily ration of the Catholics was cakes made of chaff, sorghum seeds, wheat, and the leaves of elm trees. The Protestants, confident now that they had enough food for themselves and their converts allocated additional grain to the Catholics. Dogs over seven pounds in weight were ordered killed as food if running loose. Two horses condemned as unfit for human consumption because of disease were butchered and their carcasses were sent over to the *Fu*. In idle hours the soldiers shot dogs, cats, magpies, crows, and sparrows for the Chinese.[28]

On August 12, the Chinese opened up a round-the-clock barrage at the legations. "Hell cannot be worse than what we had to endure.... Three powers were fighting us at the same time — extreme heat, fleas, and these devils of Chinese; it is hard to say which one was the worst. Firing did not cease during the whole night."[29] Two French soldiers were killed. A German was wounded in the temple; the doctor cleaned blood, bone, and brains out of the open wound and left the bullet inside. He lived.

Despite the renewed Chinese attack, the besieged were inured to the sound of gunfire and hardly altered their daily schedule. At the chapel, where the missionaries made their home, the scene was almost casual — although punctuated with the sound of gunfire. Gilbert Reid, the wounded missionary, was up and around again and he sat at the end of a table, dictating to Mary Andrews. At the same table sat Dr. James Ingram making a map of the defenses which he would later see published in *The Independent*, a weekly newsmagazine. White-bearded Chauncey Goodrich, thirty-five years in China, was at the other end of the table. He was the author of *Goodrich's Pocket Chinese-English Dictionary*.[30]

George Morrison was up and around, walking with a cane, almost recovered from the wound in his thigh. He had written most of his account of the siege and was awaiting his first opportunity to send it to the *Times*. William Ament was sorting confiscated goods for the next auction. His auctions, thus far, had netted $681 for a fund to benefit Chinese Christians. The American sailor, Gunner's Mate Joseph Mitchell, was probably sleeping. Nearby was his creation, "Betsy," the homemade cannon. Were a vote taken of the most valuable of the legation guards, Colonel Shiba would win easily but Mitchell might come in second. Frank Gamewell, the consensus selection as most valuable civilian, was working as usual, repairing weak spots in the defense, supervising a gang of Chinese workers digging a counter-mine, and chinking a few last cracks with sandbags. Gamewell was always busy — but never too busy, it seemed, to miss breakfast with the charming Miss Condit-Smith.

Mary Porter Gamewell prepared, as were many of the women, for the arrival of their rescuers. Later, she would write. "One of the army officers asked, if we had the siege to go over again what we would do? I said there was one thing we would not do, and that was to take extra trouble to have on clean clothes to welcome the relieving army. I do not like to recall how I ironed the day before the troops came. I had been sick and was just up and able to get around. My knees trembled under me while standing, and two bullets struck the roof of a little house five or six feet from where I was standing, and sent the brick dust over my clean skirt and shirt waist. We had one iron for I don't know how many people to use, at least twenty-five. These ladies were waiting for me to get through so they could iron."[31]

Up on the Tartar Wall, the American marines improvised flagstaffs to fly the flags of the United States, Russia, Germany, and Great Britain. The flags, they hoped, would guide foreign soldiers to the base of the Tartar Wall and the water gate, the easiest entrance into the Legation Quarter.

* * *

Chinese attacks on the Peitang had slackened. The main problem was food. Favier reduced the daily ration for 3,000 Chinese Christians to two ounces per person. "The horrors of the famine make themselves harshly felt," said Favier. "Bodies lengthen, color vanishes, an air of death reigns among us. Walking corpses still move about, but with effort ... leaves of trees of every sort, remains of every kind, all are gathered up with care, with rapacity, one might say.... Our Christians are so enfeebled that they lie out on the verandas, thin, pale, almost dead."[32]

The worst was yet to come. On August 12, at 6:30 in the morning, the Chinese exploded a huge underground mine in the northeast corner of the orphanage beneath a building full of families, another building housing several Italian sailors, and the house where lived Lt. Olivieri, the Italian naval officer in command of the defenders. The mine swallowed up a hundred yards of wall and collapsed the buildings. When the mine exploded, the Italian nun, Sister Vincenza, was at mass. She ran to the spot of the explosion. Sister Vincenza saw that among the ruins was Lt. Oliveri's house. She and others sorted through the ruins, moving beams and rocks to see if Olivieri was alive under the rubble. All was silence.

The Catholic priests and nuns moved on to the ruin of another building where they heard the cries of women buried in the debris. One of the women was trying to get out and a Marist priest ran to help her. As he reached the house a bullet hit him in the chest. "He had just time to begin the Act of Contrition. He finished it in Heaven."

Sister Vincenza tells her story.

> I ran back to the house of Signor Olivieri, where I found the five Italian sailors, who were still alive. And once more we began to pull away the beams and the rubble and the iron bars. Seventeen big beams had fallen from the floor above. After more than an hour's work we heard a voice, a groan! What a moment! "He is not dead. He is alive!" we shouted at one another. At last we managed to uncover him. He was sitting on his bed with his chin pressed against his knees because of a heavy beam which weighed down on him. What had saved his life had been the mosquito curtain. The net was wound round his head and kept the dust from his face. But how had he been able to breathe down there during an hour and a half or two hours?
>
> His first words were: "And the nuns? Are there any victims among the nuns? And my sailors?"
>
> We told him that all were safe. He was too weak as yet to be told the truth. The two bishops came at once to see him, and everyone hailed the miracle! ... Signor Olivieri had only one small wound on his head, but he was racked with anxiety. The wall which separated us from the Boxers had fallen down, and they could have entered easily. But our Angels kept guard."[33]

The great mine killed 137 people, including eighty-one adults, fifty-one children, and five Italian sailors. The next day another mine, smaller than the first, exploded near the earlier crater but it did little damage. The mines were the last attempt of the Chinese to annihilate the defenders of the Peitang. Lt. Olivieri, a man of miraculous escapes, Sister Vincenza, and Monsignor Favier would survive.

* * *

On August 12, the allied armies gathered at Tungchou The Japanese, without waiting for their allies, blew a gate open, shot a few Chinese, and entered the city without a fight. Tungchou was undefended and depopulated. The Chinese armies had disintegrated and the residents of the city had fled. By noon all the allied forces had settled down in comfortable camps. The Americans found a shady spot near the west gate, a clear stream of flowing water nearby. The soldiers and marines took an afternoon's rest in cool, watered ease — or, for the most adventurous, a looting expedition into Tungchou.

The generals met that afternoon. All the allied commanders except Lineivitch, the Russian, wanted to press on to Peking the next day. General Lineivitch said his men were tired and demanded a day's rest before undertaking the assault on Peking. They reached a compromise. Next day, each of the allies would scout their route and establish forward outposts. In the afternoon, their soldiers would march forward to the outposts, about five miles from Peking, where they would camp for the night. The next day, August 14, the foreign armies would advance, batter their way into the city, and relieve the siege of the legations.

All apparently in accord, the generals returned to their camps to prepare their soldiers for the march. The allied armies in Tungchou, decimated by sunstroke and heat exhaustion, probably did not number more than ten thousand men. The ten thousand would attack the capital of the oldest and most populous nation on earth.

* * *

From Tungchou multiple routes led to the gates of Peking. The foreign armies would approach side by side, like runners moving up to the starting line, and, at the crack of a figurative pistol, begin a race to be first to reach the legations. It was to be, in Olympic terms, a run for the gold — and may the best army win.

The Russians would take the northernmost route, the right flank of the allied advance, their objective the Tung Chih gate in the Tartar Wall, the most distant gate from the Legation Quarter. Next, would come the Japanese, their objective the Chi Hua gate north of the Imperial canal. On the south side of the canal the Americans would advance toward the Tung Pien gate where the Tartar Wall meets the Chinese Wall, the nearest of the outer gates to the Legation Quarter. The Americans had drawn a good route, and would have an advantage in the race. Next, on the left flank and the most southerly of the armies, would come the British with their objective the Sha Wo (Hsia Kuo) gate in the wall of the Chinese city.

A fifth runner arrived at the starting line. General Frey, the glory-minded French commander, caught up to the main body of allied troops with a contingent of several hundred exhausted French and Tonkinese soldiers. The French were sandwiched into the race between the Japanese and the Americans. Frey would get about one-half a lane to run in. Undaunted, he came out with the most inspirational of the general orders which each commander issued to his army on August 13. "Tomorrow, under the walls of Peking, when the foreign national anthems are played, a complete silence will be maintained; each anthem will be heard with respect. When the French national anthem is played, it will be sung as loudly as possible, in tune, by the whole of the French Expeditionary Corps. Our compatriots and the occupants of the foreign Legations beleaguered on the other side of the walls of the Chinese capital will know, when they hear our noble war-chant, that deliverance is at hand."[34] Frey was not deterred from glory by such minor matters as a shortage of men and material. If nothing else, the French would sing better than anyone else.

* * *

General Adna R. Chaffee moved out early August 13 to scout the route. His outpost established, about five miles from Peking, as agreed among the commanders, Chaffee leisurely moved all his troops forward and the Americans settled down for the night, ready to wake up and assault the massive walls, battlements, and pagoda gate-houses of Peking, now in sight through the dusty haze of a hot China evening. Ahead, from within the city, were the sounds of battle. A passing storm mixed the boom of thunder and artillery. The barking of small arms floated across the distance. Was this the last stand of the legations while idle rescuers slept within sight of their objective?

At daybreak, the Americans put cavalry out front to scout the route for the infantry forming up to march. A Japanese staff officer interrupted Chaffee's preparations. "Where," he asked, "were the Russians?"[35] They were not on the Japanese right where they were supposed to be. The question was soon answered. Fighting was going on now in front of the American and Japanese lines. It was the Russians. General Lineivitch's "exhausted" soldiers had stolen a march on the other allies and were already on the attack. Moreover, rather than north where they were supposed to be, the Russians during the night had crossed the Japanese front and were attacking the Tung Pien gate, the assigned objective of the American army. The Russians had jumped the gun, but no referee existed to call them back to the starting line and force them into their proper lane.

The race was on.

17

Rescue

On August 13, the allied armies only five miles away, the Chinese attacked the legations from the Mongol Market just after dark. They fired a two-inch Krupp gun from the Imperial City, apparently on this occasion by gunners who knew how to hit what they intended. "In ten minutes this gun did more damage than the smooth-bores had effected in a five week's bombardment."[1] One of the shells hit the dressing room off the bedroom of British minister Sir Claude MacDonald and made a wreck of it. Another came through the fortress at the front gate of the British Legation and knocked the guards down, stunning them. The Chinese fired the Krupp cannon only seven times before Joseph Mitchell, the gunner of the Colt machine gun, found its location and loosed a long burst. The cannon was heard no more.

Twice during the night a general alarm called all volunteers, including the members of the dubious Carving Knife Brigade, to their posts. The Anglican priests, Norris and Allen, armed themselves for the first time during the siege. Many of the women tucked pistols in their clothing in the expectation that, if worse came to worse, they would shoot themselves and their children. At the barricades, Chinese officers urged their troops forward — but the soldiers declined. They blustered, yelled, trumpeted, and fired rifles into the air but they would not leave cover and rush the walls behind which were the foreigners. The red-headed devils did not save their ammunition tonight. Ever man and every gun blazed away. The heavens replied in kind with a storm that sent rain down in torrents and punctuated the cries of "Sha, Sha" with thunderclaps.

For five volunteers from Sir Robert Hart's Imperial Customs occupying a trench in the *Fu*, it was the worst night of the siege. The men faced a large number of Chinese as little as five yards away on the other side of a barricade. They shredded the barricade with their rifle fire. But the Chinese soldiers in the *Fu*, as they had in the Mongol Market, declined to assault the handful facing them in the trenches. The foreigners survived the withering fire passing a few inches over their head while standing in knee-deep mud. They feared they had been abandoned, that the Italians to one side had retreated and they were isolated and surrounded. Only their confidence in the capability of Colonel Shiba kept them in their trench — and then, about 2:00 A.M. they heard heavy guns in the distance. Rescue was at hand! The Chinese heard it too and their attack in the *Fu* slacked off.[2]

There were casualties. A French priest and a Belgian doctor were slightly wounded. The Japanese doctor at the *Fu* was shot in the leg. A British marine was wounded in the shoulder. A German soldier was killed as was a Russian on the Tartar Wall. Joseph Mitchell, the American gunner of "Betsy" had an arm shattered by a rifle ball while he fired his homemade cannon from the strong point fort overlooking the Mongol Market.

"We passed the most dreadful night of the whole siege. We were grouped together as closely as possible, and had to yell at the top of our voices to make ourselves heard."[3] At two in the morning came the sound of a machine gun —"like a rapping of hard wood on hard wood"—

from the east—the direction of Tungchou and the relief force.⁴ The American missionaries gathered outside the chapel. Was it the foreign troops? Nobody could say—but the Rev. John Wherry offered thanks and they stood in the moonlight, heads bowed, while Chinese bullets whistled overhead and the five heavy guns of the foreigners—"Betsy," the Italian one-pounder, and the three machine guns: the American Colt, the Austrian Maxim, and the British Nordenfelt—sounded their distinct voices. The missionary women made coffee and cocoa for everyone in the chapel. There seemed no need to ration luxuries now. Death—or salvation—was at hand. Bessie Ewing "was the only grown person who slept."⁵ She was tired and weak from three weeks of sickness and five months of pregnancy. People came to her bedside and asked if she heard the machine gun. She sent them away and went back to sleep.

An American soldier puts cream in his coffee. The British ridiculed the slouch hats of the Americans as inadequate to protect them from the hot Chinese sun (National Archives, ca. 1900. Public Domain).

At five came the sound of big guns to the east to go along with the rat-tat-tat of the machine guns. Now, there could be no doubt. The foreign armies were at the gates of Peking. The last attempt of the Chinese to annihilate the defenders had failed.

* * *

The first among the relief force to enter the city of Peking was a character from the underbelly of Chinese politics, a Norwegian named J. W. N. Munthe, a Chinese-speaking mercenary, former cavalry instructor, and a guide, scout, and interpreter for the Russians. Munthe led the Russian general Vassilevski, a battalion of Russian soldiers, and an artillery battery to the Tung Pien gate about midnight. Under cover of a heavy thunderstorm they approached within two hundred yards of the Tartar Wall without drawing fire, crept forward, crossed a bridge across the moat and surprised thirty Chinese soldiers at the gatehouse. In a brief battle with rifle and bayonet they killed the Chinese. But the alarm had been sounded and Chinese soldiers in the pagoda over the gate fired down at the Russians. The massive outer door to the gate was closed. The Russians brought forward two field artillery pieces to knock a hole in it. Twenty shots were necessary to blast a small hole in the iron-clad wooden gate. Vassilevski and Munthe squeezed through the hole and bid their soldiers follow. Now, they were inside a courtyard between the outer and the inner doors of the Tung Pien, trapped as if in a well, surrounded by towers with Chinese soldiers above and around shooting down into them. "It was a scene of the wildest excitement.... The savage yells of the Chinese from above, the flashes of musketry playing along the edge of the wall, the deafening din of their gingals and of the Russian rifles, drowned the moaning of those unfortunates who fell, wounded and dying, in scores."⁶

The Tung Pien gate was a trap. The gate, with its five-story tower, intersected the walls of the Tartar and Chinese cities. The Russians would have been massacred had they not managed to force their way through two posterns—side doors—of the massive gate and into the open,

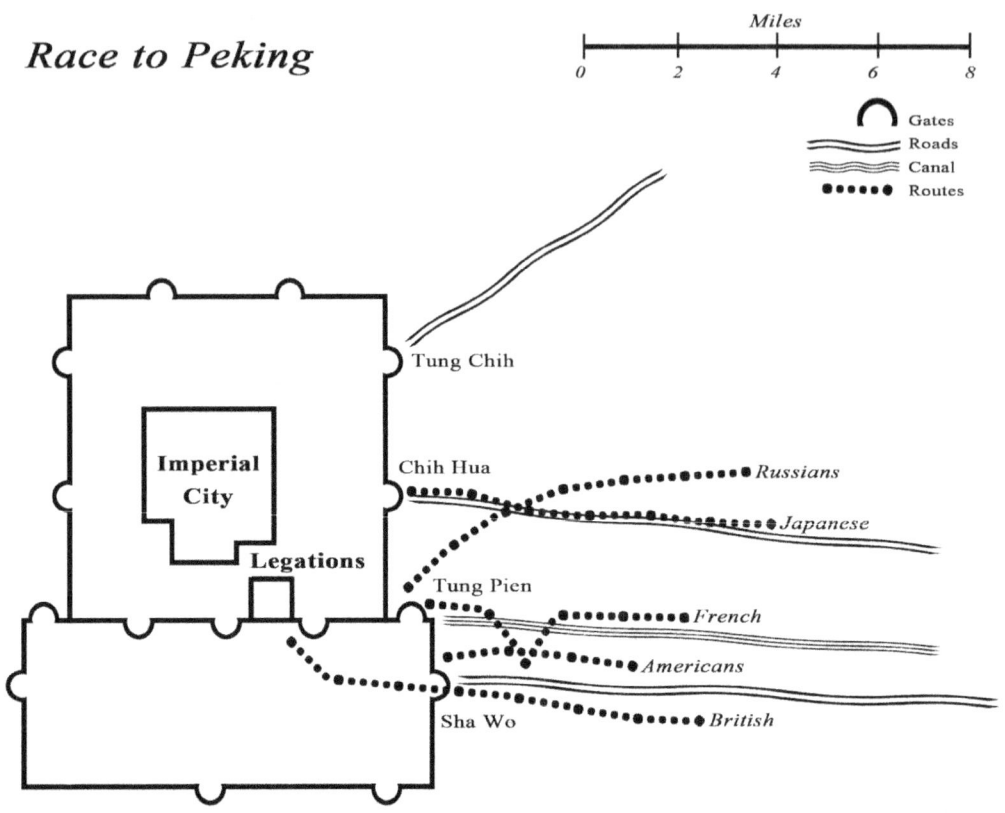

The Race to Peking. The allied armies set out from Tungchou on August 14. Each nationality wanted to be first to relieve the siege of the legations (by Kathryn Kelly-Hensley, 2008).

inside the Chinese City, at the foot of the Tartar Wall. They proceeded carefully along the edge of the wall. But their troubles were just beginning. From the wall, the Chinese poured fire down upon them, killing the horses pulling their guns and several men. It was impossible to move without abandoning their guns, so the Russians dug in to wait for daylight and reinforcements. Their little excursion had cost them twenty-six men dead and 102 wounded, including General Vassilevski. The Russians' premature attempt to relieve the siege of the legations stalled.

* * *

While the Russian adventure at the Tung Pien gate was going awry, the other allies were advancing on schedule. The two American correspondents, Frederick Palmer and Oscar King Davis, tossed coins to see who would accompany the Japanese and who would stay with the Americans. Palmer won — or so he thought — and went with the Japanese. As the Japanese had led the allied column most of the way to Peking, chances were they would reach the legations first. Palmer carefully packed the bottle of Bass's ale in his haversack. He had been tempted during the hot, dusty march to drink the ale, but conscience prevailed. His friend Bill Bainbridge in the legation had endured incredible privations. He would appreciate beyond measure the gift of a bottle of ale.

The Japanese proceeded according to plan and pulled up in front of their assigned gate, the Chi Hua, at their assigned time of eight A.M. Chinese soldiers awaited them. The Japanese rushed the gate shoulder to shoulder and were repulsed by rifle fire and artillery. They brought their field artillery up and spent the rest of the day shelling the gate and the Tartar Wall. The shells bounced off the gate without doing much damage, but Chinese resistance slowly evaporated. That night, about nine P.M., repeating their exploit at Tientsin, Japanese engineers blew the gate down with an explosive charge and their infantry raced into the city meeting little opposition. Palmer was with them, but by that time he knew that the Japanese had lost the race to relieve the legations. The Japanese, as usual, suffered heavy casualties: two hundred men killed or wounded.

U.S. commander Adna R. Chaffee was a man of limited imagination. He knew the Russians were somewhere in his front doing something they were not supposed to, but, like the Japanese, he followed the plan, sending his cavalry out to scout his route at first light. The cavalry ran into opposition and the missionary scout E.K. Lowry, whose wife was among those in the legations, rode back to Chaffee to request help. Chaffee and a battalion rushed down the road to rescue the cavalry.

The Americans encountered two hundred French troops on the road. The French commander said he was marching to join the Russians. Chaffee told the French to get out of his way and, as the chronicler delicately puts it, "it was with much difficulty that he persuaded the French commander to let the Americans pass."[7] Shoved off the road, the French disappeared from the assault on Peking. Where they spent the rest of the day nobody knew or cared.

The American cavalry having been rescued from a few Chinese snipers, Chaffee advanced to the northeast wall of the Chinese City, two hundred yards from his assigned objective, the Tung Pien Gate, where the Russians were pinned down. The Americans took shelter in the lee of the wall. Every loophole in the tower pagoda of the Tung Pien spouted fire as Chinese soldiers shot at the Russians below them, huddled just inside the Chinese City or sheltered in the dark corners of the gate tower. The Russians were going nowhere, shot to pieces. The Americans would try a different strategy.

The most lasting image of the siege of the legations is that of American soldiers scaling the walls of Peking. That is exactly what happened. The Chinese City wall under which the American soldiers crouched was not as massive as the Tartar Wall, but it was thirty feet high and ten feet broad on top. The soldiers had no ladders or tools, nothing except their rifles and the ropes they used to draw water out of wells. Captain Learnard, the senior officer present, noticed, however, that the facing of the wall had crumbled, leaving crevices and projections usable as hand and foot-holds by an agile climber.

Learnard called for volunteers. "Immediately there stepped forward a young soldier who had been noted for his unspotted character and clean life. It was Trumpeter Calvin P. Titus, Company E, Fourteenth Infantry. He said: 'I will try.'"[8]

Titus, small and slight, left rifle and trumpet behind, stripped off his pack and began the climb, clinging like a fly to the crumbling brick and feeling his way from crevice to crevice, his boots finding toe-holes in the pitted, ancient surface of the wall. Near the top he peeked through the embrasure. Not a Chinese soldier was near. One last push and he was on top calling down encouragement. Before the Chinese two hundred yards away noticed, five American soldiers and two rifles were on top. The two riflemen took shelter and returned the Chinese fire and the others dropped ropes to haul up more rifles and ammunition.

The Americans on the wall worried that they might be confused for Chinese and shot by other American or allied soldiers. Private Detrick, a mounted orderly, was sent to get a flag. At a full gallop he dashed through the battle to headquarters where he borrowed an American flag and rode back the same way, the Chinese on the wall sniping at the running horse, the rider, and the flag whipping in the wind.[9]

At 11:03 A.M. on August 14, the American flag was raised. The Americans cheered and the Russians nearby, pinned down for hours, joined in the jubilation. The Chinese directed their artillery at the Americans on the wall, but American guns quickly silenced the Chinese.

A few American soldiers climbed down the wall into the Chinese City and joined the Russians in the shadowy inner courtyard of the Tung Pien gate. Chinese bodies littered the road and floated in the shallow water of the moat. Inside, dead and dying Russians were in dark corners. Bullets fired by Chinese from the tower looming over the courtyard ricocheted from wall to wall, the sound magnified in the close quarters. Russian soldiers exchanged fire with the Chinese in the towers, their unmanned field artillery nearby, horses shot dead in their traces. Amidst the crowded confusion of the courtyard, American artillerymen forced two field guns through the gate and courtyard and out into the open air. From there, they pointed the guns nearly straight up and fired into the five-story tower until the Chinese ducked or ran. The entrance was open. Americans poured into the Chinese City, past the battered Russians.

While the army was scaling the walls, the American marines were guarding the supply train, but about noon they also reached Peking. As he hustled his company forward, Captain Smedley Butler was hit in the chest by a bullet. It knocked him unconscious and when he woke up he had been carried to the shelter of the guardhouse outside the gate. He heard someone comment, "He's shot through the heart."[10]

Butler had the wind knocked out of him but he managed to suck enough air to mutter, "No, not the heart." The bullet had flattened a brass button on his uniform and dug a hole into his chest, carrying "off part of 'South America' from the Marine Corps emblem" tattooed on his chest. It was a bad bruise, and for weeks afterwards his chest was black and he coughed up blood. Butler's company continued on into Peking leaving him to rest at the gatehouse. He tried to follow, but nearly collapsed and was leaning against the gate when a mounted officer came by. He saw Butler staggering and gagging, and lifted him onto his horse and carried him forward to his company.

The legend of Smedley Butler was born. The skinny, underage marine — son of a pacifist Quaker congressman — had been twice wounded in China before his nineteenth birthday. He was the youngest captain in the U.S. Marines and the most celebrated. He would become the most famous marine of his day. Thirty years later, he said, "I haven't forgotten those times; I was just a boy at the time, and still consider the Boxer campaign as the most interesting period of my life."[11]

Just about everyone else in Peking in 1900 would agree.

The marines, however, were only supporting players for an army show. Now inside the Chinese City, with artillery at their rear shelling the Tartar Wall, Colonel A.S. Daggett and two companies of his regiment advanced west, down a street two hundred yards distant but parallel to the Tartar Wall. A mile and a half away, through a gauntlet of Chinese riflemen on the wall was the Legation Quarter, best entered, according to messages from the besieged, through the water gate beneath the positions held by the U.S. Marines.

It was a spectacular fight. Daggett advanced down the street, his progress covered by men running from rooftop to rooftop, keeping up a steady fire on the Tartar Wall, forcing the Chinese to keep their heads down. But a few hundred yards from his objective, Daggett called a halt. His men and his ammunition were exhausted. He sent a messenger back for reinforcements and ammunition. It was three o'clock in the afternoon. A little more bravado, a little more dash, a little less regard for the lives of his men and Daggett's Americans might have been the first to reach the Legation Quarter.

* * *

The amiable General Gaselee woke at one A.M. August 14 to the sound of firing north and west of the British army. The general divined that all the careful plans of the allies for an orderly advance to Peking were off and it was every army for itself. The British hurried up their advance and at two A.M. they set out through a quagmire of mud. They followed a ravine rather than a road, eroded twenty feet below the cultivated plain. The British heavy artillery was left far behind, the naval officers and the Chinese regiment trying to wrestle the big guns through the mud and muck. The big guns weren't needed. Hardly a shot was fired at the British, but the heat became oppressive. By noon, when the British reached the Sha Wo gate to the Chinese City, horses were dying and men were dropping. A few Chinese marksmen from the wall shot at them but field artillery answered and drove them away. Roger Keyes, the daring captain of HMS *Fame*, raced forward on his horse, Torpedo, a Union Jack between his teeth, scaled the wall, and planted the flag, a sign to the artillery that the gate was now in the hands of the British. A disorganized mass of infantry — Rajputs, Bengal Lancers, Sikhs, and British officers — rushed through the gate into the Chinese City. On the right, flankers rubbed elbows with Daggett's American troops advancing along the south side of the Tartar Wall.

With the Americans on their right and nothing on their left, the British tramped through the Chinese City, turned north on the wide street leading to the Hata Gate, and deployed through the narrow, winding alleys. General Gaselee was with the advance units. Shortly, the general, his staff, and a few Sikhs and Rajputs were facing the Tartar Wall, guided by a merchant named Boyce Kup.

> The heat was stifling, the stinks were sickening and the progress was slow as the exhaustion was considerable. But at last at about 2:45 pm we struck the moat nearly opposite the water gate and there on the wall in front of us we saw the flags of England, America, and Russia just as described in the cipher message. There was, however, an ominous silence and not a defender to be seen. For a moment we feared the worst had happened and that the flags were but a lure to draw us into the open between the Chien and Hata Gates. Suddenly we saw a flag waving, "Come in by the water gate," in the best English style of flag signaling. With a cheer we, some seventy officers and men, dashed across the moat under an ill-directed fire from the Hata Men and in a few moments were safe under cover of the vaulted arch of the water gate. It was barred against us but we quickly burst our way through, assisted by eager hands from inside, and then amidst the clapping of the Chinese Christians and the frantic cheering of the Europeans on the canal bank we struggled through the slime and mud and up the bank and found ourselves at 3 pm the first to achieve the rescue of the Legations, with Sir Claude [MacDonald] waiting to welcome us, clad in immaculate tennis flannels.[12]

The British won the race. Their only casualty all day was one man dead of sunstroke.

Lt. Roger Keyes claimed to be the first man inside the Legation Quarter. Small and slender, he squeezed through the wooden bars on the water gate. He raced through the compounds of the American and Russian legations to the British Legation with the flag of HMS *Fame* and saw that it was hoisted over the British Legation.[13] A second source, Frederick Brown, a Methodist missionary on General Gaselee's staff, gave the honor of being the first British officer inside the Legation Quarter to Captain Pell, aide de camp of the general.[14]

Other observers saw it differently. Mrs. W. P. Ker, watching the gate to the British Legation, said, "The first man through the green door was a Sikh. He rushed up to the lawn and then toured the compound; an unforgettable sight, naked to the waist, sweating like a pig, hair tumbling from his shoulders. He kept waving his rifle and shouting 'Oorah!' There was no doubt about his joy at our relief. The next man was Tom Scott (Bengal Lancers) hard on the Sikh's heels ... Major Vaughn, the cousin of the headmaster of Rugby, *really* was the first man to reach the gate, but sat himself down in a ditch to light his pipe, and so got left."[15] Sir Claude MacDonald gave the credit for being the first to Major Scott and a few of his Sikhs and he seems most likely to be accurate.[16]

Major Vaughan had the most pleasant reception. While lighting his pipe, "a young lady without a hat and carrying a fan" met him and showed him the way to the British Legation where he and his men could get a badly needed drink of water. Vaughan passed through the Russian Legation, the cemetery and cheering Chinese schoolgirls, and onto the lawn of the British Legation. "The whole place was crowded with Europeans, cheering and waving their hats,

The Water Gate. The foreign forces entered the Legation Quarter on August 14, 1900, through this passage beneath the Tartar Wall. The gate was barred at the time. The canal flowing out of the city through the gate bisected the Legation Quarter and drained the Imperial and Forbidden cities (Savage Landor, *China and the Allies,* 1901).

and perfectly indifferent to the hail of bullets which were pattering against the roofs and upper parts of the walls around them."[17]

The besieged were thrilled. An Englishman named Moore, father of Siege Moore, the only European child born in the Legation Quarter during the siege, had spotted the British troops from the wall. Captain Newt Hall sent Moore to tell Sir Claude MacDonald. MacDonald and the idle among the besieged rushed out of the British Legation to the water gate to welcome the soldiers. Chinese Christians and American marines joined the well-dressed crowd. The marines descended into the slime of the half-dry canal to help the British break down the wooden bars of the water gate.

Oberlin graduate Luella Miner was one of the idlers. She was sitting under the trees by the tennis court when "an American marine from the city wall ran into the yard shouting, 'The troops are inside the city—almost here!' There was a wild rush for the south end of the compound, and there sheltered by barricades we stood and saw the first of the relief army straggling up the streets.... Black-faced, high-turbaned troops, Rajputs from India — great, fierce-looking fellows, but their faces were beaming with joy, and they hurrahed louder than we did. There were British officers with them, and one of them stooped in passing and kissed a pale-faced girlie who looked as if she needed to be rescued by a relief army."[18]

Luella Miner, a strait-laced thirty-eight-year-old missionary, might have liked to be kissed — and perhaps she was. There was a great deal of kissing. And some scandal. A journalist reported with shock that "an unconfirmed rumour says that the bronzed faces of the Hindoos were even kissed."[19] For the British a kiss planted on the cheek of a turbaned Indian soldier by a European woman plumbed the depths of moral deprivation. Polly Condit-Smith, eminently kissable — but not by anyone below her social class — confirmed this shocking rumor. "A little blond Englishwoman was so overcome at the relief really being here that she seized the first one she could get to and threw her arms around him and embraced him. The Sikh was dumfounded at a *men-sahib* apparently so far forgetting all caste."[20]

Miss Condit-Smith and Harriet Squiers saw General Gaselee arrive, riding his horse through the water gate in the midst of a group of Sikhs. The general "jumped off his horse on seeing us, and showing on every inch of him the wear and tear of an eighty-mile midsummer relief march, he took our hands, and with tears in his eyes said, 'Thank God, men, here are two women alive,' and he most reverently kissed Mrs. Squiers on the forehead."[21] Gaselee, followed by the admiring women, made his way to the British Legation. Here, he found that not only were the women alive, they were decked out in their Sunday best. "The scene on coming to the British Legation lawn was extraordinary," said Roger Keyes. "All the ladies looked nice in clean white and light-coloured dresses, strolling about on the lawn. Some of the men, who had run in from the barricades, looked rather fierce, with arms of sorts festooned round them, but most were in flannels, having a quiet afternoon off — a very enthusiastic and friendly garden party — they all wanted to shake hands and seemed very pleased to see us — a very dusty and disreputable looking lot of ruffians."[22] Problems between the triumphant troops, however, and missionaries broke out immediately. The missionaries complained to General Gaselee that their Chinese converts were being robbed and harassed by the soldiers.[23]

Frank Gamewell never even turned his head when the relief arrived. His crew of missionaries and Chinese were strengthening a barricade in the ruins of the Hanlin Academy. To remind the foreigners that a war was still going on, Chinese soldiers ringing three sides of the Legation Quarter opened fire. A Sikh was wounded and a Belgian woman out to see the soldiers was hit in the leg — the only woman wounded during the siege. Polly Condit-Smith also paid a price for her boldness. A bullet nipped her ear and another grazed her ankle. The celebration halted briefly until the Sikhs and Rajputs were deployed at the barricades. Over at the *Fu* Colonel Shiba led his little band of Japanese marines on one last sortie. The last few Chinese soldiers slipped away.

The Americans arrived — dirty, travel-worn, and dog-tired — two hours after the British, General Chaffee hustling up to the front to lead his troops. The hardships of the day had been wearing but casualties were light: one man killed, nine wounded, and one man seriously injured from a fall while climbing the wall. General Chaffee and his escort rode through the slime of the water gate and were led to the American Legation past cheering lines of the besieged where, in the residence of the American minister — which was pock-marked by bullet holes — the Congers had organized a reception. The soldiers stacked arms in the shade of the trees, dusted themselves off, and drank cool, sweet water from the well. Then, they entered the Congers' house where a delegation of Americans welcomed them. Rescuers met rescued and a curious silence ensued. Nobody knew what to say. Finally, former missionary W.A.P. Martin, the seventy-three-year-old president of the Imperial University of Peking, broke the ice. "We are glad to see you."[24]

Sarah Pike Conger recalled that General Chaffee had tears in his eyes, uncharacteristic of the blunt old soldier. "We heard the fierce fighting last night," he said, "and knew that you were still alive. We pushed forward, but when the fighting ceased for a time, we were sure that we were too late, that it was all over, that you were massacred. The awful thought of defeat, of failure, came over me. But it was not defeat!"[25]

The British were first to reach the legations; the Americans second. An hour later the

Russians arrived. At dark, the Japanese finally fought their way into the city. A few French officers stumbled in that evening, but the French troops, wherever they were, did not arrive until the next morning.

* * *

At the siege hospital Dr. Anna Gloss attended to Captain Jack Myers, the American marine who led the critical sortie on the Tartar Wall, July 3. Wounded in the leg by a spear, Myers suffered first from infection and later typhoid fever. Now, still feverish, he heard the ruckus on the tennis courts and asked what was happening. "The troops are in," replied Dr. Gloss.

She moved the screen so he could look out a window and he saw the dark-skinned Indian soldiers marching by. "Tears coursed down his haggard cheeks as he saw for himself that help had come and the terrible siege had ended. 'Are you not glad?' the nurse inquired. 'God knows that I am glad,' he said."

The patients and the nurses at the hospital were caught up in the jubilation and every patient who could walk or find a crutch joined the celebration. Nurses and missionary doctors slipped away. Dr. Gloss "stood, with hypodermic syringe in a hand that trembled with excitement and weariness, over one wounded and suffering man, to turn and find the next escaped." Soon, there were new patients. The wounded Belgian woman was brought in as was a Sikh soldier badly wounded in the face and shoulder. Dr. Wordsworth Poole was bandaging the Sikh while his assistants "with thoughts on the tennis court where the American troops were being welcomed, were rendering him very ineffectual assistance." For the first time in the siege he showed irritation. "I have but two hands; I will be obliged if some one will hold this bandage for me." Poole had an unhappy end. He was exhausted and would sicken and die soon.

Within a day, the siege hospital emptied as the allied armies took its patients to their field hospitals for care. "The wonderful organization ... ceased ... and the Siege Hospital became an empty, desolated, dwelling house."[26]

* * *

It was a public relations blunder for Sir Claude MacDonald to greet the rescuers wearing immaculate tennis flannels. The rescuers anticipated they would find a pitiful remnant of bedraggled humanity in the legations, noble in their rags but worn down to bronzed skeletons, wounds bandaged with dirty rags, demeanor humbly thankful. What they found were well-dressed men and women, thin and drawn, but healthy in their jubilation, attended by ragged but efficient Chinese servants. Quite a few of the rescued were on their way to being the worse for drink — champagne being the beverage of choice for this festive day — supplied from the ample cellars of the M. and Mme. Chamot.

The soldiers, by contrast, looked the worse for wear. They had marched through terrific heat for ten days to reach Peking. The Americans had gone all day without food and little water, had scaled a wall, and fought a running battle on the rooftops. It had been, someone said, the hottest day in the history of the world. While the rescued reveled in their tennis flannels, the rescuers collapsed in the shade of trees, accepting cups of water and too tired to move.

Frederick Palmer, the American correspondent, did not arrive at the legations until the next day, but he expressed the feelings of many of the rescuers. "It was not the first time in history there was an edge between the besieged and the relievers, the one asking, 'Why were you so slow?' And the other saying, 'You don't seem so badly off, after all' ... If the Legation folk had put on their old siege clothes, the men allowed their beards to grow, and the women had not powdered their faces, they would have made a more realistic impression on the weary men of the relief column.... I confess myself — I am so tired, so filthy, and so generally 'out of sorts' — to being a little exasperated that everybody in the legations looks so well fed."[27]

Palmer's exasperation began when he reached the Legation Quarter and went to hunt for his friend Bill Bainbridge. He still had the bottle of Bass's ale in his haversack and he anticipated that he would meet Bainbridge crawling "out of his bomb-proof, emaciated and famished." Instead, Bainbridge greeted him by saying, "'What will you drink? We have beer and we have Scotch, but no soda to go with it, only water.' He had gained ten pounds since the last time I saw him. Rice and horse-meat seem to be fattening."[28] Palmer didn't take the bottle of ale out of his haversack.

* * *

MacDonald greets General Gassele. Not a good photograph, but it shows Sir Claude MacDonald clad in "immaculate tennis flannels" with hand upraised greeting British general Gassele, right, on his entry to the Legation Quarter (Smith, *Convulsion in China*, 1901).

The champagne, the tennis flannels, and the clean, pressed sundresses of the women did not negate the fact that the legations had been in a fight — one in which nearly 50 percent of the legation guards had been killed or wounded. With German thoroughness, Dr. Velde, the surgeon at the siege hospital, kept a record of the dead and wounded.

Casualties During the Siege of the Legations

Legation Guards	Number	Killed	Wounded	% casualties
American	56	7	10	30.3
Austrian	37	4	11	40.5
British	82	3	10	15.9
French	47	11	37	102.1
German	52	12	15	51.9
Japanese	25	5	21	104.0
Russian	81	6	19	30.9
Italian	29	7	12	65.5
Total	409	55	135	46.5

The 100 percent plus casualties listed for the Japanese and French reflect that among their dead and wounded were men who were wounded, returned to the firing lines, and were wounded a second time. In one estimate, only five of 25 Japanese guards escaped being wounded or killed during the siege.[29] Also, two Russian guards who died of disease rather than wounds are listed in the above table. The Americans, British, and Russians got off lightly among the legation guards compared to the Continentals and the Japanese.

Velde also totaled civilian casualties.

Casualties Among Volunteers and Civilians

	Killed	Wounded	Total
American	0	1	1
Austrian	0	0	0
Belgian	0	1	1
British	3	6	9
French	2	6	8
German	1	1	2
Japanese	5	8	13
Russian	1	1	2
Italian	1	0	1
Total	13	24	37[30]

The last killed was old, addled Padre d'Addosio. The day after the arrival of the foreign troops he left for Peitang alone on a donkey to see his colleagues there. Along the way, Chinese soldiers killed him. At the beginning of the siege, the good father had prophesied that he would receive his reward in paradise for having preached to the heathen. He ensured the truth of his prophecy.

Minister Conger summed up the damage to the American Legation. "Four shells struck our gatehouse, tearing away our flagstaff; four shells exploded in our servants' quarters; three struck my residence, two of them exploding inside; two struck the office building, and two the house of Mr. Cheshire, while the roofs of nearly all the buildings were sadly damaged by innumerable bullets. To show in what storms they came, five quarts of them were picked up to be remolded into new ammunition in one hour in our small compound."[31]

* * *

The missionaries who weathered the siege soon learned how lucky they were. Their colleagues around north China were slaughtered. William Ament had special reason to grieve the murder of three American Board missionaries in his old home of Paoting along with a dozen more — men, women, and children — from the Presbyterian and China Inland Mission. In far away Chekiang province, inspired by the Boxers, eight Protestant missionaries and their three children were killed. Shantung, the origin of the Boxers, saw only the murder of Sidney Brooks, the first foreign victim of the Boxers. Timely rains and a stern governor, Yuan Shih Kai, stamped out the movement there.

Shansi province and the Mongolian borderlands witnessed the greatest bloodbath. On July 9, 1900, Governor Yu Hsien had presided as judge and jury over the execution of thirty-three British, Scandinavian, and American Protestant missionaries and twelve French Roman Catholic missionaries. Oberlin College saw its ambitious attempt to conquer for Christ a whole Chinese province end in the most disastrous of failures — the extermination of the "Oberlin Band."

Nineteen hundred was the most disastrous year in the history of Protestant missionaries. A total of 136 Protestant missionaries and 53 children were killed in China.[32] Catholics suffered in similar proportions with 47 foreign priests and nuns killed. Surviving missionaries told of miraculous escapes on foot through hostile China, or even across the Gobi desert into Siberia. Chinese Christians died in wholesale numbers. Thirty thousand Catholics and two thousand Protestants were killed. A third branch of Christianity, the Russian Orthodox mission in Peking, lost between 200 and 400 of its 700 converts.[33] In addition, more than one thousand Western and Japanese soldiers died in the Boxer Rebellion.[34] No estimate is possible of the Chinese soldiers, Boxers, and innocent Chinese killed or dying of causes related to the war of 1900. Surely it amounted to hundreds of thousands.

18

Ament's Palace

At three A.M. August 15, twelve hours after foreign troops relieved the siege, the Empress Dowager, the Emperor, the heir to the throne, and thirty members of the court slipped out of the Forbidden City. The Dowager was said to have dressed as a common peasant, her six-inch long fingernails snipped, her hair tied in a simple knot. The court fled north to the Great Wall, suffering unaccustomed hardships, and then southwest to Shansi where a favorite, Yu Hsien, was governor.

Governor Yu Hsien, flushed with self-pride at his success in rooting out hated Christians from his province, may have felt a premonition of his fate when a fleeing court took up residence with him after being chased out of Peking by a foreign army. He installed the royals and their shrunken entourage in his palace and entertained them grandly during their three-week stay. The Empress Dowager was undoubtedly aware of the massacres of Christians carried out at the direction of the governor. She hinted to him that his fate was to be sacrificed to the wrath of the foreigners.

The allied conquerors in Peking later demanded that Yu Hsien be executed and in February 1901 the Dowager ordered his decapitation. He was one of two high Chinese officials executed in the aftermath of the Boxer Uprising. Three other high officials were given the less severe punishment of being allowed to commit suicide. Prince Tuan, the enthusiastic partisan of the Boxers, was exiled to distant Sinkiang province. General Tung Fu-hsiang, leader of the Kansu soldiers who led the assault on the legations, was dismissed from imperial service.

After her sojourn in Shansi, a rested Dowager and her retinue continued on to Sian, 600 miles southwest of Peking, and there she halted and reestablished her government and awaited developments. Manchu historians called the Dowager's flight across north China a tour of inspection.[1]

* * *

The rescue of the foreigners in Peking ended the breathless summer-long drama of the siege. Christianity had triumphed over the heathen — but every great event has its melancholy aftermath. The communion of the besieged in the legations had molded itself into an instrument of survival. This community fell apart after the relief.

> In twenty-four hours the whole aspect of the Legation had been changed, and the moral atmosphere was as changed as the outward aspect.... Then each one had his own place, his own work; people moved to and fro quietly, or collected at the Bell Tower in animated groups to discuss the latest news or probabilities.... But now the whole place was in a turmoil.... There was no longer the regular routine of watch and other duties for the besieged. The daily ration of flour, rice, and horseflesh to which we had grown accustomed ceased; everyone had to forage for himself. We had hoped that the arrival of the relief force would restore order and bring us plentiful supplies. For the moment it seemed as if confusion was worse confounded, and supplies more scanty and difficult than ever.... Already many of the refugees were busy packing up and preparing to return to their own Legations; already men in small parties were beginning to go out in search of loot."[2]

Harriet Squier's elegant mess dined together for the last time on August 14. Polly Condit-Smith lamented, "There is sadness about the last time of everything. And truly," she said, "it was so with us ... as we dined together last night there was a strong feeling, although we did not speak of it, that nobody but ourselves, who went through this incredible eight weeks of horror, were ever going to know really what the siege in Peking has been, and that we might all talk until doomsday, but the world will never understand. Perhaps it is too busy to try."[3]

The first to disappear were the soldiers, sailors, and marines who had defended the legations for so long and so well. In a moment, these men "folded their tents like the Arabs, and silently stole away." Reunited with the relief armies, they melded into the thousands of new faces and "were to be seen and heard no more."[4]

* * *

The American missionaries were prepared. These seventy people — whose practicality belied their spiritual profession — had plans. Arthur Smith crafted a message to tell the world that the missionaries in Peking had been saved. Smith found, of course, a biblical passage to celebrate the event. "Our soul is escaped as a bird out of the snare of the fowlers; the snare is broken and we are escaped" (Psalms 124).[5]

Smith also had a hand in a more secular document — one that amused several journalists when it was handed to them along with a loaf of bread as they were making a meal out of a can of sardines on the lawn of the British Legation. As Henry Savage Landor said, "The business capabilities of the American missionaries ... were active even at this time, when everybody was jubilant over relief at last having arrived, and most people could think of nothing else." The subject was indemnity — how much the Chinese government should be forced to pay, to whom, and for what, and the missionaries were the first to have their claims ready The document of the missionaries read:

Resolved:
That in claiming indemnity from the Chinese Government, we consider that adequate allowance be made:
1. For loss of time caused by the Boxer disturbances.
2. For all traveling expenses, including those to and from foreign lands, necessitated by missionaries being peremptorily ordered to leave China.
3. For future rise of prices in building materials and labour.
4. For rent of premises until new ones can be built.
5. For literary work destroyed.[6]

The correspondents "could not repress our astonishment at the claim for loss of time and literary work destroyed." Savage Landor added, with puckish amusement, that "had the Chinese any humour, it would not be unreasonable to expect a counterclaim for time wasted by their subjects over the efforts of the missionaries to convert them. As for literary work destroyed, it is safer not to discuss the question, as I am still too grateful for my share of the loaf of bread." Throughout the siege, and thereafter, the American missionaries were fixated on an indemnity for losses of personal and mission property during the siege. Almost immediately they began making lists of their losses and giving them to Conger. "And we're making the losses pretty large," said one missionary woman, "so as to be sure that we get all that we are entitled to."[7] That seemed to be the intention of all the surviving foreigners.

For William Ament it was his surviving Christian converts who mattered. As the siege ended, Ament's real work was just beginning. He wrote his wife in the United States. "If we get out [alive] most of the missionaries talk of going home as they have no place to go here and have no clothing or articles for housekeeping ... I think I shall remain here and gather up the fragments that are left.... Our poor people — those who are saved — not many, must be settled in homes and efforts made to secure indemnity for them as well as for ourselves. My heart bleeds for them. They are aliens in their own country and pronounced as 'bandits' by imperial decree."[8]

Ament's sadness had a dark side. The comfortable American Board compound — his home for most of twenty years— was burned and the members of the fledgling churches he had established were dead or scattered. For Ament, life after the Boxer rebellion was to rebuild the Christian community he had created with so much dedication and at the cost of three of his four children — their carefully tended graves in the Protestant cemetery of Peking desecrated by the Boxers, bones scattered or burned, stones broken, trees cut down, and walls tumbled over.[9]

Ament recognized that his faith was endangered by bitterness and the stress of months of danger and hardship. "I am gathering in 'confiscated goods' and distributing to needy Chinese. The selfish side of human nature comes out in the work assigned me. Good garments are greedily called for, and many want more than their share. I am afraid that too serious a draft is made on my religion, and I am growing callous and cynical." He added, "I must go now and hold morning prayers in the chapel."[10]

Before the end of the siege, Ament had asked U.S. minister Edwin Conger if he could take possession of a palace adjoining the destroyed American Board Mission, to house and care for his surviving Christians after the siege. Conger consented. The owner of the palace, a Mongol prince, was known to have been a Boxer supporter and Ament had no qualms about displacing him from his property. Of the Boxers he said: "They are a set of cowards and well merit the punishment they will receive."[11]

Ament's planning was justified. The day after the foreign soldiers arrived in Peking, Sir Claude MacDonald let it be known that refugees were no longer welcome in the British Legation. The arriving armies and the diplomats, businessmen, and missionaries whose homes and offices had been destroyed scrambled to seize palaces and Chinese buildings as homes and headquarters. Ament and Elwood Tewksbury anticipated the rush. In the late afternoon of August 15, they ventured out to visit what was left of the American Board Mission. The mission was in the eastern Tartar City. The two ragged missionaries, Ament, forty-eight years old, stern and solid, his mouth sore from scurvy and looking more like a down-on-his luck captain of industry than a missionary, and Tewksbury, thirty-five, a Harvard man, a talented pianist, as were his wife and oldest son — his disheveled appearance not concealing a tall, slender, elegant, and aristocratic bearing—walked together down Hata Street. The street, formerly crowded with people and shops, was empty. They turned left onto a small lane Ament's mission was there, the street deserted, the chapel and houses destroyed. Across the street a lumber yard burned, set afire for who knows what reason. No buildings were left standing in the American Board compound to house the Chinese converts.

Ament insisted on taking possession immediately of the intact Mongol palace next door. The two missionaries pushed open the outer gate and rushed inside, not knowing whether they might meet resistance. Only the corpse of a gateman greeted them. Exploring the palace and its gardens they found a room full of guns and ammunition. Ament decided to remain for the night. He was afraid that if he were not present soldiers of the foreign armies might take the palace for their own. Tewksbury, concerned that his family would be worried if he didn't reappear, tried to dissuade him but returned alone to the British Legation. He informed Minister Conger that Ament was alone in the Mongol palace and Conger — not wishing to be held responsible for the follies of a missionary who might turn up dead — sent a squad of soldiers with Tewksbury to retrieve him. They found Ament in the arsenal of the palace preparing to defend it against anyone — Chinese or foreign — who might try to take it from him. On the promise of the soldiers that the palace would remain in the possession of the American Board, Ament consented to return to the British Legation for the night.

Ament's Palace. Ament confiscated the palace after the siege as a base of operations and to house his surviving Chinese Christians. Delegations of Chinese from the countryside visited him at the palace to pay indemnities he imposed and beg protection from foreign soldiers (Porter, *William Scott Ament*, 1911).

The next morning the American Board missionaries decided among themselves that Tewksbury and Ament would remain in China to "arrange for the indemnities and possibly lay again the foundations of our Peking and Tungchou compounds and mission work."[12] That day, August 16, 1900, like Moses leading the children of Israel, Ament led two hundred surviving Chinese converts from the Legation Quarter to his expropriated palace. Ament's lieutenants were young, kindly Baptist William Stelle and Miss Nellie Russell of Michigan, thirty-nine years old and a patroness of Chinese women. Ada Haven and the beautiful Elizabeth Sheffield would also assist him briefly. Ament's progress to the new home of the American Board Mission was unheralded by trumpets or heavenly harps. "Most of our people are going away and I feel lonesome. I am tired out. Have not taken my clothes off for some time and the heat is terrific. Then I have no clothes, and my one pair of shoes are [*sic*] dropping from my feet. I have not worn a linen collar or shirt for two months and feel as rough as our soldiers look. Well," he added, laconically, "we are free, for the present at least."[13]

Tewksbury — the adjective used to describe him is indefatigable — took up residence nearby in another expropriated palace with the Tungchou group of American Board missionaries who would remain in Peking: Mrs. Tewksbury and children, Luella Miner, Jane Evans (Aunt Jennie), Abbie Chapin, Mr. and Mrs. Arthur Smith, and the Wycoff twins. Arthur Smith had already started writing his book about the siege. With them were the remnants of the Christian population of Tungchou and the surviving students of North China College. Georgina Smith took over another palace for the London Missionary Society and would also remain in Peking to reconstitute the society's work.

Most of the missionaries of all denominations returned to their homelands within a few days. The heavy burden of resurrecting the missions from the ashes fell on Ament, Tewksbury and Georgina Smith. They would navigate, without the counsel of wise friends and colleagues, the shoals of international politics, revenge, and retribution in which they would be embroiled.

* * *

Glory eluded the French. On the morning of August 16, French troops sallied out of the Legation Quarter to relieve the siege of the Peitang. Alas, they were too late. The industrious Japanese had stumbled across the Peitang earlier that morning and the good fathers, the French and Italian sailors, and the starving masses of Chinese beheld the arrival of several hundred Japanese soldiers at their front gate. The Japanese were welcomed, albeit with some linguistic confusion. The French arrived a little later and saw 250 Japanese already inside the Peitang. The Japanese, being polite, stepped aside to let the French take center stage, and the siege of the Peitang, to the great excitement of its inmates, was declared at an end.[14]

Bishop Favier survived the siege but his love for China did not. He cut off his pigtail, doffed the silk robes he customarily wore, and took up the miter and cassock of a Roman Catholic bishop. In the aftermath of the siege the Catholics would extract an eye for an eye and a tooth for a tooth. China would pay twice, in silver and in blood, for every Catholic life lost and every Catholic property destroyed. For all their lack of participation in the relief of the legations and the Peitang, however, the French would soon bring thousands of soldiers to Peking and, along with the Germans, become enthusiastic scourgers of the China countryside in support of the Catholics.

If the survival of the legations seemed miraculous, the survival of the Peitang was a full-fledged miracle. The Legation Quarter might have been overwhelmed by a coordinated attack of three or four thousand Chinese soldiers; in the Peitang a determined attack of a few hundred Chinese soldiers would have overwhelmed the forty-three French and Italian guards, several armed priests, and a few hundred Chinese with spears and swords. Chinese tactics against the Peitang were even more cautious than against the legations. They relied on artillery — with the main objective, it seems, of knocking down the high towers of the cathedral which offended *feng shui* — burrowing mines, and starvation. The impact on people at the Peitang continued, as did that of the legations, beyond the relief date. The Sister Superior of the Peitang died on August 20, unable to recover from the hardships of the siege.[15]

* * *

On Sunday, August 19, the people of the siege came together one last time for a thanksgiving service on the tennis court at the British Legation. Arthur Smith delivered the sermon on

American Missionaries in the Siege. A photograph of 53 of the more than 70 American missionaries who survived the siege in Peking. 1. G. W. Verity; 2. Amy Brown; 3. Mrs. Arthur H. Smith; 4. W. T. Hobart; 5. John A. Wherry; 6. W. F. Walker; 7. Dr. James H. Ingram; 8. H. E. King; 9. George R. Davis; 10. Arthur H. Smith; 11. Charles A. Killie; 12. William B. Stelle; 13. Gilbert Reid; 14. Grace Newton; 15. Sarah Luella Miner; 16. Nellie Russell; 17. Dr. Maud Mackey; 18. Elizabeth Martin; 19. Mrs. Frank D. Gamewell; 20. Gertrude Gilman; 21. Dr. Anna Gloss; 22. Charlotte M. Jewell; 23. Gertrude Wyckoff; 24. Ada Haven; 25. Mrs. Howard Galt; 26. Mrs. James H. Ingram; 27. Franklin M. Chapin; 28. Janet C. McKillican; 29. Mrs. Gilbert Reid and child; 30. Dr. Eliza Ellen Leonard; 31. Mrs. Charles A. Killie; 32. Alice Terrell; 33. Jane Evans; 34. Mrs. Chauncey Goodrich; 35. Mrs. W. F. Walker; 36. Dr. Emma E. Martin; 37. Mrs. Charles E. Ewing and child, Ellen; 38. Mrs. Franklin M. Chapin; 39. Mary Andrews; 40. Mrs. John L. Mateer; 41. Dr. Chauncey Goodrich; 42. Deborah Matilda Douw; 43. Ruth and sister Ingram; 44. Grace Goodrich; 45. Esther Walker; 46. Ewing Marion; 47. Dorothea Goodrich; 48. Carrington Goodrich; 49. Ernest Chapin; 50. Ralph Chapin (Smith, *Convulsion in China, 1901*).

the theme: "The Hand of God in the Siege of Peking." After the sermon, several of the American marines were heard to comment loudly that Smith had rendered more credit unto God than was his due and less unto the U.S. Marines.

Polly Condit-Smith's last few days in Peking were crowded with affairs of society. The amiable young lady helped Harriet Squiers host crowds of handsome, dashing military officers at the Squierses' abundant table. First, however, they had to move their baggage from their room at the British Legation to their bullet-spattered residence in the American Legation. Horror of horrors, Chinese servants were hard to come by. They had abandoned their masters and "were off looting or trying to find places for their families." Moreover, Harriet Squiers—who truly was an benevolent angel—was nursing her son, Bard, who had typhoid; the wounded Captain Jack Myers, who also had typhoid; and Navy Surgeon Lippett, who was still disabled from the wound he suffered in the siege. Instead of abundance, they found scarcity. So did missionary Charles Ewing who was a member of a foraging committee which sought its daily bread in the abandoned shops near the Legation Quarter. They found cattle and chickens, but no eggs or fresh fruit and vegetables. Frightened of the foreign soldiers, the farmers were not coming into the city.[16]

But the tribulations of moving were overcome and Polly enjoyed several days of attention from dashing military officers—many of them bearing gifts to show their pleasure at her favor.

She refused a looted sable coat from Baron von Rahden, a Russian military officer, and quickly regretted that her American sensibilities had gotten in the way of accepting a priceless gift. When a Belgian offered her an elaborate looted pearl bracelet, she abandoned the etiquette of her upbringing and accepted it — immediately. She also gave a Sikh soldier two dollars for "an exquisite gold-mounted cloisonné clock and two huge, struggling hens!" The hens made wonderful soup.[17]

Two days later, forty American missionaries and several civilians, including Polly, Frank and Mary Porter Gamewell, and Charles and Bessie Ewing departed Peking for home. The Gamewells were overdue for furlough in the United States and needed to attend to Mary Gamewell's anemia, a problem that would kill her six years later. Frank Gamewell had been the indispensable man in the siege of the legations and was returning home a hero — bright, shining, and untarnished. In his pocket he had a letter from American minister Conger. "Dear Mr. Gamewell. You deserve and will receive the lasting gratitude of all the Peking besieged ... to your intelligence and untiring effort, more than to that of any other man, do we owe our preservation."[18]

The hardships of the Gamewells and their colleagues were not quite over. The American refugees rode from Peking to Tungchou in U.S. army wagons drawn by four mules each. Along with them were a few Chinese servants, twenty wounded men, and an escort of one hundred and fifty soldiers. It was a strange journey through "villages and scattered farms, all absolutely deserted. The crops were ripening in the fields, but there was no one to look after them or to reap them.... We went into house after house, broken plates and cups lay upon the floor, an evil stench warned the intruder from corners, the water from the wells had a strange taste savouring of disease and death. 'Where can the people all be?' we asked.... Doubtless many of them were hiding in the crops from fear of the foreign invasion. The inevitable result was plain — famine and nakedness in the coming winter."[19]

Tungchou was worse. "We thought that we had seen ruin and destruction enough in Peking, but we had seen nothing to compare with Tungchou. The havoc wrought by war was appalling. The city had been sacked by the Russians: the gates were destroyed; the main street a mass of debris.... Fires still smouldered on every side.... In our journey across the city I saw only two Chinese."[20]

The Americans were loaded on boats to float and sail down the river to Tientsin. Polly Condit-Smith — of course — got on the best riverboat and she and the military officers in the expedition sailed away in relative comfort. The less fortunate missionaries and other civilians were crowded onto three other boats, each with a crew of three Chinese boatmen and eight marine guards. The marine officer commanding the riverboats was drunk and, as a result, the Ewings' boat didn't get any supplies. When they complained, the officer threatened them with courtmartial if they did not obey him. They watched ruefully as the other boats loaded bags of potatoes and onions for the journey as well as army rations. The uppity attitude of some of the missionaries toward the soldiers may have caused the problem. One of the American soldiers told of being called a "tramp" and "lousy" by a missionary mother and her daughter.[21] The missionaries believed they deserved more respect for the ordeal they had survived; the soldiers believed they deserved respect as the rescuers.

However, the marine enlisted men on the Ewings' boat shared their rations with the missionaries. Dinner their first night on the boat was canned salmon and hardtack, a rock-like biscuit which endured all things and remained as it began, more-or-less edible. Bessie Ewing pronounced the meal delicious after siege fare, and the next morning it got even better: fried bacon, which "melted in our mouths," hardtack, and all the coffee they could drink. There were some problems. None of the missionaries had cups, saucers, plates, or eating utensils. They ate meals with their fingers and used tin can lids for plates and empty sardine tins for cups. The

River Boats on the Pei Ho. Missionaries and other civilians leaving Peking after the siege traveled to Tientsin in river boats like these (Savage Landor, *China and the Allies,* 1901).

women were sick or burdened with children and it fell to the men to do the cooking over the charcoal stove on each boat. Courtenay Fenn was pronounced an excellent cook; his specialty was Saratoga chips, which would come to be better known as potato chips.[22]

The canned food and potatoes were a treat but the journey was far from luxurious. "Nine of us lived, ate and slept for five days on bare boards, in a space of less than thirty feet, not once taking off our clothing. All the shelter we had from rain and sun was a straw matting placed over the sail-beam ... so low we could barely sit up straight under it. The heat was intense, and we were devoured by fleas. Along the banks and floating on the river we encountered quantities of dead bodies, which did not add to our comfort."[23]

The boatmen—farmers impressed into the service of the marines—had little notion how to handle the ungainly rice boats and the convoy spent much of its time on sandbars. The marines were in the water for hours each day, pushing the boats off mud and sandbanks. The boats passed and re-passed each other as they each, in turn, ran aground and were shoved free. Races enlivened the dull, horrid stretches of the river. Two of the marines came down with fever and Lt. Waldron, the commander of one of the boats, was shot in the hand by a sniper—a reminder that Boxers still survived in the countryside.

The riverbanks, normally teeming with life, were deserted. Before, the river had been crowded with boats bearing rice, tea, copper, and brass; now it was empty of Chinese traffic. "The foreigners seemed to be the only people in a land of deserted wealth."[24] The villages were burned; the population dead or in hiding. North China was a devastated land.

The convoy of Americans arrived at Tientsin "tired, worn out, completely exhausted, when we met with an accident, which was the finishing stroke to our already overflowing cup of hardship."[25] The rice boat ran into a sailboat and the mast of the sailboat came crashing down onto the women resting on the deck. The falling mast nearly killed Ellen Terry, a missionary doctor, and Miss Ione Woodward, a guest of the Congers' during the siege. Miss Woodward's mother said dryly: "It is to be hoped that better accommodations were secured for those in the following convoys."[26] The soldiers, as soldiers do, probably enjoyed watching the discomfort of their civilian charges.

The reception of the refugees in Tientsin was less than ceremonial. "An army officer was on hand to show us where to land and to request that we hurry as they wished to send the boats back with more soldiers. But he was much put out when we asked where we were to go and how we and our baggage were to be transported."[27]

Military discourtesy aside, the missionaries and the other civilians sorted themselves out and passed out of each other's lives. The Congregational missionaries went to the American Board Mission; the Methodists and the Presbyterians to their respective missions. The society women were entertained by the generals and the rich businessmen of Tientsin. After a few days rest, they were all on their way home, first, by steamer to Nagasaki, then to San Francisco or Tacoma — or in the case of Miss Condit-Smith via Paris to replenish her wardrobe. To her dismay, when she arrived in New York two days before Christmas, customs authorities confiscated her newly-acquired clothes and Chinese jewelry until duties could be assessed. Her argument that she had lost all her clothes in the siege of the legations fell on deaf ears.[28]

For Mary Porter Gamewell, the float down the Pei River was to be her farewell to China. After a few days in Tientsin, the Gamewells boarded the P & O ship *Ballarat* and steamed for Japan and the United States. Mary would never return.

19

The Looting of Peking

The defeat and the humiliation of China in the summer of 1900 reaffirmed to many the superiority of Western civilization. "Once more," said *The Times* of London, in the rolling prose of untroubled imperialism, "a small segment of the civilized world had exhibited those high moral qualities the lack of which renders mere numbers powerless."[1] The assumption by *The Times* of the high moral qualities of the Christian and Japanese conquerors of Peking was contradicted by that new species of journalist, the foreign correspondent. They followed the allied army to Peking. The euphoria of the rescue, of people glad to be alive after a siege, quickly gave way to disquieting reports of appalling misbehavior by Christian soldiers and civilians — including missionaries. These reports resonated loudest in the United States. The voices deploring the atrocities of the allied soldiers and the excesses of the civilians came from the journalists — not noted for being especially scrupulous, but crime made for good copy. The voices of the missionaries who might have been expected to lead the chorus of protests were absent. In the words of correspondent George Lynch, "they stood by silent spectators of this crucifixion of Christianity."[2]

American newspapers compared the cruelties of the allied occupation of Peking to the wars of Attila, Genghis Khan, and Tamerlane. The image of the siege, so noble and uplifting in the moral lesson it taught of the superiority of Western civilization, was erased in its aftermath by an orgy of slaughter, looting, and destruction. In that summer of 1900, the domination of the West over the East may have reached its zenith. By Christmas many in the United States were disgusted. A brave expedition to save the lives of besieged countrymen had become — in the words of one correspondent — "the biggest looting excursion since the days of Pizarro."[3] A Chinese diplomat expressed the view that the eighth of the ten commandments be rewritten to read, "Thou shalt not steal, but thou mayest loot."[4]

The Boxers began the destruction of Peking. Large sections of the city were burned, one-half of the population had fled, and long-dead bodies littered the streets when the foreign armies arrived. What the Boxers began, the foreigners completed. Peking was a treasure trove. Wealthy Chinese, Manchus, and Mongols stored their wealth in possessions: furs, silks, jewelry, porcelain, bronze statues, and silver *sycee*— ingots of pure silver cast in the shape of a shoe weighing four and one-quarter pounds and worth seventy dollars each.[5] The court, the wealthy, and many of the poor fled Peking to escape the foreigners and left their houses empty and their valuables open to predation. The allied armies occupying the city were allied only in the face of a common enemy; no central authority among them commanded obedience from the unruly soldiers and officers of eight nations. The political competition among the allies spread to matters of loot. Who could get more than the others?

Few foreigners in Peking resisted the temptation to loot or buy loot. Each nationality accused the other of atrocities and looting while minimizing its own culpability. All were guilty. It appears that the American soldiers were the least guilty. Each allied power occupied a sector of Peking, somewhat like post World War II Berlin, and General Chaffee, stern and unbending, banned looting in the American sector. Shortly thereafter, an American patrol surprised two Indian soldiers of the British army looting in the American sector. They were ordered to halt and surrender, but fled to the British Sector and — once across the boundary — fired their rifles at the Americans. The American soldiers fired back and killed both Indians.[6] A serious international incident had taken place. The soldiers of one ally had killed soldiers of another. Quick action on the part of the Americans was essential to calm the enraged British. Chaffee ordered an immediate court-martial of the two Americans. They were quickly acquitted and — to make sure the British got the point — Chaffee gave them commendations for marksmanship. "The good effect on the situation was marked," according to Chaffee's biographer.[7]

But Chaffee's ban on looting was more symbolic than real, a warning to other nations not to trespass on the American domain. A chaplain with the American forces said, "Our rule against [looting] is utterly ineffectual & those who disobey do so with impunity & get many interesting articles thereby."[8] The American marines were a rowdy crew. Lt. Frederick Wise tells of Peking after the conquest.

> We went through streets along which staggered Chinese and allies alike, their shoulders loaded down with loot. We passed pawnshops with looters swarming like ants around sugar.... Each palace we entered in the Imperial City had been pretty well ransacked. There was any amount of stuff left. But silks were unrolled and tossed aside. Vases, porcelain, and cloisonné were knocked to the floor and lay in broken bits everywhere. It was chaos.
>
> But in several places we managed to lay to one side furs and bolts of silk to gather up later. We went back to our quarters through streets where severed heads were hanging from walls by their long queues; where men and women still dangled from the ropes with which they had been hanged; where dogs snarled and left off gnawing the dead to slink away as we neared.[9]

The looting expeditions of Wise and his fellow marines were assisted by the American missionary Gilbert Reid, the founder of the Mission to the Higher Classes. Reid's strategy to make China Christian was to convert the country's leaders in the expectation that the common people would follow. Ament, to the contrary, was the proponent of building up Chinese Christianity one convert at a time, striving for a self-sustaining network of Christian churches. The only American missionary wounded in the siege, his faith in the higher classes destroyed, Reid had a thirst for revenge. He loaned the marines his English-speaking servant to assist them. Wise does not mention what Reid received in return for the favor. Other unnamed Christian missionaries claimed to know where gold could be found. For a share of the proceeds, the missionaries would guide Wise and his marines to the spot. Wise came to have a dim view of the supposed information of the missionaries. "I went on several of these treasure hunts with missionary guides," he said with disgust. "We drew a blank every time."[10]

Most of the missionaries who helped plunder Peking had the discretion to keep their mouths shut. Reid trumpeted his looting for the world to hear. "I only regret I didn't have more time to loot ... instead of leaving so much to others, including not a few loot critics." He wrote a magazine article called "The Ethics of Loot."[11] The New York *Evening Post* said of the article: "It turns out on reading to be much loot and not much ethics."[12]

The stories of looting by missionaries creep out. William Stelle, who remained in Peking with Ament, sent four trunks of furs to New York to be sold "for the benefit of suffering Christians."[13] Dr. Emma Martin helped herself to several items: a garment of taffeta silks, sandalwood fans, jade, a hair ornament, and embroidered shoes. "I had just the best time ... it was such fine sport. I could hardly believe it was me. It was surely the gayest 'lark' I ever had." The joy of finding luxury items for the taking overwhelmed her. The Martin sisters were not rich; their claim for possessions destroyed in the siege amounted to a modest $652.00.[14] Emma was unaccustomed to luxury. Later, on reflection, she had second thoughts: "It is just outrageous the way the allied powers, especially the soldiers have behaved in China. If our indemnities have to come out of the poor people I don't feel as if I want any."[15]

Four American soldiers wrote about missionary looting to the Baltimore *Sun*. The soldiers admitted that they had done their share of looting and would do it again if they had the chance, but they came down hard on the missionaries. "Speaking of looting, who did the most.... The missionaries did the most of it all ... they knew where the mostly costly goods were, while the soldier would have to search before he could find the goods." They continued, "A batch of missionaries came down from Peking [to Tungchou] on the wagon train, and as sure as a God is above they had enough trunks for a hundred families. There were only about ten families that came down.... I overhead a girl about 12 years old say to another member of the missionary party ... What do you think? Mama had to leave a lot of dresses and lace behind to make room in the trunks for the silks."[16] It seems likely that the "twelve year old" girl speaking of her mother's "silks" was eleven-year-old Grace Goodrich, the daughter of Chauncey and Sarah, as she was the only American missionary child of about that age. Her father, Chauncey Goodrich, 64 years old, was revered as a "saint," his third wife, Sarah, "impressively-buxom" and 45 years old, was "very aggressive and outspoken" and "concerned with living today rather than going to heaven."[17] There was no love lost between the missionaries and the soldiers in China in 1900.

The British justified their looting: "Looting on the part of the British troops was carried on in the most orderly manner, and the houses of all those known to be friendly were protected. It should be remembered," the officer continued, "that it is one of the unwritten laws of war that a city which does not surrender at the last and is taken by storm is looted."[18] The British held loot auctions every afternoon except Sunday in front of the main gate to the British Legation. Richard Herring, the elderly constable of the British Legation, was the auctioneer and the auctions were well attended — except by the French and Russians, who objecting to paying when there was plenty to steal. Sir Claude and Lady Ethel MacDonald frequently were in the crowd of bidders. Herbert Squiers, the handsome American diplomat, was an active bidder, as was George Morrison, the correspondent of the *Times*. Sikhs and Royal Marines, Americans, Japanese, and Germans, diplomats, missionaries, and correspondents all mingled looking for a bargain. The Scottish missionary, the well-named Dr. Dudgeon, was an astute bidder and a man who did not pay too much.[19]

Unrestrained theft by the better class of people probably reached a peak on August 28 when the military commanders opened up the Forbidden City to visitors. A contingent of British women headed by Lady Ethel visited the palace and observed Japanese soldiers "cramming things into their haversacks" and German officers "laden with loot." The British women could not "stand to see these things going to the common Japanese soldiers" so they helped themselves to several choice items. "I hustled a Jap out of the way and got it just before him," was the account of how one good jade piece found its way into a worthy English pocket. Lady MacDonald apparently did not participate directly in the pilfering, but she was presented with a "beautiful clock inlaid with stones" by a Japanese general who no doubt had looted it only a few minutes before.[20] Lady Ethel accepted the clock as a gift. Later, it was reported later that the MacDonalds possessed 87 large packing cases filled with the most valuable treasures and "had not yet begun to pack."[21]

The least likely of all the Americans to loot would seem to have been the stuffy, upright Congers, Edwin and Sarah, and their daughter, Laura. But a niece, Mary Pierce, who weathered the siege, wrote a letter home describing the Congers' visit to the Forbidden City. "We were told that nothing should be carried away, consequently we were abiding by that to the very end, when we went into a room full of nice little snuff boxes and jade dishes and the officer in charge turned his back and all of the other officers filled their pockets.... We followed their example, and brought home a few little things.... Young M. de Giers [the son of the Russian minister] gave us girls some handsome jade pieces and the next day he gave Laura a sleeve pug that was found in the Empress Dowager's room the first day that the Russian General went through the palace. Laura has always wanted a real Peking pug, but they were hard to get and exceedingly high priced.... This dog is called a 'sleeve' pug because the Chinese carry them in their sleeves, they are so small."[22] Apparently even the Congers were not immune to stealing a "few little things." We have no record of what happened to the dog.

The correspondent of *The Times*, Dr. George Morrison, was one of the most successful looters. Morrison confiscated a palace for himself after the siege and — familiar with Chinese ways — unearthed two chests containing "gold things of much value." Later, he had the audacity to purloin a "beautiful piece of jade" from the emperor's palace in the Forbidden City. However, he said sadly, it was "of no value, having a blemish." Undaunted, he acquired the finest piece of jade in Peking" which he sold to Herbert Squiers for 2,000 taels — about $1,500.[23] Herbert Squiers was one of everyone's best customers. He paid Bishop Favier $5,000 for a collection of porcelain.

A year later, on his departure from China, *The New York Times* reported that "H.G. Squiers, Secretary of the United States Legation, started for home to-day on leave of absence. He takes with him a collection of Chinese art, filling several railroad cars, which experts pronounce one of the most complete in existence. Mr. Squiers intends to present the collection, which consists largely of porcelains, bronzes and carvings from the palaces, bought from missionaries and at auctions of military loot, to the New York Metropolitan Museum of Art."[24]

For those few not "consumed with lust for loot" or the necessity of finding their next meal, the days after the relief of the siege were passed in visiting the holy places in Peking which had previously been closed to foreign eyes. The upright Anglican Roland Allen employed his time visiting the great shady parks within the walls of the Temple of Heaven and the Temple of Agriculture and the artificial mountain called Coal Hill by the foreigners. Even here, in the outer courts of the great temples, turbaned Indian soldiers hawked their looted articles, some priceless, some worthless, the soldiers having no idea which was which. Allen saw Russian soldiers rob two peaceful, well-dressed Chinese men. "The Russians simply made them undo their girdles and hold up their tunics whilst they felt all around their waists for watches or money — mere highway robbery. That was a trifle, but it made an honest man feel cross."[25]

Bertram Simpson abandoned the Legation Quarter and became the captain of a roving gang of bandits and the owner of a harem of concubines. Simpson passed by the Peitang one day and found that the Catholics were seized with looting fever. "There was no one to be seen. Everybody was away.... The sailors and the priests and their converts, remembering that Heaven helps those who help themselves, had sallied out and were reprovisioning themselves and making good their losses. Indeed, the only men we could find were some converts engaged in stacking up silver shoes, or *sycee*, in a secluded quadrangle. These had become the property of the mission by the divine right of capture."[26] In the words of a correspondent, "the Catholic Cathedral here has at times been turned into a salesroom for stolen property."[27] Bishop Favier was accused of looting by a French general. He denied the charge, but his initiative in raising money to support his surviving converts raised a few eyebrows.

The most shameless and successful looters of all were the Chamots, August and Annie. The Chamots journeyed to the United States with a fabulous fortune, arriving in San Francisco on January 1, 1901. Among their possessions was Pepper Pot, one of the few Mongolian ponies who survived uneaten during the siege. In addition to the proceeds of his looting, Chamot collected $200,000 as an indemnity from the Chinese government for the destruction of his hotel. He built a mansion on San Francisco Bay, decorating it with choice items such as a jeweled headdress which once belonged to the Empress Dowager. Chamot was not modest about his accomplishments during the siege. He said he had been wounded seven times — the meticulous German

Annie Chamot. Born Annie Elizabeth McCarthy in San Francisco, Annie was the female hero of the siege, celebrated for her marksmanship on the front lines of the defense (Coltman, *Beleaguered in Peking*, 1901).

doctor Velde did not record any of these wounds — and that he killed 520 Boxers and Annie bagged 180. On Annie Chamot's best day, her husband bragged, she killed seventeen Chinese[28] — an exaggeration of monumental proportions. After the first flush of Boxer enthusiasm, the Chinese showed the remarkably intelligent and human characteristic of preserving their lives.

* * *

The Germans had played no part in the raising of the siege of the legations in Peking, but they would become paramount among the occupying forces. All agreed that the Germans, aggrieved at the murder of their minister, Baron von Ketteler, would be first among equals in the occupation. Field Marshal Count Alfred von Waldersee became the commander in chief of the allied armies in northern China and charged with rooting out the surviving Boxers, punishing Boxer supporters, and negotiating a peace agreement, including indemnities, with Chinese diplomat Li Hung-chang, the best-known and most experienced diplomat of the Ching dynasty. Soon, 10,000 German troops were in northern China, mostly in Peking; the French and the British had nearly equal numbers.[29] In the beginning the allies cooperated in sending out punitive missions to scour the countryside of surviving Boxers and accept the surrender of Chinese soldiers. The Germans were the most enthusiastic of nationalities contributing to the punitive missions. Between December 1900 and April 1901, 46 military expeditions were sent out of the cities, and thirty-five were composed of Germans only.[30] This was a period during which Will Ament was journeying frequently to the countryside without military escort, fearing the foreign soldiers more than he did remnant Boxers. The Americans were the least enthusiastic of the allies in taking part in these punitive expeditions. "The

German contingent," said an American officer, "not having arrived in season to take part in the relief expedition, they were anxious, as most military men are, to engage in active service, and these expeditions afforded the only field for the indulgence of these desires."[31] American journalists were more explicit in their criticisms. "It is difficult to avoid the conclusion that the greatest single obstacle to peace in China is the intransigent attitude of Germany.... Is it to Germany that the primacy belongs in aggression and mischief-making."[32]

Among the humiliations imposed on China by the allies was the construction of a monumental gate dedicated to Baron von Ketteler at the site of his assassination on Hata Street. With glee, the Chinese renamed the gate Victory of Virtue after the German defeat in World War I.[33] The baron had probably done more than any single person to incite the Chinese government and people to rage. Ketteler's legacy was quickly erased as was German influence in China.

* * *

In Peking, those missionaries who stayed — Will Ament, Elwood Tewksbury, Georgina Smith and others — were busy. Ament soon found that his new-found position as the Moses of the Chinese Christians had gratifying aspects. The first priority was food for the converts, nearly starved after the siege. Ament was persuasive with his Chinese neighbors. In a letter to his wife written only six days after the end of the siege, he said that he was taking food from rich families near his palace. "They ought to suffer in view of all the misery they have created.... I have suddenly developed into a man of influence ... and the neighbors treat me as though I were a prince. They have brought me in eggs, chickens, ducks, and grapes galore." He added, "Our poor people come in with their tales of woe that would break a heart of stone. Many have been killed and I shall act as avenger."[34] And later he wrote, "I shall soon begin some punitive measures on Boxers."[35] It was those punitive measures that would get him into trouble.

The missionaries had problems with the foreign soldiers, especially the Russians who controlled the southeastern area of the Tartar City where their palaces were located. Peking was divided into occupation sectors with a different power controlling each. The Russian sector was the worst. "The Russian soldiers are ravishing the women and committing horrible atrocities."[36] But the Russians were not the only violators. Bertram Simpson came across a company of British Indian troops in a palace filled with converts: "these black soldiers were engaged, amidst cries and protests, in plucking from their victims' heads any small silver hairpins and ornaments which the women possessed. Trying to shield them as best she could was a lady missionary. She wielded at intervals a thick stick and tried to beat the marauders away.... Some also tried to caress the women and drag them away.... Then the lady missionary began to weep in a quiet and hopeless way, because she was really courageous."[37] Simpson said that he rescued the converts and the missionary by sticking his revolver in the face of an Indian soldier and ordering them to leave.

Ament, Tewksbury, and Georgina Smith operated in a similar manner, copying the British Legation in holding loot auctions and selling off treasures they acquired to support the Chinese Christians. They gathered food and other necessities in anticipation of a hard winter coming after a summer in which the Christians had been unable to harvest crops. They collected goods that could be sold to help maintain the converts or replace their destroyed possessions. There is no evidence that Will Ament personally benefited from the looting and auctions. More than two weeks after the siege ended, when the chaotic phase of the looting was ending, Ament was still writing his wife that he was destitute, needing shoes and underclothes and with no book other than a Bible.

The missionaries, with the help of their Chinese Christians, also began to hunt down Boxers who had now taken off their red and yellow headbands and attempted to blend into the population. Georgina Smith was the most enthusiastic of the Boxer hunters. "Miss Smith had

Georgina Smith and Chinese Christians. As did Ament and Tewksbury, Smith stayed in Peking after the siege to protect her Chinese converts. The man at lower left is Joseph Stonehouse, later murdered, the last foreign victim of the Boxer Rebellion (Ricalton, *China through the Stereoscope*, 1901).

arrested a Boxer who burned the mission and thrown two children into the flames. Sir Claude had him shot," read Morrison's diary entry on September 6. "Miss Georgina Smith is our Boxer catcher. General staff dreads the name of Miss Smith," reads another entry. The strong-minded Miss Smith demanded that the British army assist her in Boxer hunting, And on October 8, "Miss Smith has hunted down several Boxers and had them executed. She has blackmailed a respectable Chinese who fed the Boxers taels 500 [about $350] to be devoted to the Mission. Money well spent."[38]

Moreover, the doughty Miss Smith established a protection racket to protect people in her neighborhood from Russian soldiers. Shopkeepers menaced by Russians would run to her and she would rectify the situation. "Everything is [mine] in this neighborhood now," she said.[39] She set up work gangs among her Chinese, paying them with money that she obtained on the black market. When the family Georgina had displaced from the palace asked her to give them back their winter clothes, she was reported as saying that "when she recovered her lost clothes they would get theirs."[40] Miss Smith was a one-woman mafia.

Ament and Tewksbury also lorded over their neighborhoods as judge and jury, keepers of valuables, paymasters for wages, goods, and largesse. Although both were American Board missionaries they operated independently. Ament's priority was the survival and the recoup of losses of his Chinese converts and the reestablishment of the churches he had created; Tewksbury seemed more focused on gathering resources for the future expansion of the American Board Mission, especially for those activities in which he was interested. Their lack of cooperation and coordination with each other was probably based on personalities. Ament was the senior missionary, but Tewksbury, from Harvard, listened only to God — and sometimes it seems not even to him.

Ament and Tewksbury both stimulated missions by American soldiers to the countryside to rescue surviving Chinese Christians and wipe out the Boxers, who were still considered a threat. In September, Ament served as guide and interpreter for Captain Forsythe and 200 cavalry to the east of Peking. "We burned two Boxer headquarters, destroyed some arms and brought in sixteen refugees, Christians who had been in hiding.... The Boxers ran like wild deer from us, and we found it impossible to catch them in the high grain. The expedition did great good in stilling the people and causing bad people to fear."[41] Later, he wrote to Mary: "You may not know that I led a troop of horsemen through San Ho district, and because I wanted certain Boxers hunted out and punished I was spoken of as vindictive and bloodthirsty. Now it comes out that this expedition has to be repeated because of the softness of the Americans in dealing with the Chinese!"[42]

Forsythe told a different story in his official report. The Chinese Christians who accompanied the expedition as guides, he said, looted the house of a suspected Boxer sympathizer. Forsythe threatened to terminate the expedition if Ament did not stop the looting by the Christians and return all the stolen property. Reluctantly, the Christians gave back their loot and the soldiers fired the house and the loot. The strained relations between the Chinese Christians and the army may also have been due to the American soldiers killing by mistake one of the Chinese Christians and also shooting another unarmed Chinese.[43] Later, talking to the press, Forsythe was more vituperative. He was quoted as saying that "bloodthirsty" missionaries wanted him to shoot "suspected Boxers" on the spot "and burn down the towns in which they were harbored."[44]

Tewksbury also ran afoul of the army. In September he requested an army escort for a visit to villages near Tungchou to settle claims for destruction of Christian property by Boxers. General Chaffee granted his request and assigned an officer and 20 men as an escort, but, wary of missionaries, he stated a condition that the escort was only for the purpose of protecting Tewksbury and could be terminated at any time at the discretion of the officer, Lt. P.W. Guiney. Moreover, Chaffee said that he "doubted the propriety of Mr. Tewksbury entering upon the settlement of any claim for damages" and instructed Lt. Guiney to make a list of all claims and settlements. Chaffee specified that his military escort was not to "use aggressive measures toward the Chinese unless absolutely necessary to protect themselves and those under the protection."[45]

Tewksbury paid little attention to Chaffee's restrictions and made the purpose of his mission clear in a threatening letter he wrote to the villages he planned to visit. "I am now bringing soldiers, intending to visit each village where our Christians have been living and investigate the destruction of life and property of our church members. We have heard that you have allowed in your village villains to persecute malignantly the church.... Our church however has a heart of love ... [but] for massacre and pillage of Christians and their property the whole village must be held responsible.

"If you wish to arrange with us, you may appoint 2 or 3 elders who will come within three days to Tungchou ... and consult there with us as to indemnity.... If after the given time you do not come we must understand that you do not wish to arrange for settlement.... Do not say that you have not been informed. E. G. Tewksbury."[46]

He appended to the letter a listing of the indemnities he would expect for each Chinese Christian killed or displaced by the Boxers to include burial expenses, pensions for survivors, monetary compensation for property destroyed, and the designation by the village of a location for a Christian chapel. Chinese villages who agreed to his terms received a proclamation, signed by Tewksbury, asking foreign soldiers to protect the village, women, and homes.[47]

Problems quickly arose between Tewksbury and his army escort. He refused to give Lieutenant Guiney an accounting of what he had collected.[48] General Chaffee apparently recalled the military escort in disgust before the end of Tewksbury's visit[49] and the U.S. Army thereafter ceased its missions to the countryside — partially because it feared it was being used by the missionaries to enhance their power and prestige[50] and partially because "the sentiment of the Americans was opposed to the slaughter of inoffensive Chinese."[51] At Chaffee's insistence, Tewksbury later made a report of the money and property seized during the mission. From 23 villages in which 166 Christians were killed and 184 houses destroyed, Tewksbury collected 16,150 taels (about U.S. $12,000) and 96 acres of land to be used for chapels, cemeteries and rented out to benefit widows and orphans.[52] This was a large amount of money, representing the annual income of several hundred peasant families.

Back in Peking, like Solomon of old, Ament became a judge. "Day after day, Dr. Ament held an impromptu court. Men from villages who had been guilty of destroying either chapels, or the homes of the Christians, came to him. It was as good as a theater to see him administer justice, and there were many ludicrous scenes. He was like a father. Many of them he knew by name or reputation. Often, while we were at meals, the door would suddenly open and some one would drop on his knees, saying: 'Forgive me, old pastor, forgive me.' Some he scolded roundly, especially the gentry and men who should have known better. He made his settlements according to Chinese law, dealing directly with the offenders, saving thereby all cost of lawsuits and the extra squeezes of the underlings."[53] Ament also took non–Christians under his wing. Chinese, especially women, came to his palace to seek protection from criminals and foreign soldiers. "It was a daily sight to see him dashing out of his court, stick in hand, to drive out marauders, either foreign, or Chinese in foreign dress, or lawless soldiers."[54]

Ament paid little attention to the declining but continued danger from Boxers in the countryside and soon journeyed to his old preaching grounds south of Peking around Cho Chou accompanied only by his Chinese assistants. He knew the people and their leaders and Nellie Russell gave him credit from saving Cho Chou from destruction by French and German soldiers occupying the region.[55] Ament negotiated an agreement between the soldiers and city officials under which the city agreed to supply the soldiers with grain. He received a royal reception in Cho Chou. Donations flowed into him from the gentry and the magistrate gave him a palace formerly occupied by Boxers. This humble missionary now saw himself as the savior of the Christians and the scourge of the Boxers. "Twenty Boxers have been beheaded by the French soldiers who patrolled this region and others driven away, and property confiscated. We are not through with them yet. The devil overdid himself this time in this masterpiece. It will recoil on his own head. No religion ever had such an advertisement as ours has had. I could open the doors and take in multitudes." His high-flying enthusiasm was tempered when his pony went lame and he had to walk; he lost his appetite and felt a sense of weakness.[56]

"The entire winter was spent in the reestablishing of the Christians in their homes ... Dr. Ament personally saw each family relocated. He called on the head men of the village and made them responsible for peace and quiet.... One of the hardest struggles Dr. Ament had with himself and some of his flock was when a noted Boxer was caught and brought to him to be handed over to the Germans. This man had killed eleven members of one family. For a night and a day he was kept bound in a side room while the pastor was seeing what was best to do. Much to the displeasure of the men who caught him Dr. Ament told him that if he would pay enough money to support a young widow and her little child he would spare him. This the man agreed to and the next day the money was brought."[57]

Ament also had to protect converts from foreign soldiers, especially French and Germans scouring the countryside for Boxers in search-and-destroy missions. The soldiers were not selective in the Chinese they chose to afflict. George Wilder found one convert recovering from bayonet wounds given him by German soldiers. He had tried to save his house from being burned down. Moreover, "the doors and the windows in these unburned villages are being all walled up by their owners to prevent the woodwork from being taken for fuel by the poor freezing Sikhs. A Chinaman cannot keep wooden doors or windows these days to shelter himself from the cold."[58] Wilder continued, "We [the missionaries] are welcomed when we go into the country as a protection from the soldiers" who replaced the Boxers as the terrors of the countryside.[59]

Later, in November, Ament expressed qualms about the severity of the punishment being inflicted on the Chinese. "I am very sober over what I hear as to the behavior of the German soldiers in Cho Chou. They behave more like demons than men. The city had been fairly well punished. Boxers had been decapitated. Others had been fined and passing troops had taken grain and animals to eat it. Then these Germans came along, with no right, as it is really French territory, and strip the people of even the clothes they wear, and it is cold weather."[60] Ament was not the only missionary complaining about the Germans. Near Tientsin, George Wilder heard of three German officers going to houses and demanding "pao wa wa ti" which literally translated means "women who carry babies in their arms," that is, young women."[61] In Peking, "beastly" German soldiers attacked, for no apparent reason, and almost killed a houseboy of the Bainbridges. Bill Bainbridge saved the boy.[62] Ament was also critical of American soldiers. "More Americans are seen drunk than other nationalities and in many ways our soldiers are a disgrace to the republic," and he added, "I have been protecting villages from our soldiers."[63]

Ament railed against the collusion between the French and Catholics. "The worst of it is that the miscreants under the flag of the Catholic Church are collecting money from the people. With the aid of a Catholic priest and twenty-five soldiers, French, thirteen men were shot in Tou Tien including one church member ... the people are ground between the upper and the nether millstones."[64] Ament did not perceive that the justice he meted out to the Chinese might be seen in the same light as that of the Catholics.

Ament's letters reveal his conflict, expressing both sympathy for the Chinese and a conviction that a hard hand was needed in China. On January 27, 1901, he did what he had never done before: he stayed away from Sunday church services to rest and reflect.[65] William Scott Ament was tired and sore in spirit.

Ament, the most visible and talkative missionary in Peking, attracted the attention of journalists and criticisms of him and others began to appear in the press. None of the missionaries in China seem to have realized that their words might be perceived by citizens at home as vindictive, revengeful, and un–Christian. A statement by former missionary W.A.P. Martin, the president of the Imperial University in Peking — the most respected American in China — is typical. He spoke against "moderation and mercy in dealing the Chinese. No punishment can be too severe," he said in a letter to the *San Francisco Call*, "for the murder of missionaries and innocent children."[66] While Ament's actions were questioned and condemned in the American press, his fellow missionaries in China were more than supportive. Their statements were often more inflammatory than his own.[67] The missionaries' long years of failure in China, the contempt heaped upon them by the heathen Chinese, the murder of their converts and fellow missionaries, and the accumulated stress and hardships of the siege upset their moral equilibrium. Much as they deplored French and German excesses, they were united in their opinion that a hard hand was the appropriate policy for the United States in China. Given that opportunity, and with foreign armies in northern China to protect them, the missionaries abused their newly gained power.

* * *

The commanding general of the American forces, Adna Chaffee, was determined not to play into the hands of the imperialists and the missionaries, and it is from him rather than the missionaries that we get one of the most realistic assessments of the impact of the foreign occupation of Peking and northern China. "It is safe to say that where one real Boxer has been killed since the capture of Peking, fifty harmless coolies or labourers on the farms, including not a few women and children, have been slain. The Boxer element is largely mixed with the mass of the population, and by slaying a lot one or more Boxers might be taken in."[68] The foreign troops, especially the Germans and the French, occupying northern China and sending out punitive expeditions made the countryside a wasteland. "Wherever the allied troops are, the country is almost deserted."[69] The French and Germans were practicing military maneuvers in the China countryside using live ammunition and Chinese for target practice. A missionary said, "The people have a hunted look and the fear of us foreigners is upon them."[70]

The American army, despite its more humane policy toward the Chinese than the other allies of the occupation, did not escape censure for both brutality and arrogance. On a different theme, the photographer James Ricalton summed up one complaint of the civilians against the military. "It would seem that under even a quasi-military rule, civilians have few if any rights.... Many citizens, both American and English, complained bitterly of the high-handed, unlawful and impudent way in which officers took possession of private homes.... Three times I had received permission from agents of the owners to occupy private houses ... when American officers came, and in a way which I fear is somewhat characteristic of my countrymen said: 'Get out of this; we want these rooms!'"[71] The army on its part complained bitterly that civilians often tried to charge the military exorbitant sums for its use of buildings, supplies, and transport.[72] Smedley Butler summed up his opinion of war in his autobiography, *War is a Racket*.

20

Mark Twain and Will Ament

William Ament would be recalled as a hero of the Boxer Rebellion if not for a new species of journalist, the foreign correspondent. With the steamship and the telegraph, newspapers entered a golden age in which brave and dashing young men — and a few women — wandered the world to report the instant history of stirring events. One of the correspondents in Peking was Wilbur J. Chamberlin of the *New York Sun*. Chamberlin delved into the soft underbelly of the foreign occupation.

Chamberlin had dinner with Ament on October 14. He said:

> The Rev. A. is a missionary, and he appears to be a very good sort of a fellow, but I cannot for the life of me approve of his methods. I think I shall have to write a story about him and some of the other missionaries. You see, when the soldiers came to Peking and these missionaries were safe, some of them began at once to clamor for damages that they said they had sustained. The first thing they did was to get for living places the palaces of the rich Chinese Princes, and when they had them they started in clearing them out. Then they let their native Christians go out hunting and stealing more loot, and they sold that. They said it was no sin and they eased their consciences by saying that they had the right to reimburse themselves for the losses that they had sustained. It was just as if a man had stolen something from me, and to get square, I went and stole something from him. In other words, two wrongs make a right. They may be all right, but I don't think so.[1]

Chamberlin wasn't himself immune to the attractions of stolen goods. He bought a pile of Chinese brass for five dollars from Ament. "They are so cheap I think I'll invest in some more. I also arranged to get a couple of Chinese gowns of silk."[2] Chamberlin also visited the loot auctions at the British Embassy and bought two fur coats. He records no disapproval of his own actions.

What seemed appropriate for journalists and soldiers was apparently not appropriate for missionaries. "The more I see of Christianity in practice in a heathen country, the more convinced I become that there is a heap of hypocrisy in this world of ours and in this Christian civilization. What with missionaries running around selling things that they know are stolen, calling for blood to avenge blood, and in all ways demanding an eye for an eye and a tooth for a tooth ... it certainly seems that there is a heap more of the 'do others, or they will do you,' than there is of the 'do unto others as you would have them do unto you.'"[3] For Chamberlin, Ament was the perfect target. He was open, argumentative, morally righteous, and proud of his accomplishment of reestablishing his churches and preserving the lives of his converts. Chamberlin both admired Ament and was appalled by him. He called him a friend — but friendship and admiration did not get in the way of a good story.

* * *

Back in the United States, the Rev. Judson Smith, the corresponding secretary of the American Board, was beside himself. Newspaper stories told of missionary misdeeds and cited Ament and Tewksbury as the principal malefactors. Ament sent Smith reports of his activities, but it took weeks for a letter to get from China to the U.S. Journalists telegraphed in their stories at one dollar per word and their stories appeared the next day. Smith was behind the time in the information he received from the field to respond to criticism in the press. Tewksbury did not even bother to reply to Smith's urgent inquiries for information.

Smith's concerns were real. The missionary movement depended upon the favorable opinion of the American public, especially the moneyed classes, for its revenue. Bad publicity about missionaries in China harmed the reputation of the American Board, the oldest and most prestigious of missionary organizations. Frustrated and under attack, on January 2, 1901, Smith suggested that Ament and Tewksbury "come home." Later, his letters got more insistent, hinting that he thought the missionaries may have suffered a breakdown in their mental health.[4]

Ament was only partially aware of Smith's concerns and the furor in the United States. He was still feeling good about himself. He wrote proudly, "Every one of our dispossessed church members ... has been reinstated, and money compensation made for his losses. This has been done by appealing to the sense of justice among the villagers where our people lived, and where they were respected by all decent people. The villagers were extremely grateful that I brought no foreign soldiers, and were glad to settle on the terms proposed."[5]

On January 29, 1901, Ament set out on his third visit to Cho Chou since the siege. He had finished his most urgent work. He had collected indemnities for his church members, the congregations were reestablished, and new chapels were under construction. The Chinese countryside, in its timeless routine, was returning to normal, shaking off the turmoil of the previous year. The Boxers had disappeared as quickly as they had arisen. Ament was now planning to go back to the U.S. on a well-deserved furlough to see his wife and son for the first time in more than two years. He had earned a rest.

Ament planned to dedicate a new chapel at Cho Chou and to perform a wedding. The Chinese officials of Cho Chou greeted him like visiting royalty. They decorated the streets and the new chapel with gaudy banners and umbrellas. However, his triumphant entry into the city was short lived. A Jesuit priest and French and German soldiers — 3,200 of whom occupied the city — arrested him.[6] They searched his belongings and dragged him away to French headquarters. Subsequently the priest arraigned him before the city magistrate. He was accused of extortion. One of Ament's converts, the priest charged, had extorted 3,000 taels from a pawnshop owner. The uneasy magistrate, faced with foreigners on both sides of the case, determined the facts. The extortion turned out to be a bribe of 150 taels rather than 3,000, but Ament's convert was declared guilty. The French priest demanded that the young Chinese receive the maximum sentence of five years imprisonment. The magistrate complied — but later told Ament that the boy's sentence would be reduced when the furor died down. The priest also demanded that Ament be imprisoned as an accessory to the extortion. From captivity, Ament sent word back to Peking of his plight. U.S. minister Conger protested vigorously to the French Legation and the missionary was soon released. He complained that the French stole 600 taels from him and demanded — to no avail — that the Jesuits be expelled from Cho Chou.[7]

Chamberlin wrote a sardonic analysis in a letter home.

> Quite a long while ago he [Ament] had a scheme for collecting damages for all of his native Christians and his church from the Chinese themselves. He went around to some forty villages and collected about 80,000 taels [$60,000]. A few days ago, he went back there and was promptly arrested at the instigation of some Roman Catholics. It appears that they had the same sort of a scheme, but A[ment] got there first, and when they went around to these same villages to make their collections, they found that he had all the money there was. Naturally, they were enraged, so they made complaint against A., and declared that he had been blackmailing the villages.
>
> The French and Germans, both of whom are notorious blackmailers out here, went after A. as soon as they heard that he was back in Cho Chou — rather resented anybody else blackmailing in

their field, don't you see?—and they arrested him. He sent in to the Minister here and we kicked up such a row about the matter that A. has been released, and both the French and the Germans insist that he has never been under arrest. You see, they are a little afraid of your Uncle Samuel when he has troops around.... I really think, myself, that A. might have left a little for the Catholics. I don't like to see a man take it all, even if he is a missionary.[8]

The Cho Chou incident illustrated the bitter competition of Catholic and Protestants in the promotion of Christianity in the Chinese countryside. "In some cases," said the American Board, "the Catholic Church was found actively engaged in drawing the discontented and worldly-minded to its communion by the promise of help in securing indemnity and in the punishment of those who have persecuted them." In other words, some of the Chinese Christian were comparison shopping the benefits of allying themselves with the Catholics or with William Ament. In such an atmosphere, "it was difficult to turn their attention to spiritual matters."[9]

* * *

The newspaper stories about Ament's arrest were another dagger in the heart for Judson Smith in Boston, faced with a rising crescendo of bad publicity about the activities of his missionaries in China. And it got worse. Ament probably would have escaped with only a scourging in the ephemeral press and the criticism of the missionaries would have died down if not for two mistakes Chamberlin made in his reporting that attracted the attention of the American humorist Samuel Langhorne Clemens, better known as Mark Twain. Chamberlin claimed in a *Sun* article that Ament "assessed fines amounting to thirteen times the amount of the indemnity" and that this additional money was to be used "for the propagation of the gospel," rather than for the benefit of the persons who had suffered damages.[10] Twain read Chamberlin's story and was outraged. He had recently returned to the United States after ten year residence in Europe "to an ovation that went on the rest of his life." He was a celebrity, "a person who is known for his well-knownness," and his opinion on every conceivable topic was sought out, debated, and digested. "What a fame and force he is," said his old friend William Dean Howells.[11]

On February 6, Twain published an essay in the *North American Review* entitled, "To the Person Sitting in Darkness." The Rev. William Scott Ament was Exhibit A of what Twain called "The Blessings-of-Civilization Trust." The essay would become one of Twain's most influential. He seized on the theme that Ament had collected thirteen times the amount of damage done to church property and converts. Quoting from Chamberlin, but adding italics, he wrote:

"The Rev. Mr. Ament, of the American Board of Foreign Missions, has returned from a trip which he made for the purpose of collecting indemnities for damages done by Boxers. *Everywhere he went he compelled the Chinese to pay.* He says that all his native Christians are now provided for. He had 700 of them under his charge, and 300 were killed. He has *collected 300 taels for each of these murders, and has compelled full payment for all the property belonging to Christians* that was destroyed. He also assessed *fines* amounting to THIRTEEN TIMES the amount of the indemnity. *This money will be used for the propagation of the Gospel.*

"Mr. Ament declares that the compensation he has collected is *moderate* when compared with the amount secured by the Catholics, who demand, in addition to money, *head for head.* They collect 500 taels for each murder of a Catholic. In the Wenjiu country, 680 Catholics were killed, and for this the European Catholics here demand 750,000 strings of cash and 680 *heads.*

"In the course of a conversation, Mr. Ament referred to the attitude of the missionaries toward the Chinese. He said: 'I deny emphatically that the missionaries are *vindictive,* that they *generally* looted, or that they have done anything *since* the siege that *the circumstances did not demand.* I criticize the Americans. *The soft hand of the Americans is not as good as the mailed fist of the Germans.* If you deal with the Chinese with a soft hand they will take advantage of it.'

"'The statement that the French government will return the loot taken by the French soldiers is the source of the greatest amusement here. The French soldiers were more systematic looters than the Germans, and it is a fact that to-day *Catholic Christians*, carrying French flags and armed with modern guns, *are looting villages* in the province of Chihli.'"

Twain played with the words of the Chamberlin article. "Taels, I win. Heads, you lose," was his atrocious pun. He continued.

Our Reverend Ament is the right man in the right place.... His magnanimity has won him the approval of a nation, and will get him a monument.... Subscriptions for it can be sent to the American Board; designs for it can be sent to me. Designs must allegorically set forth the Thirteen Reduplications of the Indemnity, and Object for which they were extracted; as ornaments the designs must exhibit 680 Heads, so disposed as to give a pleasing and pretty effect, for the Catholics have done nicely, and are entitled to notice in the monument....

Mr. Ament's financial feat of squeezing a thirteen fold indemnity out of the pauper peasants to square other people's offenses, thus condemning them and their women and innocent little children to inevitable starvation and lingering death, in order that the blood money so acquired might be "*used for the propagation of the Gospel*," does not flutter my serenity; although the act and the words, taken together, concrete a blasphemy so hideous and colossal that, without doubt, its mate is not findable in the history of this or of any other age....

We have Mr. Ament's impassioned assurance that the missionaries are not "vindictive." Let us hope and pray that they will never become so, but will remain in the almost morbidly fair and just and gentle temper which is affording so much satisfaction to their brother and champion today."[12]

Twain's essay rolled on, citing the atrocities of Christians and Christian soldiers in China, South Africa, and the Philippines. It was a powerful anti-imperialistic diatribe, doing what Twain did best — pinpointing the hypocrisy of those who claimed to be benevolent agents of civilization and Christianity while the bayonet was their most useful tool and the bulging pocketbook their reward. For the American public, already suspicious of imperialistic adventures, Twain exposed the savagery underlying the pious language of the proponents of spreading the "Blessings of Civilization." Never again would the missionaries — especially those of the venerable American Board — sally forth with as much confident surety of their moral and spiritual correctness. A biographer later said that Twain "never wrote anything more scorching, more penetrating in sarcasm, more fearful in its revelation of injustice and hypocrisy" than "To the Person Sitting in Darkness."[13] Ament's reputation was forever tarnished.

A few days passed before Ament, back from his joust with the French in Cho Chou, learned of his scourging by Twain. Nellie Russell, his fellow missionary in Peking, told the story.

When he was weary in body and mind, there came like a thunderbolt the article by Mark Twain in the *North American Review*. I remember that day I went to his study on a matter of business and found him sitting at his desk, as if stricken at the heart. I exclaimed, "What is it? Are you ill?" "If I am what that man says, I am not fit for you to speak to me! I feel as though I should go off and hide myself in a cave in the mountain, never again to be seen of man." I thought he had gone out of his head with all his cares, and I replied, "What you need is rest and a doctor, and I am going to send for one." If the writer of that article could have seen how he suffered he would have felt that every cent he received for that article would be a red hot coal of fire. A brave, masterful man he was, ever ready to relieve, not to add to the sum of human suffering, and while in some things he may have been unwise, his mistakes, whatever they may have been, were of the head and not the heart.[14]

Ament was devastated. Instead of an all-conquering hero he was portrayed as a villain. His position was that of a military officer who anticipates a medal for bravery after completion of a difficult and dangerous mission but is instead accused of cowardice.

The missionary establishment in China and the United States rallied around Ament and struck back quickly at Mark Twain — but wary of his formidable jabs and japes and respectful of his mighty reputation. Three days after Twain's article appeared in the *North American Review* Judson Smith, the long-suffering corresponding secretary, responded. Smith complimented

Twain on his "brilliant article" and expressed "great admiration" for his genius. But, he went on:

> I observe that in commenting on affairs in China you select the Rev. Mr. Ament, D.D., one of our missionaries at Peking ... and that you base all you have to say of him on a single press despatch printed in the *Evening Sun* of December 24th, and that you assume the accuracy of this despatch as though it were Dr. Ament's frank and full confession of deeds and motives. The arraignment is severe, the effect on Dr. Ament's name and reputation must be very damaging. The prejudice thus awakened against the missionaries, mission work and the American Board is serious and likely to be of long consequence....
>
> It should require, as you will see, the ample warrant of unquestioned facts to justify a public arraignment of so wide a scope and far-reaching influence as you have made against this man—a man of hitherto unblemished character, of singular Christian devotion, of heroic courage and splendid deeds.... You are too experienced an author to rest so terrible an accusation against a man whose reputation is as dear to him as yours to you, and who is engaged in missionary work on the other side of the globe, upon a single newspaper despatch. I wonder what other information you possessed, what inquiries you made concerning Dr. Ament's record and of whom those inquiries were made....
>
> I know that you will not unwillingly do any man an injustice, and I have written freely and at once that you may have the facts before you such as are known to me and to all of us in these rooms, and be able duly to amend what has been written.
>
> Assured of your good sense of fair play and with highest regards, I am,
>
> Very truly yours,
>
> JUDSON SMITH[15]

Twain answered Smith's letter, but refused to recant. Pandora was out of the box and the great debate about missionaries in China was underway. The Rev. William Scott Ament was the centerpiece. Ament's defense was based on the two misstatements of fact in the newspaper article quoted by Twain. Judson Smith sent a telegram to Ament on February 13 to verify the misstatements. It was brief. Telegrams were costly. "Ament, Peking. Laffan's News Agency [e.g. Chamberlin] reported New York *Sun*, December 24th, your collecting thirteen times actual loss, using for propagating the Gospel. Are these statements true?"

Ament answered two days later. "Statements untrue. Collected *one-third* for church purposes, additional actual damages now supporting widows and orphans. Publication 'thirteen times' blunder cable company. All collections received approval Chinese officials, who urging further settlements same line. Ament."[16]

Armed with facts to prove Twain wrong on two key points, the powerful missionary establishment counterattacked on all fronts. From Peking came a telegram to the *North American Review*. "Peking Missionary Association demands public retraction. Mark Twain's gross libel against Ament utterly false."[17] The blue-blooded *Boston Journal,* in the home of the American Board, chastised Twain in an editorial entitled, "A Humorist Astray." A newspaper in Hartford, Connecticut—where Twain had lived and still owned a house—had unkind words to say about him. Chamberlin of the New York *Sun*—Twain's inspiration—was induced to modify the record.[18] The *Sun* published an article on March 5, "A Clean Bill for the Missionaries."

"Minister Conger will give a letter to the missionaries here stating that the collection of indemnities was not extortion, but the payment was voluntary on the part of the Chinese officials, and was moderate in amount. The seizure of the property was justified by the prospect that a severe famine was inevitable, and there was no government to look after the distressed people. The proceeds of the seizures were used entirely for these people."[19] The *Sun*, however, did not back away entirely. It reasserted that Ament had broken "one of the Commandments conveyed to Moses on Sinai" that he had probably taught his Chinese converts.[20] Finally, *The New York Times* was persuaded to retract an unfavorable editorial. "It seems we have been led into doing an injustice to him [Ament] by adopting the less authentic [statement], in ignorance of the more authentic. In that case we have to express our sincere regret."[21]

Twain, however, did not back down. In the April issue of the *North American Review* he lashed back in an article titled "To my Missionary Critics." The Reverend Ament — no doubt to his relief — receded to second place in Twain's statute of particulars; Twain fired broadsides at Judson Smith, the American Board, and missionaries in general. He admitted the error of his statement that Ament charged the Chinese an indemnity of thirteen times actual damages. But he turned Ament's admission that he assessed one-third more as damages into a debating point rather than an apology.

Twain extended an olive branch to Ament and other front line missionaries but damned the missionary establishment.

> A missionary is a man who is pretty nearly all heart, else he would not be in a calling which requires of him such large sacrifices of one kind and another. He is made up of faith, zeal, courage, sentiment, emotion, enthusiasm; and so he is a mixture of poet, devotee, and knight errant. He exiles himself from home and friends and the scenes and associations that are dearest to him; patiently endures discomforts, privations, discouragements; goes with good pluck into dangers which he knows may cost him his life; and when he must suffer death, willingly makes that supreme sacrifice for his cause.
>
> Sometimes the headpiece of that kind of a man can be of an inferior sort, and error of judgment can result — as we have seen. Then, for his protection, as it seems to me, he ought to have at his back a Board able to know a blunder when it sees one, and prompt to bring him back upon his right course when he strays from it. That is to say, I think the captain of a ship ought to understand navigation. Whether he does or not, he will have to take a captain's share of the blame, if the crew bring the vessel to grief.[22]

Twain's second article was gasoline on the fire of the debate. Judson Smith responded the following month in the *North American Review*. This time, he was less respectful of Twain.

> These points, therefore, seem clear: 1. The efforts of the missionaries have saved the lives of hundreds of the Chinese refugees, who with them went through the siege of Peking and helped to save the Legations, and thus placed the Allied Powers in their debt.
>
> 2. The utterly abnormal conditions which have prevailed since the siege have demanded exceptional treatment, and in dealing with them the missionaries have shown great caution, courage, and wisdom.
>
> 3. The indemnities secured were wholly for the Chinese whom the Boxers had robbed and outraged; not a penny has been asked or used for missionary losses of any kind....
>
> In extraordinary and abnormal conditions, these men have carried through a necessary, but delicate and perplexing, undertaking, in a large-hearted, high-minded way, which has enhanced their personal reputation and reflected fresh credit on the missionary name.... It is not a light thing to speak evil of these men without the amplest reason.... We grant that nothing can excuse evil deeds in a missionary; but we also insist that nothing can excuse the traducing of an honest man's good name. It is true of the missionaries, as of any others, that every man is to be adjudged innocent until he is proven guilty. No such proof in this case has yet been furnished. The more we hear from them, the closer we investigate, the clearer is their course, the nobler seem their deeds. Their vindication, if not already complete, is sure to come."[23]

* * *

Elwood Tewksbury was also coming under fire from within and without the American Board. Tewksbury was especially unpopular with the American army, and unlike Ament he requested an escort of American soldiers to accompany him to the countryside. Tewksbury wrote Minister Conger on March 10, 1901, requesting a cavalry escort for himself, other missionaries, and Chinese to visit villages near Tungchou and hold funeral services for Christians killed by Boxers. General Chaffee responded in the affirmative, although his response indicated in full undiplomatic measure his opinion of the Rev. Tewksbury and missionaries. "It is my opinion that Mr. Tewksbury and his party may visit the places named by him safely, without a military escort and be unmolested and that if he is himself not of that same opinion he should forego his visit, as no good can come to his cause from action obtained only through fear caused by the presence of foreign soldiers.... Nevertheless a detachment of cavalry will be ready to proceed in accordance with the itinerary submitted in his letter."[24] The missionaries had political power—and Tewksbury exerted it. General Chaffee did not want to be criticized for refusing to cooperate, however grudgingly, with the missionaries.

With the criticism leveled at Ament, Tewksbury suddenly became communicative with the American Board in Boston. He wrote a very long letter to Judson Smith, the core of which was a theological justification of himself: "If Jesus were here now in our place, he would wish us to secure certain security against crime, i.e. legal punishment for the criminals in terms *that common heathen can understand.*" (One looks in vain for thunderbolts from heaven striking down the Rev. Tewksbury after that statement.) "This appears to me the crucial point where American policy is criminally weak both in the Philippines and in China. Forgiveness of crime—moral suasion—demands an educated intelligence to understand, and this does not exist plentifully among the heathen natives here! Leniency, forgiveness, are called cowardice."[25]

* * *

The veteran China missionary Devello Z. Sheffield went to Peking a few months after the end of the siege, apparently as an unofficial investigator to ascertain the truth of the charges against Ament and Tewksbury. Sheffield gave Ament a clean bill of health in his letters to Judson Smith. "The charge that Dr. Ament compelled payment was false.... Dr. Ament went without military escort and accomplished his work not only to the satisfaction of the Christians but even more to that of officials and villages. No one has left a better name among the people, or done more to prepare the way for beginning again direct mission work—no one has done so much!" Sheffield reports one mistake Ament made in trusting a Chinese assistant too much, but excused it: "Dr. Ament has a wide field and has been one man to cover it."[26]

Tewksbury gets a much more equivocal review. "Your letters have at last taken terrific effect on Tewksbury and he has written a letter that will make a book! I have read it—with much interest and satisfaction, though I have not heartily approved of all his lines of activity."[27] Sheffield advises Smith that Tewksbury is in "poor health and needs to have a change, as does his family"—missionary code, perhaps, to argue in favor of removing Tewksbury from his post.[28]

In a later letter, however, Sheffield showed more awareness of Tewksbury's virtues although still disapproving of his tactics. "During last winter Mr. Tewksbury had several carts in charge and gave employment to native Christians and others in supplying grain, hay, etc to the British army. He has not reported these accounts to the mission, rather he has stated that he has money in hand from this source which he regards as belonging to himself to use for Christian work. He announced his plan to use it to build up a Summer Christian School.... This announcement was cheered by the mission. Mr. Tewksbury is getting his feet as a strong Christian worker, but he must work in his own lines.... He has done noble work for the mission, no one better in this time of trouble, and is working well at present for reconstruction. I do not think it wise to 'bring him to book' in this matter, but let the mission exercise the restraint and modification in his plans that it is able to do."[29] In other words, Sheffield advised the American Board that Tewksbury was too valuable an asset to be subject to pettifogging financial rules and to be called to task for the proceeds of grain speculation and land Tewksbury bought for a pet project. Sheffield might later have regretted his charity toward Tewksbury when he suffered the fate of having him as a subordinate. Three years later, in a stinging letter to Judson Smith he criticized Tewksbury for his "love of power and control; his use of money; erratic judgment; and irregular methods."[30]

Whether Tewksbury benefited personally from his business transactions after the siege cannot be determined, but, five years later, after the Tungchou Mission had been rebuilt a missionary child, Durand Porter, described the Tewksburys' house. "Both he [Tewksbury] and his wife were accomplished pianists.... If my mother had permitted herself the sin of envy, she would have coveted any one of the three pianos ensconced in the Tewksburys' huge living room: two Steinway Concert Grands and a Steinway Baby Grand."[31]

* * *

Will Ament was a fighter and he got off the canvas to take on the most famous man in America. He even saw some humor in the situation and compared himself to the rakish poet Byron. "Byron," he said, "woke up one morning to find himself famous. I woke up to find myself infamous."[32] In the midst of the furor, he went home to defend himself. He left China on March 29, traveling on the same steamship as Minister Edwin Conger and his wife, Sarah Pike Conger. The Congers, with negotiations on a peace treaty with China nearly concluded, were also returning to the United States for a furlough. The journey by sea restored Ament's confidence. "The Congers are full of kindness. Everybody has been kind, and so sorry that I have been abused in the newspapers. I can stand anything, if my friends who know me stand by me."[33]

Ament was a celebrity. At Nagasaki and in Hawaii the American missionaries turned out to give him a "regular ovation" and the journalists gave him a regular grilling. As usual, he talked too much for his own good; but Conger helped him with a statement of support he made to the press when their ship arrived in Victoria, British Columbia, on April 23. "There were really no acts on the part of the missionaries that were not entirely justified, when the circumstances are known. The missionaries did not loot. The missionaries there found 20,000 destitute men and women on their hands. There was no government, no organized authority. There were the houses of men who had been firing on the foreign quarter, directing the attack, leaders of the Boxers; their property had been abandoned as a result of a state of war, and was taken in order to succor hundreds of suffering and destitute Chinese, whose lives the original owners had been laboring to destroy. The winter was coming on and measures of some kind were imperative, and the appropriation of the property for the ends in view was unquestionably justified. That briefly was the situation. I am prepared to justify the conduct of the American missionaries before the siege and after the siege."[34] The British minister, Claude MacDonald, whose legation had been used for loot auctions, chimed in with a word of support.[35]

While Ament was in transit to the United States, Judson Smith was desperately trying to contact him to order him to shut up and give no press interviews before coming to Boston for consultations.[36] His attempts to communicate with his missionary missed fire because when Ament reached San Francisco, the journalists were out in force and Ament gave them good copy. He revealed that some of the indemnities collected by the missionaries had gone into grain speculation (by Tewksbury) and purchasing property for churches and schools. Judson Smith saw that Ament was a candidate for self-immolation with the press, and, finally catching up with him, ordered that he avoid referring to the charges made against him by Mark Twain. "Such words as 'seize' and 'take' in your explanations ... give peculiar offense to certain sensitive consciences in this country."[37] Smith was managing a public relations disaster for the American Board.

Ament complied with Smith's order for no press interviews, and apparently also adopted his advice on avoiding excessive, belligerent language. The press, already battered by the missionary establishment, soon gave a much more favorable hearing to Ament — who was, an assertive, persuasive, attractive man with a genuine claim to heroism during the Boxer Rebellion. Ament made his way across the United States and had a "cordial reception in Chicago." The first real test of whether he could redeem himself came in New Haven, Connecticut, with a formal address on the subject of China. He passed. The newspapers complimented him on his "lively and interesting running story of the events in the legations from day to day during the siege"[38] and his careful and lucid defense of himself from the charges of Mark Twain and others. Ament's defense of himself rested on three pillars. First, collective guilt and punishment were the norm in China and he collected indemnities from clans as the Chinese themselves would have done. Secondly, he confiscated a palace in China with the permission of Edwin Conger, the American minister. Third, the one-third extra indemnity that he collected above and beyond the damages suffered by Chinese Christians was to assist penniless widows and children.

Ament gained assurance. People wanted to believe this straight-forward, business-like missionary. His stump speech hardly referred to his own troubles. Instead, he inspired his listeners with an impassioned clarion call for Christians to rush to the opportunity for the spread of the gospel in China. His audience applauded him, loud and long, his triumph interrupted only sporadically by renewed criticisms of him in the press. In 1900, to be a missionary was to follow a romantic and heroic calling and Ament, a man of courage, faith, and intelligence, fulfilled the image. He was the missionary of the hour. He drew a crowd wherever he went. He spoke eight times in Detroit in three days, ten times in Cincinnati. He went to Chicago as guest of honor for a banquet. He now took pains to be careful with his speech around journalists. He became diplomatic, reasonable, and circumspect. The outspoken man of action and self-righteousness learned to watch his words.

Soon, the Reverend Ament was on the podiums of the most influential organizations in the United States. He was a guest at a banquet in New York at Delmonico's, the most famous restaurant in the country. Four hundred bankers and business leaders rose to their feet to cheer him when he spoke. Ament was no bearded prophet, no wild-eyed fanatic, no black-cloaked circuit rider, no Romanist priest. He seemed a man you could trust to run a railroad—the highest encomium of America's capitalists. Then, it was to Boston and the Twentieth Century Club and to Toronto to speak before the International Christian Endeavor Society. The demand for his speeches led him back to the West Coast and to the Great Plains—the small towns of the Dakotas where only eleven years before a movement similar to that of the Boxers had sprung up on the Sioux reservation and was quashed at Wounded Knee. William Ament, a China missionary, had become a celebrity. There is no evidence that he enjoyed it. He was fighting for his reputation and that of the missionary movement.

Ament snatched time to pass in Oberlin with Mary, his son Willie, now fourteen, and his mother, eighty-three years old. Ament was a husband more often gone than not. His wife, accustomed to his restless energy, tolerated the long months and years alone. Nothing in their letters indicates strain in their marriage, but introspection in a missionary marriage was not common. Devotion to spouse and family and a joyful Christian union was expected of missionaries and what was expected more often than not became the public reality.

In October 1901, Ament carried his struggle for vindication to the heart of Mark Twain country: Hartford, Connecticut, the former home of the humorist. He was the principal missionary speaker at the annual meeting of the American Board. Three thousand people came to see him and he spoke for an hour. He never mentioned Mark Twain nor said a word about the controversy swirling around him. He was inspirational, high-minded, statesmanlike, and prophetic. He spoke of the redemption of China and his confidence that Christianity would make a permanent and profound impression on China. Christianity, he pronounced, was the institution that would mold and guide the progress and the uplift of the Middle Kingdom from the low state to which it had fallen due to its transgressions and errors. "That a new China has emerged from the Darkness," he concluded, "and has come out upon the state of history to perform its part in the world's progress is evident not only from the condition of the people in China, but from the aroused sentiment throughout the Christian World."[39]

Ament entered the year 1902 satisfied that he had redeemed himself. Mark Twain receded into silence. Criticism in newspaper after newspaper turned to applause. Best of all, China, the

Boxers, missionaries, and looting disappeared from the headlines and Ament resumed the quiet life of a missionary on furlough in the United States. He was restless. He wanted to return to China.

His complacency was shaken by a letter from Judson Smith — the man who led the defense on his behalf and who had confronted Mark Twain, an American icon, on behalf of God, the American Board, and William Ament. Smith suggested that the money Ament and Tewksbury had collected in China to support their Chinese Christians be given back. China, as a requirement of a peace treaty signed in September 1901, would pay a formal indemnity to missionary organizations for the property damages they had suffered in the Boxer Uprising. Therefore, it seemed only fair, in Smith's view, that the money collected by Ament should be returned after the indemnity was received. Ament wrote back to Smith, trying to wrap his mind around this concept and its implications. "It is a hard proposition you give me to solve. Would you mean that the sum raised should be returned when the indemnity is received?"[40] Was there a criticism in Smith's suggestion. If the money should be returned, was it wrong to have collected it in the first place? Did Smith and the American Board—despite their public defense of him— believe that he had been wrong?

Ament rarely mentioned the subject again. He realized that Smith, the American Board, and church leaders in the United States had doubts that his actions following the siege of the legations were correct. They had defended him to close ranks around a colleague, to admit no evil and to manifest no cracks in the veneer of the missionary establishment. Ament had been a symbol—defended to maintain public confidence in the missionary movement, but in the back rooms of the missionary societies, in the corridor chatter outside the boardrooms, Ament was an embarrassment. In the official histories of missionary enterprise he would recede to obscurity rather than occupy the place of honor he otherwise would have merited. The missionaries had won the battle with Mark Twain, but the humorist, armed with a poisonous pen and lasting fame, won the war. Twain's essays are often reprinted and read — but Ament's defense and the defense of him by others is buried in musty archives.

William Ament, the most successful missionary in north China, the best evangelist, and the most dedicated pastor had committed a grave error. Mark Twain was right. Ament had been unwise, indiscreet, possibly dishonest. In his moment of power and glory, he had betrayed his faith and behaved as a vengeful conqueror. That others were no better, and many even worse, was no excuse.

Epilogue

The Peking to which William Ament returned in June 1902 was a different city than he had left fifteen months before. Legation Street reminded him of Europe. The street was paved and patrolled by uniformed policemen. The foreign invasion had pushed the capital of China into the modern world. The railroads had been repaired and expanded. Travel to the interior was now easier and safer. The American Board Mission was being rebuilt and expanded to encompass several properties formerly owned by Chinese. Henceforth, missionaries in China would live in greater ease and comfort. The Chinese were friendlier too, more open, and professing interest in both the religion and the science of the West. The missionaries felt almost welcome. Chinese converts, however, were still rare. Before the Boxer Uprising, the Peking station counted 811 converts, afterwards only 426. Most of the missing had been murdered by the Boxers.[1] Ament would take to the countryside to try to reverse the decline in Chinese Christians.

The missionaries preached Christianity with renewed vigor. Chinese Christians grew slowly in numbers and influence until the siren songs of two newer religions, nationalism and communism, drew them away. However, the missionaries never recovered the plenitude of their confidence in the wake of the Boxer Rebellion and the calumny called down on William Scott Ament. They had lost, for all time, the certainty of their conviction that Christianity was the cornerstone of civilization. Marxism — a confident religion of historical determinism — shoved Christianity aside and captured the hearts and minds of Chinese rebels and intellectuals as Christianity never had.

After 1900, the new breed of missionaries was more secular in outlook. Their faith in the power of evangelism had declined. They often emphasized the worldly benefits of Christianity — education, science, women's rights, and reform in addition to the pure religion of the gospel. To implant their religious message, they sought to fulfill Chinese demands for western ideas and technology. China took the ideas and the technology and mostly ignored the religion. The influence of Christianity in China would rise, peaking before World War II, but then apparently pass into history with scarcely a ripple. Only after monolithic communism was itself crumbling would Chinese Christians reappear from the shadows.

On this return to China, Mary Ament came with her husband. Willie, their 15 year old son, stayed in Ohio to attend Oberlin Academy and later Harvard. Mary, now forty-five years old, had become a woman of accomplishment — president of a church society in Michigan, renowned for her ability to manage servants and a Chinese household, and an excellent Chinese speaker. Slender and attractive, a wife of whom William Ament could be proud,[2] Mary accompanied her husband on his countryside itinerations, on at least one occasion strapping on a revolver and pistol belt for protection.[3] Always the dutiful and traditional wife, however, she left Peking in 1906 to return to Owosso to care for her husband's mother, now nearing her ninetieth year.

The Aments' life in Peking gave them great enjoyment during these years. Ament, even though now an eminence, still preached daily in the street chapel. He could easily have avoided such menial duty and devoted himself instead to missionary affairs and conferences, writing, and lecturing while recreating a good part of every summer at the missionary beach resort of Peitaiho. He still had his old evangelical militancy, but leavened with reality. He wrote, "Now is the time when men of verve and muscle are needed in China. The current is against us. The official tone is a patronizing one and seems to say we will suck your civilization dry and we do not want your religion. In fact that is what Tuan Fang [a Chinese neighbor and official] said to me in conversation the other day."[4] His interpretation of the Chinese attitude toward the West was correct.

In 1907, Ament journeyed to Shanghai to attend what would be the largest and most important gathering of missionaries ever to take place in China. One thousand one hundred and eighty-six Protestant missionaries from dozens of missionary organizations and a score of countries gathered for more than a month at the China Centenary Missionary Conference to discuss and pass resolutions about the most important issues of the day. The conference celebrated 100 years of Protestant missionary endeavor in China.

Many of the survivors of the siege of Peking were there. Arthur Henderson Smith, resembling former president U.S. Grant in his official photo, was elected co-chairman of the conference. W.A.P. Martin attended, 57 years after he first arrived in China, one of three missionaries at the conference with more than 50 years in China. In a nod toward the fact that women comprised the largest number of missionaries, a few women served on committees related to women's work. Luella Miner was the chairman of the Women's Work: Education Committee. Gilbert Reid, the only missionary wounded during the siege and the author of the notorious article "The Ethics of Loot," was there, as was Ada Haven, now the wife of C.W. Mateer. Another distinguished name and siege survivor at the conference was the gray-bearded patriarch and Chinese scholar Chauncey Goodrich.

William Ament was elected chairman of the Comity and Federation Committee.[5] Perhaps taking a page from the Catholics, his cause was to encourage union of all Protestant missionaries working in China and bring order out of a diversity of organizations and doctrines that often bordered on chaos. It was a fond, but impractical dream. In religious and humanitarian organizations, backbiting, competition, and doctrinal disputes are and were far more characteristic than comity. Moreover, union and comity among Protestants was of minor concern compared to the burning, but mostly unmentioned, tension underlying the conference: the relationship between old style evangelical work and the new philosophy which put the evangelist on a plane equal, or only barely superior to, the educator, reformer, and medical doctor. The new won a ringing victory. Evangelical work was forced to share the spotlight of missionary priorities with education, propagation of science, women's work, health, and moral issues such as opium smoking and foot binding. The sonorous voice of the preaching evangelist would no longer be the dominant means by which China would be brought to Christ. The Chinese instead would be seduced by Western science, medicine, and education to accept the tenets of Christianity.

Ament did not participate in that debate but gave an assist to his siege-mate Luella Miner in promoting a resolution about women's work, an indication that he was in sympathy with the new despite his devotion to the old.[6] But Ament undoubtedly would have agreed with old China hand Arthur Smith, who said, "Christianity always and everywhere begins with the lowest stratum of society and works upward."[7] Ament worked at the bottom.

Ament had a nagging headache during the conference and his colleague and biographer, H.D. Porter, wondered whether this was the beginning of his fatal illness.[8] After the conference, however, Ament plunged back into his wearing schedule. Several times during the following year, however, he was overcome by the sun and muscular weakness. For a change of scenery, he retired to the seaside resort of Peitaiho in July 1908. Soon he was running a high fever and suffering from pain in his ribs and shoulder. Missionary doctors believed an operation was necessary, and then another, and another. Amid a series of four operations, Mary Ament arrived from the U.S. to reunite with him.

Ament recovered from the operations only to suffer what was probably a stroke in November. His doctors recommended that he return to the United States to see a brain specialist. Dr. Lucius C. Porter and Mary Ament accompanied him. He got worse en route and when their ship arrived at San Francisco on Christmas he was in a stupor. He faded away to insensibility and passed away on Wednesday, January 6, 1909."[9] His son Willie came to San Francisco from Oberlin and was there at the end.

William Scott Ament was 57 years old. He was buried in Owosso. The eulogies in his honor extolled the man. "Will Ament embodied in his character the essential elements of a successful pioneer — self mastery, boundless energy, courage, faith, hope and charity.... He never waited for things to happen — he made them happen. Difficulties and dangers only stimulated him to greater and more determined effort." Another eulogist said: "His work was in the main strongly evangelistic and pastoral.... A preacher by birth and training, a good speaker of Chinese, his enthusiasm for preaching to the heathen was deep and abiding."[10]

The dark shadows hovering over Ament's life were the accusations against him by Mark Twain. One night in 1907 he spoke of the scandal with the Rev. J. J. Barton, a visiting churchman from the United States, during a visit to Shansi, the place of martyrdom for dozens of missionaries during the Boxer Rebellion. Ament said, "I presume there are many in the United States who regard me as little better than a thief and a robber." Barton assured him that was not the case, that the charges against him had no foundation. "That is true," Ament answered, "but do the people believe the proof, and will the truth ever catch up with the charge?"[11]

Perhaps Ament deserves better. He paid for his sins by becoming the symbol of all the sins of all the foreigners in China in 1900. The destruction of the strange, mad Boxer movement made thoughtful men and women around the world take notice of what they had wrought in the name of Christianity and civilization.

Mary Ament remained in China several years after her husband's death and taught at the Bridgman School. She died in 1928, age 71, in Cleveland, Ohio.[12]

* * *

Like an enormous pachyderm in its death throes the Manchu dynasty crumbled slowly, its passing more ludicrous than majestic. The Empress Dowager survived the Boxers by eight years. A peace treaty was signed in September 1901 and the foreign armies departed, although leaving a residual force that would remain there until World War II. The Dowager and the court returned to Peking in January 1902. She made a belated attempt to reform and modernize her empire. She opened the Forbidden City to visitors. Western ideas were sought out. Students traveled abroad to learn the wisdom and the science of the West. She abolished the age-old examination system for civil servants — a strait-jacket pedagogy which tested a candidate's skill at memorization and his dexterity at regurgitating wisdom sanctified by centuries. China began a slow movement toward a modern government. To placate her restless millions of Chinese subjects chafing under Manchu rule, the Dowager even annulled the ban on intermarriage between Chinese and Manchu and added several Chinese to her cabinet of close advisors.

It was too little and too late for the Manchus. They had lost the mandate of heaven; the Yellow River had changed course; and a new generation of Chinese nationalists was eager to root them out of power. The Dowager, however, did not die without one last dynastic shuffle. The Emperor Kuang Hsu died after a long illness. The Dowager herself was seriously ill. She ate one last enormous bowl of strawberries and cream and laid down and died the next day,

November 15, 1908. The coincidence of the nearly simultaneous deaths of the emperor and Empress Dowager inevitably aroused suspicions that the Dowager had taken measures to ensure that Kuang Hsu would not succeed her as the ruler of China.

On her deathbed, Tzu Hsi named a successor, a pathetic three-year-old boy the West came to know as Henry Puyi. Eunuchs dragged the kicking and screaming boy away from his family and installed him in lonely grandeur in the suite of the emperor in the Forbidden City. Henry Puyi was the last emperor of China. He was deposed in 1912 when a republican revolution brought down, at long last, the Manchu dynasty.

Sarah Pike Conger never lost her admiration for the Old Buddha. She became the Dowager's friend and supporter. The Congers departed China in 1905. Edmund Conger was appointed ambassador to Mexico, but he resigned due to poor health and died in 1907. Sarah retired to Pasadena, California, wrote two books about China, and became a leader in the Woman's Christian Temperance Union.

Herbert Squiers, the American diplomat, was dogged by allegations of looting which prevented him from realizing his ambition of a political career. He died in 1911 at the age of fifty-two. Harriet auctioned off part of his collection of Chinese antiques (said by *The New York Times* to have been "gathered"). The proceeds of the two-day auction were not disclosed but a single afternoon netted more than forty thousand dollars.[13] Harriet Squiers lived until 1935.

Polly Condit-Smith married A.A. Hooker and in 1910 wrote, under her married name of Mary Hooker, a lively book about the siege in Peking. She died at the young age of forty-eight in 1918. Her hero, George Morrison, remained in China and grew rich and famous as an advisor to Chinese politicians. He died in 1920, fifty-eight years old, after accumulating a huge and valuable collection of Chinese antiques and books. The ne'er do well Bertram Lenox Simpson never did do well. He became a secret agent and advisor to Chinese warlords and was assassinated in Tientsin in 1930. He gloried in his lurid life and ultimately paid the price. Sir Robert Hart retired to England in 1908 and died in 1911.[14]

For Captain Newt Hall, the unpopular and prickly second in command of the American marines in the legations, the aftermath of the siege was unfortunate. General Chaffee looked into the whispering campaign against Hall and cleared the marine officer of cowardice. Captain McCalla supported Hall and recommended both Myers and him for brevet promotions. However, Hall got attention when *The New York Times* reported that Minister Conger accused him of cowardice, insubordination, and neglect of duty. Conger denied making such comments about Hall.[15] Unfavorable mention was also made of Hall in a magazine article by William N. Pethick.[16] Hall requested a court-martial to clear his name. He was declared innocent, but the exoneration was less than complete. He was said to have shown "great caution" and declared to have been adequately punished by "the world wide publications and criticism of his conduct in Peking."[17]

Was Hall guilty? Not according to a letter written many years later to author Peter Fleming: "The court feels called upon to remark that there will be found in the record a great deal of incidental or collateral evidence going to show the prevalence of a feeling adverse to Captain Hall, officially and socially, at the United States Legation, which naturally would not tend to minimize any mistake or unpopular act on his part. Femininity figures on certain pages, and it is plainly indicated that some of the severest criticisms of Captain Hall are traceable to the same residence which extols into heroic importance a civilian (Mr. Squiers) who is incidentally condemned by evidence adduced by the defense."[18] In other words, Hall did not get along well with Herbert and Harriet Squiers. Hall, however, went on to a successful career "officially cleared and stoutly defended by many friends in the Marine Corps, got his brevet, stayed on, and ultimately retired a colonel."[19]

Dr. Emma Martin and her sister, Lizzie, stopped in Japan on their way back to America in

1900 and worked for a time with missionaries there. Returning to China, the Martin sisters had long careers, retired and in 1945, Emma, age 75, and Lizzie, age 72, were living in their home town of Otterbein, Indiana.[20] Emma always retained her forthright no-nonsense manner and a healthy respect for the moral issues of American missionary work in China.

Mary Porter Gamewell died in 1906, age 58, of the anemia that already afflicted her in China. Frank Gamewell remarried, returned to China, and later had the prestigious post of general secretary of the Methodist Board of Foreign Missions in New York. He died in 1950 at the age of 83.[21] Elwood Tewksbury never achieved his ambition to be a star in the missionary firmament. He remained in China until 1906, beset by bitter disagreements with other missionaries, and subsequently worked with missionary organizations in the United States. He died in 1945.

Lt. Colonel Goro Shiba, the best soldier in the siege of the legations, had a distinguished career. He became an author and a general in the Japanese army before retiring in 1930. He lived until 1945 when he died of complications from an attempt at suicide after Japan surrendered to the United States.[22]

Like Herbert Squiers, the ill-gotten gains of Auguste and Annie Chamot did not bring them success and happiness. Chamot lost his mansion in the 1906 San Francisco earthquake and everything else shortly afterwards, including Annie. He died an alcoholic in 1910, forty-three years old. He had fifteen cents on his person. His second wife, a manicurist named Betsy Dollar, was at his deathbed Annie had married her chauffeur in 1909. She was 38 and he was 25.[23]

* * *

Arthur Smith, the scribbling missionary and scholar, commented in 1909 about the changes wrought by the Boxer Rebellion. The Chinese saw the "necessity of many changes in government, in education, in manners, in dress, in medicine, sanitation, in social appliances, etc., and hence presumptively in religion."[24] Smith, as always, emphasized the positive aspects of the Western impact on China. He died in 1932 at the age of 87 in California after a career of 54 years in China. His wife, Emma, who had a Bible verse handy for every situation, died in 1926. Smith's finest contribution to the missionary effort came in 1906 when he helped persuade President Roosevelt that Chinese indemnity payments to the United States be used to found a national university in China and to support Chinese students in the United States. The amount returned to China was $12 million by the early 1920s.[25] Conscience money, one might assert, to redress the excesses of William Ament and other missionaries in 1900.

Sarah Pike Conger, the metaphysical, eccentric wife of the U.S. minister in Peking, has the last word on China, the Boxer Rebellion, and the missionaries.

> China belongs to the Chinese, and she never wanted the foreigner upon her soil. The foreigner would come, force his life upon the Chinese, and here and there break a cog of the wheels that run their government so systematically. Even if we grant that China's condition has been improved by these invasions, what right has the foreigner to enter this domain unbidden and unwelcomed? The foreigner has forced himself, his country, his habits, and his productions upon China, always against a strong protest. It kept getting worse for China, and she recognized the fact. At length, in one last struggle, she rose in her mistaken might to wipe the foreigner and his influence from her land. Could we, after taking these facts home to ourselves, blame the Chinese for doing what they could to get rid of what they considered an obnoxious pest that was undermining the long-established customs of their entire country?[26]

American and Canadian Missionaries in the Siege at Peking

Ament, the Rev. William Scott. b. 1851, Owosso, MI. American Board. Arrived China, 1877.
Andrews, Miss Mary Elizabeth (Aunt Mary). b. 1840, Cleveland, OH. American Board.
Brown, Miss Amy E. Presbyterian, Christian and Missionary Alliance (CMA), in Peking since 1897.
Chapin, Abbie G. b. 1868. American Board.
Chapin, Franklin M. and Flora Barret. Children: Ernest and Ralph. American Board.
Davis, the Rev. George R. Methodist. Arrived Peking, 1870.
Douw, Miss Deborah Matilda. b. 1835, Albany, NY. Independent. Arrived Peking, 1874.
Evans, Miss Jane Gertrude (Aunt Jennie). American Board.
Ewing, the Rev. Charles E. (b. 1869), and Elizabeth Goodyear Smith (b. 1870). Children: Marion and Ellen. American Board. Arrived China, 1894.
Fenn, the Rev. Courtenay Hughes (b. 1866), and Alice Holstein (b. 1865). Children: Henry and Martha. Presbyterian.
Galt, the Rev. Howard S. (b. 1872), and Louise West (b. 1876). American Board.
Gamewell, the Rev. Francis Dunlap (b. 1857), and Mary Q. Porter (b.1848). Methodist. Arrived China, 1881 and 1872.
Gilman, Miss Gertrude. Methodist.
Gloss, Dr. Anna, M.D. Methodist. Arrived China, 1885.
Goodrich, the Rev. Chauncey (b. 1836), and Sarah B. Clapp (b. 1855). Children: Grace Dorothea and Luther Carrington. American Board.
Gowans, Annie H. (British or Canadian). Presbyterian.
Haven, Miss Ada. b. 1850. American Board (later Ada Haven Mateer).
Hobart, the Rev. W.T. Methodist.
Inglis, Dr. John M., and Theodora. Child: Elizabeth (died July 22, 1900). Presbyterian. Arrived Peking, 1898.
Ingram, Dr. James H. (b. 1858), and Myrtle Prough. Daughter and stepdaughter: Ruth. American Board.
Jewell, Mrs. Charlotte M. Methodist. Arrived China, 1883.
Killie, Charles A. (b. 1857), and Louisa Scott (b. 1856). Presbyterian.
King, the Rev. H.E. Methodist.
Leonard, Dr. Eliza Ellen, M.D. b. 1866. Presbyterian.
Lowry, Mrs. Edward K. (Katharine M.). Methodist. Husband came to Peking with relief column.
Lowry, Dr. George D. Methodist.
McCoy, Miss Bessie Campbell. b. 1871. Presbyterian.
Mackey, Dr. Maud Aura. b. 1872. Presbyterian.
McKillican, Miss Janet C. (Jennie) b. 1855. (Canadian). Presbyterian.
Martin, Miss Elizabeth (Lizzie). b. 1873. Methodist. Arrived China, April 1900.
Martin, Dr. Emma E. b. 1870. Methodist. Arrived China, April 1900.
Mateer, Mrs. John L. (May La Rhue Sellers). b. 1845. American Board (widow).
Miner, Miss Luella. b. 1861. American Board.
Newton, Miss Grace b. 1860. Presbyterian.
Reid, the Rev. Gilbert (b. 1857), and wife. One child. Independent (formerly Presbyterian). Mission Among the Higher Classes of China. Wounded July 5.
Russell, Miss Nellie Naomi. b. 1861. American Board.

Rutherford, Miss Hattie E. (British?) Presbyterian, CMA.
Sheffield, Miss Elizabeth E. b. 1875. American Board. (Later Elizabeth Stelle).
Smith, the Rev. Arthur Henderson (b. 1845), and Emma Dickinson (b. 1849). American Board. Arrived China, 1872.
Stelle, the Rev. William B. Independent, later American Board.
Terrell, Alice. Methodist. Professor of mathematics.
Terry, Dr. Ellen Methodist. Arrived China, 1887.
Tewksbury, the Rev. Elwood Gardner (b. 1865), and Grace Holbrook (b. 1864). Children: Donald and Gardner. American Board.
Verity, the Rev. G.W. Methodist.
Walker, the Rev. W. F., and wife. Child: Esther. Methodist.
Wherry, the Rev. John A. Presbyterian. Arrived China, 1872.
Whiting, the Rev. John L. b. 1837. Presbyterian.
Wycoff, Miss Gertrude. b. 1864. American Board. (twin).
Wyckoff, Miss Grace. b. 1864. American Board (twin).

Former Missionaries

Coltman, Dr. Robert, Jr. (b. 1862), and wife. Six children. Formerly Presbyterian. Arrived China, 1883.
Martin, the Rev. W.A.P. b. 1827. Formerly Presbyterian, President, Imperial College. Arrived China, 1850.

Chapter Notes

Prologue

1. *The Literary Digest,* August 25, 1900, 211.
2. *Ibid.,* July 14, 1900, 34.
3. See http://www.adam-matthew-publications.co.uk/digital_guides/japan_through_western_eyes/part%204.aspx, May 20, 2008.

Chapter 1

1. *The Chinese Recorder,* 1900, 211–214; Purcell, 290; Lu Yao in Buck, 75. It is unclear who gets the honor for naming the Boxers. A letter dated September 21, 1899, from missionary Grace Newton in Pang Chuang, Shantung, is the earliest use of the name I can find. The context of the letter seems to indicate that it was a known term by that time. Either Henry D. Porter or Arthur H. Smith is the likely coiner of the term.
2. Porter, 160.
3. Ruoff, 208.
4. *Ibid.,* 58–59.
5. Ament's trip outside Peking is from Porter, 175–179. Despite what he had seen, Ament opined that the "Boxer bubble is practically burst."
6. Ruoff, 15.
7. FRUS, 1900, 107. Many other examples of similar language can be found.
8. Ruoff, 15–16.
9. Quoted from O'Connor, *The Spirit Soldiers,* 20.
10. This story was perhaps told first by Anna N. Benjamin in *Outlook* 65 (1900): 640.
11. Smith, *Convulsion,* 32.
12. *Ibid., Convulsion,* 202.
13. O'Connor, 46.
14. Quoted from Cohen, *History,* 84.
15. *Ibid.,* 83.
16. *Ibid.,* 74, 75, 316.
17. Cohen in Bickers, 183, 192.
18. The Rev. A.P. Happer, "A Visit to Peking," *The Chinese Recorder,* January-February 1879, 23–24.
19. Purcell, 93.
20. Fleming, 29.
21. Savage Landor, vol. 1, 133.
22. Esherick, 134.
23. ABCFM Papers, Ament's letter of January 16, 1900.
24. Smith, *Convulsion,* 109.
25. Barr 55.
26. *Ibid.,* 7.
27. Duff, 110–111.
28. Bigham, 45.
29. *Baptist Missionary Magazine,* April 1849, 104.
30. Smith, "Village Life in China," 350.
31. "Missionaries in China," *The New York Times,* January 29, 1901, 8.
32. Timothy Richard, "Historical Evidences of Christianity in China," *The Chinese Recorder,* March 1890, 145.
33. *The Chinese Recorder,* September 1892, 407–408.
34. Forsythe, 55.
35. Estimates of the number of Protestant missionaries is derived from a chart published in *The Literary Digest,* August 11, 1900, 167. Other sources give slightly higher estimates.
36. *The Chinese Recorder,* March 1899, 144–145.
37. Smith, *Convulsion,* 60.
38. *Ibid.,* 48.
39. Ament, "Romanism," 48.
40. Arlington, 14.
41. Lutz, 39.
42. *The Literary Digest,* September 22, 1900, 347.
43. Smith, *Convulsion,* 80.
44. Purcell, 124.
45. *The Literary Digest,* October 13, 1900, 443.
46. *The Chinese Recorder,* November 1889, 587.
47. Michie, 72–73.
48. Ruoff, 18.
49. Fairbank, *The Missionary Enterprise,* 270.

Chapter 2

1. www.Penfield.fm/genealogy, November 15, 2007.
2. Porter, 32.
3. *Ibid.,* 33.
4. *Ibid.,* 33.
5. *Ibid.,* 34.
6. www.Penfield.fm/genealogy, November 15, 2007.
7. Van Housen, 234.
8. *Light and Life for Women,* January 1881, 10.
9. Porter, 47.
10. Several of the famous Cambridge Seven — muscular, socially elite, well-educated — British missionaries who arrived in China in 1885 declined to study Chinese because they anticipated that God would grant them proficiency in the language. He didn't. See Austin, 222.
11. Porter is the source of these quotes and the biographical information on Ament.
12. Reeve, 54.
13. *The Chinese Recorder,* September-October 1880, 349–357.
14. Liu, 110.
15. Porter, 41.
16. *Ibid.,* 45.
17. *Ibid.,* 52.
18. *Ibid.,* 68.
19. "Statistics of the Shantung Protestant Missions," *The Chinese Recorder,* 1877, 381.
20. Porter, 103.
21. *Ibid.,* 116.
22. *Ibid.,* 117.
23. Hunter, 164.
24. *The Chinese Recorder,* April 1892, 183.
25. Ruoff, 18–19.
26. "In Memoriam: Rev. William Scott Ament, D.D.," *The Chinese Recorder,* May 1909, 278.
27. Ruoff, 26.
28. http://www.angelfire.com/mi2/shiawasseetours/ament.html, November 15, 2007.
29. *Missionary Herald,* July 1899, 281–282.
30. Forsythe, 25.
31. Price, xxi, xxii.
32. Calculations of the numbers of American missionaries vary between 70 and 78 depending upon who is

considered American and a missionary. See Appendix.
33. Quoted from Pruitt, who delves into the motivation of female missionaries, 1; Forsythe, 10.
34. Beaver, 178.
35. http://www.censusbureau.biz/statab/hist/HS-22.pdf, May 5, 2008.
36. Mrs. W. E. Bainbridge, *Diary*.
37. Tuttle, 42.
38. *Gospel in All Lands*, November 1894, 524.
39. Menzi, vol 3, part 3, pages 10–13 discusses servants and their wages in 1905.
40. http://eh.net/atp/answers/0789.php, January 25 1007.
41. Varg, 5.
42. Smith, *Convulsion*, 518.
43. This famous phrase was apparently coined by religious leader John R. Mott.

Chapter 3

1. Whiting in Sharf, 225.
2. FRUS, 1900, 122.
3. Morrison, *The Living Age*, February 2, 1901, 269. The two largest empires in 1900 were ruled by women: China and Great Britain.
4. Porter, 180.
5. Allen 25.
6. Allen, 25. Ament's account of the trip is shorter and he says that they spent a single night in Cho Chou and then returned to Peking. The date is estimated from Stelle having just returned on May 22.
7. FRUS, 1900, 130.
8. FRUS, 1900, 130.
9. Steiger, 196.
10. Emma Martin, Diary, 6.
11. Emma Martin, Letter, April 5, 1900.
12. *Ibid.*, Letter, May 18, 1900.
13. *Ibid.*, Letter, May 26, 1900.
14. Hoe, 20–22.
15. Measurements of the city and walls are calculated from Lin Yutang, 203 and Denby, 26. The walls of Peking were torn down to use as building materials during the Great Leap Forward in 1957.
16. Allen, 29–31, among others, has a good description of entering Peking.
17. Little, *Intimate China*, 324.
18. Scidmore, 189.
19. Krout, 498.
20. Ruoff, 20.
21. Scidmore, 61.
22. *Ibid.*, 66.
23. *Ibid.*, 146.
24. Little, *Intimate China*, 325.
25. *Ibid.*
26. Scidmore, 145.
27. Arlington, 6.
28. Biographic data concerning Hart is from Whittlesey and Weale, 63.
29. Quoted from Fleming, 65.
30. Porter, 147.
31. Little, *Intimate China*, 327.
32. Scidmore, 152.
33. Smith, A. "The Contribution of Foreigners to Chinese Discontent," *The Outlook*, December 15, 1900, 925.
34. Mateer, 48–49.

Chapter 4

1. Hooker, 6. Polly Condit Smith authored this book in 1910 under her married name of Mary Hooker. She appears in the literature as Polly Condit Smith, Polly Condit-Smith, Polly C. Smith, and Mary C. Smith. I will call her Polly Condit-Smith.
2. "Refugees Reach Tien-Tsin, *The New York Times*. August 29, 1900, 2.
3. Hooker, 10.
4. Seagrave, 7.
5. Hoe, 306.
6. Hoe, 34.
7. *Catholic Encyclopedia: Herbert Goldsmith Squiers*. http://www.newadvent.org/cathen/14238c.htm, November 16, 2007.
8. Quoted from Hoe, 37; re Dupree see Morrison, *The Living Age*. February 2, 1901, 275.
9. Morrison, *The Living Age*, November 17, 1900, 406.
10. Allen 26.
11. Vare, 209 and many other sources.
12. Biggs, 28–29.
13. Conger, 91.
14. Clemens, 97.
15. Conger, 92.
16. Allen, 54–55.
17. Myers, 542. The photographer was probably Mrs. M.S. Woodward of Evanston, Illinois, a house guest of the Congers. She was called "Mamma," helped in the siege hospital, and formed a singing quartet to entertain the besieged. Her daughter Ione was also in Peking. (Hoe, 388).
18. Conger, 92.
19. Allen, 54–55.
20. "Peking, Report of Captain John T. Myers," http://www.history.navy.mil/docs/boxer/boxer11.htm, November 16, 2007 An interesting calculation illustrating the difference between the heavy expenditure of ammunition in today's wars as compared to the past is the following. The marines arrived in Peking with precisely 27,720 rounds of ammunition. At the end of the siege, they had 7,000 remaining. Without taking into account the small amount of ammunition expended before the siege, they fired 377 rounds per day (20,720 divided by 55 days) or less than 7 rounds per marine or sailor per day.
21. I have followed FRUS, 1900, 190 in listing the numbers of legation guards. Estimates of their numbers range between 445 and 459. See Biggs, 31, Reid, Morrison, and others. The differences are because several soldiers visiting Peking are sometimes counted among the legation guards, and sometimes not.
22. Morrison, *The Living Age*. February 2, 1901 268.
23. "Peking: Report of John T. Myers." http://www.history.navy.mil/docs/boxer/boxer11.htm.
24. Myers, 542.
25. Quoted from Fleming, 69.
26. Coates, 4.
27. Davids, 63.
28. Mateer, 31–32.
29. Esherick, 291.
30. Hoe, 385.
3. Mateer, 52.
32. Mateer, 55.
33. Ransome, 48.
34. Tuttle, 185.
35. *Shanghai Mercury*, 10–11.
36. Smith, *Convulsion*, 215.
37. Porter, 183.
38. Ruoff, 73.
39. Hoe, 50.
40. Allardyce loaned him the shotgun.
41. Hoe, 50.
42. Morrison, *Living Age*, November 17, 1901, 408.
43. Porter 185.
44. Hoe, 56.
45. Menzi, Vol III, Part 3, 10. Georgina later became Mrs. Biggin.
46. Ransome 49–50.
47. Hoe, 56–59.
48. Hoe, 174.
49. Mateer, 58–62.
50. Mateer, 349.
51. Hoe, 28.
52. Two hundred Chinese school girls is the author's estimate. One hundred thirty came from Bridgman and the Methodist school; no estimate was found of the number of LMS and North China College students and other schools, but a guess of another sixty or seventy seems reasonable.
53. Mateer, 69.
54. Mateer, 83.
55. Martin, letter of June 19, 1900.
56. Martin, Diary, 48.
57. Sharf quoting Private Upham, 155.
58. Mateer, 77, 78.
59. Mateer, 79; Tuttle 198.
60. Hoe, 82–83.
61. Martin, letter of June 17, 1900.
62. Tuttle, 199.

Chapter 5

1. Mateer, 45.
2. Seagrave, 315.
3. Fleming, 72.
4. Morrison, *Living Age*, November 17, 1901, 411.
5. W. E. Bainbridge, Diary, 11. This incident is odd in that the Chinese soldiers previously had not molested foreigners in Peking. Perhaps the murder of Sugiyama came about from an old grudge or by soldiers operating outside the bounds of their orders.
6. Tuttle, 195.
7. Although Miss Douw and her four helpmates were guests of the Congers at the American Legation.
8. Porter, 185.
9. Ruoff, 78.
10. Weale, 50.
11. *Ibid.*, 51.
12. Some accounts do not state that the boy was killed.
13. Oliphant, 13–14.
14. Mrs. W. E. Bainbridge, Diary.
15. Morrison, *The Living Age*, February 2, 1901, 270.
16. Tuttle, 195.
17. Miner, "Prisoner," 642.
18. Mrs. W. E. Bainbridge, Diary.
19. Weale, 60.
20. Morrison, *The Living Age*, November 17, 1900, 413.
21. Weale, 61.
22. Myers, 544.
23. Tuttle, 196.
24. Miner, "Prisoner," 642.
25. *Ibid*
26. Tuttle, 198.
27. Hooker, 40.
28. Payen, 455.
29. Ransome, 58–59.
30. Tuttle, 206.
31. Fleming, 100.
32. Fleming, 98.
33. Fleming 100.
34. Conger, 100.
35. Morrison, 414.
36. Fleming, 95.
37. Allen, 92.
38. Hooker, 26.
39. Weale, 66.
40. Smith, *Convulsion*, 234.
41. Mateer, 96.
42. Davids, 102. Other accounts give Seymour up to 2,261 soldiers.
43. Taussig, 410.
44. Wurtsbaugh, 210.
45. Bacon, 105.
46. Taussig, 412. Casualty estimates vary from source to source.
47. Taussig, 413.
48. Davids, 107.
49. Bacon, 108.

Chapter 6

1. Vare, 194.
2. Many sources, including http://www.royalty.nu/Asia/China/TzuHsi.html, February 21, 1908.
3. The preceding story is from Conger, 39–43.
4. Rhoads, 33, 68.
5. Bland, 50.
6. This and the previous story are from Smith, *Convulsion,* 10–11.
7. Der Ling, 161.
8. Quoted from Seagrave, 308.
9. Qi Qizhang in Buck, 140.
10. Lin Huaguo in Buck, 150.
11. Thompson, 170.
12. Quoted from Clements, 116.
13. Quoted from Fleming, 79.
14. Chalmers, 53.
15. Mrs. Jones account of her adventures is from the *Shanghai Mercury,* 19–23 June 21, 1900.
16. Chalmers, 54.
17. Three hundred twenty-one British, 133 Germans, 244 Japanese, 159 Russians, 25 Italians, and 22 Austrians. Sharf, 89.
18. *Shanghai Mercury,* 19–23 June 21, 1900.
19. Sources for the Taku battle include Fleming, 80–83, and Elliott, 499–511, who gives a much more favorable account of Chinese military prowess than most authors,.
20. Esherick, 289; Tan, 72.
21. Conger, 108.
22. The full text of the Chinese diplomatic note is in Davids, 83.
23. Fleming, 103.
24. Tuttle, 208.

Chapter 7

1. Emma Martin, Diary, 56. Martin said the women did not know of the "council of war" until the following morning.
2. Smith, *Convulsion,* 249–250.
3. Lord, 143.
4. Smith, *Convulsion,* 252.
5. Porter, 187.
6. Mateer, 107.
7. *Ibid.* As Smith was the only English missionary known to be in the Methodist Mission, it is probable she was the "sweet-faced London Mission woman" making this statement.
8. Mateer, 103–104.
9. Quoted from Sharf, 173–174.
10. Mateer, 121.
11. Personal observations of the author.
12. Davids, 84.
13. Hooker, 44.
14. *Ibid.* Also many other sources.
15. Mateer, 124.
16. Tuttle, 209.
17. Miner, "Prisoner in Peking," 645.
18. Emma Martin, Diary, 56–57.
19. Smith, 253–255, and Thompson, 277. There are many accounts of the baron's last meeting with the diplomatic corps. I have pieced together the story mostly from these two sources.
20. The story of the baron's assassination is taken from Morrison, *The Living Age,* November 17, 1900, 473–474.
21. Payen, 453.
22. Among others, Fleming supports this view, 107.
23. Conger, 109.
24. Tuttle, 212.
25. Mateer, 124–125.
26. Allen, 107.
27. Quoted from Thompson and Macklin, 180.
28. Allen, 6.
29. Quoted from Pearl, 117, but also from other sources.
30. W.E. Bainbridge, Diary, 24.

Chapter 8

1. Mrs. E. K. Lowry, 69. Lowry lists 18 nationalities among the besieged. However, Swiss is not included in her list and Auguste Chamot was Swiss. Therefore, at least 19 nationalities were present.
2. Ransome 110. Three hundred fifty-six Chinese were living in the British Legation, according to a census.
3. Morrison, *The Living Age,* November 17, 1900, 475. I have corrected Morrison's addition. The sources differ slightly in enumerating the legation guards.
4. Reid in *Shanghai Mercury,* 112.
5. Emma Martin, Diary, 61.
6. Weale, 111.
7. *Ibid.*, 112.
8. Mateer, 161.
9. *Ibid.*, 132.
10. Smith, *Convulsion,* 273.
11. *Ibid.*, 274.
12. Weale, 142.
13. ABFCM Papers, Sheffield letter, February 26, 1901.
14. Anderson, 235.
15. Tuttle, 99–100.
16. Coltman, 78.
17. Mateer, 177.
18. Payen, 458.
19. *Ibid.*, 460.
20. Weale, 142–143.
21. *Ibid.*, 134–135.
22. Emma Martin, Diary, 61.
23. Tuttle, 241.
24. "Missionaries Defended," *Sun* (New York), March 24, 1901.
25. Mateer, 175, and Smith *Con-*

vulsion, 745–747, list the committees and their members.
26. Coltman, 79–80.
27. Fenn, 2919.
28. Tuttle, 243–247.
29. Weale, 120–121.
30. Morrison, 478.
31. Keown-Boyd, 105.
32. Hooker, 35–36.
33. Smith, *Convulsion,* 280.
34. Hooker, 68.
35. *Ibid.,* 62.
36. Mateer, 138.
37. Smith, *Convulsion,* 283.
38. Seagrave, 376.
39. Oliphant, 39.
40. Morrison, *The Living Age.* November 24, 1900. Oliphant's account has the ring of truth to me. The British began the destruction of the Hanlin which was completed by a fire set by the Chinese, whether purposely or accidentally.
41. Weale, 136.
42. Smith, *Convulsion,* 282–283.
43. Oliphant, 55.
44. National Archives, Microfilm group 62–02, Roll 378.
45. Seagrave, 396.
46. Tan, 75, 93.
47. *Ibid.,* 95.
48. Lin Huaguo in Buck, 152–153.
49. Ding Mingnan in Buck, 37.
50. Tuttle, 236.

Chapter 9

1. Beach, 413.
2. Mrs. W. E. Bainbridge, Diary.
3. Hoover's story of his adventures in China are in Hoover, 35–72.
4. Nash, 119.
5. Chalmers, 56.
6. See Schmidt, 21, for examples of the special consideration Butler got from another officer.
7. Andrews, 254.
8. Schmidt, 21. Daggett, 18–19, counts a total of 169 men under Waller's command, but only 131 of them made the assault on Tientsin.
9. Thomas, 45.
10. Daggett, 18–19.
11. Thomas, 49–51. The tales of both Hoover and Butler may have improved with the telling — but are too good to resist repeating.
12. *Ibid.,* 52.
13. Hoover, 52.
14. Thomas, 54.
15. Hoover, 51.
16. *Ibid.,* 52.
17. Menzi, 118.
18. Taussig, 413.
19. Bacon, 109. Times and distances differ according to source.
20. *Ibid.,* 111.
21. Taussig, 416.
22. Wurtzbaugh, 215.
23. Bacon, 112–113.
24. Taussig, 419.
25. Bigham, 187.
26. Thomas, 57.
27. Bacon, 116.
28. Fleming, 89.
29. Bigham, 190.
30. Quoted from Bickers, 186.
31. Seymour, 350.
32. Lynch, *War,* 306–307.
33. Landor, vol. 1, 133.
34. Quoted from Duiker, 133.

Chapter 10

1. *Shanghai Mercury,* 101.
2. See, among others, Ransome, 93.
3. Weale, 126. Except as otherwise noted the description of the defenses is from Weale, 120–135.
4. Lynch, 89.
5. http://en.wikipedia.org/wiki/Shiba_Goro, February 9, 2008.
6. Weale, 130.
7. Hoe, 379.
8. Weale, 131.
9. Hart, 268.
10. Giles, 145.
11. *Ibid.,* 129.
12. Weale, 150–151,.
13. *Ibid.,* 151.
14. *Ibid.,* 152–153.
15. Smith, *Convulsion,* 468.
16. *Ibid.,* 272.
17. Hart, 268.
18. Morrison, *The Living Age.* November 24, 1900, 476.
19. *Ibid.*
20. Measured on contemporary maps.
21. Ingram, 3030.
22. Hart, 276.
23. Weale, 123.
24. *Annual Reports of the War Department,* 1901, 456.
25. *Ibid.*
26. Smith, *Convulsion,* 316–317.
27. Davids, 80. This translation of a Chinese document affirms that that government knew the guards numbered only about 400.
28. Smith, *Convulsion,* 286–287.
29. *Ibid.,* 287.
30. Keown-Boyd, 109–110. David Oliphant in this party "had the satisfaction of killing his first man"— apparently a rite of passage for young men of that era. Oliphant was in turn killed a few days later. His brother Nigel survived. Oliphant, 43.
31. Smith, *Convulsion,* 292.
32. Tan, 113–114.
33. Hooker, 81.
34. Allen, 187.
35. Emma Martin, Diary, 75.
36. Hooker, 116.
37. Quoted from Cameron, 384.
38. Favier, 545–546, 553–554.
39. Quoted from Fleming, 225.

Chapter 11

1. Oliphant, 72.
2. Davids, 132–133.
3. Mateer, 216.
4. Oliphant, 51, 54, 70.
5. Thompson, 184–185.
6. Smith, *Convulsion,* 297.
7. Quoted from Fleming, 132.
8. Myers, 545–546.
9. Several sources describe a major German-American offensive on the Tartar Wall on June 24, but Myers does not mention American participation in any such attack; rather, he says that the Americans were unsuccessful in creating a post on the wall.
10. Smith, *Convulsion,* 289.
11. Myers, 545–546.
12. *Ibid.,* 550.
13. *Ibid.,* 542.
14. Upham in Sharf, 160, and Pethick, 310. Pethick claims that Hall was on the wall at the time of the retreat; others do not make the same claim. Myers ("Report, 4) said that "I ... withdrew into the Legation," it being unclear whether the "I" was him personally or the men under his command. That Pethick didn't like Hall is readily apparent from his account, and I have accepted Upham's statement that Myers "ordered all hands off the wall." The unpopular Hall was blamed for most of the deficiencies of the American marines — although it was probably Myers who located the American barricade in an untenable position in the first instance.
15. Allen, 166.
16. Fenn, "The American Marines," 2848.
17. Mateer, 187.
18. Mrs. W. E. Bainbridge, Diary. Emma Smith's role during the siege seemed to have been to hand out Bible verses to people in the British Legation. Some appreciated them; some probably did not. See W.A.P. Martin, 118.
19. Biggs, 95.
20. See Oliphant, 67: "We can only hope now that the Americans will hang on to the wall at all costs."
21. Giles, 129.
22. Emma Martin, Diary, 73.
23. Allen, 146.
24. Giles, 139.
25. Smith, 306.
26. Coates, 192; Sharf, 160–161. Biggs, 95, says that the American marines again abandoned the wall and withdrew to the foot of the ramp.
27. Pethick, 310.

28. Smith, *Convulsion*, 315.
29. Oliphant, 78–79.
30. *Ibid.*, 78–80.
31. Coltman, 84.
32. W. A. P. Martin, 97.
33. Pethick, 311.
34. W. A. P. Martin, 83.
35. Giles, 141.
36. Smith, *Convulsion*, 324–325.
37. Keown-Boyd, 122.
38. Smith, *Convulsion*, 747.
39. Coates, ed., 149.
40. Fenn, 2919–2920.
41. Allen, 256.
42. *Ibid.*, 182.
43. Report of Army, 1901, 458.

Chapter 12

1. Aspinall-Oglander, 57.
2. Palmer, *With My Own Eyes*, 174–175.
3. We have only Hoover's word for it that he accompanied the marines as a guide. Apparently nobody else involved in the battle mentions him.
4. Thomas, 59.
5. Schmidt, 18.
6. Daggett, 28.
7. American Diplomatic Papers, 133.
8. Hoover, 53. Most of previous story is derived from Hoover.
9. Thomas, 61–65.
10. Palmer, "With the Peking Relief Column," 303.
11. Savage Landor, vol. 1, 186.
12. Palmer, "With the Peking Relief Column," 304.
13. H.H. Lowry, 745.
14. McCloskey, 117.
15. Quoted from *The Literary Digest*, August 4, 1900, 121.
16. Wise, 38–42.
17. Menzi, vol. 2, 111.
18. McCloskey, 115.

Chapter 13

1. Quoted from Fleming, 157.
2. Weale, 210.
3. Allen, 204.
4. "The Fortification of Peking During the Siege," *The Gospel in All Lands*, February 1902, 83.
5. Smith, *Convulsion*, 340–341.
6. Coltman, 110.
7. Miner, "A Prison in Peking," 703.
8. Hoe, 214–215.
9. Lord, 35.
10. Quoted from Biggs, 116.
11. Upham in Sharf, 163.
12. "Report of Captain John T. Myers." http://www.history.navy.mil/docs/boxer/boxer11.htm, December 10, 2007.
13. Mrs. W.E. Bainbridge, Diary.
14. Hoe, 261.
15. Quoted from Thompson, 190–191.
16. Hooker, 126.
17. Emma Martin, Diary, 82.
18. Conger, 135.
19. Giles, 88.
20. *The New York Times*, July 16, 1900, 1.
21. Quoted from *The Literary Digest*, July 21, 1900, 61.
22. *The Philadelphia Press.* Quoted from *The Literary Digest*, August 4, 1900, 121.
23. Tan, 95.

Chapter 14

1. Smith, 279.
2. Trevor-Roper, 34.
3. Hooker, 124.
4. *Ibid.*, 69.
5. *Ibid.*, 112–113.
6. Coltman, 79.
7. Mrs. W. E. Bainbridge, Diary.
8. Mateer, 105.
9. Davids, 170.
10. Morrison, December 1, 1900, 552.
11. Fenn, "The Food Supply," 2919.
12. Weale, 216.
13. Tuttle, 248.
14. Mateer, 197.
15. Tuttle, 248.
16. Payen, 466.
17. Tuttle, 244.
18. Mateer, 203–204.
19. Hooker, 148–49.
20. Upham in Sharf, 165.
21. Weale, 190–191.
22. Hooker, 129–130.
23. Tuttle, 254–55.
24. *Ibid.*, 256.
25. "In Memoriam, Rev. William Scott Ament, D.D.," *The Chinese Recorder,* May 1909, 281.
26. Matter, 173.
27. *Ibid.*, 172.

Chapter 15

1. Vare, 309.
2. Cameron, 391.
3. http://www.chinahistoryforum.com/index.php?act=Print&client=printer&f=34&t=19868, February 12, 2008.
4. Most of the information on the hospital, except as otherwise noted, comes from Ransome. Also from Hoe, quoting Lillie Saville, 142.
5. Mateer, 231, 237.
6. Emma Martin, Diary, 67.
7. *Ibid.*, 62.
8. *Ibid.*, 63.
9. Hooker, 74.
10. Mateer, 231.
11. Statistics of deaths from wounds were computed from Ransome, 17–18, and Myers, 552.
12. Mateer, 247–48.
13. *Ibid.*, 236–237.
14. Hoe, 146.
15. Emma Martin, Diary, 69. Hoe, page 198, believed that this remark might have been directed at Marian Lambert rather than Ransome.
16. Emma Martin, Diary, 86.
17. *Ibid.*, 105.
18. *Ibid.*, 68.
19. *Ibid.*, 69, 94, 98, 99.
20. Mateer, 297.
21. Mrs. W. E. Bainbridge, Diary.
22. Mateer, 314–316.
23. Coates, 253.
23. *Ibid.*, 253.
24. Morrison, *The Living Age*, December 1, 1900, 645.
26. Hooker, 148, 150.
27. Allen, 236.
28. Mateer, 288.
29. Ransome, 106.
30. Mateer, 209.
31. Allen, 229.
32. Miner, "Prisoner in Peking," 735.

Chapter 16

1. Aspinall-Orlander, 60.
2. Thomas, 68.
3. Holbrooke in Sharf, 236.
4. Whiting in Sharf, 218.
5. McCloskey, 133. Most of the previous details are also from McCloskey, 17–21 and 129–138.
6. Holbrook in Sharf, 236.
7. This is the reported strength of the Allied armies: 18,600. Actual strength was under 16,000. Daggett, 59.
8. Aspinall-Oglander, 57.
9. Steel, 9.
10. Thomas, 68–69.
11. Palmer, *With My Own Eyes*, 199.
12. Daggett, 64.
13. Wise, 50–51.
14. The account of the battle of Yang Tsun is mostly from Daggett, 59–69.
15. Wise, 46.
16. Palmer, *With My Own Eyes*, 193.
17. Savage Landor, vol. 1, 375.
18. Thomas, 70.
19. Aspinall-Oglander, 61.
20. Daggett, 72.
21. Thomas, 69. Statistics for marines dropping out are from Millett, 161–162.
22. Quoted from Keown-Boyd, 168–169.
23. Quoted from *The Literary Digest,* February 2, 1901, 141.

24. Sorley, 75.
25. Coates, ed., 267.
26. Giles, 175.
27. Hooker, 169.
28. Mateer, 347.
29. Payen, 467.
30. Mateer, 375–377.
31. *Ibid.*, 377.
32. Quoted from Cameron, 391–392.
33. Vare, 310–311.
34. Quoted from Fleming, 194.
35. Carter, 191.

Chapter 17

1. Quoted from Fleming, 198.
2. Lynch, 130–133.
3. Payen, 467.
4. Hewlett, 32.
5. Mateer, 382.
6. Savage Landor, vol. 2, 175.
7. Daggett, 78.
8. *Ibid.*, 81.
9. Sorley, 81.
10. Thomas, 73.
11. *Ibid.*, 26.
12. Fleming, 203.
13. Quoted from Keown-Boyd, 180.
14. Aspinall-Oglander, 64.
15. Frederick Brown, 112.
16. Quoted from O'Connor, 244.
17. Coates, 277.
18. Vaughan, 101.
19. Miner, "Prisoner in Peking," 741.
20. Hooker, 175.
21. *Ibid.*, 176.
22. Aspinall-Oglander, 65.
23. Lynch, 84.
24. Daggett, 88.
25. Conger, 161.
26. This and previous quotes from Anna Gloss are from Mateer, 398–400.
27. Palmer, *With My Own Eyes*, 201–202.
28. *Ibid.*, 201.
29. W.E. Bainbridge, Diary.
30. Dr. Velde's tables of casualties had several arithmatic errors which I corrected. It was published by various sources including Myers, 552, and Daggett, 235. I have altered Velde's statistics to include Padre d'Addosio, killed the day after the siege ended, and the Belgian woman wounded on the last day of the siege. In addition to battle casualties, six foreign children died of disease during the siege. At least one of the wounded men — and probably several — in Velde's table later died.
31. Davids, 183.
32. Glover, 1. Calculations of missionary deaths differ slightly depending upon the source.
33. See Latourette, 508–519; Martin, 66.
34. Author's estimate based on totaling casualty estimates for the various battles.

Chapter 18

1. There are many accounts of the Dowager's flight from Peking. Preston is the most recent, 255–261.
2. Allen, 276.
3. Hooker, 183.
4. Smith, *Convulsion*, 434.
5. Mateer, 395.
6. Savage Landor, vol. 2, 193.
7. Palmer, "With the Peking Relief Column," 307.
8. Porter, 191–192.
9. Smith, *Convulsion*, 498.
10. Porter, 190.
11. *Ibid.*, 191.
12. *Ibid.*, 196. The Methodists and Presbyterians also left representatives behind to help their surviving Christians and rebuild their missions. We hear much less of them. Either they were more discreet or less aggressive in confiscating palaces and goods.
13. *Ibid.*, 192.
14. Fleming, 220–221.
15. Oliphant, 197.
16. Ruoff, 102.
17. Hooker, 179.
18. Brown, *From Tientsin*, 120.
19. Allen, 293.
20. *Ibid.*, 293–94.
21. *The Sun* (Baltimore), January 16, 1901, 2.
22. Ruoff, 104–105.
23. Payen, 468.
24. Allen, 297.
25. Payen, 468.
26. Woodward, 279.
27. Ruoff, 105.
28. *The Washington Post*, December 23, 1900, 1.

Chapter 19

1. Quoted from O'Connor, 286.
2. Lynch, 375.
3. *Ibid.*, 179.
4. *Sun* (New York), January 10, 1901, 1.
5. Wise, 40.
6. Steel identifies the soldiers as from the 24th Punjab Infantry, 58. The word "loot," incidentally, found its way into English from Hindustani.
7. Carter, 214.
8. Hevia in Bickers, 98.
9. Wise, 55–56.
10. *Ibid.*, 69.
11. Gilbert Reid, "The Ethics of Loot," *The Forum*, July 1901.
12. Quoted from *The Literary Digest*, July 13, 1901, 36.
13. W.A.P. Martin, 136. Martin denied that he looted, other than taking a goat-skin rug on the floor of the house in which he lived for a time after the siege. However, he was afflicted by Indian, Russian, and American soldiers who invaded the premises, took some things, and opened his trunks to search for valuable items.
14. Emma Martin, Diary, 111, 112. The missionary's claims for indemnities were modest. Not so Herbert and Lou Hoover. The Hoovers submitted a claim for $52,707 which included three lost years of salary for Hoover. He was awarded, however, only $10,759. Varg, 49. The journalist George Morrison submitted a claim for 5,804 pounds (about US $24,000) which included 2,625 pounds for his wound. Thompson, 200.
15. Mathisen, 430.
16. *Sun* (Baltimore), January 16, 1901, 2.
17. Menzi, vol. 3, part 3, 7; Porter, 285, note 2. The Goodriches journeyed from Peking through Tungchou about the time the soldier recalled this incident and they are the only American missionaries who had a daughter about 12 years old. See also Ruoff, 105.
18. Vaughan, 121.
19. Lynch, 177–178.
20. Quoted from Hoe, 319.
21. Whiting in Sharf, 223; Hevia in Bickers, 109.
22. *The Sun* (New York), January 28, 1901, 5.
23. Pearl, 130.
24. *The New York Times*, September 3, 1901, 3.
25. Allen, 282.
26. Weale, 364–65.
27. Chamberlin, 191.
28. New York *Sun*, January 2, 1901; Hoe 332–333.
29. Morse, 319.
30. *Ibid.*, 317.
31. *Ibid.*, 318–319.
32. *New York Nation*, October 18, 1900, quoted from Morse, 319.
33. http://en.wikipedia.org/wiki/Klemens_von_Ketteler.
34. Porter, 197.
35. *Ibid.*, 198.
36. *Ibid.*
37. Weale, 327–28.
38. Quoted from Hoe, 322–323.
39. Quoted from Hoe, 324.
40. Miller in Fairbank, 277.
41. Porter, 207. Dr. Robert Coltman, a former missionary, also accompanied this expedition.
42. *Ibid.*, 219.
43. *Annual Report of the Secretary of the Army, 1900*, 138–140; James L. Hevia in Bickers, 99.
44. Miller in Fairbank, 276.
45. ABCFM, Tewksbury Letter, February 18, 1901.

46. *Ibid.*
47. *Ibid.*
48. Hevia in Bickers, 111.
49. ABCFM, Tewksbury Letter, February 18, 1901.
50. Hevia in Bickers, 99.
51. Sorley, 97.
52. Annual Report of the Secretary of War, 1901, 454.
53. Porter, 208.
54. *Ibid.*, 240–241.
55. *Missionary Herald*, June 1901, 226.
56. Porter, 213.
57. *Ibid.*, 209–210.
58. Menzi, vol. 2, 116–117.
59. *Ibid.*, vol. 3, 10.
60. Porter, 233.
61. Menzi, vol. 2, 122,.
62. Mrs. W. E. Bainbridge, Diary.
63. Porter, 217.
64. *Ibid.*, 218.
65. *Ibid.*, 221.
66. Miller in Fairbank, 274–275.
67. *Ibid.*, 275.
68. Lynch, 84.
69. Menzi, vol. 2, 111.
70. *Ibid.*, 122.
71. Ricalton, 253–254.
72. See, for example, Sharf, 120.

Chapter 20

1. Chamberlin, 98.
2. *Ibid.*, 102.
3. *Ibid.*, 116–117.
4. ABCFM Papers, Smith letters to Mary Ament, January 2, February 12, and February 20, 1901.
5. Quoted from Lindbeck, 402–403; *Missionary Herald*, February 1901, 46.
6. *Annual Reports of the War Department, 1901*, 467.
7. Porter, 250. ABCFM Papers, Ament's letter dated February 18, 1901; *The Sun* (New York), February 6, February 8 and February 9, 1901, 2.
8. Chamberlin, 263–264.
9. ABCFM Annual Report, 1902, 117.
10. *Sun* (New York), December 24, 1900.
11. Quoted from Kaplan, 358, 361, 362–363. "Known for his well-knownness" originated with Daniel Boorstin.
12. Twain, "To the Person Sitting in Darkness," *North American Review*, February 1901.
13. Albert Bigelow Paine. Quoted from Young, 278.
14. Porter, 210.
15. Quoted from Porter, 233–234.
16. *Ibid.*, 231–232.
17. *Ibid.*, 236.
18. *Ibid.*, 236–238.
19. Quoted from Porter, 236.
20. *The Sun* (New York), March 30, 1901, 1.
21. *The New York Times*, February 18, 1901, 18.
22. Twain, "To My Missionary Critics," *North American Review*, April 1901.
23. The Rev. Judson Smith, "The Missionaries and their Critics," *The North American Review* (May 1901).
24. ABCFM Papers, Tewksbury Letter to Judson Smith, February 19, 1901 (a very long letter of many sections. The exact date of which is uncertain to this chronicler).
25. *Ibid.*
26. ABCFM Papers, Sheffield letter to Judson Smith, Item 17, March 26, 1901.
27. ABCFM Papers, Sheffield letter to Judson Smith, Item 16, February 26, 1901.
28. ABCFM, *Ibid.*, March 26, 1901.
29. ABCFM, Sheffield letter to Judson Smith, n.d.
30. ABCFM Papers, Sheffield letter to Judson Smith, June 17, 1904.
31. Menzi, vol. 3 of the Wilder Stanley Saga, part 3, 7.
32. Porter, 231.
33. *Ibid.*, 253.
34. *The Literary Digest*, May 11, 1901, 578.
35. Porter, 213–214.
36. ABFCM Papers, Judson Smith letters to Mary Ament, April 18, 1901, and William Ament, May 2, 1901.
37. Miller in Fairbank, 279; Young 195.
38. Porter, 259.
39. "Status of Foreign Missions," *The New York Times*, October 10, 1901, 9.
40. I find only Ament's response to Smith in the voluminous papers of the ABCFM. However, Ament's letter is clear that Smith had written him on this subject. ABCFM Papers, Ament's letter of January 22, 1902.

Epilogue

1. Porter, 269.
2. *Ibid.*, 264.
3. *Ibid.*, 581.
4. *Ibid.*, 307.
5. *China Centenary Missionary Conference Records.*
6. *China Centenary*, 583–584.
7. "Smith, Arthur Henderson" http://www.bdcconline.net/bdcc_stories/china/tianjin/smith_ah.html.
8. Porter, 325.
9. *Ibid.*, 342.
10. *Ibid.*, 350, 352.
11. *Ibid.*, 366.
12. http://www.penfield.fm/genealogy/wc01/wc01_144.html.
13. *The New York Times*, April 10 and April 12, 1912.
14. Keown-Boyd, 249.
15. "Mr. Conger Accuses Captain of Marines," *The New York Times*, October 28, 1900; Biggs, 117; Heinl, 142.
16. Pethick.
17. Biggs, 117; Heinl, 142. "Capt. N. H. Hall Exonerated," *The New York Times*, May 24, 1901.
18. Hoe, 375.
19. Biggs, 117.
20. *Old China Hands*, 1945.
21. Anderson, 235.
22. http://en.wikipedia.org/wiki/Shiba_Goro., January 30, 2008.
23. Hoe, 333; Seagrave, 369.
24. Quoted from Varg, 86.
25. http://www.bdcconline.net/bdcc_stories/china/tianjin/smith_ah.html and http://links.jstor.org/sici?sici=0002-9300(192407)18%3A3%3C544%3AROTCI%3E2.0./CO%3B2-N, December 28, 2007.
26. Conger, 189.

Bibliography

Abbreviations: ABCFM Papers—Papers of the American Board of Commissioners for Foreign Missions, original papers at Houghton Library, Harvard University, microfilm edition available at Howard University Divinity Library; an enormous collection of letters and other documents. **ABCFM Annual Reports. FRUS**—*Foreign Relations of the United States, 1899, 1900, 1901,* Government Printing Office, Washington, 1900, 1901, 1902

Selected Periodicals and Newspapers

The Chinese Recorder
The Independent
The Gospel in All Lands
Light and Life for Women
The Literary Digest
The Living Age
The Missionary Herald
The Missionary Review of the World
New York *Sun*
The New York Times
New York *World*
The Outlook
The Shanghai Mercury
The Times of London
Washington Post

Books, Articles, and Unpublished Sources

Agnew, James B. "Coalition Warfare—Relieving the Peking Legations, 1900." *Military Review*, October 1976: 58–70.

Allen, the Rev. Roland. *The Siege of the Peking Legations.* London: Smith, Elder, 1901.

Austin, Alvyn. *China's Millions: The China Inland Mission and Late Qing Society, 1832–1905.* Cambridge, UK: Wm. B. Eerdmans, 2007.

Ament, the Rev. William S. "The Charges against the Missionaries." *The Independent,* 19 May 1901: 1051–1052.

Ament, the Rev. W.S., D.D. "A Bishop's Loot," *The Independent,* 19 September 1901: 2217–2218.

_____. "The Chinese Settlement Once More." *The Independent,* 12 September 1901: 2147–2149.

Anderson, Gerald H. *Biographical Dictionary of Christian Missionaries.* Grand Rapids, MI: Wm. B. Eerdmans, 1999.

Annual Reports of the War Department, 1900, 1901.

Andrews, Roy Chapman. *Under a Lucky Star.* New York: Viking Press, 1943.

Arlington, L.C., and William Lewisohn. *In Search of Old Peking.* Peking: Henry Vetch, 1935.

Aspinall-Oglander, Cecil. *Roger Keyes.* London: Hogarth Press, 1951.

Bacon, Admiral R.H. *The Life of John Rushworth, Earl Jellicoe.* London: Cassell, 1936.

Bainbridge, W.E., and Mrs. W.E. Bainbridge. Diaries. Herbert Hoover Presidential Library.

Barnard, John. *From Evangelicalism to Progressivism at Oberlin College, 1866–1917.* Columbus: Ohio State University Press, 1969.

Barr, Pat. *To China with Love: The Lives and Times of Protestant Missionaries in China, 1860–1900.* London: Secker & Warbuck, 1972.

Beach, Harlan P. "In China's Ancient Holy Land." *The Chautauguan,* January 1906: 403–417.

Beaver, R. Pierce. *American Protestant Women in Mission.* Grand Rapids, MI: Eerdman's, 1980.

Berkhofer, Robert F., Jr. *Salvation and the Savage.* Lexington: University of Kentucky Press, 1965.

Bickers, Robert, and R.G. Tiedemann. *The Boxers, China, and the World.* Lanham, MD: Rowman and Littlefield, 2007.

Bigham, Charles Clive. *A Year in China.* London: Macmillan, 1901.

Bland, John Otway Percy. *Recent Events and Present Policies in China.* New York: J.B. Lippincott, 1912.

The Boxer Rising: A History of the Boxer Trouble in China. Reprinted from the *Shanghai Mercury.* New York: Paragon Book Reprint Corp., 1967

Brown, the Rev. Frederick. *From Tientsin to Peking with the Allied Forces*. London: C.H. Kelly, 1902.

Brown, Fred R. *History of the Ninth U.S. Infantry: 1799–1909*. Chicago: Donnelley, 1909.

Buck, David D., ed. *Recent Chinese Studies of the Boxer Movement*. London and New York: M.E. Sharpe, 1987.

Cameron, Nigel. *Barbarians and Mandarins*. Chicago: University of Chicago Press, 1976.

Carter, W.H. *The Life of Lieutenant General Chaffee*. Chicago: University of Chicago Press, 1917.

Chalmers, Rear Admiral W.S. *The Life and Letters of David, Earl Beatty, Admiral of the Fleet*. London: Hodder and Stoughton, 1951.

Chamberlin, Wilbur J. *Ordered to China*. London: Methuen, 1904.

Chinese Centenary Missionary Conference Records. New York: American Tract Society, n.d.

Chuan Sen. "A Chinese Account of the Siege of the Legations." *The Independent*, 22 November 1900: 2776–2781.

Clemens, Paul H. *The Boxer Rebellion: A Political and Diplomatic Review*. New York: Columbia University Press, 1915.

Coates, Tim, ed. *The Siege of the Peking Embassy 1900*. London: The Stationery Office, 2000.

Cohen, Paul A. *China Unbound: Evolving Perspectives on the Chinese Past*. New York: Taylor and Francis, 2003.

_____. *History in Three Keys: The Boxers as Event, Experience, and Myth*. New York: Columbia University Press, 1997.

Coletta, Paolo E. *Bowman Hendry McCalla: A Fighting Sailor*. Washington: University Press of America, 1979.

Coltman, Robert Jr., M.D. *Beleaguered in Peking: The Boxer's War Against the Foreigner*. Philadelphia: F.A. Davies, 1901.

Conger, Sarah Pike. *Letters from China*. Chicago: A.C. McClurg, 1910.

Covell, Ralph. *W.A.P. Martin: Pioneer of Progress in China*. Washington: Christian University Press, 1979.

Crozier, Capt. William. "Some Observations on the Pekin Relief Expedition." *North American Review*, February 1901.

Daggett, A.S. *America in the China Relief Expedition*. Kansas City, MO: Hudson-Kimberly, 1903.

Darcy, Eugene. *La Defense do la Legation de France a Pekin*. Paris: Challamel, 1901.

Davids, Jules, ed. *American Diplomatic and State Papers: The United States and China: Boxer Uprising*. Series 3, vol. 5. Wilmington, DE: Scholarly Resources, 1981.

Davidson, Lt. W.C. "Operations in North China." *Proceedings of the U.S. Naval Institute*, December 1900: 637–646

Der Ling, Princess. *Two Years in the Forbidden City*. New York: Moffat, Yard, 1911.

Dillon, E.J. "The Chinese Wolf and the European Lamb." *The Contemporary Review*, January 1901: 2–31.

Dorn, Frank. *The Forbidden City*. New York: Charles Scribner's Sons, 1970.

Duff, Alexander. *The Indian Rebellion: Its Causes and Results*. New York: Robert Carter & Bros, 1858.

Duiker, William J. *Cultures in Collision*. San Rafael, CA: Presidio, 1978.

"Duthine." "A Visit to Peking in 1899." *The Living Age*, 13 October 1900.

Edwards, E.H. *Fire and Sword in Shansi: The Story of the Martyrdom of Foreigners and Chinese Christians*. Reprint of 1903 edition. New York: Arno, 1970.

Elliott, Jane E. *Some Did It for Civilization, Some Did it for Their Country*. Hong Kong: Chinese University Press, 2002.

Esherick, Joseph W. *The Origins of the Boxer Uprising*. Berkeley: University of California Press, 1987.

Fairbank, John K., ed. *The Cambridge History of China*. Vol. 10, *Late Ch'ing, 1860–1911, Part 1 and 2*. Cambridge: Cambridge University Press, 1978.

Fairbank, John King. *The Great Chinese Revolution: 1800–1985*. New York: Harper and Row, 1986.

Fairbank, John K., ed. *The Missionary Enterprise in China and America*. Cambridge, MA: Harvard University Press, 1974.

Favier, Monsignor. "Deux Mois de Siege: Journal de Monseigneur Favier." *Les Missions Catholiques*, 16 and 23 November 1900.

Fenn, the Rev. Courtenay Hughes. "The American Marines in the Siege of Peking." *The Independent*, 29 November 1900: 2845–2850.

_____. "The Food Supply During the Siege." *The Independent*. 6 December 1900: 2917–2920.

Feuerwerker, Albert. *The Foreign Establishment in China in the Early Twentieth Century*. Ann Arbor: University of Michigan Press, 1976.

Fleming, Peter. *The Siege at Peking*. New York: Harper, 1959.

Forsythe, Sidney A. *An American Missionary Community in China, 1895–1905*. Cambridge: Harvard University Asia Center, 1971.

Gamewell, Mary Ninde. *Ming-Kwong: "City of the Morning Light."* West Medford, MA: Central Committee for the Study of Foreign Missions, 1924.

Gamewell, Mary Porter. "Across Chili from the Sea to Peking." *The Chautauquan*, December 1905.

_____. "Up the Yangtse to Tibet." *The Chautauquan*, January 1906.

Garrity, John. "Which of these Men is the Real Herbert Hoover?" *Smithsonian*, May 1985.

Giles, Lancelot. *The Siege of the Peking Legations: A Diary*. Edited and Introduction by L.R. Marchant. Nedlands, Western Australia: University of West Australia Press, 1970.

Gipps, G. *The Fighting in North China (Up to the Fall of Tientsin City)*. Shanghai: Kelly & Walsh, 1901.

Glover, Archibald B. *A Thousand Miles of Miracle in China*. London: Hodder and Stoughton, 1904.

Gracey, the Rev. J.T., D.D. "Missionaries and 'Loot' in Peking." *Missionary Review of the World*, March 1901: 206–208.

Greenwood, Frederick. "The Missionaries and the Empire," *The Nineteenth Century*, July 1901.

Hart, Sir Robert. "The Peking Legations: 'A National

Uprising and International Episode.'" *The Living Age*, 2 February 1901.

_____. *These from the Land of Sinim: Essays on the Chinese Question*. London: Chapman & Hall, 1903.

Heinl, Robert Debs, Jr. *Soldiers of the Sea: The United States Marine Corps, 1775–1962*. Annapolis: United States Naval Institute Press, 1962.

Hewlett, William Meyrick. *Forty Years in China*. New York: Macmillan, 1943.

Hohenberg, John. *Foreign Correspondence: The Great Reporters and their Times*. New York: Columbia University Press, 1964.

Hooker, Mary (Polly Condit-Smith). *Behind the Scenes in Peking*. New York: Brentano's, 1911.

Hoover, Herbert. *The Memoirs of Herbert Hoover: Years of Adventure, 1874–1920*. New York and London: Hollis and Carter, 1952.

Hubbard, Ethel Daniels. *Under Marching Orders: A Story of Mary Porter Gamewell*. New York: Missionary Education Movement, 1911.

Hunt, Michael H. "The Forgotten Occupation: Peking, 1900–1901." *Pacific Historical Review*, November 1979.

Hunter, Jane. *The Gospel of Gentility: American Women Missionaries in Turn-of-the-Century China*. New Haven, CT: Yale University Press, 1984.

Hykes, the Rev. John R., D.D. "The Martyr Missionaries in China." *The Missionary Review*, February 1901.

Ingram, James H., M.D. "The Defense of the Legations in Peking." *The Independent*, 3 December and 10 December 1900: 2979–2984, 3035–30340.

Kaplan, Justin. *Mr. Clemens and Mark Twain*. New York: Simon and Schuster, 1966.

Kempff, James. "Letter from the Senior Squadron Commander U.S. Naval Force on Asiatic Station." *Proceedings of the U.S. Naval Institute*. June 1901.

Keown-Boyd, Henry. *The Fists of Righteous Harmony*. London: Leo Cooper, 1991.

Ketler, Isaac C. *The Tragedy of Paotingfu*. New York: Fleming H. Revell, 1902.

Krout, Mary H. "By Rail to Peking." *The Chautauguan*, August 1900.

Kwong, Luke S.K. *A Mosaic of the Hundred Days*. Cambridge MA: Harvard East Asia Monographs, 1984.

"Lansdowne." "The Fortifications of Peking During the Siege." *The Gospel in All Lands*, February 1902: 80–86

Latourette, Kenneth Scott. *A History of Christian Missions in China*. New York: Macmillan, 1929.

Leech, Margaret. *In the Days of McKinley*. New York: Harper and Bros. 1959.

Lin Yu-tang. *Imperial Peking: Seven Centuries of China*. New York: Elek Books, 1961.

Lindbeck, John M.H. *American Missionaries and the Policies of the United States in China, 1898–1901*. Diss., Yale University. Ann Arbor, MI: University Microfilms International, 1986.

Little, Mrs. Archibald (Alicia Helen). *Intimate China*. London: Hutchison, 1901.

_____. "Peking Revisited. An Anniversary Study of August 1900." *The Eclectic Magazine of Foreign Literature*, October 1901.

_____. *Round About My Peking Garden*. London: T. Fisher Unwin, 1905.

Liu, Kwang-Ching, ed. *American Missionaries in China: Papers from Harvard Seminars*. Cambridge, MA: Harvard University Press, 1970.

Lord, Walter. *The Good Years*. New York: Harper and Bros., 1960.

Lowry, Mrs. E.K. "A Woman's Diary of the Siege of Pekin." *McClure's Magazine*, November 1900.

Lowry, H.H. "The Chinese Resentment." *Harper's Monthly Magazine*, October 1900: 740–747

Lutz, Jessie G., ed. *Christian Missions in China—Evangelists of What?* Lexington, MA: DC Health, 1965.

Lynch, George. "Vae Victis! The Allies in Peking after the Siege." *The Independent*, 8 November 1900: 2681–2683.

_____. *The War of the Civilizations: Being the Record of a 'Foreign Devil's' Experiences with the Allies in China*. London: Longmans, Green, 1901

MacCloskey, Monro. *Reilly's Battery: A Story of the Boxer Rebellion*. New York: Rosen, 1969.

MacDonell, John. "Looting in China." *The Contemporary Review*, March 1901: 444–452

Martin, Dr. Emma. *Diary and Letters*. University of Illinois at Champaign-Urbana Library.

Martin, W.A.P., D.D., LL.D. *The Siege in Peking*. New York: Fleming H. Revell, 1900.

_____. "The Siege of Pekin." *National Geographic Magazine*, February 1901: 53–62.

Mateer, Ada Haven. *Siege Days: Personal Experiences of American Women and Children during the Peking Siege*. Chicago: Fleming H. Revell, 1903.

Mathisen, Robert R. *Critical Issues in American Religious History: A Reader*. Waco, TX: Baylor University Press, 2001.

Menzi, Donald Wilder. *The Wilders of North China*. Vol. 3 of the Wilder-Stanley Saga: 1894–1900, 1901–1904, 1904–1909. http://reced.org/dmenzi/wilders/Downloads.htm, November 22, 2007.

Michie, Alexander. *Missionaries in China*. London: Edward Stanford, 1891.

Millett, Allan R. *Semper Fidelis: The History of the United States Marine Corps*. New York: The Free Press, 1980.

Miner, Luella. *China's Book of Martyrs*. New York: Pilgrim Press, 1903.

_____. "The Flight of the Empress Dowager." *The Century Magazine*, March 1901: 777–780.

_____. "A Prisoner in Peking: The Diary of an American Woman During the Siege." *The Outlook*, 10, 17, and 24 November 1900.

Moncrieff, Col. G.K. Scott. "Peking, August 1900." *Blackwood's Edinburgh Magazine*, November 1905: 627–638.

Moncrieff, Major General G.K. Scott. "Recollections of the Germans in China, 1900." *Blackwood's Edinburgh Magazine*, July 1915.

Morrison, Dr. George E. "The Siege of the Peking

Legations." *The Living Age*, 17 and 24 November 1900; 1, 8, and 15 December 1900. Originally published in *The Times* of London.

Myers, Captain John T. "Military Operations and Defenses of the Siege of Peking." *Proceedings of the U.S. Naval Institute*, September 1902.

Nash, George H. *The Life of Herbert Hoover: The Engineer, 1874–1914*. New York: W.W. Norton, 1983.

Nicholls, Bob. *Bluejackets and Boxers: Australia's Naval Expedition to the Boxer Uprising*. Sidney: Harper Collins, 1986.

O'Connor, Richard. *The Spirit Soldiers: A Historical Narrative of the Boxer Rebellion*. New York: Putnam's, 1973.

Old China Hands: A Roster. Berkeley Chamber of Commerce. 1945.

Oliphant, Nigel. *A Diary of the Siege of the Legations in Peking*. London: Longman, Greens, 1901.

Palmer, Frederick. "Mrs. Hoover Knows. " *Ladies Home Journal*, March 1929.

_____. *With My Own Eyes*. Brooklyn: Bobbs-Merrill, 1932.

_____. "With the Peking Relief Column." *The Century Magazine*, December 1900.

Paine, Ralph D. *Roads of Adventure*. Boston: Houghton Mifflin, 1922.

Payen, Cecile E. "Besieged in Peking." *The Century Magazine*, January 1901.

Pearl, Cyril. *Morrison of Peking*. Sydney: Harper Collins, 1967.

Peffer, Nathaniel. *The Far East*. Ann Arbor: University of Michigan Press, 1958.

Pethick, W.N. "The Struggle on the Peking Wall." *The Century Magazine*. December 1900.

Porter, Andrew. *Religion versus Empire? British Protestant Missionaries and Overseas Expansion, 1970–1914*. Manchester: Manchester University Press, 2004.

Porter, Henry D. *William Scott Ament: Missionary of the American Board to China*. New York: Fleming H. Revell, 1911.

Preston, Diana. *The Boxer Rebellion*. New York: Berkley Books, 1999.

Price, Eva Jane. *China Journal: 1889–1900*. New York; Charles Scribner, 1989.

Pruitt, Lisa Joy. *A Looking Glass for Ladies*. Macon, GA: Mercer University Press, 2005.

Purcell, Victor. *The Boxer Uprising: A Background Study*. Cambridge, MA: Harvard University Press, 1963.

Ralph, Julian. "Women who Make Trouble: Missionary Methods Must Change in China." *The Chinese Recorder*, November 1900.

Ramsay, Alex. *Peking Who's Who: 1922*. Peking, 1922. Republished Taipei, 1971.

Ransome, Jessie. *The Story of the Siege Hospital*. London: SPCK, 1901.

Reeve, the Rev. B. *Timothy Richard, D.D.* London: S.W. Partridge, n.d.

Reid, Gilbert. "The Ethics of Loot." *The Forum*. July 1901.

Report of the Secretary of the Navy, 1900, 1901.

Rhoads, Edward J. *Manchus & Han*. Seattle: University of Washington Press, 2000.

Ricalton, James. *China through the Stereoscope*. New York: Underwood & Underwood, 1901.

Rockhill, William Woodville, ed. *Treaties and Conventions with or Concerning China and Korea*. Washington: Government Printing Office, 1904.

Ruoff, E.G., ed. *Death Throes of a Dynasty: Letters and Diaries of Charles and Bessie Ewing, Missionaries to China*. Kent, Ohio, and London: Kent State University Press, 1990.

Savage Landor, A. Henry. *China and the Allies*. 2 vols. New York: William Heinemann, 1901.

Schmidt, Hans. *Maverick Marine: General Smedley D. Butler and the Contradictions of American Military History*. Lexington, KY: University Press of Kentucky, 1987.

Scidmore, Eliza Ruhamah. *China: The Long-Lived Empire*. New York: Macmillan, 1900.

Seagrave, Sterling. *Dragon Lady: The Life and Legend of the Last Empress of China*. New York: Vintage, 1992.

Seymour, Admiral Sir Edward. *My Naval Career and Travels*. London: Smith, Elder, 1911.

Sharf, Frederic A., and Peter Harrington. *China 1900: The Eyewitnesses Speak*. London: Greenhill Books, 2000.

Smith, Arthur H. "China a Year after the Siege in Peking." *The Outlook*, August 24, 1901: 969–975.

_____. *China in Convulsion*. 2 vols. New York: Fleming H. Revell, 1901.

_____. "China Six Months after the Occupation of Peking. *The Outlook*, April 13, 1901: 865–871.

_____. "The Contribution of Foreigners to Chinese Discontent. "*The Outlook*, December 15, 1900: 923–926.

_____. "The Punishment of Peking." *The Outlook*, October 27, 1900: 493–501.

_____. "The Transformation of Peking." *The Outlook*, May 18, 1901: 157–162.

_____. "Why the Chinese Dislike Foreigners. "*The Outlook*, January 26, February 2 and February 23, 1901: 216–221, 400–406, 631–666.

_____. *Village Life in China: A Study in Sociology*. New York: Fleming H. Revell, 1899.

Smith, the Rev. Judson. "The Missionaries and their Critics." *The North American Review*, May 1901.

Smith, Stanley. *China from Within, or the Story of the Chinese Crisis*. London: Marshall Brothers, 1901

"Some Missionary Experiences in China." *The Missionary Review*. January 1901.

Sorley, Capt. L.S. *History of the Fourteenth United States Infantry from January 1890 to December 1908*. Chicago: Lakeside, 1909.

Spence, Jonathan D. *The Gate of Heavenly Peace*. New York: Viking Adult, 1981.

Sprague, the Rev. W.P. "Flight from the 'Boxers' by Way of Siberia." *The Missionary Review of the World*, February 1901.

Steel, Richard A. *Through Peking's Sewer Gate: Relief of the Boxer Siege, 1900–1901*. New York: Vintage, 1985.

Steiger, George Nye. *China and the Occident: The Origin and Development of the Boxer Movement*.

New York: H. Milford, Oxford University Press, 1927.

Tan, Chester C. *The Boxer Catastrophe*. New York: Columbia University Press, 1955.

Taussig, Captain J.K. "Experiences during the Boxer Rebellion." *Proceedings of the U.S. Naval Institute*, April 1927: 403–420.

Thomas, Lowell. *Old Gimlet Eye: The Adventures of Smedley D. Butler*. New York: Farrar and Rinehart, 1933.

Thompson, Michael Don. *The Holy Spirit and Human Instrumentality in the Training of New Converts: An Evaluation of the Missiological Thought of Roland Allen*. Diss., Golden Gate Baptist Theological Seminary, Mill Valley, CA, 1989.

Thompson, Peter, and Robert Macklin. *The Man who Died Twice: The Life and Adventures of Morrison of Peking*. Crow's Nest, Australia: Allen & Unwin, 2005.

Thomson, John. *Through China with a Camera*. London: Harper & Bros., 1899.

Trevor-Roper, Hugh. *Hermit of Peking: The Hidden Life of Sir Edmund Backhouse*. New York: Knopf, 1977.

Tuchman, Barbara. *Stilwell and the American Experience in China, 1911–1945*. New York: Macmillan, 1970.

Tuttle, A.H. *Mary Porter Gamewell and Her Story of the Siege in Peking*. New York and Cincinnati: Eaton and Mains, 1907.

Twain, Mark. "To My Missionary Critics." *North American Review*, April 1901.

_____. "To the Person Sitting in Darkness." *North American Review*, February 1901.

Van Hoosen, Bertha. *Petticoat Surgeon*. Manchester, NH: Ayer, 1980.

Vare, Daniele. *The Last Empress*. New York: Doubleday, Doran, 1938.

Varg, Paul A. *The Making of a Myth: The United States and China, 1897–1912*. East Lansing, MI: Michigan State Press, 1968.

_____. *Missionaries, Chinese, and Diplomats: The American Protestant Missionary Movement in China, 1890–1952*. Princeton, NJ: Princeton University Press, 1958.

Vaughan, Lt. Colonel H.B. *St. George and the Chinese Dragon*. London: C. Arthur Pearson, 1902

Waite, Carleton Frederick. *Some Elements of International Military Cooperation in the Suppression of the 1900 Anti-Foreign Rising in China with Special Reference to the Forces of the United States*. Los Angeles: University of Southern California Press, 1935.

Waldersee, Alfred, Count von. *A Field Marshal's Memoirs*. London: Hutchinson, 1924.

_____. "Plundering Peking." *The Living Age*, June 9, 1923: 563–569.

Weale, B.L. (Bertram Lenox Simpson). *Indiscreet Letters from Peking*. New York: Dodd, Mead, 1907.

Wehrle, Edmund S. *Britain, China, and the Antimissionary Riots, 1891–1900*. Minneapolis: University of Minnesota Press, 1966.

Whiting, the Rev. J.L. "Besieged in Peking." *The Independent*, 11 October 1900: 2422–2423.

Whittlesey, H.C. "Sir Robert Hart." *The Atlantic Monthly*, November 1900: 699–705.

Wilson, James H. *Under the Old Flag*. 2 vols. New York: Appleton, 1912.

Wise, Col. Frederick May. *A Marine Tells It to You*. New York: J.H. Sears, 1929.

Witte, Count. *The Memoirs of Count Witte*. Edited by Adam Yarmolinsky. London: Heinemann, 1921.

Woodward, Mr. M.S. "The Personal Side of the Siege of Peking." *The Independent*, 22 November 1900: 2782–2792.

Wurtsbaugh, Lt. Daniel W. "The Seymour Relief Expedition." *Proceedings of the U.S. Naval Institute*, June 1902: 207–219.

Young, Marilyn Blatt. *The Rhetoric of Empire: American China Policy, 1895–1901*. Cambridge, MA: Harvard University Press, 1968.

Index

HMS Algerine 71
Allen, Roland 39, 43, 51, 57, 123, 128, 161, 174, 197
Allied army 1, 129, 155; atrocities 168–169, 204; attack on Tientsin 130–135; looting Tientsin 136–137; march to Peking 163–175; Taku 68–69
Ament, Emily 17, 213
Ament, Emily Hammond 23
Ament, Margaret 22
Ament, Mary Alice Penfield 19, 20, 201, 213, 217; description 215; marriage 18; poor health 22–23
Ament, Phillip Wyett 22
Ament, William Scott 12, 13, 14, 28, 30, 38, 39, 46, 90, 160, 170, 184, 198, 211, 221; arrested 206–207; childhood 17; children 22–23; college 17–18; confiscated goods 153–154; confiscates palace 186–188; criticized by Twain 207–210; defends himself 212–214; "ideal missionary" 2; illness and death 216–217; journey to China 18–19; "judge" 202–203; life in Paoting 20–22; looting 199; married 18; meets Boxers 3–6; military escorts 201; as missionary 23–24; Peking after siege 199–201; Peking home 24–25; preaches 216; press 205–207; remains in Methodist Mission 52–53; rescues missionaries 47; resigns 23; return to Peking 215; returns to Methodist mission 81; returns to U.S. 212; saves boy 55; stays in China 188; street urchin Li Wuyuan 126–127, 160–161; transfer to Peking 22; visits to countryside 3–6, 23–24, 30–31, 201–202, 206; volunteer 110
Ament, William Sheffield 23, 213, 215, 217
America and Americans 29, 42, 43, 182, 206; Ament returns to 212–213; Chaffee arrives 181; damage to Legation 184; Fourteenth Infantry 167, 168, 177, 167; looting Peking 194–195; military rule 204; Ninth Infantry 132–133; relief force 163–164; relations with missionaries 137–138, 191, 204; scale Peking Wall 177–178; shoot Sikhs 195; trade 11; with Seymour 58; Yangtsun 166–167; see also Marines
American Board Mission (Peking) 52, 221, 222; annual conference 46; description 24–27; mission burned 54, 187
American Board of Commissioners For Foreign Missions (ABCFM) 18, 19, 22, 24, 26, 39, 45, 47, 49, 55, 205
Andover Theological Seminary 18
Andrews, Miss Mary Elizabeth ("Aunt Mary") 76, 168, 221
Andrews, Roy Chapman 99
Austria and Austrians 29, 42, 43, 54, 69, 71; abandon Legation 81; in French Legation 107; with Seymour 58

Backhouse, Sir Edmund Trewlawny 147
Bainbridge, Mary 27, 53; refuses to pray 121–122
Bainbridge, William E. (U.S. diplomat) 6, 165, 176, 183
Baptists 5
Barr, Pat 12
Barton, J. J. 217
Bayly, Capt. 99, 102, 130
Beatty, Capt. David 69, 104; attacks military college 98–99
"Betsy" (homemade cannon) 114–115, 140, 170, 175
Big Swords (sect) 7
Bigham 48
Boxer Rebellion 1, 2, 184, 205; changes after 219; see also Boxers
Boxers 45, 49, 50, 73, 96, 113, 140, 145, 160; abandonment of Christians 75; Ament meets 3–6; arrive in Peking 44; atrocities 105; attack foreign buildings 53–57; attack Peitang 115–116; battle Catholics 5; battle Seymour 60–62, 103–104; burn Feng-tai 40–42; burn grandstand 51; destruction of Peking 194; disappear 111, 146; executions 105, 155; hunted by Smith 199–200; in countryside 5, 30–31, 46, 202, 204; in Peking 53–55, 94; in Tientsin 69–70, 98; invulnerability 10; Ketteler attacks 53; kill Brooks 3; missionaries killed 184; origins and description 7–12; "rabble" 67; slogans 7–9; prisoners 131
Bridgman School 39, 49, 217
Bristol, H. H., kills Chinese 51
Britain and England 66, 145, 146; trade 11
British Legation 29, 30, 52; after siege 185–187, 189–190; auctions 196; beginning of siege 77, 81–85; bombproof shelters 140; census 83; deaths 160; defenders 110–111; described 37, 83, 101; fires 92–94, 112–113; flies 150–151; hospital 157–159; relief arrives 179–181; water 151
British soldiers 42, 43, 52, 57, 71, 195; attack Tientsin 130–135; described 110, 164; looting 196; relief force 163; relieve siege 178–181; with Seymour 58; on Tartar Wall 121, 125–126
Brooks, Sidney M. 30, 184; murdered 3
Brown, Mrs. Amy E. 221
Brown, Frederick 179
Butler, Lt. Smedley 102, 104, 142, 163, 167, 168, 204; battle of Tientsin 100–101, 133–134; bio 99–100; describes marines 130; enters Tientsin 101; wounded 178

Caetani (It. officer) 143
Camden, SC 87, 88
Carles, W. R. (Consul), Letter 160–161
Carter, Pvt. 100
Carving Knife Brigade 111, 174
Casualties 167; hospital 157–159; legations 145, 183–184; missionaries and Chinese Christians 184; Seymour 104; Tientsin 138
Catholics see Christians, Chinese; Missionaries, Catholic
Chaffee, Maj. Gen. Adna R. 163,

172, 177; atrocities 204; bans looting 195; bio 163; court martial 195; enters Legation Quarter 181; and Tewksbury 201–202, 210–211
Chamberlin, Wilbur J. 208, 209; writes about Ament 205–207
Chamot, Annie Elizabeth 42, 47, 107, 109, 149, 159, 197, 219; kills Chinese 198
Chamot, Auguste 47, 77, 84, 182, 219; baker 149; hotel manager 109; looting 77, 197–198; rescues railway workers 42
Chang Hsin Tien (Zhang Xian Dian) town 41–42
Chapin, Miss Abbie G. 75, 157, 189, 221
Chapin, Ernest 221
Chapin, Flora Barret 221
Chapin, Franklin M., photo 89, 221
Chapin, Ralph 221
Chekiang (Zhejiang) province 11; missionaries killed 184
Cheshire, Fleming D. 6, 30, 56, 73, 119, 148, 184
Chi Hua gate 172, 176
Chien Gate (Qian) 35, 36, 43, 59, 109, 112, 160, 179; burned 57–58
China and Chinese 42; defeat 194; disintegration 94–95; famine 21–22; "first shot" 51; population 1; massacre 105; opposition to missionaries 2, 12, 15–16, 20–22, 28; prestige 155; religion 14–15; request truce 113–114, 156; southern provinces 146; transliteration 2; world view of 66–67; see also Ching, Empress Dowager
Chinese Centenary Missionary Conference 216
Chinese City see Peking
Chinese soldiers: attack from Fu 112–113; attack from Mongol market 174; attack Peitang 116–117; attack Tartar Wall 120–121, 124–126; attack Seymour 62, 104; cadets 98–99; "darkest day" attack 139–140; fires 92–93; forces and artillery 111–112; guard Squires 40; kill James 82; performance 112, 117, 126; "round the clock" barrage 169–170; tactics 118–119; "ten thousand" 82; Taku 68, 70–73, 94–95; Tientsin 135–136
Ching, Prince 67, 76; letter to MacDonald 140–141, 145, 162
Ching (Qing) Dynasty 2, 17, 67, 146; decline 97; ends 217–218; establishment 65; Ketteler 79; relations with diplomats 38; secret societies 9; supports Boxers 67–68
Cho Chou (Zhuozhou) city 5, 30–31, 202, 206, 207, 208
Christianity and China: civilization 12–16; opposition 15–16, 20, 208–210, 213; debate 216

Christians, Chinese 1, 13–14, 15–16, 24, 47, 80, 119, 123; battle with Boxers 5–6; Catholics neglected 127–128, 170; desert missionaries 44–45; in Fu 107, 127, 170; installed in palace 188–189; killed by Boxers 184, 215;in Legation Quarter 127; moved out of Fu 122–23; numbers 13–14, 128, 168;numbers in siege 85; question of abandonment 75–76; rescued 55–57; Russian rape 123; starvation 127; taken to Legation Quarter 80; in Tientsin 98–99;work details 88–90; see also Schoolgirls
Cohen, Paul 10
Cologan, Sr. 63
Coltman, Dr. Robert 54, 110, 222
Condit-Smith, Polly 77, 92, 93, 119, 147, 158, 161, 170, 180, 186, 218; courage failing 168; customs problems 193; departs Peking 191; dressing gown 114; nipped by bullet 181; receives gifts 190–191; rescued 40–41; sees Strouts 143–144; serves coffee 148; shirkers 152; steals chicken 151
Conger, Edwin H. (U.S. diplomat) 31, 41, 44, 47, 53, 55, 67, 75, 76, 77, 78, 80, 85, 119, 120, 121, 122, 124, 142, 143, 146, 149, 181, 184, 186, 206, 218; Chinese ultimatum 73–74; defends missionaries 209; description 29; letters to Gamewell 52, 74, 191; looting 196–197; meets with Ament 6; message from Ching 144–145; permission to Ament 187
Conger, Laura 29, 92, 196, 197
Conger, Sarah Pike 43, 57, 73, 82, 88, 114, 160, 181, 218; call on Empress 63–65; cheers up E. Martin 157; China and Chinese 219; description 29; loots 196; reassures women 92; tells Mrs. Ketteler of husband's death 79
Cordes, Heinrich, wounded 78–80
Cousins, Edmund 102

D'Addosio, Father 55; killed 184
Daggett, Col. A. S. 133, 167; battle inside Peking 178
Daly, Pvt. Daniel J. 99, 143; Medal of Honor 142
D'Arc, Mme. 107, 109
Darcy, Lt. 107, 139
Davis, the Rev. George 90, 221
Davis, Oscar King 165, 176
Dering, Herbert 83
Detrick, Pvt. 177
Dhuysberg, W. J. von 142, 143
Diplomats 2; and missionaries 6–7; appoint MacDonald 91–92; call on Tsungli Yamen 38; Chinese messenger 113, 161; Chinese ultimatum 73–74; delay 76–77; in Peking 29–30; letter from Favier 31; letter to MacDonald 140–142; notes to Tsungli Yamen 32, 76–78; request soldiers 42; send patrols 56, 57; wives 63–65
Dollar, Betsy 219
Dorward, Gen. 133, 134
Douw, Miss Deborah Matilda 39, 221
Drought 9, 30; see also Famine, Great
Dudgeon, Dr. 196; and Nostegarde 152–153
Dupree, Willie 42

Empress Dowager Tzu Hsi (Cixi) 2, 38, 39, 113, 197; childhood 64–65; Chinese humiliation 155, 73; death 217–218; during siege 146; flees Peking 185; orders foreigners killed 95; receives diplomatic wives 63–64; relations with Boxers 67–68; rule 66–67; supports Boxers 67–68; ultimatum to Legations 73–74
Eunuchs 39, 63, 66
Evans, Miss Jane Gertrude ("Aunt Jennie") 189, 221
Ewing, the Rev. Charles E. 3, 6, 7, 16, 24, 46, 53, 160, 190, 221; departs Peking for Tientsin 191–192; photo 89
Ewing, Elizabeth Goodyear Smith (Bessie) 24, 27, 77, 78, 80, 175, 191, 221; eggs 162; flees Tungchou 46; sick children 160
Ewing, Ellen 24, 46, 77, 162, 221; sick 162
Ewing, Marion 24, 221

HMS Fame 71, 129
Famine, Great (1877–79) 21–22
Favier, Bishop 54, 170, 189; letter to diplomats 31; looting 197; Peitang siege 115–117; hunger 170–171
Feng shui (Fengshui) 10, 39, 115
Feng-tai (Fengtai) town, burned 40–42
Fenn, Alice Holstein 151, 221
Fenn, the Rev. Courtenay Hughes 45, 90, 127, 149, 192, 221; on Tartar Wall 121; steals eggs 151
Fenn, Henry 221
Fenn, Martha 221
"Fighting Parsons" 111, 156; photo 89
Fists of Righteous Harmony see Boxers
Fleming, Peter 218
Food 117, 190, 199; missionary's diet 147–148; stolen chicken 151; eggs 151, 162; melons 162; horsemeat recipe 150; Squiers' mess 147
Forsythe, Capt. 201
Fortifications see Gamewell, Francis; Hoover, Herbert; sandbags
France and French 29, 43, 202; arrest Ament 206–207; attack on Tientsin 131; atrocities 203; Catholics 14, 203; Chaffee orders 177; imperialism 11; in Legation

Index

107, 139; looting 203; mines 139; relief force 165; relieve Peitang 189; with Seymour 58
Frey, Gen. 172
Fu, the 80, 83, 85, 90, 112, 113, 118, 139, 154, 170 181; Chinese in 127–128; defenses 106–107, 140; given to Christians 56; last night 174; schoolgirls in 122–123; Strouts killed 143–144
Fuller (hospital steward) 157
Fukushima, Gen. 134–135, 166

Galt, the Rev. Howard S. 221
Galt, Louise West 221
Gamewell, Francis Dunlap (Frank) 46, 50, 52, 55, 90, 93, 121, 156, 158, 168, 170, 181, 219, 221; appointed fortification chief 87; bio 87–88; defense of Mission 53–54; departs Peking 191; description 148; farewell to China 193; fortifications 88–90, 110, 140; photo 89; tries to leave Peking 45
Gamewell, Mary Q. Porter 32, 45, 46, 50, 76, 77, 95, 219, 221; bio 87–88; departs Peking 181;photo 46; recipe 150; sick 170
Garrigues, Father 54
Gaselee, Gen. Alfred 167, 178; commander 163; enters Legation Quarter 179–181; message to Legations 168
Germany and Germans 29, 42, 43, 202; atrocities 203; Chinese attack 139–140; imperialism 11–12; occupation of Peking 198–199; in Legation 107–108; kill Boxers 55; on Tartar Wall 108, 119–120; relief force 165; transport Ketteler's body 79–80; with Seymour 58
Ghost dance movement 10, 41
Giers, M. de 196
Giles, Lancelot 145
Gilman, Miss Gertrude 221
Gloss, Dr. Anna 157, 158, 182, 221
Goodrich, the Rev. Chauncey 170, 196, 216, 221
Goodrich, Grace Dorothea 196, 221
Goodrich, Luther Carrington 221
Goodrich, Sarah B. Clapp 196, 221
Gordon, "Chinese" 70; pamphlet 118
Gowans, Miss Annie H. 157, 221
Guiney, Lt., with Tewksbury 201–202

Hall, Capt. Newt 47, 50, 53, 79, 120, 121, 122, 124, 143, 180; court martial 218; described 110; "drinking and cowardice" 142, 144; relations with Squiers 142
Hall, Private 48
Halliday, Capt. Lewis 88, 144, 157; wounded 112–113
Hanlin Academy 92, 181; burned 93–94

Harding, Lt. 100
Harllee, Lt., trek to Tungchou 168
Hart, Sir Robert 47, 56, 67, 73, 81, 82, 109, 110, 111, 149, 174; bio 37–38; reads message 113; letter 119
Hata gate and street (Hatta) 36, 53, 107, 112, 179, 199; Ketteler assassinated 78–79
Hattori, Capt. 72
Haven, Miss Ada (later Mateer) 24, 162, 188, 216, 221; flight to Methodist mission 49
Hay, John 145
Henry, Paul, commander at Peitang 116; killed 156–157
Herring, Richard 196
Hobart, the Rev. W. T. 90, 127, 221
Hooker, A. A. 218
Hoover, Herbert 129, 132, 165; and missionaries 97; battle of Tientsin 132–133; demeanor 130; fortifications 99, 101; guests 129–130; protects Chinese 101–102; travels and work 96–98
Hoover, Lou 97, 98, 129; dairy herd 102; with Joaquin Miller 130
Horse meat 1, 149–150
Hospital, Legation Quarter 157–159
Hsien Feng (Xianfeng) Emperor 65
Hsiku Arsenal(Xiku) 103 -104
Hunt, Corporal 49, 125

I Ho Chuan (Yi He Chuan) *see* Boxers
Imperial and Forbidden City (Peking) 66, 67, 112, 117, 174, 176; Winter Palace 63
Imperial Maritime Customs 37, 47, 73, 174
Imperial University 37, 222
Ingles, Theodora 48, 221; baby dies 160
Inglis, Elizabeth 221
Inglis, the Rev. John M. 221
Ingram, Dr. James H 170, 221
Ingram, Myrtle Prough 221
Italian Legation, lost 91
Italy and Italians 11, 29, 43, 71; in Fu 91–92, 107; Taku 72; with Seymour 58

Jackson, the Rev. Jesse 9
Jackson, Pvt. Joseph 167
James, Huberty 56; killed 82
Japan and Japanese 29, 42, 43, 52, 67, 71, 72; assault on Peking 176–177;battle of Tientsin 132–136; capture Tungchou 171; in Fu 106; in Peitang 189; march 167–168; murder of Sugiyama 52; Peitsang 165–166; relief force 164; Taku 71–72; war with China 11; with Seymour 58
Jarlin, Bishop 115
Jellicoe, Capt. John R. 59; wounded 103
Jen Chiu (Renqiu) town 5

Jen Mu Shih (Christian) 47
Jewell, Mrs. Charlotte M. 49, 75, 221
John, Griffin 16
Jones, Mrs. James, visit to Tientsin, Taku 69–73
Jung Lu (Rong-lu) Gen. 67, 94, 111, 153; and Empress 63;letter to foreigners 113–114

Kalgan 97
Kansu (Gansu) soldiers 43, 52, 57, 119, 121, 195
Kempff, Adm. James 31; declines to attack Taku 69
Ker, Mrs. W. P. 179
Ketteler, Baron Clemens von 29, 55, 74, 141; attacks Boxer 53; assassination 78–79; monument 198–199
Ketteler, Maud Ledyard 29, 82, 95; reaction to death of husband 79
Keyes, Roger 71, 165, 168; in Legation Quarter 181; in Tientsin 129; scales wall 179; "Torpedo" 163, 179
Killie, Charles A. 221; photo 89
Killie, Louisa Scott 121, 221
King, Pvt. C. B., killed 158
King, the Rev. H.E. 90, 221
Kipling, Rudyard 1
Knobel, steals chicken 151
Koo, Mrs., saved by Hoover 102
Kuang Hsu (emperor) 39, 63, 217
Kup, Boyce 179

Lambert, Marian 157
Learnard, Capt. 177
Legation Guards: arrival 42–44; disappear 186; distrust 111; numbers 85; panic 91–92; rescue Chinese 56, 57; stress 152; wounded 157–159
Legation Quarter (Peking) 1, 29, 30, 41, 43, 44, 57, 67; after siege 185–186; Americans arrive 181; civilian deaths 160; defenses 88–90, 106–111; description 36–38; discipline 152; map 108; messengers 126–127; population 85; siege begins 82; truce 156, 160–161
Leonard, Dr. Eliza Ellen 45, 157, 221
Leonard, Lt. 134
Li Hung-chang (Li Hong-zhang) 198
Li Wuyuan, carries message to Tientsin and returns 126–127, 160–161
Liang Cho (Liangzhuo) town 5
Lights in the sky 123–124
Lineivitch, Gen. 171, 172
Lippet, Naval Surgeon 56, 110, 190; wounded 120
Liscum, Col. Emerson H. 132; killed 133
Lister and Listerine 158
Little, Mrs. Archibald 37
Lofa (RR station) 59, 60

London Missionary Society 39, 47, 49, 189; burned 54
Looting 77, 128; auctions 196, 199; Peking 194–198; Tientsin 136–137
Lowry, Edward K. 177
Lowry, Mrs. Edward K. 221
Lowry, Dr. George D. 32, 92, 221
Lowry, Katherine 121
Lynch, George 194; describes desolation 105

MacDonald, Sir Claude 9, 29, 31–32, 42, 44, 47, 55, 56, 73, 83, 85, 92, 109, 111, 120, 121, 124, 154, 157, 174, 187; appoints Gamewell 87–88; argument with Saville 48; darkest day 139–140; establishes committees 86; greets relief force 179–182; letter from Ching 140–142; lights 123–124; loots 196; marines dislike 151–152; obituary 145–146; requests troops 51–52; sends message 126–127, 160–161; takes command 91; tours wall 155–156; truce 156
MacDonald, Lady Ethel 51, 65, 79, 81, 88, 147, 148; call on Empress 63–64; loots 196
Machia pu (Majiabao) RR station 10, 35, 43, 51, 52
Mackey, Dr. Maud Aura 45, 157, 221
Manchu Dynasty *see* Ching Dynasty
Manchuria 11
Manchus 9, 42, 73, 78, 79, 80, 95, 146, 217; rule 65
Marines, American 43, 47, 54, 55, 92, 190; abandon and return to Tartar Wall 121; appearance 130; arrival in Peking 43; attack Chinese 124–126; battle near Tientsin 99–101; battle of Tientsin 132–134; charge Chinese mob 53; Chinese attack German Legation 139–140; description of 130; dislike diplomats 151–152; doubts about 122; expand position 142–143; funeral 143; looting 135–136, 195; on wall 108–110, 119–120; sharpshooters 110; steal turkey 152
Martin, Miss Elizabeth (Lizzie) 33, 49, 78, 81, 218–219, 221; trip to China 32
Martin, Dr. Emma E. 19, 33, 75, 81, 142, 218–219, 221; "darkest day" 144; loots 195–196; Mrs. Conger 157; packs 78; romance with Fuller 159; shoots pistol 49; trip to China 32; working in hospital 157–159
Martin, W. A.P. 37, 90, 181, 216, 222; punish Chinese 203
Mateer, C. W. 216
Mateer, Mrs. John L. 24
McCalla, Capt. Bowman Hendry 52, 59, 103; fights Boxers 60–61; wounded 104

McCoy, Miss Bessie Campbell 45
McCreary, Lt. Wirt 165
McKillican, Miss Janet C. 158, 221
McKinley, President William 29
Meade, Col Robert L. 132, 138
Medina, Ohio 23
Methodists and Mission 39, 53, 67, 221, 222; abandon Mission 77, 80–81; Ament collects goods 81; and Gamewells 87–88; fortification 49–50, 53, 55; Ketteler's assassination 79–80; missionaries gather 45–48; religious services 58
Miller, Joaquin, with Hoovers 130
Miner, Luella 53, 54, 55, 78, 88, 148, 180–181, 189, 216, 221
Mines and countermines, legation quarter 139–141, 156; at Peitang 56, 171
Missionaries, Catholic 2, 10, 82; arrest Ament 206–207; converts 13–14, 55; indemnities 207–208; looting 197, 203; massacre 17; Paoting 19–20; cathedrals 39; cathedrals burned 54–55
Missionaries, Protestant 2, 9, 82, 205; abandon converts 75–76; after siege 215; committees 87–91; conference 216; converts 12–14; deserted by Chinese 44–45; eating and sleeping 86, 148; flee stations 68; hardships 21, 25–28; in chapel 80–81; indemnities 186, 188, 201–202, 209; in Peking 39; killed by Boxers 184; leave China 191–193; leave Methodist Mission 77–78, 80–81; life in Peking 24–28; numbers 14; looting Peking 195–196; photo 190; punish Chinese 203–204; rescued by Ament 47; salaries 27; relations with military 137–138, 190, 191, 193, 196, 199; support Ament 203, 208–209, 212; women 26–27
Mitchell, Gunner's Mate Joseph "Betsy" 114–115, 170; wounded 174
USS Monocacy, Battle of Taku Forts 70–71
Moore, Siege 180
Morrison, Dr. George E. 43, 47, 52, 54, 58, 67, 77, 80, 82, 93, 118, 122, 147, 148, 161, 170, 196, 200, 218; "carving knife brigade" 111; kills Boxers 57; looting 197; rescues Chinese Christians 54; rescues women 40–41; saves books 81; wounded 143–144
Mott, John R. 86
Mount Holyoke 26
"Mud Wall" 132
Munthe, J. W. N. 175
Murphy, Sgt. 82, 125
Myers, Capt. John T. 47, 50, 55, 119, 120, 121, 122, 124, 126, 142, 144, 152, 155, 190; calls meeting

44; described 110; in hospital 182; speech 125; wounded 125

Nakagawa 143
Nan Meng (Nanmeng) town 5
USS Newark 42, 61
Newton, Miss Grace 45, 221
Nieh Shi Cheng, Gen. 59, 73
North China College, Tungchou 39, 46, 47, 49, 189
Norris, Frank 139, 174
Nostegarde 152–153

Oberlin College 17–18, 26; Oberlin band 25
Oliphant, Nigel 93, 118, 125
Olivieri, Ensign, at Peitang 116, 156; buried 171
Otterbein, Indiana (town) 32, 219
Owosso, Michigan (town) 12, 17, 24

Palmer, Frederick 129, 130, 134, 135, 136, 165, 176; describes Legation Quarter 182–183; trek to Tungchou 167–168
Paolini, Lt. 107
Paoting (Baoding) City 2; Aments' travel to 18–19; message from missionaries 45; missionaries killed 184; mission 19–21
Partridge, Pvt. 134
Pei Ho River (Beihe) 42, 59, 68, 71, 97, 99, 146; boat traffic 10, 165; dead Chinese 103; missionaries travel 191–192; Seymour's retreat 102–103
Peitaiho (Beidaihe) Beach Resort 160, 217
Peitang (Beidang) Cathedral 1, 67, 197; babies die 156; Henry killed 156–157; mines 171; population 85, 116; relieved 189; siege 115–117
Peitsang (Beicang) city, battle of 165–166
Peking (Beijing): changes 215; climate 40, 159–160; description 32–39; diplomats 29–30; fires 51, 54–58; Legation Quarter 36–38; looting 194–198; map 34; missionaries 24–28; Missions 17; occupation 199; siege 1; Sugiyama killed 52; *see also* Legation Quarter; Tartar Wall; Imperial City
Peking Hotel 83–84, 109
Pell, Capt. 179
Pethick, William N., rescues Catholics 55, 56, 148
Philippines 43
Pichon, Madame 139
Pichon, Stephen 29, 31, 74, 116, 139
Pierce, Mary 143, 196
Pierson, Isaac 19–21
Ping Ting (Ping Ding) town 5
Pokotilov, Baron de 149
Pokotilov, Mrs. 162
Ponies, Mongolian 83, 197
Poole, Capt. F. G. 93, 111
Poole, Dr. Wordsworth 157, 159, 182

Port Arthur (Lushun) city 11
Porter, Durand 211
Porter, H. D. 216
Porter, Lucius C. 217
Presbyterians 45, 49, 221, 222; flee Mission 48; Mission in Peking 30, 39
Puyi, Henry 218

Ragsdale, James W. 6, 94, 133
Rahden, Baron von 191
Railroads 10–11, 40–42, 68; Seymour expedition 59–62; Tientsin to Peking 33–34
Ransome, Jessie 48, 56, 157, 159
Red Lanterns (sect) 7
Reid, Gilbert 39, 43, 149, 168, 216, 221; defends looting 195; wounded 128
Reid, Mrs., and child 221
Ricalton, James, civilian rights 204
Richard, Timothy 13, 21, 23
Rosthorn, Dr. Arthur von 107; buried in explosion 139
Rosthorn, Paula von 107, 159
Russell, Miss Nellie Naomi 24, 80, 157, 188, 221; on Ament 202–203, 208
Russia and Russians 29, 41, 42, 43, 58, 68, 96, 120; attack Tientsin 100–101, 130–135; at Taku 71; brutality 104–105, 199; enter Peking 175–176; in legation 109; in Manchuria 11; in siege 149; in Tientsin 69; on Tartar Wall 121, 125–126; rape of schoolgirls 123; relief force 164–165, 168; steal a march 172–173; with Seymour 58
Russian Orthodox Mission 184
Rutherford, Miss Hattie E. 222

Sandbags 88–90, 121, 158, 159
Savage Landor, Alfred Henry: describes massacre 105; missionary's letter 186
Saville, Dr. Lillie 157; argument with MacDonald 48
Schoolgirls, Chinese 76, 80; go to Methodist compound 48–49; in Fu 107; moved to Legation Quarter 122–123; rapes 123, 152
Scott, Mrs. 104
Scott, Maj. Tom 179
Secret Societies 9
Seymour, Adm. Edward Hobart 44, 67, 68, 73, 85, 88, 96, 98, 100, 160; expedition 58–62; letter to MacDonald 56; rescues Chinese woman 105; retreat 102–104; summoned to Peking 51; See-no-more 57
Sha Wo gate (Hsia Kuo) 172, 176, 179
Shanghai 69, 73
Shansi (Shanxi) 184, 217; missionaries killed 184, 185
Shantung (Shandong). Province 3, 7, 8, 9, 11, 23, 30, 145, 184

Sheffield, Devello Z., investigates A and T 211–212
Sheffield, Miss Elizabeth E. (later Stelle) 24, 80, 159, 188, 222
Shiba, Lt. Col. Goro 57, 90, 123, 143, 170, 174, 181; death 219; defends Fu 91, 106–107
Sian (Xian) 185
Siege of Legations 1; population 85; "Continentals" 147; truce 156, 161–162; see also British Legation; Legation Guards; Legation Quarter; Marines, American; Tartar Wall
Sikhs and other Indian troops 191; enter Legation Quarter 179-182; killed by Americans 195; rob converts 199
Simpson, Bertram Lenox 58, 86, 91, 149, 197, 218; describes defenses 106–111; discontent 152; military service 90; on Am. Missionaries 90; saves converts 199
Smith, the Rev. Arthur Henderson 8, 12, 13, 30, 66, 86, 90, 04, 110, 112, 121, 128, 189, 216, 222; abandonment of Chinese Christians 75–76; indemnities 186, 219; meets Ament 18–19; on Continentals 147; preaches 58, 189–190
Smith, Emma Dickinson 18–19, 75, 189, 219, 222; prays 122
Smith, Georgina 39, 41, 54, 75, 189; description of 47–48; hunts Boxers 199–200; looting 199; Peking after siege 199–201; photo 200
Smith, Judson 211, 212, 214; indemnity 214; Mark Twain 207–210; press furor 205–207
Smith, Mrs. Mary 49
Smith, Capt. Percy 125
Society for the Propagation of the Gospel 39
Spain and Spanish 65, 89
Squiers, Bard 190
Squires, Fargo 77, 148
Squires, Harriet 80, 181, 190, 218; rescued 40–41; room and mess 147–149, 186
Squires, Herbert G. 6, 41, 80, 120, 143, 147, 196, 218; art collection 197; chief of staff 155; marines dislike 151; relations with Hall 142; orders Myers to attack 124–125; turkey stolen 152
Stanley 159
Stelle, William B. 5–6, 30, 42, 90, 110, 127, 188, 195, 222; and Nostegarde 153; missionary women 159; photo 89
Stonehouse, Joseph 111; photo 89, 200
Strouts, Capt. B. M. 82, 88, 93, 112, 155; killed 143–144
Su, Prince 56, 80, 83, 113
Sugiyama, Akira 57; murdered 52

Taiping Rebellion 15
Taku (Dagu) banks, forts, and city 7, 18, 31, 42, 44, 62, 76, 95, 99, 123; Battle of Taku Forts 68–74, 98
Tan, Chester 95
Tangku (Tanggu) 71, 101
Tartar City see Peking
Tartar Wall 33, 35, 44, 55, 57, 80, 107, 112, 118, 155, 160, 170, 177, 178; Americans expand positions 142–143; defenses 119–122;description 38–39, 119; marines attack 124–126
Taussig, Capt. 61
Temple of Agriculture 35
Temple of Heaven 35
Terrell, Miss Alice 222
HMS Terrible 123, 163
Terry, Dr. Ellen 192, 222
Tewksbury, Donald 222
Tewksbury, Elwood G. 46, 47, 149, 162, 188, 200, 206, 219, 222; accompanies Ament 187; confiscates Palace 189; house 211–212; indemnities 202; leads missionaries 80, 86–87; looting 199; military escorts 201–202, 210–211; Peking after siege 199–201; Sheffield criticizes 211–212; talks to Chinese 113
Tewksbury, Gardner 222
Tewksbury, Mrs. 189, 222
Thomann, Capt. Von 77, 90; death 92
Thomas, Armorour's Mate J. T., "Betsy" 114–115
Thornhill's Roughs 111
Tiananmen Square 36
Tien Chu Chiao (Dian Ju Jiao) 15
Tientsin (Tianjin): allied army 7, 10; casualties 138; conquest of 130–136; foreign settlements 97–98, 129; Hoover in 96; looting 136–137; massacre 17; marines attack 100–101; refugees arrive 192–193; Seymour's retreat 102–104; siege of 1, 98–99, 129–130, 155; see also Butler, Lt. Smedley; Hoover, Herbert; Seymour, Adm. Edward Hobart
Titus, Calvin P., scales wall 177
"To the People Sitting in Darkness" 207–208
"To my Missionary Critics" 210
Tours, Mr. 82
Truce in Legation Quarter 113–114; 161–162
Tsingtao (Qingdao) city 11
Tsungli Yamen (Zongli Yamen) Foreign Office 30, 31, 57, 63, 67, 145, 162; description 38; guards 42–43; Letter from Ministers 76
Tuan (Duan) Prince 67, 73, 76, 94, 185
Tung Chih gate 172, 176
Tung Shaoyi 102
Tung Fu-hsiang, Gen. (Dong Fu-xiang) 43, 52, 111, 113, 121, 146, 185

Tung Pien gate 172, 173, 175, 176, 177, 178
Tungchou (Tongzhou) city 10, 39, 171, 175, 189, 202, 210; captured 171–172; destruction 191; missionaries flee 46–47; road to Peking 10–11
Turner, killed 125
Twain, Mark 2, 213, 214; and missionaries 207–210
Tzu Hzi *see* Empress Dowager

United States *see* America and Americans
Upham, Pvt. 142
Usedom, Capt. Von 62

Vassilevski, Gen. 175, 176
Vaughn, Maj. 179
Velde, Dr. Carl 142, 148, 157, 183, 198
Verity, the Rev. G. W. 222
Victoria, Queen 30
Vincenza, Sister: rescues Olivieri 171; starving children 156

Volunteers, in Legations 110–111

Waldersee, Count Alfred von 198
Waldron, Lt. 192
Walker, Esther 222
Walker, Mrs. 222
Walker, the Rev W. F. 222
Waller, Maj. Littleton W. T. 100, 101
Warren, Henry 142, 144
Water gate 155, 179
Wen An (Wenan) 6
Western Hills 30, 33, 40, 80, 160; Buddhist temples 40
Wherry, the Rev. John A. 143, 175, 222
HMS Whiting 71
Whiting, the Rev. John L. 222
Wilder, George 137; protects converts 203
Wilhelm, Kaiser 11, 12
Wise, Commander 71
Wise, Lt. Frederick: Peking looting 195; Tientsin looting 136–137; Yangtsun battle 166–167
Wogack, Capt. 99, 102

Woodward, Ione 192
Woodward, Mrs. 192
Wounded Knee 10, 41
Wray, Capt. 88, 144
Wu, Minister 145
Wurtzbaugh, Lt. 103
Wycoff, Miss Gertrude 189, 222
Wycoff, Miss Grace 189, 222

Yang Tsun (Yangcun) 59, 61, 102; battle of 166–167
Yehonala (Empress Dowager) 64, 65
Yu Hsien (Yu-xian), Governor 184; executed 185
Yu Lu (governor) 73, 94–95
Yuan Shi Kai 184
Yung Lo Ta Tien (Yong Le Da Dian), burned 93
Yungting Gate (Yongding) 35, 52

www.ingramcontent.com/pod-product-compliance
Lightning Source LLC
Chambersburg PA
CBHW080803300426
44114CB00020B/2808